BRITANNIA

Also by Graham Stewart

Burying Caesar: Churchill, Chamberlain and the Battle for the Tory Party

His Finest Hours: The War Speeches of Winston Churchill

The History of *The Times*: The Murdoch Years

Friendship and Betrayal: Ambition and the Limits of Loyalty

BRITANNIA

100 DOCUMENTS THAT SHAPED A NATION

GRAHAM STEWART

Atlantic Books
London

First published in hardback in Great Britain in 2010 by Atlantic Books and Callisto, imprints of Atlantic Books Ltd.

This hardback edition published in Great Britain in 2011 by Atlantic Books.

10 9 8 7 6 5 4 3 2 1

A CIP catalogue record for this book is available from the British Library.

ISBN: 978 1 84354 998 7

Design and layout by www.carrstudio.co.uk
Printed in Malta by Gutenberg Press Ltd

Atlantic Books
An imprint of Atlantic Books Ltd
Ormond House
26–27 Boswell Street
London
WC1N 3JZ

www.atlantic-books.co.uk

For my young nephew,

Rufus Stewart

CONTENTS

I THE DARK AGES

II THE MEDIEVAL AGE

LIST OF ILLUSTRATIONS

First Picture Section

Page from the *Lindisfarne Gospels*. © The British Library Board/HIP/TopFoto.

Bayeux Tapestry. akg-images/Erich Lessing.

Magna Carta. © The British Library Board/HIP/TopFoto.

Map of Great Britain from *Abbreviatio Chronicorum Angliae*. © The British Library Board.

Declaration of Arbroath. SCOTLANDSIMAGES.COM/Crown Copyright 2007. The National Archives of Scotland.

Second Picture Section

Founder's Charter upon Act of Parliament. The Master and Fellows of King's College, Cambridge.

Mary Rose from the Anthony Roll. The Art Archive/Magdalene College Cambridge/Eileen Tweedy.

Monteagle Letter and Guy Fawkes's Confession. The National Archives, London. SP14/216 (11a).

Union Flag design. © National Library of Scotland.

Scottish National Covenant. © National Library of Scotland.

Third Picture Section

Death Warrant of Charles I. Houses of Parliament, Westminster, London, UK/The Bridgeman Art Library.

Act of Union. SCOTLANDSIMAGES.COM/Crown Copyright 2007/The National Archives of Scotland.

The Plum-Pudding in Danger. Library of Congress Prints and Photographs Division, LC-USZC4-8791.

Poverty map of London. Atlantic Books Collection.

Fourth Picture Section

War recruitment poster. The Granger Collection/Topfoto.

British Empire map. The Art Archive/Lords Gallery/Eileen Tweedy.

London Blitz damage map. The City of London, London Metropolitan Archives.

Sgt. Pepper album cover. © Apple Corps Ltd.

The Dodi and Diana condolence book at Harrods. Courtesy of Harrods.

INTRODUCTION

≈

In the summer of 1647, Britain was slipping towards anarchy. Five years of civil war had left the Royalist forces broken and scattered. Although King Charles I was held captive, his enemies remained hesitant and unsure. Parliament was in disarray, its politicians reduced to making self-serving gestures having long since lost control of the revolution they had helped set in motion. Only one power in the land seemed capable of restoring order, but even the New Model Army, for all its battle-hardened prowess in war, was riven with dissent in the moment of its apparent victory. Belligerent and unpaid, it marched on the capital. On arrival, its commander-in-chief, Sir Thomas Fairfax, was appointed Constable of the Tower of London. As he was given a tour around the mighty fortified keep, a selection of its treasures was presented for his inspection. Eventually he was shown a fragile document that was already over 400 years old and not even written in English. Nonetheless, it was what the general had specifically requested to see. 'This is that,' he declared, gazing reverentially at the Magna Carta, 'which we have fought for, and by God's help we must maintain.'

Was the Civil War really a contest over an aged scrap of manuscript? Could the English, so often derided for their indifference to grand ideas, have made such a big issue out of a thirteenth-century set of dictates? In the search to find meaning out of the internecine conflict that gripped the British Isles in the 1640s, historians have identified many strands of discord – social, national, political, economic and religious. There is, however, no reason to assume that those who accompanied Sir Thomas Fairfax on his tour of the Tower looked at him strangely when he pronounced on the importance of Magna Carta. In assembling their case against the Crown, Parliamentarians had spent much of the previous twenty years searching out old documents that they believed provided the legal proof that their case was just and that arbitrary rule was alien to the ancient constitution.

At the beginning of the twenty-first century, Magna Carta still receives an occasional mention in the press and in Parliament, and most Britons are aware of its importance, even if they cannot exactly recall why. Actually, most of it was repealed in the nineteenth century and the provisions that remain tend to make the news only because they are perceived to be under threat. The Act of Union of 1707 is another national treasure that crops up in modern debate, principally because of a Scottish nationalist movement whose aim is to have it consigned to the dustbin of history. For all the opinions expressed about the Act of Union, how many people have seen it, or even have a mental picture of what it looks like? Much the same may be said of the Bill of Rights, whose 300th anniversary in 1989 was greeted with nationwide indifference.

The contrast with the United States of America could not be sharper. Daily, queues shuffle slowly and reverentially through the neoclassical portico of the National Archives in Washington, DC, for a glimpse of the documents that founded the nation. A high proportion of Americans not only know what their Declaration of Independence and Bill of Rights look like, they even have a pretty good recollection of what they say. In fact, America's Founding Fathers did not hit upon all their deep philosophical ideas, albeit neatly wrapped up in a few choice expressions, in one blinding flash of original genius. For, like Sir Thomas Fairfax, they had an almost mystical reverence for the eloquent defence of rights, freedoms and equality before the law that had been scratched upon the historic parchments of the country they had left behind.

The Founding Fathers of the United States borrowed liberally from Britain's archival heritage, even as they were trying to set themselves apart from Britain. Crucially, however, a fundamental difference divided the two English-speaking nations. The Americans – thereafter copied by most of the world – opted for a written constitution while the British persevered with their uncodified system of laws and precedents. Perhaps an absence of what are generally perceived as 'founding documents' has made modern Britons believe that their country's venerable statutes and charters are not especially relevant and that their only real appeal lies in their charming calligraphy.

Certainly, many of the documents collated in this book are a visual delight, but that is not why they are here. They cover a wide range of national endeavours, from law and politics, literature and science, inventions and city planning to sport, economics and religion. The principle guiding their selection is that they definitely shaped their age, and most of them still resonate today. For while we may not be governed by a single constitutional document, we are governed by many, drawn from the better part of two millennia of history – and a representative sample of the greatest of them are collected and contextualized here.

What is more, the term 'governed' is meant not only in a narrow administrative sense. Our expressions have been shaped by the great translations of the Bible, by the works of Shakespeare and by the extraordinary compilation of words and meanings made by Dr Samuel Johnson. The influence of Adam Smith's treatise guides the way in which we do business. We may no longer travel on trains designed by George and Robert Stephenson, nor do we toil over one of Richard Arkwright's water frames, but we must make a trip (not by rail) to some exceptionally remote parts of Britain to avoid evidence of their influence in industrializing, moulding and uniting the country. All, once, had to be imagined and developed, using ink and paper and, as such, deserve recognition here.

Restricting the number of documents presented to one hundred is, intentionally, a tight discipline. No matter how carefully considered, the choice is ultimately based on personal opinion and therefore open to debate. One could easily fill the entire book with Acts of Parliament and still lament the lack of space available to include many more with a sound claim to fame. To do so, though, would be at the expense of presenting a reasonable spread of documents from across a wider range of national activity. Providing this range necessarily involves selecting some documents as representative of their theme. In this way, the 1832 Reform Act represents legislative measures towards greater democracy. The absence here of subsequent reform acts is not intended to diminish their importance, merely to recognize that they carried on a process that the 1832 Act started. Nor is this book just a compendium of 'firsts' – the *Rocket* was not the original steam train, nor the Spitfire the pioneer fighter plane, nor were the MCC's Laws the first rule book on cricket. Sometimes it is the document that best expresses an idea, rather than the one that takes the earliest crack at it, that makes the more persuasive case for inclusion. Ultimately, this is a book about documents that have made Britain what it is today, a national focus that must automatically shut out concepts that, while conceived by Britons, are not primarily or exclusively rooted in British society. British inventions that have shaped the world really need a book of their own. An attempt to do them all justice here would only blur the purpose of the compilation.

This is an attempt to tell the history of Britain through its seminal documents. It is not, of course, the whole story, any more than the history of a nation can be told purely through the lives of its monarchs, or the tales of its writers, or the body-counts from its battlefields. There are, therefore, limits to this approach. For instance, serfdom withered and died during the Middle Ages. It was not abolished by any single statute. Sometimes it is the absence of a document that changed the course of British history. The freedom of the press was not created by the stroke of a legislative diktat. Rather, it began to take shape after Parliament's failure to renew the Licensing Act in 1694. Thereafter, press censorship was primarily regulated by the libel laws (although, famously, in the theatre, the Lord Chamberlain endeavoured to keep a lid on smut and sedition between 1737 and 1968). Nonetheless, for a nation that prides itself on its empiricism and 'muddling through' attitude, it is striking how elemental some statues have proved.

Finally, it is important to recognize that, despite centuries' worth of destructive wars, fires, deliberate desecration, ignorance and absent-mindedness, we are still in possession of so much of our archival inheritance. Not all nations are equally blessed. Britain's good fortune in this respect owes much to the actions of a few individuals. For instance, many of the most important manuscripts to have survived from Anglo-Saxon England might have been lost following the dissolution of the monasteries and the political traumas of the early seventeenth century, had they not been collected and preserved by two men. One of them was Matthew Parker (1504–75), archbishop of Canterbury, who bequeathed his manuscript library to Corpus Christi College, Cambridge. The other was the seventeenth-century MP, Sir Robert Cotton (1571–1631).

Having failed to interest the state in establishing an academy 'for the study of antiquity and history', Cotton began buying as many historic documents as he could afford for the library that he built for Cotton House, his four-storey home adjoining the House of Commons. Politicians as well as antiquarians were given free rein to examine his collection, finding numerous historical precedents with which to challenge the increasingly arbitrary rule of King Charles I. Cognizant of the danger contained in the manuscripts, the king had the library impounded and Cotton briefly imprisoned. Upon his release, he was denied access to his own collection and was still petitioning for readmission when he died, in May 1631, apparently of grief at his library's fate. Seemingly, Charles I – as much as Sir Thomas Fairfax – was fully aware of the potency of old documents.

Yet Cotton's irreplaceable collection – which included not just Magna Carta but also the Lindisfarne Gospels, *Beowulf* and the *Anglo-Saxon Chronicle* – remained intact. In 1701 his grandson, fearful of what might happen when his 'two illiterate' grandchildren inherited it, sold it to the nation. It was the first time that an Act of

Parliament secured books and manuscripts for the benefit of the public. Cotton's collection is now in the safe care of the British Library. Truly, we owe a profound debt of gratitude not just to Cotton and Parker but to all those men and women in private houses, churches, libraries, universities and museums who across the centuries dedicated themselves to preserving manuscripts for posterity, often when others struggled to see the point. It is thanks to their efforts that we can examine the documents that shaped a nation.

I

THE DARK AGES

1ST CENTURY A.D.
THE VINDOLANDA TABLETS

ROMAN EXPERIENCES OF LIFE IN BRITANNIA

Britannia was a province of the Roman Empire from the first to the fifth century AD, as long a period as separates the English Civil War from the present day. Yet what do we really know about this long period of Roman rule? Thankfully, accounts such as that by the great historian Tacitus (c. AD 55–120) have survived. For all their contemporary propaganda and rhetorical passages coloured with artistic licence, they tell us much about how Britain was conquered. However, what happened there during the following 300 years has been more a matter for archaeologists.

It is primarily from the remains of its desecrated monuments and hidden treasure that a picture of Roman Britain has emerged. This is because after the Roman legions departed in AD 410, a 'Dark Age' descended during which neglect, adaptation and outright destruction did so much to erase testimonies from the land that Romans thought of as the end of the known world.

Intricate floor mosaics and indoor plumbing provide evidence of domestic comfort in the villas of the wealthy and the influential (by comparison, such plumbing was beyond the grasp of even an eighteenth-century British aristocrat). The remains of forts and cities offer a sense of Rome's ambitious military and civic planning. The network of roads provided an infrastructure so valuable that, resurfaced, parts of it still connect the country nineteen centuries later.

Following Julius Caesar's abortive expeditions in 55 and 54 BC, in AD 43 the emperor Claudius launched an invasion of the province that the Romans had named Britannia. Although their grip was briefly imperilled during the rebellion of Queen Boudicca of the Iceni tribe in AD 60–61, the invaders clung on and proceeded to consolidate their hold, either by pitting their military might against the hostile British tribes or by bribing the biddable ones into collaboration. Leaving Ireland well alone, the legionaries moved into southern Wales and pushed up into northern Scotland, where their general, Agricola, defeated the Caledonian tribes in

AD 84. Thereafter, the Romans fell back to a tighter west–east defensive line roughly between the River Clyde and the Firth of Forth. However, after the emperor Hadrian visited Britain in AD 122, that boundary was redrawn to the south by the construction of his great seventy-three-mile wall running from the Solway Firth to the Tyne. This northern perimeter of Roman rule has furnished some of the most important insights into the lives of the conquerors.

Ironically, the really poignant narratives are not the testaments intended to endure but rather those consciously dumped in the rubbish pit. During the 1970s, discarded writing tablets began to be unearthed from the site of the Roman fort of Vindolanda, west of Hexham. These were, for the most part, ink inscriptions written on the smooth surfaces of thin leaves of wood, between one and three millimetres thick and postcard-sized. Although they are charred or broken fragments the damp environment has, remarkably, helped preserve them over the better part of two millennia. The earliest appear to date from around AD 90, when Vindolanda was already a fort but before Hadrian's defensive wall system was built nearby.

Many of the writing tablets, now held in the British Museum, are examples of Roman army bureaucracy: receipts for provisions and other commercial transactions, inventories, work assignments, requests for leave and appeals for clemency. From one report, we learn that the fort was garrisoned by soldiers of the First Cohort of Tungrians. The nominal strength was 752 men, but many of them were in fact posted elsewhere. At other times, it was garrisoned by the Ninth Cohort of Batavians. The Tungrians came from the area

THE ROMANS IN BRITAIN

55 BC Julius Caesar launches the first Roman expedition to Britain, landing near Deal.

54 BC Julius Caesar's second expedition to Britain.

AD 43 The emperor Claudius orders a full-scale invasion of Britain.

AD 47–50 Londinium (London) founded.

AD 51 Revolt by the British chieftain Caratacus is crushed and Caratacus is paraded through Rome.

AD 61 Boudicca, Queen of the Iceni, revolts and sacks Colchester, London and St Albans before being defeated.

AD 84 The Battle of Mons Graupius during the invasion of Caledonia (Scotland) by Agricola, governor of Britannia.

AD 122 Work begins on the construction of Hadrian's Wall.

AD 142 The Antonine Wall is constructed between the Forth and the Clyde. It is abandoned by AD 164.

AD 216 Roman Britain is administratively divided into two: Britannia Superior (the South) and Britannia Inferior (the North).

AD c.270 Construction begins of the 'Saxon Shore' of coastal forts to repel Germanic pirates.

AD 306 Constantine is proclaimed Roman emperor at York.

AD 369 Mounting numbers of attacks by Picts and Irish-Scots are repelled by the Roman general Theodosius.

AD 396 The Roman general Stilicho assumes authority in Britain and organizes a defence against attacks by Picts, Irish and Saxons.

AD 402 The Sixth Victrix Legion is withdrawn from Britain.

AD 407 The remaining legion, the Second Augusta, is withdrawn from Britain.

AD 410 The emperor Honorius confirms the Roman departure from Britain.

around the River Meuse and the Batavians from the mouth of the Rhine and the Scheldt, which makes these Roman soldiers, in modern-day terms, Germans and Dutch.

Such documents provide a sense of where Vindolanda's troops came from, how they were organized and even what they were eating. However, they also provide many more personal details. The extent of literacy is evident from the fact that some of the letters are written by – rather than about – slaves. There are the familiar gripes and expressions of lofty condescension voiced by occupying forces down the centuries. Their relations are either being tapped for useful presents or badgered to send money to cover accrued debts. They are also chided for not writing more often. There is the grim reality of being posted far from home. One soldier refers

The writing on this tablet from Vindolanda, dating from c. AD 97–103, reads in translation: 'the Britons are unprotected by armour. There are very many cavalry. The cavalry do not use swords nor do the wretched Brits mount in order to throw javelins.'

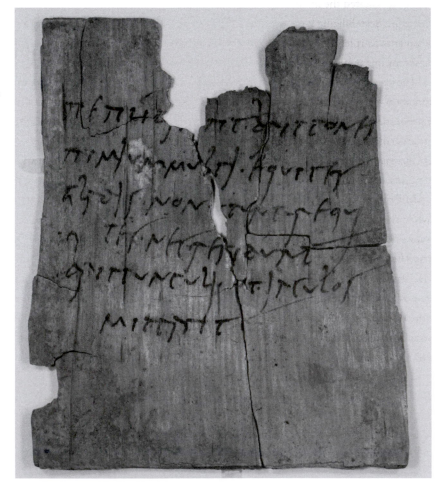

to the natives, the Brittones, by a derisory nickname, Brittunculi, which, roughly translated, means 'Wretched Brits'.

It was not just at javelin distance that Roman soldiers could expect interaction with the natives. Even after Hadrian's Wall was constructed as a heavily fortified barrier, it was also a customs post for cross-border trade, suggesting continuing dealings with those who lived on the far side. Nonetheless, any attempt by Hadrian's successor, Antoninus Pius, to re-establish the Clyde–Forth frontier along the turf ramparts of his Antonine Wall had been abandoned by AD 164, not much more than twenty years after its construction.

Thereafter, while Roman civilization appeared entrenched in the English South and the Midlands, the evidence suggests there were recurring revolts in the North. This necessitated the maintenance of a Roman army in Britain so powerful that it became a destabilizing force in imperial politics, nominating its own – often rival – claimants as rulers. It was, for instance, at York that Constantine was proclaimed emperor in AD 306.

The breakdown of direct authority from Rome was matched by the deteriorating situation elsewhere along the fringes of imperial territories. Troops that ought to have remained in Britain were transferred to the continent, both as part of the internecine struggle for political supremacy between rival power-brokers and in increasingly desperate efforts to hold back the Barbarian onslaught along the empire's contracting Germanic frontiers.

In Britain, Rome's enemies seized their chance. Picts attacked from the north while the defences of the southern English coast were probed by Saxon pirates. Nevertheless, Britannia was still essentially an imperial province when, in AD 410, the Visigoths sacked Rome. In that year an appeal was sent from Britannia to the emperor Honorius requesting help. From Ravenna, where his court had removed itself, Honorius replied that he no longer had any soldiers to spare and that, consequently, Britannia would have to fend for herself. Although he may have meant it as a temporary expedient, the decision ensured the collapse of Roman Britain.

c.710
THE LINDISFARNE GOSPELS

AN ILLUMINATED MASTERPIECE FROM THE DARK AGES

A page from the Lindisfarne Gospels is depicted in the first plate section.

During the fourth century, Christianity spread throughout Britain. Tolerated by the Roman occupiers from AD 313, following the emperor Constantine's Edict of Milan, it was the state religion by 382. The test, however, was whether it could survive the legions' departure in 410.

It fell to the new generation of Romano-British chiefs – among them perhaps a leader later mythologized as King Arthur – to defend the faith against pagan invaders: the Germanic tribes that poured into the country from the mid-fifth century onwards. In the sixth century, as the Britons largely lost the fight, the tenets of Christianity were rubbed out in the wake of the incomers.

In the lands they now occupied, the Germanic immigrants established regional kingdoms. Tribes of Angles settled in the Midlands and the North, giving their name to a new geographical expression – England. Their intermingling with Saxon settlers first led Europeans in the seventh century to coin the term 'Anglo-Saxon' to distinguish them not only from Britain's Celtic inhabitants but from the Saxon tribes remaining on the continent. In turn, Anglo-Saxons described the Celtic Britons they displaced as *wealas*, the Old English word for 'stranger' from which the modern English word 'Welsh' is derived.

During this bleakest period of the 'Dark Ages', Christianity survived only where it lay out of the Anglo-Saxons' reach. St Patrick (c.385–461), a Romano-Briton by birth, took the Christian message across to Ireland. In turn, the Irish missionary St Columba established his monastery on the southern Hebridean island of Iona in 563. From such outposts, the faith was spread throughout the Irish kingdom of Dalriada in western Scotland and to the native Picts beyond.

Christianity returned to England by two routes, one Celtic, the other Roman. In 597, Pope Gregory the Great sent (St) Augustine on a mission from Rome to Canterbury where he baptized the Anglo-Saxon king of Kent, Æthelbert. Converting royalty proved a shrewd 'top-down' means of securing powerful protectors for the

Roman Church. Æthelbert's daughter, Æthelburga, married Edwin, king of the Deiran dynasty in Northumbria. At Easter 627, this most powerful of northern rulers followed his wife's example and converted to Christianity along with his court. After Edwin's death, the Northumbrian throne passed to Oswald, a member of the rival Bernician dynasty. Oswald had previously been exiled on Iona and he encouraged its missionaries to settle in Northumbria.

Among Oswald's gifts to them was Lindisfarne. This small island, which twice daily is both connected to and cut off from the Northumbrian coast by the tide, became one of the focal points for the Columban mission spreading out from Ireland and Scotland. While the Church in northern England was staffed largely by Celtic monks, the doctrine became more identifiably Roman during the later years of the seventh century and, in particular, after 664 when the Synod of Whitby pronounced against the Celtic calendar for Easter. Like the other monastic settlements, the monastery at Lindisfarne acclimatized itself to the universal claims of the Roman Church. Over a period of years, a specifically Celtic Christian tradition in the British Isles began to wane.

Lindisfarne was particularly fortunate in enjoying the strong patronage of Northumbria's monarchs. When the relics of St Cuthbert, its former bishop, were brought there in 698, it became a place of pilgrimage. It was probably with the intention of their being set on the high altar next to St Cuthbert's shrine that the Lindisfarne Gospels were written.

Bound together after completion in a metal-framed cover (subsequently lost), the book contains the gospels of the four evangelists. It is written

EARLY CHRISTIANITY IN BRITAIN

AD 63 According to the twelfth-century chronicler William of Malmesbury, Jesus' disciple, Joseph of Arimathea, reaches Glastonbury.

c.209–304 St Alban becomes Britain's first Christian martyr, although the exact date is disputed.

313 The emperor Constantine legalizes Christianity throughout the Roman Empire.

314 The bishops of London, York and Lincoln attend the Council of Arles.

382 Christianity becomes the state religion throughout the Roman Empire.

5th century Christianity in Britain is in decline following the withdrawal of Rome and the invasion of pagan Germanic tribes.

563 The Irish missionary St Columba establishes his monastery on Iona. The conversion of Scotland follows.

589 St David, a Welsh preacher who founded monastic settlements in Wales and Cornwall, dies.

597 Pope Gregory the Great sends Augustine on a mission to England. Augustine becomes the first archbishop of Canterbury and converts the Kentish king, Æthelbert.

627 The Northumbrian king, Edwin, is converted to Christianity.

635 Aidan of Iona founds the Lindisfarne monastery.

664 The Synod of Whitby accepts the Roman rather than the Celtic calendar for Easter.

735 Bede translates the Gospel of St John into Old English.

793 Vikings sack Lindisfarne monastery.

c.990 Alfric, an English abbot, translates part of the Old Testament into Old English.

in Latin, the source for which was an edition, probably Italian in origin, of the Vulgate. In this respect it was far from unique, but what made it one of the highest manifestations of Anglo-Saxon culture was the rich artistry with which it was illustrated.

Remarkably, it appears to be the work of one hand. If we are to believe the assurance of Aldred – a monk who, in the mid-tenth century, inserted between its Latin lines a word-for-word translation into Old English – we even know the identity of this gifted and extraordinarily patient artist-scribe. He was Eadfrith, Lindisfarne's bishop from 698 to 721.

Although we cannot be certain that Aldred's attribution is accurate, subsequent scholarship generally supports the book's likely provenance as Lindisfarne in the period of Eadfrith's bishopric. Certainly, the monastic community there was sufficient to support him in his undertaking. An extensive library of books, gathered from across Europe, was also available for consultation in the nearby monasteries of Monkwearmouth and Jarrow. Familiarity with such sources may also help explain the Lindisfarne Gospels' eclectic borrowing from different artistic styles. The result was a work that developed a new English art form, which harmonized influences from Celtic, Germanic, Anglo-Saxon, Roman, Byzantine, Middle Eastern and even Coptic art.

Each of the four gospels is introduced with a portrait of the evangelist and his symbol (a man for Matthew; a lion for Mark; a calf for Luke; an eagle for John). A 'carpet page' follows in which the symbol of the cross is contained within a pattern. This form of decoration was common to the Coptic art of the Egyptian Christians, but is augmented in the Lindisfarne Gospels by especially elaborate interwoven rhythmic patterns, with geometrical knots and depictions of birds and animals in the Celtic style. Next comes the 'incipit page'. Here the opening capital letter and the first words of each gospel are surrounded by rich ornamentation, with the first words transcribed in runic fashion. The attention to detail is astounding. For instance, in the incipit page (folio 139r) of the Gospel of Luke, there are 10,600 individually painted red dots in the adornment surrounding the initial.

This level of laboriously executed intricacy is all the more remarkable given that much of it would have been done with relatively primitive implements, without means of magnification and by candlelight. The personal cost of creating such a visual masterpiece must surely have been considerable eye-strain for its lone artist-scribe. Given Eadfrith's other burdensome monastic duties, it represented an extraordinary dedication to art and devotion to faith.

Costs of a different kind were incurred in the luxurious nature of the materials. The Lindisfarne Gospels were written on 259 folio sheets of vellum, whose quality of calfskin far exceeds that generally found in other important documents of the period. Nor were the pigments exclusively derived from local sources. Among the colours used appears to be lapis lazuli, which was quarried in Afghanistan.

The fact that a monk, working on a tiny windswept Northumbrian island, could draw on the resources of much of the known world demonstrates the extent to which this corner of Anglo-Saxon England not only connected itself with the visual remnants of Celtic faith but also fully acknowledged its place within the Roman orthodoxy of European Christendom.

Just as it was not cut off from that greater community, so neither was it spared from its assailants. In 793, Vikings launched a surprise attack on Lindisfarne, sacking the monastery. Further assaults followed, forcing the bishop and most of his monks to flee to the greater safety of the mainland. With them, they took St Cuthbert's remains and the Lindisfarne Gospels, first to Chester-le-Street and later to Durham. It was probably at Chester-le-Street that Aldred added his between-line textual translation into Old English. In doing so, he gave the work an additional importance as the oldest surviving example of the gospels in the English language.

The Lindisfarne Gospels eventually became part of the Cottonian Library after its removal from Durham during the Reformation, and at length found their way, first to the British Museum, and later to the British Library, where they remain to this day.

731

BEDE'S *HISTORIA ECCLESIASTICA GENTIS ANGLORUM*

THE FIRST GREAT HISTORY
OF THE ENGLISH CHURCH AND PEOPLE

While the gospels were being adorned on the island of Lindisfarne, a mere six miles away on the mainland another monk was writing one of the most important English documents of the first millennium. His name was Bede and the masterpiece on which he was working was his *Historia Ecclesiastica Gentis Anglorum* ('Ecclesiastical History of the English Nation').

Born around 673 in the nearby environs of what is now Tyneside, Bede was entrusted at the age of seven to the local monastery, which had two closely affiliated endowments, six miles apart, at Monkwearmouth and Jarrow. This twin monastery had been newly founded by Benedict Biscop, an abbot who had amassed a wealth of manuscripts from a life spent travelling through Europe.

By contrast – and despite living to the age of about sixty-two – Bede may never have ventured further than York. His window on the world was the scholarly treasure-trove at his disposal in Biscop's library. It was there that, having learned Latin, Greek and even some Hebrew, he was able to immerse himself not only in the works of Pope Gregory the Great but even in such non-Christian writers as Vergil.

Bede's interest was not merely in obtaining knowledge but in adding to it. He wrote poems, songs, biblical commentaries and biographies of St Cuthbert as well as of his local abbots. His enquiring mind ranged over subjects as diverse as the calendar and chronology, grammar and natural science. Yet it was in his devotion to the history of England that he made his greatest contribution.

Written in Latin, the *Historia Ecclesiastica* is Bede's attempt to relate England's story from the invasion of Julius Caesar to the year 731. Although primarily the account of how Christianity – and, in particular, the Roman Church – came to establish itself in England, Bede remains our principal source for early Anglo-Saxon England's political and military history.

It is through Bede that the most coherent attribution of early Germanic settlement has been handed down. He was insistent that the Angles colonized the North and the Midlands, the Saxons the South-West and South-East, and the Jutes Kent. He was also a detailed chronicler of the early Church in his native Northumbria, providing a lengthy account of the Synod of Whitby's debate over when to hold Easter and the reign of his hero, King Edwin. One of Bede's most celebrated passages relates Edwin's analogy of the acceptance of Christian teaching, using the image of the flight of a sparrow, passing briefly from the dark and cold of a winter's night through the warmth of a lighted hall and back into the unknown: 'Somewhat like this appears the life of man, but of what follows or what went before, we are utterly ignorant.'

From Chapter 14: The Conversion of King Edwin

So King Edwin with all the nobles of his nation and very many of the people received the faith and the laver of holy regeneration in the eleventh year of his reign, which was the year of our Lord's incarnation 627, and about 180 years from the coming of the English into Britain. He was baptised at York on the holy day of Easter, 12 April, in the church of the Apostle Peter which he himself had hastily built there in wood, while he was a catechumen [one undergoing conversion] receiving instruction for his baptism. In that city also he gave an episcopal see to his teacher and bishop, Paulinus. But as soon as he was baptised, he was eager by Paulinus's direction to construct in that place a larger and more majestic church of stone, in the middle of which might be enclosed the oratory which he had made before. When the foundations had been laid around the former oratory, he began to build the church foursquare. But before the walls reached their full height the king himself was wickedly killed, and left the work to be completed by his successor, Oswald. However, for six years on end from that time, that is, until the end of the reign of the king, Paulinus by his consent and favour preached the word of God in that province; and as many as were foreordained to eternal life believed and were baptised, among whom were the sons of King Edwin, Osfrith and Eadfrith, who had both been born to him in his exile by Cwenburh, daughter of Ceorl, king of the Mercians.

How reliable is Bede's scholarship? As he put it in a brief autobiographical note, he drew his narrative 'either from ancient documents, or from the tradition of the elders, or from my own knowledge'. For the period of the Roman conquest, he relied upon classical authors and, for the coming of the Anglo-Saxons, on the sixth-century Welsh monk Gildas, whose [*Liber Querulus*] *De Excidio Britanniae* ('On the Ruin of Britain') was a diatribe against the sins of his fellow Britons. Inevitably, Bede's chronology was patchy for this Dark Age, until he was able to build into a flowing narrative with the re-emergence of English Christianity in the seventh century. He was firmly on the side of buttressing religious faith in England and, in particular, was determined to inculcate the English with a sense of being part of a greater Roman Christendom. Holding strong beliefs in papal authority, he intended his readers to draw the appropriate conclusions from his chronicle of a young nation stumbling from pagan superstition to religious certainty. Despite these pedagogic aims, Bede's scholarship lifted him beyond the narrow channels of propaganda and patronage. He made every effort to ensure that his research was based on the most reliable information rather than simple regurgitation. Furthermore, his writing style showed a very human sensibility as well as a gift for storytelling.

Perhaps inevitably, Bede was particularly conscious of events in his native Northumbria. However, far from being parochial in intent, his bias is, if anything, weighted towards an over-emphasis on the extent of English unity. Reviving echoes of Roman Britain, he believed that several of the Anglo-Saxon rulers, including the Northumbrian monarchs Edwin and Oswald, should be recognized not just as the leaders of their own regional kingdoms but as effective emperors of all England. To such rulers the *Anglo-Saxon Chronicle* would later designate the title of 'Bretwalda' ('Britain ruler'). In depicting history in this way, Bede helped create the perception of a common English identity and destiny. Indeed, it was his usage that did much to popularize the use of the terms 'England' and 'English'.

In 735, four years after he had completed his great history, Bede lay dying. Despite his physical decline, he endeavoured to keep his mind active by translating the

BEDE'S LIST OF 'BRETWALDAS'

Ælle of Sussex, reigned 488–c.514

Ceawlin of Wessex, reigned 560–92

Æthelbert of Kent, reigned 590–616

Raedwald of East Anglia, reigned c.600–24

Edwin of Northumbria, reigned 616–33

Oswald of Northumbria, reigned 633–42

Oswiu of Northumbria, reigned 642–70

To which list the *Anglo-Saxon Chronicle* added:

Egbert of Wessex, reigned 802–39

Gospel of St John into Old English and composing a five-line 'death song' musing on the thought that mortals can never know how a man's soul will be judged in the afterlife. What most endured of Bede's own reputation rested with his *Historia Ecclesiastica*. Copies were made soon after his death and were translated into Old English in the ninth century. Other editions in the original Latin were exported across a European continent that was at last able to enjoy the fruits of Anglo-Saxon scholarship where previously the literary traffic had flowed only in the other direction. As the first historian to systematically use the *anno domini* dating chronology, he eventually influenced its adoption across Europe.

Meanwhile, in the small corner of England where Bede had spent his entire life, the culture that had nurtured him was under renewed assault. The Viking raids that harassed Lindisfarne also forced the monasteries of Monkwearmouth and Jarrow to be evacuated by the beginning of the ninth century. However, in the eleventh century Bede's presumed grave was discovered and his remains were re-interred in Durham Cathedral. The tradition of describing him as 'Venerable' survived long after the custom for so entitling other monks had withered. The other title that has stuck to him over the centuries, which no amount of subsequent discovery and research has diminished, is 'the Father of English History'.

8TH–10TH CENTURY
BEOWULF

THE GREATEST SURVIVING WORK
OF ANGLO-SAXON LITERATURE

We do not know who wrote the epic poem *Beowulf*, nor whether its eponymous hero sprang from the creator's imagination or was at least distantly based on a long-dead and subsequently mythologized figure whose deeds grew more extraordinary with repeated telling. An inter-generational debate among historians has failed to determine the century from which the story dates or even the English kingdom in which it was written. However, there is no disputing that *Beowulf* is the greatest surviving poem written in the Old English language.

The story is set in sixth-century Scandinavia, yet draws on aspects of old Germanic legends. Some of the words used suggest it may have been produced in one of the kingdoms settled by the Angles. Although the central characters belong to a pagan world, there are biblical references. For instance, it is stated that the monstrous Grendel is Cain's descendant. The work is assumed not to pre-date the eighth century nor to be later than the tenth century.

Beowulf is 3,182 lines in length and is written in the alliterative metre typical of most Old English poetry. It is about a hero governed only by duty, honour and bravery, who finds all too often that his supposed companions either fight among themselves or run away at the first sign of danger. As might be expected of a story set in a warrior society, it is suffused with strong and masculine descriptions; but far from merely being a blood-curdling tale of gore and brutality, its tone is frequently philosophical and reflective.

Grendel, a terrifying semi-human monster, makes repeated attacks on the great hall of Heorot, a Danish kingdom, dragging off and killing one unsuspecting victim after another. Wracked by fear, the community faces disintegration. Hope arrives in the shape of Beowulf, who travels from the land of the Geats in southern Sweden with fourteen warriors bent on freeing the people of Heorot from Grendel's terror.

When Grendel arrives for another raid on the hall, Beowulf wrestles with him, tears off his arm and inflicts a mortal injury. Grendel's mother, more terrible still, seeks revenge and carries off one of the king of Heorot's closest henchmen. Beowulf, having volunteered to track down Grendel's mother, finds her in her lair at the bottom of a lake. A great underwater fight ensues in which Beowulf succeeds in killing the monstrous matriarch.

Beowulf returns to Sweden a hero and is eventually elevated to the throne. He rules long and wisely over his people until a dragon, which has guarded treasure for 300 years, is disturbed and goes on the rampage, burning Beowulf's hall to cinders. Despite his now advanced age, Beowulf summons up his courage and pledges to slay the dragon. However, so fearsome is the beast that Beowulf's followers flee in terror, leaving him to his fate. Only a young kinsman, Wiglaf, stands by him. Beowulf gets the upper hand in the fight but, just as he is about to slay the dragon, his sword shatters and the creature inflicts a poisonous wound. Wiglaf helps him kill the beast but the venom takes its effect and Beowulf's life ebbs away.

By his fidelity, Wiglaf has shown himself Beowulf's worthy successor and becomes king. He berates those who left the fallen hero to his nemesis, bringing dishonour on themselves and giving hope to the kingdom's enemies. The poem concludes with Beowulf's interment in a great barrow with the dragon's treasure. Around him, his people lament 'that of all the kings upon the earth he was the one most gracious and fair-minded, kindest to his people and keenest to win fame'.

With themes that embrace the hero as saviour, the testing of bravery, the nobility of the quest and the pitting of man against monster, *Beowulf* contains many staples of Western storytelling. J. R. R. Tolkien's *The Hobbit* and his *Lord of the Rings* trilogy are perhaps the greatest of the twentieth-century works for which it has been an inspiration. While Professor of Anglo-Saxon at the University of Oxford in the 1930s, Tolkien did much to popularize *Beowulf* as a great work of poetry rather than merely as a document of historical importance. Indeed, for many centuries it was scarcely known and it was not until 1815 that the first published edition appeared. It had survived in the meantime in only one manuscript – whose whereabouts prior to the sixteenth century are not recorded – and was acquired by the British Museum in the eighteenth century. Fortunately, the museum had two copies made, a decision that proved indispensable to future generations of scholars who would otherwise have been unable to decipher passages in the original manuscript after it was damaged in a fire not long afterwards.

878–890

THE TREATY OF
ALFRED AND GUTHRUM

ESTABLISHING THE BOUNDARY BETWEEN ANGLO-SAXON
AND VIKING-OCCUPIED ENGLAND

The survival of Christian Britain was as fragile as the parchments upon which the monks of Jarrow and Lindisfarne chronicled and commemorated it. During the eighth century, fresh waves of invasion by a new pagan foe, the Vikings, threatened to drive it back to the periphery.

Sailing from Scandinavia, the Norsemen and Danish warriors reached far-flung corners of the island. Wales suffered least, beyond some incursions along the coast. In Scotland, however, the Vikings seized the northern and western isles, sacking the monastery at Iona in the process. England came under intense attack, with the looting of Lindisfarne just a foretaste. In 867 the previously dominant kingdom of Northumbria fell to the invader. The Midlands kingdom of Mercia capitulated the following year. By 871 every kingdom had been overwhelmed – with the exception of Wessex. If it fell, Anglo-Saxon England was lost.

The fate of Wessex rested with its new king, the twenty-two-year-old Alfred. He had become battle-hardened the previous year, helping his brother to see off one Viking assault at Ashdown in Berkshire, only to lose successive encounters thereafter. Further battles and parleys followed, with the Vikings penetrating deep into Wessex. They held Reading; then even Exeter fell to them. In January 878 their warlord, Guthrum, launched a surprise onslaught, seizing Chippenham and almost capturing Alfred.

Slipping from his pursuers' grasp, Alfred became a fugitive, seeking sanctuary in the reed beds and bogs around Athelney in Somerset. Despite the reality that much of his kingdom was overrun, he refused to give up, instead sending word that his followers should meet at the stone of his grandfather, King Egbert. Gathering them around him, he marched to meet Guthrum's army. At Edington in Wiltshire

This silver penny was minted during the rule of King Alfred over Wessex (871–99). It depicts Alfred on the obverse while on the reverse a cross and a monogram of Londonia acknowledge the absorption of London into his realm.

23

The Treaty of Alfred and Guthrum. The words describing the Saxon–Viking boundary line appear, in Old English, in the last paragraph on the right-hand side of the document (a translation appears on the facing page).

in May 878 the two sides fought one of the decisive battles of English history. Alfred was victorious. The Vikings were routed.

Stunned and impressed, Guthrum came to see Alfred at Aller in Somerset and in the church there a remarkable ceremony took place. Guthrum converted to Christianity. Alfred became his godfather, even raising him from the baptismal font. The two Christian leaders then spent a fortnight together at Wedmore where they drew up a peace treaty. The Vikings would hold on to their conquests in Northumbria and East Anglia (where Guthrum would rule), while agreeing to leave Wessex alone.

Although the peace did not hold, the treaty brought Alfred sufficient breathing space to strengthen both his army and his personal authority. Thus when fresh Viking attacks were made on Kent in 885, Alfred was able to see them off and

From the Treaty of Alfred and Guthrum

This is the peace which King Alfred and King Guthrum and the councillors of all the English race and all the people which is in East Anglia have all agreed on and confirmed with oaths, for themselves and for their subjects, both for the living and those yet unborn, who care to have God's grace upon ours.

First concerning our boundaries: up the Thames, and then up the Lea, and along the Lea to its source, then in a straight line to Bedford, then up the Ouse to the Watling Street. . . .

enter London. He rebuilt the city on the largely abandoned site of the Roman Londinium. Sometime shortly thereafter, he renewed the treaty with Guthrum. This is the version of the treaty that survives, with London in Alfred's domain, demarcating Anglo-Saxon from Viking-occupied England. (It can be found today at Corpus Christi College, Cambridge.) As the first clause makes clear, the new boundary line ran along the Thames estuary, up the Lea, thence to Bedford, then up the Ouse and along Watling Street.

This agreement represented only a partial victory for the Anglo-Saxons. It accepted rather than challenged Viking authority over eastern and northern England, the territory that became known as the Danelaw. However, such acknowledgement was the prerequisite of containment, the real achievement of the treaty. And in containing the Viking threat behind this line, it not only gave Alfred time to build forts, construct a navy and reform his army, it also helped solidify the political unity of the non-Danelaw areas of England under the rule of the royal house of Wessex. Some of the coins minted during the remainder of Alfred's reign proclaimed him *rex Anglorum*. Even if he could not really claim to be king of England, he was at least ruler of the free English. It would be for his tenth-century successors – Edward the Elder and, in particular, Athelstan – to defeat the Danelaw and unify all England under one rule.

c.890–1116
THE *ANGLO-SAXON CHRONICLE*

SHINING LIGHT UPON THE DARK AGES

The *Anglo-Saxon Chronicle* is the most comprehensive record of English history in the first millennium. It is also the most immediate account extant from the reign of King Alfred through to the middle of the twelfth century. Furthermore, it is the oldest surviving significant set of annals of any European people written in their native language.

The fact that it is in Old English is important in itself. Following the example of Bede's *Historia Ecclesiastica*, we might expect works compiled in places of learning to be in Latin. However, during the ninth century the reach of Latin as a common spoken language was diminishing even among some of the country's cultured elite. English had become the usual language in which laws, wills and even many charters were expressed, an assertion of national identity that King Alfred actively encouraged. Not only did he personally work on translating into English such Latin works as Pope Gregory's *Liber Regulae Pastoralis* ('Pastoral Cares'), he also sponsored a programme of scholarship to make available in English what he believed were those 'books which may be most necessary for all men to know'.

Whether Alfred directly commissioned the *Anglo-Saxon Chronicle* cannot be confirmed, for the oldest such written claim dates from after the Norman Conquest. Nevertheless, its composition began in Wessex during his reign. It may have been driven by the desire to collect and preserve what was known of earlier events, as well as to relate them to the contemporary achievements of Alfred's victories over the Danes and the growing sense of Wessex's role in holding together Anglo-Saxon England.

The *Chronicle* is not one document but several, for it was copied and updated in a number of locations. It is not known how many copies may once have existed, but nine have survived, either complete or in fragment. The earliest version is no

inn to exanceaſtɾe · 7 þy ȝeaɾe healfdene noɾþanhymbɾa
land ȝedælde 7 eɾȝende ƿæɾon 7 hiɾa tilȝende ƿæɾon ·

her com ſe heɾe to exanceſtɾe fɾam ƿeɾeham · 7 ða meɾehɾe
micel myſt onfoɾ · 7 þæɾ foɾ ƿeaɾð · cxx · ſcypa æt ſƿaneƿic ·
7 ſe cing ælfɾed æfteɾ þam ȝehoɾſodan heɾe mid fyɾde ɾad
oþ exanceſteɾ · 7 hi hindan oɾ ɾidan ne mihte · 7 hi him ȝiſlaſ
ſealdon ſƿa feɾla ſƿa he habban ƿolde · 7 micle aþaſ ſƿoɾon
7 ða ȝode fɾið heoldon · 7 þa on hæɾfeſte ȝefoɾ ſe heɾe on
myɾcena land · 7 hit ȝedældon ſum · 7 ſum ceolƿulfe ſealdon ·

her hine beſtæl ſe heɾe on midne ƿinteɾ ofeɾ · xii · niht
to cyppanhamme · 7 ȝeɾidon ƿeſſexna land 7 þaɾ ȝeſæton
7 micel þæſ folceſ ofeɾ ſæ adɾæfdon · 7 þæſ oþeɾ þone mæſtan
dæl hi ȝeɾidon 7 þ folc him to ȝebiȝde buton þam cinȝe
ælfɾede he lytle ƿeɾede uneþelice æfteɾ ƿudum foɾ · 7 on
moɾfæſtenum · 7 þæɾ ilcan ƿintɾeſ ƿæſ inƿeɾeſ bɾoðoɾ
7 healfdeneſ on ƿeſſexna ſtɾe mid · xxiii · ſcypa 7 hine mon
þæɾ ofſloh 7 dccc · manna mid him 7 lx · manna hiſ heɾeſ ·
7 þæɾ ƿæſ ſe ȝuðfana ȝenumen þe hie hɾæfn heton ·

Ond þæſ on eaſtɾon poɾhte ælfɾed cinȝ lytle ƿeɾede ȝeƿoɾc
æt æþelinȝa iȝȝe · 7 of ðam ȝeƿoɾce þæſ ƿinnende ƿið
þone heɾe · 7 ɾumuſ ſætena ſe dæl · ſe ðæɾ nehſt þæſ · þa on
þæɾe · ſii · ƿucan ofeɾ eaſtɾon he ȝeɾad to ecȝbɾihteſ ſtane
be eaſtɾn ſealƿuda · 7 him comon þæɾ onȝen ɾumuſ ſæte
ealle · 7 ƿilſæte 7 hamtunſciɾ ſe dæl þe hiɾe beheonan ſæ ƿæſ
7 hiſ ȝefæȝne ƿæɾon · 7 he foɾ þæſ embe ane niht of þam picu
to iȝlea · 7 ðæſ eft embe ane niht to eðandune · 7 þæɾ ȝefeaht
ƿið eal ne þone heɾe 7 hine ȝeflymde 7 him æfteɾ ɾad

From the *Anglo-Saxon Chronicle*, 1016

[King Edmund overtook the Danes] at Ashingdon, and there a fierce battle was fought. The ealdorman Eadric did as he had often done before: he and the men from Herefordshire and south Shropshire were the first to set the example of flight, and thus he betrayed his royal lord and the whole nation. Cnut was victorious, and won all England by his victory. Among the slain were Bishop Eadnoth, Abbot Wulfsige . . . and all the flower of England.

longer extant, but, once copied and distributed, it provided the common source material upon which the succeeding versions drew, especially in their coverage of the period between the first and ninth centuries. Thereafter, these copies were separately updated from their various locations by a succession of scribes, with all the varying emphases and detail that such a process entailed.

The 'Parker Chronicle', now kept at Corpus Christi College, Cambridge, appears to have been started around 891 in Winchester and covers the years from 60 BC to AD 1070. The Bodleian Library in Oxford holds the 'Laud Chronicle', written in Peterborough from a copy probably originating in Canterbury. Updated regularly until 1154, it continued the annals furthest, beyond the Anglo-Saxon age and into the troubled reign of King Stephen. The other versions are in the British Library. These were written in Canterbury, Abingdon and Worcester (the latter containing much material gleaned from northern English sources). With no collective cut-off point, they finish their accounts at various dates in the tenth and eleventh centuries. So arbitrary are some endings that one of the Abingdon scribes stopped abruptly halfway through a report on the Battle of Stamford Bridge in 1066. The paragraph was eventually finished by a much later twelfth-century hand.

That these chronicles remain far and away the most important and reliable source for Anglo-Saxon history does not mean that they are without bias or devoid of propaganda. There is, for instance, a presumption in favour of Wessex, the rights of the Church and of the Anglo-Saxons over the Vikings. Yet by its nature, the *Chronicle* – unlike Bede's history – ranges beyond the work of a single historian imposing his personal interpretation upon events. Thus, despite the elements that the different versions have in common, it is often their points of factual variation and differing regional emphasis that undermine the notion of the *Chronicle* as merely an exercise in composing an 'official' version of events.

II

THE MEDIEVAL AGE

LATE 11TH CENTURY
THE BAYEUX TAPESTRY

THE STORY OF THE NORMAN CONQUEST

Part of the Bayeux Tapestry is depicted in the first plate section.

Can the Bayeux Tapestry be considered a document, let alone a British one? Technically, it is not even a tapestry, for that would mean it was woven by a shuttle and loom. It is in fact an embroidery, created by needles threading dyed wool through linen cloth. Although only fifty centimetres high, its nine sections were sewn together so that it stretches over seventy metres in length.

That it is an artwork should not detract from its primary importance: it was made to document and justify events perhaps as little as a decade after they occurred. Like a newsreel delivered in the format of a comic strip, it tells in sequential words and images the story of the Norman Conquest of England. In doing so, it represents the opening salvo of 900 years of Anglo-French rivalry. Celebrating a French achievement and displayed in the French city from which it takes its name, it would later enthral Napoleon Bonaparte who declared that it 'records one of the most memorable deeds of the French nation and preserves the memory of the pride and courage of our ancestors'.

Given that he hoped to launch a cross-Channel invasion of his own, Napoleon's boast was understandable, but he was actually admiring what is almost certainly an English work of art, most probably made in Kent by English embroiderers. The superiority of English needlework during the period was widely acknowledged. Furthermore, although the inscriptions are in Latin, there is a familiarity with the way English names are spelled. Some of the more standardized images appear to have been copied from the Canterbury scriptoria of St Augustine's Abbey and Christ Church.

The version of events related by the Bayeux Tapestry is central to our understanding of one of the most important events in British history. Its narrative commences in 1064, with the Anglo-Saxon king Edward the Confessor dispatching his brother-in-law, Harold Godwinson, earl of Wessex, on a trip to

Normandy. The son of Æthelred the Unready, King Edward was childless and, at different times, seems to have made various (not legally binding) promises as to his preferred heir. One recipient of his approval was William, duke of Normandy. Although William was only Edward's second cousin at one remove, he was looked on favourably by Edward, who had spent much of his youth in Normandy as a refugee when the Danish king Canute and his sons occupied the English throne.

It is not clear from other sources what spurred Harold to make his fateful crossing of the English Channel to visit William's court. It may have been an accidental shipwreck. The Bayeux Tapestry implies that it was an official mission that went wrong, forcing William to rescue the young English prince from the clutches of Normandy's enemy, Guy of Ponthieu. In return, Harold is depicted, his hands placed on religious reliquaries, under the caption 'UBI HAROLD SACRAMENTUM FECIT WILLELMO DUCI' ('Where Harold made an oath to Duke William'). The assumption is that he made a solemn vow to support William's claim to the English throne on Edward the Confessor's death.

Subsequently, the tapestry shows Edward on his deathbed, affirming Harold as his chosen heir. Backed by the high council, the Witan, Harold is crowned king, but a comet in the sky portends ill fortune (Halley's Comet passed over England in April 1066). In the lower margin, the ghostly image of ships is thinly picked out. Taking his horses with him, William duly sails to England to stake his claim to the throne. The last third of the tapestry narrates the course of the Battle of Hastings. Its most famous sequence depicts Harold's death. Tantalizingly, there is more than one way to read this section. The words 'HAROLD REX INTERFECTUS EST' ('Here King Harold was killed') appear to connect not one but two Anglo-Saxon warriors. 'HAROLD REX' is above a soldier who appears to have been struck in the eye by an arrow, but the rest of the description seems to relate to a soldier being felled by Norman cavalry.

THE END OF ANGLO-SAXON ENGLAND

5 January 1066 King Edward the Confessor dies.

6 January Harold II is crowned king, probably in Westminster Abbey.

20 September At the Battle of Fulford, the invading force of Earl Tostig and Harald Hardrada, king of Norway, defeats the forces of the earls of Mercia and Northumberland.

25 September At the Battle of Stamford Bridge, Harold defeats the invaders; Tostig and Hardrada are killed.

28 September William, duke of Normandy, lands with his army at Pevensey.

14 October At the Battle of Hastings (Senlac Hill) Harold is killed.

November William takes London.

25 December William is crowned king of England in Westminster Abbey.

1069–70 During the 'Harrying of the North', William crushes dissent by laying waste to northern England.

1071 Hereward the Wake's revolt in the Fens is suppressed.

1086 The Domesday Book is collected.

1087 William is fatally injured while laying siege to Mantes in France.

The seal of William the Conqueror.

The most plausible explanation is that both men are Harold, struck first by an arrow and then felled by the horseman's sword. Holes in the linen suggest the felled warrior may originally also have had an arrow in his eye.

William was the illegitimate son of Duke Robert of Normandy and a tanner's daughter, who was officially the duke's mistress. The tapestry aimed to legitimize his seizure of England. Accordingly, it shows how Harold paid the consequence for breaking a solemn oath that William should be given the throne, even if as a captive he had given it only under duress. Yet as a work of propaganda, the tapestry is surprisingly sympathetic to the vanquished foe. Harold is depicted as a heroic and noble figure. Indeed, the first half of the tapestry seems to be far more about him than about William. During his stay in France, Harold is shown personally rescuing men from dangerous quicksand. In contrast, after they land in England Norman troops are depicted burning down the homes of innocent women and children. Far from being a divinely ordained walkover, the Battle of Hastings is accurately depicted as a close encounter, full of twists and turns. Nor are inconvenient details excluded, such as Edward's dying affirmation of Harold as his successor. Perhaps the most substantive omission is Harold's startling victory against an invading force led by the king of Norway at Stamford Bridge, outside York. The battle was fought only eighteen days before the exhausted English army, force-marched to the south coast, found itself facing the Norman cavalry at Hastings.

Who might have commissioned such a work? It was long assumed that the patron was William's diminutive wife, Queen Matilda. However, given the sympathetic rendering of Edward the Confessor and Harold, an intriguing alternative has been suggested in the personality of another queen depicted in the work: Edith. Despite being both Edward's widow and Harold's sister, Queen Edith played a politically skilful hand after the Norman Conquest, thereby ensuring – unusually – that she was not stripped of her estates. It is possible that the tapestry was her way of threading a path between honouring her Anglo-Saxon past and collaborating with a Norman future. If so, it must have been commissioned before her death in 1075.

Odo, bishop of Bayeux, remains another strong possibility. Odo was William's half-brother and he was created earl of Kent, where the Bayeux Tapestry was most likely made. However, having been appointed regent of England during William's absences in Normandy, he overreached himself by attempting to become pope too and fell out with William in 1082. The tapestry may have been a futile attempt to flatter his half-brother. It certainly flatters Odo, whose own prominence in the success of the events is highlighted.

The final section of the tapestry – which may have depicted William's coronation – is lost, but it is more astonishing that the rest has been preserved. The property of Bayeux Cathedral since at least the fifteenth century (it is first mentioned in an inventory of 1476), it was lucky to survive both the destructive zeal of Calvinist despoilers, who ransacked the cathedral in 1562, and the order for it to be torn up and used as canvas covers by French revolutionaries in 1792. In 1944, Heinrich Himmler – who decided it was 'important for our glorious and cultured Germanic history' – made a last-minute attempt to cart it off via Paris to Berlin and was prevented only by the speedy advance of the Allied armies following D-Day. It was a timely rescue, not least since it might not have survived in the ruins of the Third Reich. Bayeux itself was the first city to be liberated by British troops in the Normandy landings. A monument to their casualties subsequently placed there reads 'NOS A GULIELMO VICIT VICTORIS PATRIAM LIBERAVIMUS' – 'We, once conquered by William, have now set free the Conqueror's native land.'

1086
THE DOMESDAY BOOK

WILLIAM THE CONQUEROR'S SURVEY OF THE NATION
AND THE CENTRALIZATION OF STATE POWER

In the twentieth year of his English rule, William the Conqueror ordered a comprehensive assessment of his kingdom, in terms of who owned what, how much each holding was worth, what it might yield in taxes, and the services that tenants owed. The result was the Domesday Book. It listed not only the names of the landowners and the extent of their property, but also the use to which their land was put, right down to its ploughing capacity and the presence of fishponds. As such, the Domesday Book was unparalleled in scope and purpose, for nowhere else in Europe had so detailed a record been attempted. It is central to our understanding of the feudal state created by the Norman Conquest.

It was at Christmas 1085, while William was with his court at Gloucester, that he directed the work to commence. The contemporary account in the *Anglo-Saxon Chronicle* struggled to conceal its sense of awe when describing the extent of the ambition: 'So very thoroughly did he have the inquiry carried out that there was not a single "hide", nor one virgate of land, not even – it is shameful to record it, but it did not seem shameful for him to do – not even one ox, nor one cow, nor one pig which escaped notice in his survey.'

The principal omissions were Cumbria, Northumberland and County Durham, the northern territories not fully under Norman control and hotly disputed with the Scottish king, Malcolm Canmore. Although no record survives for Winchester and London, this may be because the relevant manuscripts are lost rather than because the two great cities were deliberately excluded. However, full surveys were made of all the counties of England south of the River Tees as well as the Welsh border areas. In all, the Domesday Book makes reference to 13,418 places. For many villages, this is their first recorded mention in history.

34

Remarkably, the information was gathered within seven months. The well-organized system that delivered these results subdivided England into multi-county regions and designated a panel of commissioners to each. These teams travelled to every village and borough, taking down evidence testified to under oath in the local provincial courts. Careful note was made of the leading landowners, the manors and estates, their extent and the features of the holdings, subtenures, slaves and value, both in 1086 and at the end of Edward the Confessor's reign in 1066. The information was then sent for analysis and revision to Winchester.

At Winchester, the vast quantity of material was summarized so that it could be made available in a readily accessible format. This version is known as 'Great Domesday' and is written in a single hand (with some insertions and corrections in a second hand). However, it excludes Essex, Suffolk and Norfolk. Perhaps because they filed late, no summary was created for these counties. Instead, for them we have the full and unabridged circuit returns, bound together in a second volume known as 'Little Domesday'. In addition, the circuit returns for Cornwall, Devon, Dorset and Wiltshire have been preserved at Exeter Cathedral. This 'Exon Domesday' allows historians to compare the raw data directly with the overview provided in 'Great Domesday'.

It is hardly surprising that so thorough an exercise acquired the epithet Domesday. To all those brought forth to testify under oath, its result must indeed have seemed as final as the Day of Judgment. The entire process was clearly an assertion of the intrusive powers of the Norman state, an authority far more centralized than Anglo-Saxon forms of government, even if it was partly dependent upon the latter's old tax records. Yet although it showed that the king owned a fifth of the country (with a further quarter owned by the Church), Domesday's instigation was in some ways the consequence of Norman insecurity.

Much of William's reign was devoted to building strong castles and suppressing revolts, both in England and back in Normandy, where he died after injuring himself sacking Mantes the year after Domesday's completion. The need to suppress repeated insurrections stretched the capacity of the Norman war-machine. Furthermore, in 1085 a costly army had to be garrisoned in readiness for an expected – but ultimately aborted – invasion by the allied armies of the Danish king and the count of Flanders (the last Scandinavian invasion attempt in English history). It is in this light that the Domesday project must be seen: as an attempt to update the tax assessments as well as to assert the feudal dues upon which the survival of this security-conscious Norman state depended.

Erchenger ten' de rege in æccta de CANTETONE ii. virg' træ 7 dimid'. Tra. ē. ii. car'. In dnio. ē dimid' car'. cu. i. uillo 7 vi. bord'. Ibi. vij. ac' pasturæ. 7 xxx. ac' pti. 7 iiij. ac' siluæ minutæ. Valet. xxx. sol'.

Stefan' capellan' ten' ecctam de MILVERTONE cu una v træ 7 uno ferding. Tra. ē. i. car'. Ibi. x. ac' siluæ.

Aluuet pbr' ten' de rege. i. hidam in SUDPERETONE. Tra. ē. i. car'. q' ibi. ē cu. i. bord' 7 uno seruo. Ibi. viij. ac' pti. Valet. xx. solid'. Val. xl. sol.

In æccta CARENTONE iacet. i. hida 7 dim'. Ibi. ē in dnio. i. car' 7 dimid'. cu pbro 7 i. uillo. 7 viii. bord'. Ibi. xl. ac' pasturæ 7 xv. ac' siluæ. Valet. xxx. solid'.

In æccta de PERETUNE. iacent. iii. virg' træ. Tra. ē. i. car'. q' ibi. ē. Valet. xx. solid'. Has. ii. æcctas tenuit Petrus eps'. Modo st in manu regis.

Leofus ten' ESSA. q' 7 tenuit de rege. E. 7 geldb' p una v træ. Tra. ē. i. car'. q' ibi. ē cu. i. seruo 7 ii. bord'. Ibi molin' redd'. vi. den' 7 vi. ac' pti. Valet. x. solid'.

Turstin' ten' LEGE. p'at' ei' tenuit T.R.E. 7 geldb' p. i. hida. Tra. ē. i. car'. Ibi st. ii. bord'. Valet. x. solid'.

Goduin' ten' dimid' hid' in ā qd uocat' Ragiol. de rege in elemosina. Valet. iii. sol'. Valet. xii. sol.

In æccta de CURI. ē dimid' hida. Ibi h't pbr. i. car'.

Eddida monialis ten' in elemosina de rege. xii. ac' træ. Ibi h't qc' xx. ac' siluæ 7 pasturæ. Val. v. solid'.

Due nonnæ ten' de rege in elemosina. ii. v træ 7 dimid' in HONECOTE. Tra. ē. ii. car'. Ibi. ē. i. car' 7 v. ac' pti. Valet. v. solid'.

In CHENEMERESDONE. ē dimid' hida træ. Val. x. sol. Petrus eps' tenuit. Modo. ē in manu regis.

·XVII· TERRA COMITIS EUSTACHIJ.

COMES EUSTACHIUS tenuit de rege DUDESTONE. Leuuin' tenuit T.R.E. 7 geldb' p una hida 7 una v træ. Tra. ē. iiij. car'. De ea. ē in dnio. i. virg' træ 7 dim'. 7 ibi. i. car' 7 ii. serui. 7 iii. uilli 7 vi. bord' cu. iii. car'. Ibi molin' redd'. xx. den' 7 iii. ac' pti. 7 xxiii. ac' pasturæ 7 xviii. ac' siluæ. Valuit 7 uat. iiij. lib. Aluredus ten' de comite.

Ipse Alured' ten' de co. CELDRA. Leuuin' tenuit T.R.E. 7 geldb' p. i. hida 7 dim'. Tra. ē. vi. car'. In dnio. ē. i. car' 7 ii. serui. 7 ii. uilli 7 i. bord' cu. ii. car'. Ibi. xxvi. ac' pti. 7 x. ac' pasturæ 7 ii. ac' siluæ. Valuit. l. sol. Modo. xl. solid'.

Euuard' ten' de co. LECHESWRDE. Aluuard' tenuit T.R.E. 7 geldb' p una v træ. Tra. ē. ii. car'. In dnio. ē dimid' car' 7 iii. serui. 7 iiii. uilli 7 iii. bord' cu. i. car' 7 dimid'. Ibi. ii. molini redd'. ii. plūbas ferri. 7 iii. ac' pti 7 xx. ac' siluæ. Valuit 7 uat. xxx. solid'.

Ipse comes ten' LOCHESTONE. Uluiet tenuit T.R.E. 7 geldb' p. v. hid'. Tra. ē. vii. car'. De ea st in dnio. iij. hidæ 7 ibi. ii. car' 7 ii. serui. 7 v. uilli 7 vi. bord' cu. iii. car'. Ibi molin' redd'. vi. den' 7 l. ac' pti. 7 lx. ac' pasturæ 7 vi. ac' siluæ minutæ. Valuit 7 uat. c. solid'.

Alured' ten' de co. CELESWORDE. Thuri tenuit T.R.E. 7 geldb' p. iii. hid'. Tra. ē. iii. car'. De ea st in dnio. ii. hidæ 7 dim'. 7 ii. uilli 7 ii. bord' cu. i. car'. In dnio aliu. Ibi. v. ac' pti. Silua. v. qc lg. 7 una qc lat'. Valet. lx. sol.

Alured' ten' de co. BELSETONE. Toui tenuit T.R.E. 7 geldb' p. iiii. hid'. Tra. ē. iiii. car'. In dnio. ē. i. car' 7 dim'. cu. i. seruo. 7 v. uilli 7 ii. bord' cu. ii. car'. Ibi molinu' redd'. xv. solid'. 7 xxii. ac' pti. 7 xx. ac' pasturæ. Silua. iii. qc lg. 7 ii. qc lat'. Valuit. iii. lib. Modo. iiij. lib.

bolonens'.

Comitissa bol' ten' de rege CHINEWARDESTUNE. Uluiet tenuit T.R.E. 7 geldb' p. v. hid'. Tra. ē. viij. car'. De ea st in dnio. ii. hidæ 7 iii. virg'. 7 ibi. ii. car'. 7 vi. serui. 7 viii. uilli. 7 viii. bord' cu. v. car'. Ibi. xxv. ac' pti. 7 xxii. ac' pasturæ. Silua. iij. qc lg. 7 una ac' lat'. Valuit 7 uat. xi. lib.

Machildis ten' de co. CONTITONE. Wlnod tenuit T.R.E. 7 geldb' p. v. hid'. Tra. ē. v. car'. De ea st in dnio. iii. hidæ 7 ibi. ii. car'. 7 iiij. serui. 7 v. uilli 7 x. bord'. cu. iii. car'. Ibi molin' redd'. lxiiij. den' 7 v. ac' pti. Pastura. iiij. qc lg. 7 ii. qc lat'. Valet. c. solid'.

·XVIII· TERRA HUGONIS COMITIS.

COMES HUGO ten' de rege TEDINTONE. 7 Witts de eo. Ednod tenuit T.R.E. 7 geldb' p una hida. Tra. ē. iiij. car'. In dnio. ē una car' 7 iiii. serui. 7 v. uilli 7 viii. bord' cu. ii. car'. Ibi. v. ac' pti 7 c. ac' pasturæ. 7 xl. ac' siluæ. Valuit 7 uat. xl. solid'.

Witts ten' de co. SANFORD. T.R.E. geldb' p. ii. hid'. Tra. ē. v car'. In dnio. ē. i. car'. cu. i. seruo. 7 viii. uilli cu. i. car'. Ibi. xx. ac' pti. 7 l. ac' siluæ. 7 molin'. Valuit 7 uat. iii. lib.

Witts ten' de co. ALRE. Ednod tenuit T.R.E. 7 geldb' p dim' hida. Tra. ē. ii. car'. cu. i. seruo. 7 i. bord' 7 i. uillo. 7 i. ac' pti. 7 xxxvi. ac' pasturæ. 7 vi. ac' siluæ. Valuit. xx. sol'. Modo. xv. sol'.

Eccta S' SEUERI ten' de co. HENGESTERICH. Ednod tenuit T.R.E. 7 geldb' p. iiij. hid'. Tra. ē. iiij. car'. De ea st in dnio. iii. hidæ 7 dim'. 7 ibi. ii. car' 7 iiii. serui. 7 vi. bord' cu. i. car'. Ibi. xxx. ac' pti. 7 xx. ac' pasturæ. 7 silua. iiij. qc lg. 7 i. qc lat'. Valet. iiij. lib. 7 x. sol'.

·XIX· TERRA COMITIS MORITONIENS'.

COMES MORITON' ten' de rege CRUCHE. 7 Turstin' de eo. Syuuard tenuit T.R.E. 7 geldb' p. vi. hid'. Tra. ē. v. car'. De ea st in dnio. iij. hidæ. 7 ibi. iii. car'. 7 ii. serui. 7 vi. uilli 7 v. bord' cu. iij. car'. Ibi molin' redd'. xii. solid'. 7 una ac' pti 7 dimid'. Silua. vii. qc lg. 7 ii. qc lat'. Valuit. iiij. lib. Modo. c. solid'.

Malger' ten' de co. SEUENEHANTONE. Aluuard tenuit T.R.E. 7 geldb' p. vii. hid'. Tra. ē. vii. car'. De ea st in dnio. v. hidæ 7 dim'. 7 ibi. iij. car'. 7 vi. serui. 7 viii. uilli 7 vii. bord' cu. iii car'. Ibi molin' redd'. v. solid'. 7 xl. ac' pti. Valuit. viii. lib. Modo. c. solid'.

De hoc ā st ablatæ. x. ac' siluæ 7 xxv. ac' moræ 7 pti. 7 sunt in Sudperet ā regis.

Malger' ten' de co. CONTUNE. Godric tenuit T.R.E. 7 geldb' p. iii. hid'. Tra. ē. iij. car'. In dnio. ē. i. car' 7 vi. uilli cu. vi. bord' hnt. i. car'. Valet. lx. solid'.

Ansger' ten' STANTUNE de com'. Aluuard tenuit T.R.E. 7 geldb' p. iij. hid'. Tra. ē. viij. car'. In dnio. ē. i. car' 7 dim'. 7 vi. serui. 7 xviij. uilli 7 iiij. bord' cu. iii. car' 7 dim'. Ibi molin' sine censu 7 cc lx. ac' siluæ. 7 l. ac' pasturæ redd'. iiii. blomas ferri. Val. lx. sol.

Ipse comes ten' SCEPTONE. Algar tenuit T.R.E. 7 geldb' p. vi. hid'. Tra. ē. iiij. car'. De ea st in dnio. iii. hidæ 7 dim' virg' min'. 7 ibi. i. car' 7 dim'. 7 iii. serui. 7 x. uilli 7 iiij. bord' 7 x v. ac' pti. Valuit. c. solid'. Modo. iiij. lib.

Gerard' ten' de co. LOPENE. Aluuard' tenuit T.R.E. 7 geldb' p. i. hida. Tra. ē. i. car'. Ibi. ē. i. bord' cu. i. seruo. 7 x. ac' pti. Valet. xx. solid'.

Robtus ten' de co. CRAFUECUMBE. Eccta S' Suuithuni Wintoni tenuit T.R.E. Ibi st. x. hidæ. sed n' geldb' nisi p. iiij. hid'. Tra. ē. xii. car'. De ea. ē in dnio. i. hida 7 ibi. iij. car' 7 vi. serui 7 xxvi. uilli 7 x. bord' cu. x. car'. Ibi. xi. ac' pti. 7 xx. ac' siluæ. Pastura. i. leuu lg. 7 dimid' leu lat'. Valuit 7 uat. viij. lib.

Ansger' ten' de co. IOLE. Ulnod tenuit T.R.E. 7 geldb' p. vi. hid'. Tra. ē. vi. car'. In dnio st. ii. car' 7 v. serui. 7 v. uilli 7 iiij. bord' cu. ii. car'. Ibi molin' redd'. xxiiij. solid'. 7 xviii. ac' pti. Silua. iii. qc lg. 7 dimid' lg. 7 ii. qc lat'. Valet. c. solid'.

Ipse com' ten' LUTCHALLE. Eccta Glastingbie tenuit T.R.E. Ibi st. vii. hidæ 7 una v træ. sed p. v. hid' geldb'. Tra. ē. x. car'. De ea st in dnio. iii. hidæ. 7 ibi. iii. car'. 7 v. serui. 7 xix. uilli 7 x. bord' cu. viij car'. Ibi molin' redd'. xxx. denar'. 7 lx. ac' pti. 7 cc. ac' pasturæ 7 c ac' siluæ. Valet. xvi. lib. Drogo ten' de co. unu v de ipsa tra. 7 uat. i. marka argenti.

From the Domesday Book's survey of Somerset, 1086

XVII The Land of Count Eustace

COUNT EUSTACE held of the King (North or West) NEWTON. Leofwine held in TRE [tempora regis Eduardis (in the time of King Edward the Confessor)] and it paid geld for 1 hide and 1 virgate of land. There is land for 4 ploughs. Of this 2½ virgates of land are in demesne, and there is 1 plough and 2 slaves; and 7 villans and 6 bordars with 3 ploughs. There is a mill rendering 15d. and 7 acres of meadow, and 33 acres of pasture and 17 acres of woodland. It was and is worth £4. Alvred of Marlborough holds it of the count.

The recording scribe provides plenty of grim evidence of William's brutality. The Conqueror quelled dissent by laying waste large swathes of northern England and killing, disinheriting or forcing into exile the old Anglo-Saxon nobility. So comprehensive was the Norman land-grab that Domesday's statistics suggest that, by 1086, only 8 per cent of England was still in the hands of its pre-1066 native English owners. What did survive, however, was the traditional unit of local administration, the county or 'shire'.

The fraught circumstances of its production should not distract from the scale of the Domesday Book's achievement. Not only did it surpass anything of its kind attempted previously, but nothing as comprehensive would again be attempted in Britain until the introduction of national censuses in the nineteenth century. More than 900 years after its completion, Domesday remains a legally admissible source of evidence for property entitlement.

The Domesday Book itself, in addition to the 'Domesday chest' in which it was formerly kept, can be seen at The National Archives in Kew. A version is now available online, with an English translation of the original Latin.

OPPOSITE: A page of the Domesday Book for the county of Somerset. A translation of one of the entries in the first column, for land held by Count Eustace, can be seen above. A 'hide' was a measure of land (between 60 and 120 acres) used to assess liability for land tax, while a 'virgate' was equivalent to one-quarter of a hide.

1166
THE ASSIZE OF CLARENDON

THE DEVELOPMENT OF CRIMINAL COURTS, THE COMMON LAW AND TRIAL BY JURY

William the Conqueror may have imposed the feudal social order upon England, but because neither he nor his successors passed much fresh legislation, Norman England's legal customs changed little from Anglo-Saxon practices. Furthermore, while the task of presiding over county courts was assumed by the senior Norman baron in the area – acting in his role as sheriff – it was the Anglo-Saxon administrative and legal jurisdiction of the shire that defined the limit of his authority.

It was during the reign of Henry II (1154–89) that the barons' judicial powers began to be weakened. Henry set in motion reforms that shaped the English legal system for the next 800 years. In addition to his judges sitting as the King's Bench at Westminster, royal judges were instructed to tour the country administering justice. This 'assize system' continued until it was replaced by crown courts in 1971. Thus it was that serious crimes came to be treated less as localized disputes, affecting chiefly those they concerned, but rather as breaches of the 'King's peace', to be dealt with by representatives of the royal court adhering to and extending a single body of precedent, the common law.

Initially, these reforms did little to change the lot of the lowest ranks of the peasantry. Tied to a baronial estate, they could still expect judgment from their lord and master. 'Freemen', on the other hand, with the money and inclination to pursue justice further, gained the opportunity to have their cases heard before royal justices, sitting with a jury.

Trial by jury is the most famous clause of the Assize of Clarendon, a set of royal instructions for justices dating from 1166. It mandates twelve 'of the more lawful' men from each 'hundred' (the shire subdivision) and four from every town to declare on oath before the county sheriff, or district justices, the

The Assize of Clarendon, 1166

Here begins the assize of Clarendon made by King Henry II with the assent of the archbishops, bishops, abbots, earls and barons of all England.

1. In the first place the aforesaid King Henry, on the advice of all his barons, for the preservation of peace, and for the maintenance of justice, has decreed that inquiry shall be made throughout the several counties and throughout the several hundreds through twelve of the more lawful men of the hundred and through four of the more lawful men of each vill upon oath that they will speak the truth, whether there be in their hundred of vill any man accused or notoriously suspect of being a robber or murderer or thief, or any who is a receiver of robbers or murderers or thieves, since the lord king has been king. And let the justices inquire into this among themselves and the sheriffs among themselves.

2. And let anyone, who shall be found, on the oath of the aforesaid, accused or notoriously suspect of having been a robber or murderer or thief, or a receiver of them, since the lord king has been king, be taken and put to the ordeal of water, and let him swear that he has not been a robber or murderer or thief, or receiver of them, since the lord king has been king, to the value of 5 shillings, as far as he knows.

3. And if the lord of the man, who has been arrested, or his steward or his vassals shall claim him by pledge within the third day following his capture, let him be released on bail with his chattels until he himself shall stand his trial.

4. And when a robber or murderer or thief or receiver of them has been arrested through the aforesaid oath, if the justices are not about to come speedily enough into the county where they have been taken, let the sheriffs send word to the nearest justice by some well-informed person that they have arrested such men, and the justices shall send back word to the sheriffs informing them where they desire the men to be brought before them; and let the sheriffs bring them before the justices. And together with them let the sheriffs bring from the hundred and the vill, where they have been arrested, two lawful men to bear the record of the county and of the hundred as to why they have been taken, and there before the justice let them stand trial.

5. And in the case of those who have been arrested through the aforesaid oath of this assize, let no man have court or justice or chattels save the lord king in his court in the presence of his justices; and the lord king shall have all their chattels. But in the case of those who have been arrested otherwise than by this oath let it be as is customary and due.

6. And let the sheriffs, who have arrested them, bring them before the justice without any other summons than that they have from him. And when robbers or murderers or thieves, or receivers of them, who have been arrested through the oath or otherwise, are handed over to the sheriffs, let them receive them immediately and without delay.

7. And in the several counties where there are no gaols, let such be made in a borough or some castle of the king at the king's expense and from his wood, if one shall be near, or from some neighbouring wood at the oversight of the king's servants, to the end that in them the sheriffs may be able to guard those who shall be arrested by the officials accustomed to do this, or by their servants.

8. Moreover, the lord king wills that all shall come to the county courts to take this oath, so that none shall remain behind on account of any franchise which he has, or any court or soke, which he may have, but that they shall come to take this oath.

9. And let there be no one within his castle or without, nor even in the honour of Wallingford [a large estate in Oxfordshire], who shall forbid the sheriffs to enter into his court or his land to take the view of frankpledge [a collective guarantee of good conduct made by a group of householders in early medieval England] and to see that all are under pledges; and let them be sent before the sheriffs under free pledge.

10. And in cities or boroughs let no one hold men or receive them into his house or on his land or in his soke, whom he will not take in hand to produce before the justice, should they be required; or else let them be in frankpledge.

11. And let there be none in a city or a borough or a castle or without it, nor even in the honour of Wallingford, who shall forbid the sheriffs to enter into their land or their soke to arrest those who have been accused or are notoriously suspect of being robbers or murderers or thieves or receivers

of them, or outlaws, or persons charged concerning the forest; but the king commands that they shall aid the sheriffs to capture them.

12. And if anyone shall be taken in possession of the spoils or robbery or theft, if he be of evil repute and bears an evil testimony from the public and has no warrant, let him have no law. And if he has not been notoriously suspect on account of the goods in his possession, let him go to the ordeal of water.

13. And if anyone shall confess to robbery or murder or theft, or the harbouring those who have committed them, in the presence of the lawful men or in the hundred court, and afterwards he wish to deny it, let him not have his law.

14. Moreover the lord king wills that those who shall be tried by the law and absolved by the law, if they have been of ill repute and openly and disgracefully spoken of by the testimony of many and that of the lawful men, shall abjure the kings lands, so that within eight days they shall cross the sea, unless the wind detains them; and with the first wind they shall have afterwards they shall cross the sea, and they shall not return to England again except by the mercy of the lord king; and both now, and if they return, let them be outlawed; and on their return let them be seized as outlaws.

15. And if the lord king forbids that any vagabond, that is, a wanderer or unknown person, shall be given shelter anywhere except in a borough, and even there he shall not be given shelter longer than one night, unless he become sick there, or his horse, so that he can show an evident excuse.

16. And if he shall remain there longer than one night, let him be arrested and held until his lord shall come to give surety for him, or until he himself shall procure safe pledges; and let him likewise be arrested who gave him shelter.

17. And if any sheriff shall send word to another sheriff that men have fled from his county into another county, on account of robbery or murder or theft or the harbouring of them, or on account of outlawry or of a charge concerning the kings forest, let him (the second sheriff) arrest them; and even if he knows of himself or through others that such men have fled into his county, let him arrest them and guard them until he has taken safe pledges for them.

18. And let all the sheriffs cause a record to be made of all fugitives who have fled from their counties; and let them do this before the county courts and carry the names of those written therein before the justices, when next they come to them, so that these men may be sought throughout England, and their chattels may be seized for the needs of the king.

19. And the lord king wills that from the time the sheriffs shall receive the summons of the itinerant justices to present themselves before them, together with the men of the county, they shall assemble them and make inquiry for all who have newly come into their counties since this assize; and they shall send them away under pledge to attend before the justices, or they shall keep them in custody until the justices come to them, and then they shall present them before the justices.

20. Moreover the lord king forbids monks or canons or any religious house to receive any men of the lower orders as a monk or a canon or a brother, until it be known of what reputation he is, unless he shall be sick unto death.

21. Moreover the lord king forbids anyone in all England to receive in his land or his soke or in a house under him any one of that sect of renegades who were branded and excommunicated at Oxford. And if anyone shall so receive them, he himself shall be at the mercy of the lord king, and the house in which they have dwelt shall be carried outside the village and burnt. And each sheriff shall swear an oath that he will observe this, and shall cause all his officers to swear this, and also the stewards of the barons and all knights and freeholders of the counties.

And the lord king wills that this assize shall be kept in his realm so long as it shall please him.

identity of the criminal suspect. This is not the first mention of a jury, which was an Anglo-Saxon concept. Indeed, King Æthelred the Unready issued a decree requiring 'that they will not accuse any innocent man or shield any guilty one'. However, the Assize of Clarendon makes more explicit a jury's role. Initially, its function was closer to that of a grand jury, determining whether there was sufficient evidence to justify a trial rather than to determine the subsequent outcome in court.

The Assize of Clarendon concerned charges relating to murder, robbery and theft, its provisions being revised in 1176 by the Assize of Northampton. The latter encouraged more severe penalties, identified forgery and arson as indictable crimes and transferred further power from the baronial sheriffs to the royal justices. Neither document abolished such ancient practices as trial by ordeal in the establishing of guilt. Specifically endorsed by both documents is the 'trial by water' (the throwing of the bound suspect into a pool, innocence being determined by an inability to float). Nonetheless, the increasing recourse to – and evolution in the role of – juries shifted procedures towards the presentation of evidence. The Church abolished trial by ordeal in 1215. Seven years later, the practice was established of calling petty juries of twelve men from the neighbourhood to determine the guilt or innocence of the accused. From 1367, a unanimous verdict from all twelve jurors was necessary, a requirement that endured until the majority verdict was deemed acceptable in 1967.

1215
MAGNA CARTA

THE 'GREAT CHARTER' LIMITS ARBITRARY POWER
AND ESTABLISHES AN ENGLISHMAN'S RIGHT
TO HABEAS CORPUS

Magna Carta is depicted in the first plate section.

In a country without a written constitution, no article of law has achieved more hallowed status than 'the Great Charter'. The document agreed between King John and his barons in the meadows of Runnymede, on the Surrey banks of the Thames in June 1215, is far more than merely a statement of the restraints placed on arbitrary power in medieval England. From the seventeenth century onwards, and throughout the expanding English-speaking world, its provisions were recalled, inspiring and fortifying those who cherished their British inheritance as well as those who sought to break away from it. The eighteenth-century radical politician John Wilkes pronounced it 'the distinguishing characteristic of all Englishmen'. For the Founding Fathers of the United States it was also a seminal text, an early draft for expressions to be extended and given new life in the US Constitution. Indeed, Magna Carta has perhaps shaped the modern world as much as any document in this book. Between a quarter and a third of mankind is governed according to the legal principles it enshrines.

It is therefore important to remember that its terms were almost immediately breached and that, despite its subsequent renewal, the claim that it represented the pivotal declaration of liberties was vigorously reasserted only in the reign of Queen Elizabeth I, when printed editions of the country's statutes opened with it. Most of its provisions were abolished by the Statute Law Revision Act of 1863. The original document contained sixty-three chapters. Today, only four of them remain on the British statute book. (These are chapters 1, 13, 39 and 40 of the document drawn up in 1215, corresponding to chapters 1, 9 and 29 in the revised version of 1225.)

So, why the fuss? First, because Magna Carta enshrines a legal philosophy that became the defining statement of the curtailment of power – that the ruler is not above the law. A sovereign may be head of state, but the state itself is a greater legal entity to which he, or she, is subject. Thus a ruler is not entitled to be a despot. Second, the chapters that have endured on the British statute books are highly significant. Although chapter 1, affirming the freedom of the English Church, was effectively made redundant by the Reformation, and chapter 13 guarantees – without specifying – the ancient freedoms of the City of London and other towns, it is chapters 39 and 40 that remain, however chipped away, a cornerstone of due process. Chapter 39 articulates what later became the cherished principle of habeas corpus ('you have the body') – that nobody can be detained without being subject to a fair trial. The state cannot simply lock up whomever it pleases:

[39] No free man shall be taken or imprisoned or disseised [deprived or dispossessed of property] or outlawed or exiled or in any way ruined, nor will we go or send against him, except by the lawful judgment of his peers or by the law of the land.

[40] To no one will we sell, to no one will we deny or delay right or justice.

Chapter 39 provided the framework for the seventh article of the US Bill of Rights (the Fifth Amendment of the US Constitution) that no person shall 'be deprived of life, liberty, or property, without due process'. In Britain, this freedom from arbitrary arrest and imprisonment was given closer legal definition by the Habeas Corpus Act of 1679. It has been temporarily suspended only during war and national emergency, although the length of time that a suspect can be held without charge was extended under the anti-terrorism legislation of the first decade of the twenty-first century.

Magna Carta was born out of acute political crisis. The barons resented the taxes and impositions forced upon them by King John, whose rule (1199–1216) was marked by hardship and cruelty at home and defeat abroad. The loss to France of Normandy (save for the Channel Islands) in 1204 speeded up the process whereby the barons were forced to decide whether they considered themselves as English or Norman landowners; but at the time they considered the loss a disaster. John had compounded the situation in 1207 by refusing to confirm Pope Innocent III's choice of Stephen Langton as archbishop of Canterbury. The pope responded by placing England under an interdict that suspended the administering of religious rites, initially preventing even the conducting of marriage services or burials in consecrated ground. Having been excommunicated, John was forced in 1211 to abase himself by surrendering his kingdoms (both England and Ireland – which had been invaded by Henry II) to the pope who, in turn, leased them back to John in return for 1,000 marks a year and bonds of fealty and homage.

The feudal dues that John expected were no longer being freely given, with many barons refusing to assist in his ongoing struggle against the French king, Philip (II) Augustus. When the latter crushed John's forces at the Battle of Bouvines in Flanders in 1214, John faced outright insurrection. Whilst the dissenting barons were essentially self-interested, they were also assisted by Stephen Langton in drawing up their demands in a more moderate, inclusive language. The result was Magna Carta. It drew on the pledges to rule within constraints that Henry I had made in his Coronation Charter of 1100. However, the document framed by Langton and the barons was different. It was not a monarch's personal statement of good intent, but a hard-won declaration to which subsequent rulers found themselves legally bound.

Such an outcome was not clear when John appended his seal in 1215. Having returned to Innocent III's good graces, he wasted no time in getting the pope to annul Magna Carta. Civil war recommenced, abetted by the landing of French troops at Thanet; the future French monarch, Louis VIII, even joined forces with the barons in London. However, the crisis soon passed with John's timely demise from dysentery in 1216, to be succeeded by Henry III, aged only nine. Those around him, including Langton, ensured that Magna Carta was redrafted and reissued in 1216, 1217 and again, with further small revisions, in 1225. It was this last version that became law in 1295 and from which those articles still operable derive their statutory authority.

Of the original document of 1215, four copies survive: one at Lincoln Cathedral, one at Salisbury Cathedral and two at the British Library. Of the latter, one was damaged in a fire in 1731; the other, still complete, was allegedly found in a London tailor's shop in the seventeenth century. The remaining extant copies were made for the subsequent reissues in Henry III's reign. Among these versions, one is owned by the Australian government and displayed in the Parliament building in Canberra. Another, privately owned, is on permanent loan to the National Archives in Washington, DC, where it hangs alongside the Declaration of Independence, the Bill of Rights and the US Constitution.

*c.*1250

THE CHRONICLES OF
MATTHEW PARIS

A DISTINGUISHED EXAMPLE OF MEDIEVAL
CARTOGRAPHY AND ILLUSTRATION

It was not until the sixteenth century, with the invention of triangulation, that maps conveyed with at least some relative accuracy the shape and scale of the British Isles. Earlier generations of travellers were largely forced to rely on local knowledge or to keep to the major tracks. Indeed, before the mid-thirteenth century, the few Britons familiar with cartography had to make do with representations that were more schematic than geographical.

Matthew Paris's map of Britain is depicted in the first plate section.

Around 1250, an English monk named Matthew Paris (*c.*1200–59) drew a series of maps that are far more accomplished than anything that survives prior to that time. Although to the modern eye his depiction of Britain is greatly removed from reality, his draughtsmanship nonetheless aimed at rendering the country in an essentially accurate rather than schematic fashion.

At first glance, the claim to accuracy hardly rings true. The coastlines of Wales and Scotland (which Paris thought was almost totally dissected from the mainland by the Firths of Clyde and Forth) are not recognizable. Indeed, only the basic shape of Cornwall can be easily discerned. However, the picture becomes clearer once it is understood that the map's central artery is the road from Dover to Berwick. Thus Kent does not stick out to the south-east of London but lies due south, roughly where the Isle of Wight ought to be. Once this is comprehended, suddenly the rump of East Anglia, for instance, can be made out.

It is not just the importance of the Dover–Berwick road that should be noted but also the emphasis given to those other sources of navigation, rivers. London is clearly marked as the most important city among the over 250 places and features named. 'Snaudun' marks the mountains of Snowdonia. More surprisingly, both Hadrian's Wall and the Antonine Wall are depicted, despite having tumbled into ruin over 800 years previously. This suggests that Paris may have had access to Roman manuscripts that have since been lost. The eastern slant of Scotland replicates the cartography of the second-century Greek astronomer, Ptolemy.

On the frontispiece of his Historia Anglorum, *the monk kneeling beneath the Virgin and Child is, in fact, a self-portrait of the author, Matthew Paris.*

Paris's significance was not confined to cartography. As a chronicler of his times, he wrote over a million words and his most important work was the *Chronica Majora*. In it, he updated the *Flores Historiarum* ('Flowers of History') of Roger of Wendover, one of his predecessors at the Benedictine abbey at St Albans. To Roger's history, from the Creation to 1234, Paris added his contemporary analysis of the years 1235 to 1259. It is a remarkable narrative, suffused with news and gossip. Paris was not a detached and cocooned scholar but a man familiar with some of the greatest figures in the realm. When away from St Albans, he appears to have spent much time attending ceremonial events and court occasions, where he hobnobbed with some exceptionally well-placed sources for his testimony. A trip to Bergen even led to a meeting with Hákon IV of Norway.

Paris was a confidant of both King Henry III and his younger brother, Richard of Cornwall, who, as 'King of the Romans' and an aspirant to the throne of the Holy Roman Empire, was active in the politics of the German lands. Frequently critical of the pope, Paris was also a staunch defender of English rights, lacing his chronicles with his own opinions and prejudices. Thus, while they cannot be regarded as either impartial or, in places, strictly accurate, they do provide telling and often first-hand knowledge of English politics. Furthermore, they were written from the standpoint of someone whose independent spirit was such that he could accept King Henry's patronage and admire his piety, yet comment critically on his political skills and indecisiveness. 'The lot of historians,' Paris sighed, 'is hard indeed, for, if they speak the truth, they provoke man, and if they record falsehoods, they offend God.'

Paris decorated his chronicles with illustrations, often in the margins. Although his artistry was naive by some contemporary standards, his efforts to observe from life, as well as merely copying stylized reproduction, earn him a significant place in the development of British art. He drew some of the earliest known depictions of London and his picture of an elephant is justly famous. His *Historica Anglorum* is prefaced with tinted line-drawings of the English kings. Since he knew Henry III personally, his representation of him there may even be relatively accurate.

Matthew Paris's *Chronica Majora* is kept at Corpus Christi College, Cambridge.

Angevins and Plantagenets

Angevins

Henry II 1154–89

Richard I 'the Lionheart' 1189–99

John 1199–1216

Plantagenets

Henry III 1216–72

Edward I 1272–1307

Edward II 1307–27

Edward III 1327–77

Richard II 1377–99

(House of Lancaster)

Henry IV 1399–1413

Henry V 1413–22

Henry VI 1422–61 and 1470–71

(House of York)

Edward IV 1461–70 and 1471–83

Edward V 1483

Richard III 1483–5

1265

SIMON DE MONTFORT'S SUMMONS FOR A PARLIAMENT

THE ROOTS OF A REPRESENTATIVE PARLIAMENT

It was in 1236 that the council of the king, busy discussing legal issues and matters of state at Westminster, was first described as a 'parliament'. While the term may then have been only recently coined, the institution was already ancient. Its antecedence stretched back not only to the council of barons and clergy that had periodically advised the Norman rulers but to the traditional Anglo-Saxon convocation of nobles, the Witan ('the knowing ones'), which had surrounded Alfred the Great.

During the fourteenth century, this assembly became more recognizably the House of Lords. In contrast, Parliament's representative element – which later evolved into the House of Commons – had its roots in a power struggle between King Henry III and his opponents, led by a seemingly unlikely champion of English national consciousness, Simon de Montfort.

The circumstances of Henry III's extreme youth – his 'minority' – on assuming the throne were propitious for those who wanted to exercise power on his behalf. The re-enforcement of the previously revoked Magna Carta was one example of this; the more assertive line taken by his council of barons and clerics on appointments and expenses another. With the passing of years, his need to compensate for shortfalls in revenue from the lost French territories – and the cost of holding on to mutinous Gascony – pushed Henry into demanding significant tax rises. And, in post-Magna Carta England, he found himself having to seek Parliament's permission to do so. In 1254 two knights from each county were asked to attend Parliament in order to approve a grant of taxation.

Henry also had to deal with a particularly strong challenge from his charismatic lieutenant in Gascony, Simon de Montfort. Following a childhood spent in southern France where his father had ruthlessly suppressed Christian heretics, de Montfort inherited the earldom of Leicester. His marriage to Eleanor, the king's widowed teenage sister, in 1238, had made him Henry's brother-in-law. However, it was his removal from Gascony following claims of heavy-handedness, subjection to a show trial and his subsequent failure to be properly remunerated that helped turn this tough, driven and deeply devout natural leader into the king's critic and influential enemy.

Forgetting his own Gallic origins, de Montfort discovered the language of English patriotism, leading the campaign to rid Henry of his foreign relations and advisers. Henry's expensive attempts to secure the Sicilian throne for his second son, Edmund, particularly riled the barons. In June 1258, Parliament met in Oxford and, with de Montfort among the guiding hands, agreed a revolutionary statement known as the Provisions of Oxford. The original document is lost, but its contents are known. The king's power was to be severely curtailed by a new council of fifteen men, acting with executive authority. The concept that the monarch would henceforth cease to control his own appointments, as well as the money raised to enact his policies, was, in the context of medieval Europe, an extraordinary repudiation of the rights of crowned heads. Nor was this merely a case of a few self-serving barons muscling in upon the throne to exploit their sovereign's weakness. The work of the council was to be debated by Parliament, which should meet at least three times a year. The king's distrusted foreign relations and advisers were to be expelled. Every county would elect four knights to examine and express to the king's chief legal officer, the justiciar, local discontents with the sheriffs. When the final form of the declaration was inscribed in Latin and French the following year, it was also written – most tellingly – in English.

Financial and political necessity forced Henry to agree, temporarily, to the provisions, but in 1261 he felt strong enough, backed with the authority of a papal bull, to repudiate them. Having made their revolutionary declarations, de Montfort and the barons were in no mood to tamely acquiesce. England, once again, was plunged into civil war. De Montfort, however, had a broad following, enjoying strong popularity in the Midlands, London and the South East as well as among the bishops. At Lewes in Sussex, his army, donning the crosses of crusaders, crushed the royal forces, taking both King Henry and his son, Prince Edward, prisoner.

In the midst of this emergency (a French invasion was also expected), executive power was effectively in the hands of de Montfort, the bishop of Chichester and the earl of Gloucester who – nominally in the king's name – formed a triumvirate to

rule England at the head of a council of nine. De Montfort issued writs requesting that each county elect four 'prudent and law-worthy' knights to attend Parliament. They were joined at Westminster in January 1265 by two burgesses elected from a list of major towns. For the first time, commoners were elected to sit in Parliament.

These representatives of town and county sat with the barons and clergy in Westminster Hall. They were not yet a separate House of Commons. Their manner of election varied in the towns, but may have been open to all freeholders in the counties. Nonetheless, in the range of policy areas that it presumed to debate, in the stipulation that members must be elected and in the breadth of its composition, the 'de Montfort Parliament' denotes a significant moment in the early development of democracy. As the historian Simon Schama has put it, 'It inaugurated the union between patriotism and insubordination.'

Almost immediately, the advance seemed undone. Prince Edward escaped custody and in August 1265 his forces routed de Montfort's army at Evesham. Surrounded by the bodies of his fallen son and his supporters, de Montfort himself was cut down – characteristically – fighting on foot in the thick of the action. Although in the years after his death parliaments were convened without

his knights and burgesses in attendance, the increasing cost of government ensured that the innovation had to be returned to, and the precedent more firmly set. This was partly because after 1265 the assent of the knights and burgesses in Parliament was deemed legally necessary for the raising of taxes.

Indeed, it was to raise money for his Scottish wars that de Montfort's nemesis, now King Edward I, summoned his 'Model' Parliament of 1295. It consisted of over 500 members, including not only the lords temporal and spiritual but also knights from every shire plus two burgesses from 110 boroughs. After 1325, these representatives were a permanent feature of parliamentary government and soon after were sitting in their own chamber, distinct from the unelected barons. One nod to popular will that came in consequence was that from 1363, English – not French – was enshrined as the official language spoken at Westminster. Furthermore, by then Parliament's hearing of petitions ensured that it, rather than the monarch, drove through new laws. This legislative right was the prerogative of the nascent House of Lords until a judicial decision of 1489 stated that laws could be enacted only with the support of both houses, and by then the commoners alone could veto the king's taxes.

The writ and return from Bedfordshire and Buckinghamshire, issued in 1274 and depicted above, is the oldest surviving example of a royal writ. The practice of sending such writs, ordering the election of members to Parliament, began with de Montfort in 1265 and continues to this day.

1284

THE STATUTE OF RHUDDLAN

EDWARD I'S ANGLICIZATION OF THE PRINCIPALITY OF WALES

Three sources of authority contested Wales at the commencement of the thirteenth century. The first was the English Crown. Periodic military campaigns had scoured England's neighbour, making inroads and building strongholds without establishing total domination. The second was the Marcher lords, the descendants of Norman barons whose estates ran not only along the Welsh borderlands but also deep into southern Wales. While nominally within the English realm, these territories were essentially the fiefdoms of their barons. Marcher law, not English law, governed their inhabitants.

The third source of authority was indigenous and was exercised in the domains of the Welsh princes. There was no law of primogeniture guaranteeing the succession to the eldest son. By the end of the twelfth century, the royal houses of Powys and Deheubarth, principalities respectively of central and south-west Wales, had been weakened by internecine rivalry. However, in the north, the mountainous princely state of Gwynedd endured and became dominant. By 1257, the authority of Gwynedd's prince, Llewelyn ap Gruffudd, stretched south from Snowdonia to embrace two-thirds of the country. A decade later, via the Treaty of Montgomery, a trade was made of token diplomatic gestures, with Henry III recognizing Llewelyn's claim to be 'Prince of Wales' in return for his acknowledging the English monarch as his feudal overlord.

The ambiguous question of whose will had seniority started to resolve itself with the succession of Edward I. One of the most determined and ruthless men ever to sit on the English throne, Edward had no intention of flattering Llewelyn, who had, after all, previously sought to interfere in English politics on the side of Simon de Montfort (to whose daughter Llewelyn was betrothed). Aware of his heightening personal danger, Llewelyn refused repeated summons to do homage to Edward either at, or following, his coronation in 1274. This snub provided the

MEDIEVAL WALES

*c.*1200–1240 Llywelyn ab Iorwerth (Llywelyn the Great) is Prince of Gwynedd and effective ruler of most of Wales.

1241 With the Treaty of Gwerneigron. Dafydd ap Llywelyn, Prince of Gwynedd, pledges loyalty to Henry III, cedes much of Flintshire to him and effectively relinquishes his right to the other Welsh lands claimed by his father, Llywelyn ap Iorwerth.

1246–82 Dafydd's nephew, Llywelyn ap Gruffudd (Llywelyn the Last), is Prince of Gwynedd.

1267 In the Treaty of Montgomery, Henry III acknowledges Llywelyn ap Gruffudd as Prince of Wales.

1277 Edward I invades Gwynedd, forcing Llywelyn to agree to the Treaty of Aberconwy, curtailing his authority and acknowledging Edward as his overlord.

1282–3 In the Second War of Welsh Independence, Llywelyn's brother Dafydd rebels against Edward I.

1283 Edward I begins construction of Caernarfon, Conwy and Harlech castles.

1284 The Treaty of Rhuddlan is made.

1294–5 Madog ap Llywelyn proclaims himself Prince of Wales and leads a fresh revolt, capturing Caernarfon before suffering defeat at the Battle of Maes Moydog.

1301 Edward I revives the title of 'Prince of Wales' and bestows it on his son, the future Edward II.

1400–1412 Owain Glyndwr rebels.

1472 Edward IV's Council of Wales and the Marches is convened at Ludlow.

1485 The Anglo-Welsh Henry Tudor becomes King Henry VII of England.

perfect pretext for Edward. In 1277, he invaded Gwynedd with a mighty army swelled not only with English knights but with Llewelyn's Welsh enemies. Losing his fertile lands in Anglesey and facing a bleak winter in the mountains, Llewelyn surrendered and finally did Edward homage at a ceremony in Worcester. His reward was to be allowed to continue in a much-reduced Gwynedd that retained Anglesey but was shorn of most of its other Welsh acquisitions. Meanwhile the English refortified their castles and administered English law in a high-handed manner guaranteed to upset Welsh sensitivities.

Welsh resentment reached breaking point in 1282, when Llewelyn's brother Dafydd started a rebellion. Llewelyn felt compelled to come to his brother's aid, but early successes were quickly undone. Marching into Powys, Llewelyn was killed in a skirmish while Dafydd was betrayed and handed over to the English. He was duly hanged, drawn and quartered, his head being taken and mounted on a pike next to that of his brother at the Tower of London. Rather than complete the collection, other Welsh leaders scrambled to abase themselves before Edward.

The king responded by embarking on an even more expensive castle-building programme of such grandeur that the mighty walls of Caernarfon, for instance, were modelled on those that protected Constantinople. The framework for the new political settlement was set out in the Statute of Rhuddlan in 1284. Also known as the 'Statute of Wales', the document dismembered Gwynedd, with Snowdonia and Anglesey passing to the English Crown. Anglesey was one of the new, English-style counties created in the north, along with Flint, Caernarfon and Merioneth. Privileged boroughs were established for the benefit of English settlers. Crimes were henceforth to be judged in the courts of English law.

Yet the Statute of Rhuddlan also established limits to anglicization in North Wales that became the template for the rest of the country. Much Welsh custom was retained. In most civil law cases, Welsh practice was tolerated alongside English common law. Only the more antiquated aspects of the native customary law were abolished.

These measures were followed, in 1301, by an imaginative act of political and symbolic appropriation. Having dispensed with the royal house of Gwynedd, Edward proclaimed his own son, the future Edward II, as Prince of Wales in a ceremony at the place of his birth, Caernarfon Castle.

1320

THE DECLARATION
OF ARBROATH

A STATEMENT OF SCOTTISH INDEPENDENCE

In 1290, Scotland was set to share the same monarch as England. In northern Scotland, the Celtic traditions and Gaelic tongue seemed remote from the culture and language of its southern neighbour. It was only as recently as the 1260s that the Western Isles and the Hebrides had finally been wrestled from Norway. Nonetheless, the Scottish court was highly anglicized in its customs and outlook. Many of the great barons – such as the Balliol and Bruce families – were of Norman stock, owning land in England as well as in Scotland. Even Scottish kings had periodically done homage to the English Crown in return for holding on to their southern property, although the Scottish monarchs never accepted that these acts of abasement infringed their sovereignty over their own realm. The major source of conflict had always been where the border lay, with repeated harrying by both sides between the rivers Tyne and Tweed. However, there had been no significant conflict between the Scots and the English for over seventy years, both sides apparently accepting the previsions of the Treaty of York of 1237, which had drawn the border from Berwick-upon-Tweed to the Solway Firth. Alexander III, who had proved a wise king of Scots since 1249, was both the nephew and the son-in-law of England's Henry III.

In 1286, Alexander was thrown from his horse over a cliff at Kinghorn in Fife, plunging his realm into crisis. The heir to the Scottish throne was his three-year-old granddaughter Margaret ('the Maid of Norway'), whose father was Eric II of Norway. A period of acute instability beckoned, in which others with lesser claims but stronger wills were poised to assert themselves. A solution, of sorts, was offered by the English king, Edward I. He suggested that his son, the future Edward II, should marry Margaret of Norway. Their descendants would ensure a union of the crowns (if not, explicitly, a union of the kingdoms). The scheme was dashed by

The Declaration of Arbroath is depicted in the first plate section.

SCOTTISH WARS OF INDEPENDENCE

First War of Independence

1296 Edward I sacks Berwick and defeats the Scottish army at Dunbar. John Balliol abdicates and Scottish nobles give homage to Edward.

1297 William Wallace leads the resistance movement.

1304 The last major Scottish stronghold, Stirling Castle, falls to the English. John Comyn, joint 'Guardian of Scotland', negotiates the terms of Scottish submission.

1305 William Wallace is executed in London.

1306 Robert the Bruce murders John Comyn and is crowned king of Scots at Scone.

1307 Edward I dies and is succeeded by his son, Edward II.

1314 Robert the Bruce wins the Battle of Bannockburn.

1320 The Declaration of Arbroath asserts Scottish independence.

1327 Edward II is deposed and murdered, and succeeded by Edward III.

1328 Robert the Bruce invades northern England and signs the Treaty of Northampton–Edinburgh in which England acknowledges Scottish independence, and Bruce's son and heir, David, marries Edward III's sister.

1329 Robert the Bruce dies and is succeeded by his infant son, David II.

Second War of Independence

1332 Bruce's Scottish enemies and Edward III unite to support Edward Balliol's claim to the Scottish throne over David II and win the Battle of Dupplin Moor. Edward Balliol is crowned king but is soon forced to flee to England.

1333 Balliol invades Scotland with the support of the English, who win a devastating victory at the Battle of Halidon Hill.

1334 Unable to sustain support among the Scottish nobles, Balliol returns to England.

1335 Edward III invades Scotland and reaches Perth.

1337 The outbreak of the Hundred Years War diverts Edward III's attention to fighting the French, and Sir Andrew Murray regains strongholds in the name of David II.

1346 David II invades England and is captured at the Battle of Neville's Cross, thereafter spending eleven years in captivity.

1357 The Treaty of Berwick frees David II. Although much of the Scottish borders remain in English hands, English efforts to dictate the nation's succession are effectively ended.

an unexpected tragedy – in 1290, on her way to Scotland from Norway, Margaret died. There was no other direct claimant to the Scottish throne.

The constitutional crisis provided Edward I with his opportunity to push himself forward as Scotland's overlord. It was clear that he was the effective power-broker when the fourteen different claimants to the throne all pledged their fealty to him and the 'Guardians' overseeing this Scottish succession contest asked Edward to arbitrate. John Balliol, a direct descendant via the maternal line of the twelfth-century Scottish king David I, seemed a likely stooge, so Edward chose him.

Such was Edward's avarice and arrogance that even this arrangement fell short of his expectations. He proceeded to act in such a high-handed manner that Scotland allied with France, England's ancient enemy. Edward responded by invading Scotland in 1296, dethroning and imprisoning Balliol and ruling the kingdom as if it were his own. To drive home that this was now a takeover, not a partnership, the Great Seal was smashed and the Stone of Destiny, upon which Scottish kings had been crowned, together with the national archives and the crown regalia, were all carted off to England.

A process by which the English and Scottish courts might harmoniously have come together was replaced by a new master–servant relationship that inflamed Scotland's sense of its separate identity. A resistance movement led by William Wallace had initial success, notably at Stirling Bridge in 1297, before being crushed at Falkirk in 1298. Captured, Wallace was hanged, drawn, burned and quartered in 1305. His place was quickly taken by a new leader who had a distant claim to the throne. Robert the Bruce (1274–1329) decided he had not much to lose by staking his right to rule. Having gained little from pledging fealty to Edward, he was under censure for murdering his political rival and Balliol's nephew, John Comyn, in – of all places – a church.

In 1306, Bruce was crowned king of Scots. The following year Edward died. The inscription etched upon his tomb in Westminster Abbey lauded him as *Scottorum Malleus* ('the Hammer of the Scots'). His successor, Edward II, was an altogether weaker character and distracted by English resistance to his taking of favourites. Here was the opportunity for Robert the Bruce to seize his chance to strengthen his shaky authority, defeat his own Scottish opponents and unite the country against English domination.

After years of guerrilla warfare, the critical events took place in 1314. Edinburgh Castle was retaken from the English. Edward II dispatched an army to relieve his garrison at the other great strategic fortress at Stirling, but his forces were comprehensively routed nearby, at Bannockburn. Although sent homewards to think again, Edward still refused to recognize Robert the Bruce as Scotland's legitimate ruler and campaigns along the border continued.

It was not just the English monarch who remained hostile to the Scots king. The papacy had excommunicated Bruce. Seeking to have this revoked – as well as to secure recognition of Scottish independence and, indeed, to explain why English hostility had diverted Scots from active involvement in the crusade against Islam – eight Scottish earls and thirty-eight barons attached their seals to an appeal sent to Pope John XXII in Avignon. Although this original document was subsequently lost, a copy was kept and is now in the care of the National Archives of Scotland in Edinburgh.

Written in Latin and probably drafted by Bernard, the abbot of Arbroath Abbey and chancellor of Scotland, the Declaration of Arbroath is one of the earliest surviving, all-encompassing statements of Scottish self-determination. It also promulgated an extraordinary constitutional notion, implying that Scotland's monarch was chosen by the people (albeit, in reality, the nobles), rather than by God. Hence, if ever Bruce surrendered to England, the Scots would replace him with another king. One statement in particular expressed the strength of national feeling: '…for, as long as but a hundred of us remain alive, never will we on any conditions be brought under English rule. It is in truth not for glory, nor riches, nor honours that we are fighting, but for freedom – for that alone, which no honest man gives up but with life itself.'

This became the ringing declaration of Scotland's independent identity. It succeeded with the pope, who recognized Bruce's claim and, with it, Scottish independence, in 1324. English acceptance followed grudgingly in 1328, although the Anglo-Scottish peace lasted only four years. Dissident Scottish nobles disinherited by Bruce allied with England and won victories at Dupplin Moor in 1332 and at Halidon Hill the following year. A renewed struggle for power ensued between the followers of John Balliol's son, Edward, and Bruce's infant successor, David II.

Despite subsequent, if temporary, English occupations of southern Scotland and the Scots' 'auld alliance' with the French, a decisive reconquest did not follow, not least because of England's increasing preoccupation with fighting in France during the Hundred Years War. The spirit of cross-border hostility remained nonetheless, and it was not until the Treaty of Edinburgh in 1560 that lasting peace between Scotland and England was agreed. Its claim to nationhood acknowledged, Scotland ended up in union with, rather than conquered by, its more powerful southern neighbour.

1382–95
WYCLIF'S BIBLE

THE TRANSLATION OF THE BIBLE INTO ENGLISH

Before the Reformation in the sixteenth century, the greatest intellectual challenge to the theology and prerogatives of the Catholic Church in England was posed by a lecturer at Oxford University, John Wyclif.

Having ceased to honour paying the feudal dues to the pope agreed by King John, the government's relations with the papacy had become increasingly fractious, while the papacy itself stood on the verge of the grave schism between 1378 and 1417: rival popes based in Rome and Avignon vied for the allegiance of Christendom. But whatever grumbles existed about the Church's aggrandizement of temporal power and all the related consequences of worldliness and corruption, there remained no path to salvation other than through its good graces.

John Wyclif (c.1328–84).

Although there had, of course, been whinges about Church abuses before, John Wyclif's erudition carried a weight that added a previously absent *gravitas* to the attacks. A Yorkshireman, born around 1328, he was a student at Oxford by 1350, returning there to lecture in theology and philosophy. During the 1370s, his ideas became increasingly unorthodox. To describe his thinking as Protestant would be anachronistic, but his arguments did foreshadow many of those put forward by the shapers of the Reformation.

Wyclif was concerned by the scale of the Church's vast – and self-serving – wealth, not to mention the distraction this created from its vocation to aid the poor. He questioned the papacy's presumptions to intervene within the sphere of national governments. He attacked the claims made for transubstantiation, disputing that, in the administering of the Eucharist, bread and wine became the body and blood of Christ.

Wyclif's translation of 1 Corinthians 13

If I speke with tungis of men and of aungels and I haue not charite, I am maad as bras sownynge, or a cymbal tynklynge. and if I haue profecie and knowe alle mysteries and al kynnyng, and if I haue al feith, so that I moue hills fro her place, and I haue not charite I am nought. and if I departe alle my goodis into the metis of pore men, and if I bitake my bodi so that I brenne and if I haue not charite it profitith to me no thing. charite enuyeth not, it doith not wickidli, it is not blowun, it is not coueitous, it sekith not tho thingis that ben his owne. it is not stired to wraththe, it thenkith not yuel, it ioieth not on wickidnesse, but it ioieth togidre to treuthe, it suffrith alle thingis, it bileueth all thingis, it hopith alle thingis, it sustained alle thingis. charite fallith neuere doun. whethir profecies schulen be voidid, eithir langagis schulen ceese, eithir science schal be distried. for aparti we knowen, and aparti we profecien, but whanne that schal come that is parfyt, that thing that is of parti schal be auoidid. whanne I was a litil child I spak as a litil child, I thoughte as a litil child; but whanne I was made a man I voidide tho thingis that weren of a litl child. and we seen now bi a myrour in derknesse, but thanne face to face. now I knowe of parti, but thanne I schal knowe as I am knowun. and now dwellen feith, hope and charite these thre, but the moost of these is charite.

1 Corinthians 13 in the Authorized Version (1611)

Though I speak with the tongues of men and of angels, and have not charity, I am become as sounding brass, or a tinkling cymbal. And though I have the gift of prophecy, and understand all mysteries, and all knowledge; and though I have all faith, so that I could remove mountains, and have not charity, I am nothing. And though I bestow all my goods to feed the poor, and though I give my body to be burned, and have not charity, it profiteth me nothing.

Charity suffereth long, and is kind; charity envieth not; charity vaunteth not itself, is not puffed up, Doth not behave itself unseemly, seeketh not her own, is not easily provoked, thinketh no evil; Rejoiceth not in iniquity, but rejoiceth in the truth; Beareth all things, believeth all things, hopeth all things, endureth all things.

Charity never faileth: but whether there be prophecies, they shall fail; whether there be tongues, they shall cease; whether there be knowledge, it shall vanish away. For we know in part, and we prophesy in part. But when that which is perfect is come, then that which is in part shall be done away. When I was a child, I spake as a child, I understood as a child, I thought as a child: but when I became a man, I put away childish things. For now we see through a glass, darkly; but then face to face: now I know in part; but then shall I know even as also I am known. And now abideth faith, hope, charity, these three; but the greatest of these is charity.

Wyclif's most important claim was that the Bible, not the Church, was the only source of divine authority. Thus, adherence to the scriptures, rather than obedience to the requirements of the Church, was the path to reaching a state of grace. This was a precursor to the central tenet of Martin Luther's Protestantism – justification by faith.

Wyclif was not a natural rabble-rouser; rather, he was a distinguished scholar with influential allies, receiving protection from one of the most powerful men in the country, Edward III's third son, John of Gaunt. His message, however, was essentially egalitarian: that the poor and those of no rank should have the means to understand God's word without the intercession of an official clergy.

He recieved his first serious rebuke in 1377 when Gregory XI issued papal bulls condemning Wyclif's teaching on nineteen grounds and summoning him to face the charges. Instead, the errant academic escaped with a light admonition to keep quiet. When the Peasants' Revolt broke out in 1381, his enemies were quick to link his teaching to this violent and anarchic disorder. After the authorities at Oxford ordered him to desist from publicly disputing transubstantiation, he left the university for Lutterworth in Leicestershire where he had been rector since 1374. The archbishop of Canterbury summoned a council that condemned Wyclif's teaching (without naming him) as heretical, while for good measure Parliament made the profession of such heresies a prisonable offence. Nonetheless, Wyclif managed to avoid prosecution, continuing to write from his obscurity in Lutterworth, where he died in 1384.

Before his passing, he had begun work on a revolutionary document – the Bible in English. This was in itself a challenge to the pope, as the Church prescribed only

SPREADING GOD'S WORD IN ENGLISH

1384 John Wyclif's Bible is the first complete translation in English.

1395 John Purvey produces his amended version of Wyclif's Bible.

1408 The Synod of Oxford prohibits any unauthorized Bible translation.

1526 William Tyndale's translation is the first printed New Testament in English.

1535 Miles Coverdale's translation is the first printed complete Bible.

1537 The Matthew Bible is published by John Rodgers.

1538 The Great Bible is the first English Bible to be authorized for public use.

1539 A revised version of the Matthew Bible is produced by Richard Taverner.

1560 The Geneva Bible is the first to number the verses of every chapter.

1568 The Bishops' Bible is authorized for public use.

1609–10 The Douai–Rheims Bible is the first complete English-language Catholic Bible.

1611 The 'Authorized King James' Bible is published.

one translation of the Bible: the Vulgate, compiled – in Latin – by St Jerome at the beginning of the fifth century. Yet a Bible in the vernacular tongue was the logical conclusion of Wyclif's teaching, since the common people searching for salvation through the word of scripture had little chance of finding it if they could not understand the Latin in which it was written. An English-language Bible would mean they no longer had to rely on the clergy's potentially self-serving interpretation. At last, the unmediated scripture could be read by – or read to – the laity in their own language.

How much of the translation was personally undertaken by Wyclif remains a matter of academic debate. The chronicler Henry Knighton, writing shortly after Wyclif's death, stated that he 'translated from Latin into the language not of angels but of Englishmen, so that he made that common and open to the laity, and to women who were able to read, which used to be for literate and perceptive clerks'. This, according to Knighton, was an abhorrent development, for 'the jewel of the church is turned into the common sport of the people'. In fact, sections of the Bible had been translated into English before, but never in a comprehensive or widely available format. It was Wyclif's followers who finished the task. Nicholas Hereford completed the first attempt, generating a literal translation from the Vulgate. Then, around 1395, a smoother, more idiomatic, version came from the pen of John Purvey.

In the absence of printing, which was still to be invented, the number of copies produced was limited by the speed of scribes. To overcome this, Wyclif's followers, who became known as Lollards, travelled around the country, disseminating their Bible's contents. Although an exact number cannot be ascertained, it is clear that a great many copies came into circulation, of which 170 have survived into the modern day. To the authorities of Church and state, this was a direct challenge that had to be suppressed. In 1401, Henry IV issued a statute, *De heretico comburendo* ('On the Burning of the Heretic') which Parliament passed, making clear the justice that would be meted out to owners of Wyclif's Bible. In 1408, the Synod of Oxford prohibited all future translation of the Bible into English without official licence. In 1427, on the order of Pope Martin V, Wyclif's bones were dug up from the Lutterworth churchyard, burned and dumped in the River Swift.

In the short term, the repression was effective. Lollardy continued but only as an underground movement, although its central tenets were picked up on the continent, finding an especially receptive audience in Bohemia. Even when the most influential adherent there, John Hus, was duly burned at the stake in 1415, Wyclif's ideas could not be unthought. What was needed was a fresh crisis in the Church and a new invention – printing – that would truly put the word of scripture in the people's hands. It was in this respect that John Wyclif was 'the morning star of the Reformation'.

HENRY VI'S CHARTERS FOR ETON COLLEGE AND KING'S COLLEGE, CAMBRIDGE

EDUCATING THE ELITE

The Charter of King's College, Cambridge is depicted in the second plate section.

Where schooling was available in the fifteenth century, it was mostly offered informally through the local parish church. There, children might gain a basic acquaintance with the alphabet as well as religious instruction. At a more structured level, there were schools attached to cathedrals, of which Canterbury, Rochester and Ely pre-dated the Norman Conquest. Collegiate churches, monasteries and hospitals also founded schools. Grammar schools, offering the grounding in Latin that was deemed useful for boys (but not girls) wanting to make the study of law or theology their future profession, or to trade in Europe, were also beginning to emerge during this period.

These various forms of schooling catered primarily for local children. Less common were 'public schools', which were endowed foundations, open to boys drawn from all over the country. For much of the medieval period, the nobility had sent their heirs neither to school nor to university, preferring to see them develop chivalric, rather than scholastic, values within aristocratic households. From the fifteenth century onwards it was to public schools that the social elite increasingly sent their sons. Consequently, public schools came to play the foremost role in moulding and shaping the experiences of most of Britain's political leaders, as well as a high proportion of those distinguishing themselves in many other fields of activity as well. Although not the oldest, it was Eton College, near Windsor Castle, that emerged as the greatest of these institutions. Indeed, it would be hard to think of any other school in the Western world with a comparable predominance in national life.

Despite being an independent school, Eton was founded by a monarch and its provost was originally a state appointment. Still a nine-month-old baby when he became king in 1422, the pious and ineffective Henry VI inherited the thrones of both England and France. He had effectively lost the latter by the time he was old enough to rule in his own right and would lose the former in the civil wars known as the Wars of the Roses. Mentally unstable, he was deposed and imprisoned in the Tower of London where, in 1471, he was murdered. Nonetheless, two of Britain's most famous foundations owe their existence to him.

Henry VI was only eighteen when he founded Eton, to provide lodging and a schooling for the sons of the wealthy and influential; but it was also endowed to educate seventy poor boys. Despite the expanding proportion of fee-paying 'Oppidans' in the succeeding centuries, these seventy scholars or 'collegers' – selected by competitive examination – remained at the core of the school with initially free and later subsidized fees.

In his designs for Eton, Henry was especially influenced by the example of the leading public school, Winchester College, which had been founded in 1382 by William of Wykeham as a 'feeder' for his university foundation, New College, Oxford. To provide the same continuity of learning, Henry duly founded King's College, an institution at Cambridge to rival New College at Oxford. Like Eton, it too was to have a provost and seventy scholars, all of whom had to have attended Eton beforehand. Henry's vision for King's College was grandiose and in 1446 he laid the foundation stone for its chapel. It proved to be one of the wonders of late perpendicular architecture, but neither Henry nor his next four successors saw it completed. The Wars of the Roses so badly disrupted construction that it was not finished until the sixteenth century.

THE GROWTH OF UNIVERSITIES

1096 Teaching begins at Oxford.

1209 Cambridge University is founded.

1261 A university is founded at Northampton. It is shut by royal writ in 1265.

1413 St Andrews University is founded.

1451 Glasgow University is founded.

1495 King's College, Aberdeen, is established with university status. It merges with Marischal College (est. 1593) to formally become Aberdeen University in 1860.

1582 Edinburgh University is founded.

1592 Trinity College, Dublin, is founded.

1595 The Scottish Parliament donates a grant to erect a university at Fraserburgh. It is abandoned in 1605.

1822 Wales's oldest degree-awarding body, St David's College, is established at Lampeter. It becomes a constituent member of the University of Wales in 1971.

1826 University College London (UCL) is established as the first to admit students regardless of faith. It gains legal status in 1836.

1829 King's College, London, is established for Anglican students. It becomes, with UCL, the first constituent college of the University of London in 1836.

1832 Durham University is founded. It gains its royal charter in 1837.

1845 Queen's University, Belfast, receives its royal charter.

1880 Victoria University is established as a federal body in Manchester. Colleges in Liverpool and Leeds join it before subsequently breaking away.

1893 The University of Wales is established.

1900 Birmingham University is established and is soon followed by other 'red-brick' or 'civic' universities at Liverpool (1903), Leeds (1904), Sheffield (1905) and Bristol (1909).

Although it anomalously enjoyed (until 1853) its own degree-awarding powers, King's was a college of Cambridge University. England's second oldest university dated from the early thirteenth century when scholars seeking to escape the violence of Oxford townsfolk decamped there. By 1400, Oxford was still the dominant institution of higher education, with perhaps 1,200 students to Cambridge's 400. Henry VI, however, feared that Oxford was tainted with the Lollard 'heresy' of John Wyclif's teaching and his decision to endow Cambridge helped redress the balance, so that by the century's end the two universities were of roughly equal size and prestige.

Teaching was in Latin (although Greek was also taught in Oxford from the 1460s onwards) and the curriculum focused on theology, philosophy and the arts. Sixty of King's seventy scholars studied theology, four studied canon law, two studied medicine, two astronomy and two civil law. The collegiate

The chapel of King's College from an engraving by David Loggan, c.1660.

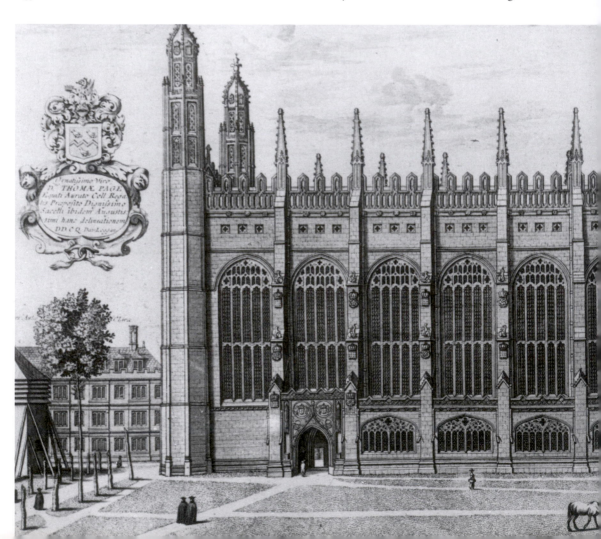

structure strengthened the sense of an inter-generational community, with undergraduates – who might be as young as fifteen in the sixteenth century – often living in the same buildings as their fellows. Yet despite the preponderance of students destined for holy orders, the colleges of Oxford and Cambridge were not comparable to monasteries. When the new humanist learning, with its reliance on classical Greek philosophers, took hold in the sixteenth century, the Dutch scholar Erasmus became one of those who studied at Queens' College, Cambridge. The wealth of both universities was massively increased as a result of Henry VIII stripping the monasteries of their assets. Henry refounded what became each institution's two grandest colleges, Christ Church at Oxford and Trinity College, Cambridge.

Throughout its first 400 years, Eton's curriculum was geared towards providing a classical education. Given that Latin was the language of the Church and the

law, this focus was not surprising in the fifteenth and sixteenth centuries. By the eighteenth century however, the justification for persevering with Greek and Latin had less to do with their vocational applicability than that they offered a sufficiently difficult test of intellectual ability. Whether the classical emphasis provided sufficient training for the Cambridge Mathematics 'tripos' was more questionable. Despite producing Kingsmen ranging from John Harington, the Elizabethan inventor of the flushing water closet, to Robert Walpole, the first prime minister, the dependence on Eton's gene pool certainly ossified King's. It finally admitted its first non-Etonians in 1865 and thereafter developed a reputation for liberal, progressive and left-wing thinking.

While retaining their social exclusivity, both Oxford and Cambridge lost some of their academic rigour in the eighteenth and early nineteenth centuries, contentedly enjoying the independence they had secured by spiralling endowment income and a virtual monopoly in producing Anglican clergymen. During this period, not only was the education offered at Edinburgh and Glasgow universities generally superior, but from 1826 competition emerged from new English foundations like University College London. However, Oxford and Cambridge restored their intellectual primacy by reforms in the mid-nineteenth century, and made their degrees available to non-Anglicans. Eton likewise reformed and broadened its curriculum, although it maintained its enduring and remarkable prominence in educating the leaders of Church and state over the succeeding 150 years. By 2010, there had been nineteen Old Etonian prime ministers, while Oxford and Cambridge had, between them, educated forty-one of Britain's fifty-five prime ministers. Other universities had educated only three.

Their predominance might have been readily understandable if Oxford and Cambridge were merely finishing schools for those seeking bureaucratic accreditation or parochial and worldly attainment, but they also enhanced their credentials as leading research institutions. As such, they attracted many of the world's finest minds, supplanting in this respect the previously dominant universities of Germany and Central Europe. By the twenty-first century, some exceptionally wealthy American universities like Harvard and Yale could claim a competitive edge, while others achieved parity. Nonetheless, it was principally Cambridge academics who achieved two of the most seismic breakthroughs of the twentieth century: splitting the atom in 1932 and unravelling the structure of DNA in 1953. Cambridge, indeed, has produced more Nobel Prize winners than the whole of France.

1485

WILLIAM CAXTON'S PUBLICATION OF MALORY'S *MORTE D'ARTHUR*

THE SPREAD OF PRINTED BOOKS AND THE ENDURING APPEAL OF THE ARTHURIAN LEGEND

By the fifteenth century, literacy in English was spreading but it still faced two significant barriers. The first was the time-consuming production, scarcity and great cost of manuscript books. The second was the assumption that Latin should remain the language for expressing abstract or high ideas. The printing revolution, which Johann Gutenberg began at Mainz around 1454 and William Caxton brought to England, did much to remove these restraints.

Born in Kent between 1415 and 1424, Caxton was possibly the son of a merchant. Whilst he received some schooling, he was not educated with the intention of pursuing a career either in the Church or in the legal profession. Rather, he became an apprentice in the Mercers' Company in London. The Mercers dealt in haberdashery, cloth and silks, for which Britain's most important business was with the Low Countries. In order to be at the heart of this trade, Caxton moved to Bruges and there, in 1465, he became governor of the prosperous Flemish city's English community. Indeed, his evident ability was such that he found himself negotiating England's trade deals with both Flanders and the Hanseatic League.

Movable-type printing already existed in the Rhine valley and when in 1471 Caxton moved to Cologne he acquired a press. Although he did not give up his career as a textiles merchant, he realized that he was well placed to corner the market in translating fashionable texts from French into English for sale in England. Initially, he personally undertook some of the translation work, covering himself against charges that he lacked the requisite scholarly credentials by securing the unimpeachable patronage of Edward IV's sister, Margaret, duchess of Burgundy. Having completed its translation from the original French, he published the

IN SEARCH OF ARTHUR

*c.*540 Gildas in his *De Excidio Britanniae* ('On the Ruin of Britain') mentions the Battle of Mount Badon but omits any mention of Arthur.

*c.*600 The Welsh poem *Y Gododdin* refers to a heroic fighter being 'not Arthur'. The oldest surviving copy of *Y Gododdin*, however, dates from the thirteenth century.

*c.*830 The *Historia Brittonum* lists twelve battles fought by Arthur.

1125 Arthur's great deeds are lauded by William of Malmesbury in his *Gesta Regum Anglorum* ('Deeds of the Kings of England').

1136 Geoffrey of Monmouth completes his *Historia Regum Britanniae* ('History of the Kings of Britain'), which provides a full – if highly elaborated – account of Arthur's career.

1155 The Round Table is mentioned in a French version of Geoffrey's *Historia* by Robert Wace.

*c.*1160–90 The French writer, Chrétien de Troyes, introduces the Grail and the knights Lancelot, Gawain and Perceval in his cycle of Arthurian romances.

1190 A grave at Glastonbury Abbey is 'identified' as Arthur's resting place.

*c.*1198 In his *Historia Rerum Anglicarum*, William of Newburgh casts doubt on the authenticity of Geoffrey of Monmouth's claims.

*c.*1210 Robert de Boron transforms Chrétien's 'grail' into the 'Holy Grail'.

*c.*1250 (date disputed) Arthur is a character in the Welsh folk tales of the *Mabinogion*.

1278 Arthur's supposed remains are reinterred at Glastonbury in the presence of Edward I.

c. late 14th century *Morte Arthure*, a 4,346-line alliterative poem, is written in Middle English.

*c.*1370–90 The Arthurian legend is referenced in Geoffrey Chaucer's *Canterbury Tales*.

1469–70 Sir Thomas Malory writes *Morte d'Arthur*.

1485 *Morte d'Arthur* is printed by William Caxton.

1599 Edmund Spenser dies while writing *The Faerie Queene*, a poem based upon Arthurian virtues.

1691 Henry Purcell's semi-opera *King Arthur* is performed, with a libretto by John Dryden.

Recuyell of the Historyes of Troye, the world's first printed book in English, in 1474. He quickly followed it with another translation, the *Game and Playe of the Chesse*.

By 1476, Caxton had returned to England, setting up his printing press by Westminster Abbey. His first offering was a further translation, the *Dictes or Sayengis of the Philosophres*, but his emphasis soon switched from publishing translated French-language texts to the works of native authors. Of these, the first was his *editio princeps* of Geoffrey Chaucer's *Canterbury Tales*. In all, he published over one hundred works, some in Latin, but the overwhelming majority in English.

Malory's account of Arthur, Sir Bedevere and Excalibur

Therfore, sayd Arthur vnto Syr Bedwere, take thou Excalybur, my good swerde, and goo with it to yonder watersyde. And whan thou comest there I charge the throwe my swerde in that water, and come ageyn and telle me what thou seest. My lord, said Bedwere, your commaundement shal be doon and lyghtly brynge you worde ageyn. So Syr Bedwere departed, and by waye he beheld that noble swerde, that the pomel and the hafte was al of precyous stones. And thenne he sayd to hymself, yf I throwe this ryche swerde in the water, therof shal neuer come good, but harme and losse. And thenne Syr Bedwere hydde Excalybur vnder a tree. And so as sone as he myght, he came ageyn vnto the kyng and sayd he had ben at the water. What sawe thou there? sayd the kyng. Syr, he sayd, I sawe nothynge but wawes and wyndes. That is vntrewly sayd of the, sayd the kynge. Therfore goo thou lyghtelye ageyn and do my commaundemente; as thou arte to me leef and dere, spare not, but throwe it in.

Than Syr Bedwere retorned ageyn and took the swerde in hys hande, and than hym thought synne and shame to throwe awaye that nobyl swerde. And so efte he hydde the swerde and returned ageyn, and tolde the kyng that he had ben at the water and done his commaundemente. What sawe thou there? sayd the kyng. Syr, he sayd, I sawe nothynge but the waters wappe and wawes wanne. A, traytour vntrewe, sayd Kyng Arthur, now hast thou betrayed me twyse. Who wold haue went that thou, that hast been to me so leef and dere, and thou arte named a noble knyghte, and wold betraye me the richesse of the swerde? But now goo ageyn lyghtly, for thy longe taryeng putteth me in grete ieopardye of my lyf, for I haue taken colde. And but yf thou do now as I byd the, yf euer I may see the I shal slee the myn owne hands, for thou woldest for my ryche swerde see me dede.

Then Syr Bedwere departed and wente to the swerde, and lyghtly took hit vp and wente to the watersyde. And there he bounde the gyrdyl aboute the hyltes, and thenne he threwe the swerde as farre as the water as he myght. And there cam an arme and an hande about the water, and mette it and caught it, and shoke it thryse and braundysshed, and then vanysshed awaye the hande wyth the swerde in the water. So Syr Bedwere came ageyn to the kyng and tolde hym what he sawe. Alas, sayd the kyng, helpe me hens, for I drede me I haue taryed ouer longe.

The consequence of this breakthrough for English literacy and literature can hardly be overstated. Caxton, however, was no intellectual concerned with shaping academic debate, but rather an industrious businessman who recognized a gap in the market, especially for popular romantic fiction. It was not until printing presses fell into the hands of political and religious dissidents that books were to become not just a profitable industry but an effective challenge to the authority of the unreformed Church and state.

Caxton, who died in 1491 or 1492, either failed to grasp, or chose not to pioneer, this development. He did not print the works of the humanist 'new learning' let alone the arguments of identified heretics. Indeed, it was telling that perhaps his most successful publication looked not forward to the Renaissance but backwards to the myths underpinning medieval chivalry. This was the *Morte d'Arthur*.

The title resulted from a misunderstanding by Caxton. Its author, Sir Thomas Malory (c.1415–71), had actually intended it to be called *The Whole Book of King Arthur and his Noble Knights of the Round Table*. Malory had adapted a mixture of sources, such as Geoffrey of Monmouth, Layamon and Chrétien de Troyes. Many of them were French, but they also included the fourteenth-century *Morte Arthure*, an alliterative poem written in Middle English. Malory wrote in rhythmic, accessible English prose, which Caxton divided up into twenty-one books. It was not until 1934 that a manuscript was discovered in the Winchester College Library without Caxton's divisions, revealing far more clearly the eight tales of Arthurian legend upon which Malory's work was structured. It was published as a new standard edition by Eugene Vinaver in 1947.

Beyond his knighthood there was little in the recorded facts of Malory's own life that tallied with the chivalric quests of Sir Galahad. Most of *Morte d'Arthur* was written while Malory was incarcerated in the Tower of London during a period of nearly eighteen years spent in one prison or another on a variety of charges (for which he was never tried), which ranged from the attempted murder of the duke of Buckingham to cattle rustling, theft, rape, jail-breaking and robbery at his local abbey. Nevertheless, *Morte d'Arthur* was responsible for perpetuating the fame of the Arthurian legend far beyond the fifteenth century. It not only inspired the Victorian painters of the Pre-Raphaelite Brotherhood and the poet Alfred, Lord Tennyson, but helped ensure that throughout the twentieth and early twenty-first century, Arthur and the Knights of the Round Table, Guinevere, Merlin and Morgan le Fay remained familiar characters in popular culture, and Camelot and Avalon enchanting destinations for the imagination.

III

RELIGION AND
THE RENAISSANCE

1525–6
TYNDALE'S NEW TESTAMENT

THE LANGUAGE OF PROTESTANT SCRIPTURE

On the eve of the Reformation, the ban on English-language versions of the Bible was still in force. The persecution of John Wyclif's Lollard followers in the early fifteenth century stood as a warning to anyone minded to risk fresh accusations of heresy. Nevertheless, a clear opportunity to challenge authority was presented by the rising support for religious reform in Germany that followed the denunciation of Martin Luther by the imperial Diet of Worms in 1521, and the success of printing presses in disseminating dissident opinion. None were more active in mounting this challenge than those inspired and emboldened by Martin Luther's stand against papal supremacy.

The man who decided to take the risk of producing a new, and widely available, translation of the Bible was William Tyndale. Born around 1494 in Gloucestershire, he had studied at Oxford University and was ordained into the priesthood. Significantly for his later work as a translator, he also learned Greek, possibly either under Erasmus at Cambridge or by reading Erasmus's New Testament translation in Latin with the Greek original alongside. Given the politics of the time, Tyndale failed in his attempt to get his English-language translation printed legally in England, so he left London bound for Hamburg. While there, he may also have spent time in Wittenberg, possibly meeting Luther who had published a German-language version of the New Testament in 1522. Tyndale's New Testament in English was finished in 1525, but an injunction disrupted its publication in Cologne. Tyndale duly moved to Worms, a centre of Lutheran activity, where the completed work was published by Peter Schoeffer.

The next stage was getting it to England and Scotland, a feat achieved by smuggling the books concealed in bales of cloth. Henry VIII's lord chancellor, Cardinal Wolsey, led the campaign to seize and destroy the several thousand copies that reached England, in which he was largely successful. Of Schoeffer's first print run, only one complete copy is still in existence and it was discovered in Stuttgart

Opening page of
St John's Gospel
from the first edition
of Tyndale's New
Testament.

as recently as 1996. Two other largely complete copies also remain: one, in the British Library, is denuded solely of its title page, while the copy in the library of St Paul's Cathedral is less comprehensive, missing seventy leaves.

Tyndale's New Testament differed significantly from the Wyclif Bible of the Lollards. Whereas the latter had been translated from the Latin Vulgate, Tyndale achieved greater authenticity by translating from the original Greek. Being printed, rather than handwritten, it could be produced and circulated in far larger numbers. Rough copies were soon being churned out by an enterprising printer in Antwerp. This emphasis on popularizing the word of scripture and placing it at the heart of belief was central to Protestant theology, as well as making a distinct departure from the Church of Rome's approach. 'I defy the Pope and all his laws,' Tyndale proclaimed, 'and if God spare my life, I will cause the boy that drives the plough in England to know more of the Scriptures than the Pope himself.'

Hunted by the agents of both Henry VIII and the Holy Roman Empire, Tyndale had to live and work in Worms and Antwerp undercover. Despite these conditions, his output remained formidable, turning out a succession of Protestant theological tracts while also antagonizing his powerful enemies further by condemning Henry VIII's divorce from Catherine of Aragon. Nonetheless, his main task remained translating the rest of the Bible. He was hard at work on this, translating from the Hebrew Old Testament and had reached the end of Chronicles, when an Englishman named Henry Philips inveigled him out of his Antwerp safe house and betrayed him for money. Dragged off to Vilvoorde Castle outside Brussels, Tyndale was imprisoned for sixteen months, put on trial and found guilty of heresy, for which the punishment was death. A chain was fastened around his neck with which he was first strangled before being burned at the stake on 6 October 1536. His last words were recorded as, 'Lord, open the king of England's eyes.'

Although Henry VIII never adopted Lutheran beliefs, in one sense he was persuaded to permit Tyndale a posthumous victory. Only months after the translator's death, the king licensed the first official Bible in English. Also drawing on the 1535 translation of the Lutheran Miles Coverdale, it was in reality two-thirds the work of the 'heretic' Tyndale. Such was both its literary and scholarly quality that Tyndale's version shaped all subsequent translations. In particular, the committee that produced the King James Bible – the Authorized Version – in 1611 retained much of Tyndale's language.

It would have been foolish to attempt anything else. Tyndale's style was poetic, yet simple, giving preference to words that were Anglo-Saxon rather than French or Latin in derivation, which undoubtedly made his work more accessible to those with minimal education – the ploughboys of whom he spoke. He produced phrases that remain familiar to us almost half a millennium later: 'fight the good fight', 'the spirit is willing', 'take up thy bed and walk', 'no man can serve two masters', 'the powers that be'. It was a style that influenced the writers of the sixteenth century, being especially influential in the work of William Shakespeare. Indeed, Tyndale's place in the history of English literature lies not only beside his fellow theologians but alongside that of the Bard. Centuries after he met his violent fate, Tyndale is still shaping not just the way the English-speaking world praises God, but also the way that it expresses itself in day-to-day conversation.

1530

PARLIAMENT'S PETITION TO THE POPE TO ANNUL HENRY VIII'S MARRIAGE

THE ENGLISH CHURCH SPLITS FROM ROME

On 11 June 1509, the new king, Henry VIII, married his late brother's widow, the Spanish princess Catherine of Aragon. In the course of the following twenty-four years, she became pregnant six times but only a daughter, Mary, survived infancy. With his wife soon to reach her fortieth year, Henry gave up hope that she would provide him with the male heir upon which he believed the security of the Tudor dynasty depended. After all, the family had come to power only as the consequence of the thirty years of dynastic struggle known as the Wars of the Roses, and the sole precedent for an English queen attempting to rule in her own right was hardly encouraging: the Empress Matilda's failed effort in 1141.

Unfortunately for Catherine of Aragon, by 1526 Henry had fallen for one of his wife's ladies-in-waiting. Much younger than Catherine, Anne Boleyn seemed far more likely to bear him a son, but to marry her Henry needed first to receive from the pope an annulment of his first marriage. This became known, euphemistically, as the 'King's Great Matter'. Pondering his failure to produce an heir, Henry had alighted on a text in Leviticus, warning that a sexual relationship with a brother's wife would be cursed with childlessness. The case rested on the suggestion that the original papal dispensation, authorizing Henry to marry his brother's widow, should not have given because it had been based upon the belief that Catherine's first marriage had not been consummated. It was a presumption suddenly convenient to dispute. However, Pope Clement VII procrastinated, refusing to meekly do the English king's bidding. His decision was not based on doctrine alone: Rome had been sacked and Clement was the virtual prisoner

From parliament's petition to the pope, 1530

To the most holy father and Lord in Christ, Lord Clement, by divine providence seventh pope of that name, we kiss your feet in all humility and pray for your happiness which we desire to be eternal, in our Lord Jesus Christ.

Most blessed father, in the case of the marriage of our unconquered and most serene prince, our Lord, defender of the faith of England and France and Lord of Scotland, many relevant arguments on the matter have been used to entreat and petition your Holiness for help, so that a conclusion can be reached as quickly as possible – a conclusion which we have long desired with all our hearts and, so far, have awaited from your Holiness in anticipation, but without result. Consequently, because this dispute has been so long protracted that it is now critical, our kingdom finds itself in a situation where we cannot be altogether silent. Our Royal Majesty, our head and to that extent the soul of us all, and we in his words – like limbs in harmony with the head, a soundly unified body – have prayed with much anxiety to your Holiness. We have, however, prayed in vain. So we are now impelled by the weight of our grief, separately and individually, to write and make this demand.

of the Holy Roman Emperor, Charles V, who was also Catherine's nephew.

Never one to be kept waiting, Henry tried to speed up the process with a succession of diplomatic overtures to Clement. On 13 July 1530, the most elaborate of these took the form of a parliamentary petition to which the archbishops of Canterbury and York attached their seals, together with those of four bishops and the leading peers of the realm. Presumptively taking the likelihood of an annulment for granted, it urged the pope to hurry up with granting it.

His Holiness was not to be so easily swayed, with the momentous consequence that it was Henry who divorced England from Rome. Thomas Cranmer, once installed as the new archbishop of Canterbury, dutifully set to his task. In May 1533 he pronounced that Henry's marriage to Catherine was annulled and that the private marriage ceremony the king had contracted with Anne was legal. If Anne were to give birth, any child of hers would therefore be legitimate. In the same year, Parliament bowed to Henry's will and asserted Rome's jurisdiction over England to be illegal. The 1534 Act of Supremacy declared Henry to be 'the only supreme head of the Church'.

The king's personal problems led to the creation of a state Church, independent of Rome, but they did not make the country Protestant. Indeed, for the laity, the change made only superficial differences to their daily worship. The Church of England remained essentially Catholic. The 1539 Act of Six Articles not only demonstrated that Henry was still opposed to Protestant 'heresies' but reaffirmed Catholic doctrine on clerical celibacy and transubstantiation (the presence of Christ's body and blood in the bread and wine of the sacrament). The traditional liturgy was kept in place as was the power of Church courts. That the bishops were appointed by the Crown was only a formal acknowledgement that it was the monarch who had, in reality, mostly been nominating them in previous centuries.

This painting, attributed to Joos van Cleve, shows Henry VIII in c.1535 while he was married to Anne Boleyn. His scroll quotes the gospel of Mark 16:15, 'Go ye into all the world, and preach the Gospel to every creature.'

Yet while life in the parish and the cathedral continued with merely minor modifications, monastic houses fared very differently. In the wake of revelations of corruption and scandal, the minor monasteries were dissolved in 1536. This was followed in 1539 by legislation to dissolve the major monasteries. By 1540, the Crown had taken over 800 monastic houses. The primary rationale was financial. The state needed money, in particular to engage in war with France. Indeed, by 1547, two-thirds of the revenue raised from monastic dissolution had been wasted on this martial enterprise. From 1545 the wealth of the private or institutional chapels known as chantries was also appropriated by the state. This represented not just an extraordinary transferral of resources, but a frontal assault on the traditional spiritual institutions of the nation.

Alas, the woman for whom Henry deemed it worth breaking with Rome soon disappointed him. After several attempts, she produced a mere daughter, Elizabeth. Henry had Anne beheaded in 1536 on (spurious) charges of adultery, incest and treason, and proceeded to marry the third of his six wives, Jane Seymour. She died giving birth to the male heir for whom he had been prepared to go to such lengths. As Edward VI, he was to succeed his father in 1547, transforming the state religion during his brief reign to the Protestant faith. The greater irony, however, was that for all his desire for a son, it was Henry's daughter, Elizabeth, who ultimately proved the most capable and celebrated ruler of the age.

1536

THE ANGLO-WELSH
ACT OF UNION

WALES ENTERS INTO FORMAL UNION WITH ENGLAND

The victory of Henry Tudor over Richard III at the Battle of Bosworth Field in 1485 had ended the thirty-year-long Wars of the Roses and put on the English throne a family whose blood was part Welsh.

What this meant for Wales was initially unclear. Indeed, during the preceding 200 years, the constitutional relationship between Wales and England had been complicated. Conquered by Edward I, the principality of Wales in the west and north-west was carved into English-style shires. By contrast, the extension of the English Crown's authority in eastern and southern Wales was far more evolutionary. These lands were the semi-autonomous domains of earls of Anglo-Norman descent, the 'Marcher' lords.

During the reign of Henry VII (as Henry Tudor became), Wales enjoyed a form of dominion status within the English realm and was administered by a prerogative council, meeting mostly in Ludlow in Shropshire. At first, this system continued after the accession of Henry VIII, but it was not to endure. Two Acts of Parliament, in 1536 and 1543, which later became known as the Acts of Union, were passed with the explicit intention of ensuring that Wales was 'incorporated, united and annexed' by England.

Of the two acts, that of 1536 was the more important. The Marcher territories were divided into shires and administered on the same county-government model as in England. This created the shires of Denbigh, Montgomery, Radnor, Brecon, Pembroke, Glamorgan and Monmouth. Together with the shires created in the north and west by Edward I, they would be represented in Parliament by twenty-seven MPs.

The legislation struck at the heart of the old Marcher legal autonomy, by establishing that the English common law had supremacy and was to be applied

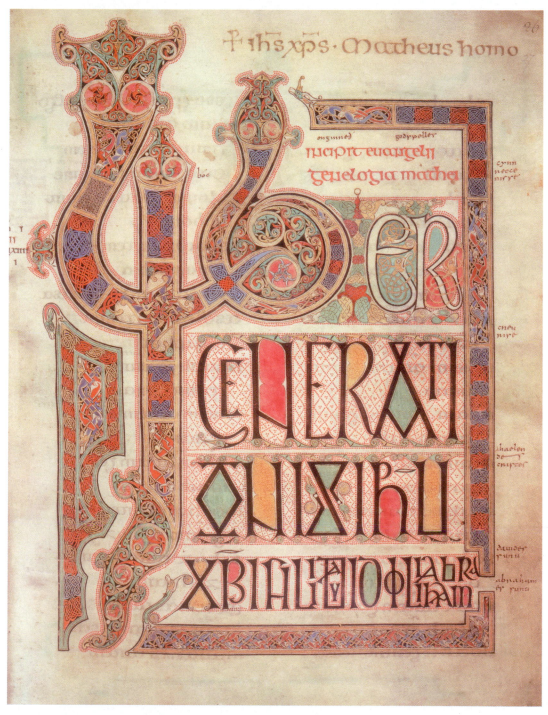

c.715 – THE LINDISFARNE GOSPELS
The opening page, known as the incipit page, of the Gospel of St Matthew. Stylistically, the decorative details share many common characteristics with Anglo-Saxon jewellery design.

LATE 11TH CENTURY – THE BAYEUX TAPESTRY

'Here King Harold was killed', states the Bayeux Tapestry. Harold is popularly assumed to be both the warrior with the arrow in his eye and the figure being felled by the Norman cavalryman.

1215 – MAGNA CARTA

Only four of the first copies issued of Magna Carta survive. This is the best-preserved of the two versions held at the British Library.

c.1250 – THE CHRONICLES OF MATTHEW PARIS

Matthew Paris's mid-thirteenth-century map of Britain is the oldest surviving example of a map that attempts – however imperfectly – to portray geographical accuracy rather than merely to present a schematic representation of the island. Over 250 places are marked as well as long-defunct features like the Hadrian and Antonine Walls.

1320 – THE DECLARATION OF ARBROATH

Eight Scottish earls and thirty-eight barons attached their seals to the Latin plea to Pope John XXII to recognize Scotland as an independent nation.

From the Act of Union, 1536

Albeit the Domynyon Principalitie and Countrey of Wales justly and rightuouslye is and ever hath ben incorporated annexed united and subjecte to & under the Imperiall Crowne of this Realme, as a verrye membre and joynte of the same, Wherfore the Kinges moost Roiall Magestie of mere droite and verye right is verie hedde King Lorde and Ruler, yet notwithstanding by cause that in the same Countrey Principalitie and Dominion dyvers rightes usagis lawes and customes be farre discrepant frome the Lawes and Customes of this Realme, And also by cause that the people of the same Dominion have and do daily use a speche nothing like ne consonaunt to the naturall mother tonge used within this Realme, somme rude and ignorant people have made distinccion and diversitie betwene the Kinges Subjectes of this Realme and hys Subjectes of the said Dominion and Principalitie of Wales, wherby greate discorde variaunce debate dyvysion murmur and sedicion hath growen betwene his said subjectes; His Highnes therfore of a singuler zele love and favour that he beareth towardes his Subjectes of his said Dominion of Wales, mynding and entending to reduce them to the perfecte order notice & knowlege of his lawes of this his Realme, and utterly to extirpe all and singuler the senister usages and customes differinge frome the same, and to bringe his said Subjectes of this his Realme and of his said Dominion of Wales to an amicable concorde and unitie, Hath by the deliberate advise consent and agreament of the Lordes spirituall and temporall and the Commons in this present assembled and by the auctoritie of the same, ordeyned enacted and established that his said Countrey or Dominion of Wales shalbe stonde and contynue for ever incorporated united and annexed to and with this his Realme of Englande; And that all and singuler personne and personnes borne and to be borne in the said Principalitie Countrey or Dominion of Wales, shall have enjoye and inherite all and singuler fredomes liberties rightes privileges and lawes within this Realme and other the Kynges Dominions as other the Kinges Subjectes naturally borne within the same, have enjoye and enherite: And that all and singular personne and personnes inheritable to any Manours Landes Tenements Rentes Revercions services or other Hereditaments, which shall discende within the set Principalitie, Countrey or Dominion of Wales, or within any particuler Lordshippe parte or parcell of the said Countrey or Dominion of Wales, shall forever inherite and be inheritable to the same Manours Landes Tenementes Rentes Revercions and Hereditamentes after the Englisshe tenure, without division or particion, and after the forme of the Lawes of this Realme of Englande, and not after any tenure ne after the fourme of any Welshe Lawes

> or Customes; And that the Lawes Ordynaunces and Statutes of this Realme of
> Englande for ever, and none other Lawes Ordenaunces ne Statutes, shalbe had
> used practised & executed in the said Countrey or Dominion of Wales and every
> parte therof, in like manner and forme and order as they ben and shalbe had
> used practised and executed in this Realme, and in such like manner and forme
> as hereafter by this acte shalbe further established and ordeyned; any acte statute
> usage custome president libertie privilege or other thing, had made used graunted
> or suffred to the contrary, in any wise notwithstanding.

throughout Wales. However, distinctive chancery and exchequer courts were
established, while four Courts of Great Sessions, equipped with their own circuit
and permanent judges, presided over twelve of the Welsh shires. Monmouth's
exclusion from this arrangement (it was attached to the Oxford circuit) left
ambiguous its status as to whether it was in England or Wales. Across Wales, law
enforcement was to be overseen by justices of the peace, chosen by the local gentry.

The growth of this powerful squirearchy class was stimulated by the
abolition of Welsh inheritance law, which was replaced by England's tradition of
primogeniture, solidifying landownership as the prerogative of eldest sons. The
social gulf between them and other freeholders widened in a society that still
had a very small merchant class. Besides wealth, the most obvious demonstration
of this gulf was language. The fact that the 1536 act established English as the
language of official business did much to separate the increasingly English-
speaking squirearchy from the rest of the native-speaking community.

However, although the Welsh language ceased to be used in legal and
administrative matters, it was not actively suppressed. Indeed, a statute of 1563
ordered the Bible and the Book of Common Prayer to be translated into Welsh,
which did much to preserve and develop the language. Nor was the imposition of
Anglicanism initially met with the same level of resentment as in Ireland. Whereas
the overwhelming majority of Irish remained implacably Catholic, in Wales by
contrast, Protestantism successfully took root across most of the country. In this
respect, Welsh society was not divided by the sort of penal laws that reduced
Ireland's majority religionists to second-class status under the law. Only in the
nineteenth century, with the Nonconformist revival, did the division between
church and chapel become one of the most contentious issues in Welsh life, forcing,
belatedly, the disestablishment of the Anglican Church there in 1920.

1546
THE ANTHONY ROLL

THE INVENTORY AND DEPICTION OF
KING HENRY VIII'S ROYAL NAVY

The Mary Rose from the Anthony Roll is depicted in the second plate section.

The Royal Navy made possible Britain's emergence as the world's foremost commercial and imperial power, yet until the beginning of the sixteenth century neither the English nor the Scottish governments owned particularly impressive navies. This began to change with the investment made by Henry VIII in building a great fleet. No document better illustrates the results of that decision than the Anthony Roll.

It is a visual depiction of the fifty-eight ships in Henry VIII's navy, accompanied by an inventory of each vessel's munitions. The roll takes its name from its compiler, Anthony Anthony, an official of the ordnance, who presented his work to the king in 1546. The fleet is depicted on three vellum rolls, each about five and a half yards long. Both the descriptions and the artwork appear to be in Anthony's hand. The result doubtless pleased Henry, who generally delighted in viewing manifestations of his own power. After the king's death, Anthony stayed at his post, serving successively Edward VI, Mary I and Elizabeth. His Dutch father had come to England to supply beer to Henry's army and, when not attending to his formal duties, Anthony found time to part-own the appropriately named Ship brewhouse by the docks of East Smithfield just beyond the Tower of London. He died in 1563.

Although the birth of the Royal Navy is traditionally ascribed to Alfred the Great, and ships sailed in successive monarchs' service in the centuries thereafter, Henry VIII is usually considered the founder of the modern navy. Not only did he order mighty warships to be constructed, he also created a naval administrative bureaucracy as well as the capacity needed to maintain and develop the 'senior service' thereafter.

It is thanks to the Anthony Roll that a contemporary depiction of what Henry's fleet looked like has survived. It starts with the grandest of them all, the *Henry*

THE GROWTH AND DECLINE OF THE ROYAL NAVY

1547 At his death, Henry VIII's navy comprises fifty-eight vessels.

1707 The 227 ships of the Royal Navy are supplemented by the three ships of the Royal Scots Navy when the two fleets are merged.

1793 At the outset of renewed war with France, the Royal Navy comprises about 500 ships.

1805 In the year of Nelson's great victory at Trafalgar, the Royal Navy has grown to about 950 ships.

1840 The first screw-propeller-powered steamship, HMS *Rattler*, is launched.

1849 The first steam-powered battleship, HMS *Agamemnon*, is ordered.

1860 The launch of HMS *Warrior*, the first all iron-hulled and armoured warship, heralds the coming of the 'ironclads' and the decline of wooden ships.

1901 The first Royal Navy submarine, HMS *Holland 1*, is launched.

1905 With ten big guns and a speed of 21 knots, HMS *Dreadnought* is both the world's best-armed and fastest battleship. She makes previous designs effectively obsolete.

1914 The Royal Navy enters the First World War as by far the globe's most powerful fleet, led by 18 dreadnoughts, 29 non-dreadnought battleships, 20 town-class cruisers, 15 scout cruisers, 200 destroyers and 150 cruisers. Almost 35,000 sailors are killed during the conflict.

1918 The first aircraft carrier, HMS *Argus*, comes into commission.

1922 The age of Royal Navy global dominance ends with the Washington Treaty, which establishes equality between the Royal Navy and the US Fleet in battleships, battlecruisers and aircraft carriers.

1939 The Royal Navy enters the Second World War with 15 battleships and battlecruisers, 7 aircraft carriers, 66 cruisers, 184 destroyers, 60 submarines and 45 escort and patrol vessels.

1945 By the end of the Second World War, there are 885 ships in Royal Naval service. During the war 278 ships have been sunk and over 50,000 sailors killed.

1960 There are 202 ships in the fleet.

1963 Britain's first nuclear-powered submarine, HMS *Dreadnought*, comes into commission.

1980 There are 162 ships in the fleet.

1982 Falklands War. Six ships are sunk and ten more damaged.

2000 There are 98 ships in the fleet.

2010 There are 88 ships in the fleet.

Grace à Dieu. Launched in 1514 and alternatively known as the *Great Harry*, she was 165 feet (50 metres) long and carried 43 cannons besides 141 smaller guns. Manned by up to 1,000 crew, she was, of her type, without comparison anywhere in Europe. Her end, nonetheless, was unheroic. During Mary's reign she burned out while in dry dock, due, it was stated to 'neckclygens and lake of over-syth'.

The fact that Henry's fleet included fourteen oar-powered galleasses (larger and taller than regular galleys) and row-barges is among the Roll's many surprises. Such craft were customary in the Baltic and the Mediterranean but had long since ceased to be native to the seas around the British Isles. Yet it is Antony's illustration of the *Mary Rose* – the only surviving contemporary depiction – that attracts the most attention. He may well have painted her just as she was about to go down. The finished rolls were presented to Henry some months after he had watched, horrified, from the shore, as his beloved warship keeled over and sank while about to engage the French fleet on 19 July 1545. Initially it was hoped she might be raised from the Solent, which may still have been the case when Henry took possession of the roll. In reality, efforts to salvage her proved fruitless. It took until 1982 for the remains of her hull and starboard side to be lifted from the Solent's protecting silt and put on display in Portsmouth, the haven she was trying to defend. The archaeological evidence suggests that Anthony's depiction was inaccurate in the siting of the gunports and contained some artistic licence, but was certainly based on her actual design rather than merely being symbolic.

In 1680, Charles II made a present of the first and third of the Anthony Rolls to Samuel Pepys, who had been temporarily forced to resign his secretaryship of the Admiralty. Cut up and pasted into two volumes, they are now in the safe keeping of the great diarist's alma mater, Magdalene College, Cambridge. The second roll remained intact and is in the British Library. It had particularly fascinated the future 'Sailor King', William IV (1765–1837), who used to bore guests by indulging in lengthy readings from its ships' inventories. He gifted it to his illegitimate daughter Mary, who married Charles Fox, a successor of Anthony as surveyor of the ordnance.

1549
THE BOOK OF COMMON PRAYER

THE LITURGY OF THE CHURCH OF ENGLAND

The Book of Common Prayer established the liturgy of the Church of England, replacing the traditional Catholic service, which had been conducted in Latin, with a simpler, uniform service said in English. Over the succeeding centuries, its evocative language accompanied generations of men and women through the most important and poignant ceremonies of their lives, from baptism, through marriage and on, ultimately, to the grave.

OPPOSITE: Title page of the first edition of the Book of Common Prayer.

Without the Book of Common Prayer there would be no 'dearly beloved'; a bride and groom would not be joined together 'in holy Matrimony which is an honourable estate' and one that 'is not by any to be enterprised, nor taken in hand, unadvisedly, lightly, or wantonly'. At the graveside, there would be no 'In the midst of life we are in death' nor 'Earth to earth, ashes to ashes, dust to dust'.

Before the break with Rome, parishes had used the Latin rite, which was universally applied across Europe, albeit in a language that only the well-educated could understand. Nor was Latin the only bar to comprehension. The rite was assembled in a confused manner and was contained not in a single book but spread across several. Throughout Britain, there was no agreement over which of the different formats to favour, although the 'uses' of Sarum (Salisbury) had become the most popular.

Such variation ended abruptly in 1549 when the Act of Uniformity imposed the Book of Common Prayer as the sole liturgy to be used in every parish of the Established Church in England, Wales and Ireland. It is of significant constitutional importance that Parliament took it upon itself to legislate in this manner. From the break with Rome until that moment, approving the doctrine and liturgy of the Church of England had been a royal prerogative. Thereafter, it was a parliamentary one.

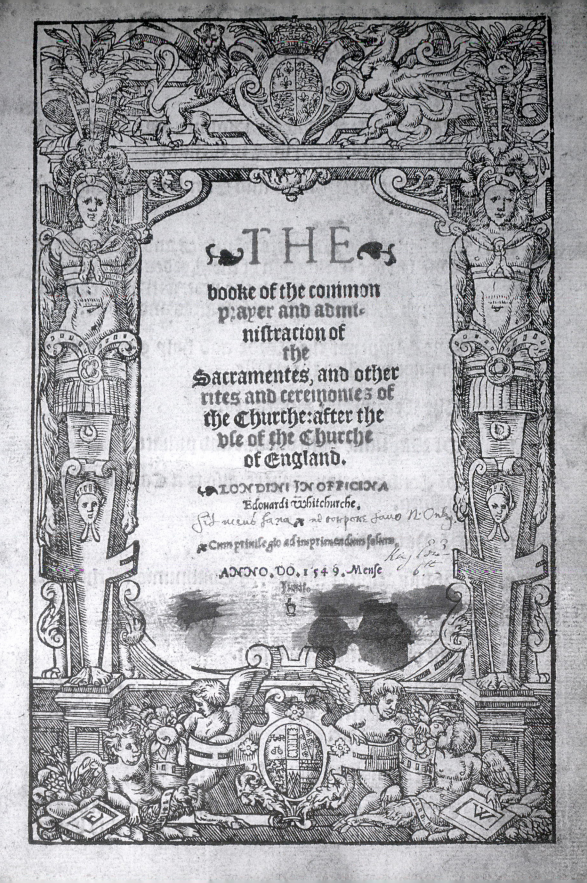

THE

booke of the common
prayer and admi-
nistration of
the
Sacramentes, and other
rites and ceremonies of
the Churche: after the
vse of the Churche
of England.

LONDINI IN OFFICINA
Edouardi Whitchurche,

Cum priuilegio ad imprimendum solum.

ANNO. DO. 1549. Mense
Iunio.

The principal author of the Book of Common Prayer was Thomas Cranmer (1489–1556), the first Protestant – and married man – to be archbishop of Canterbury. A Cambridge don who was attracted to Martin Luther's ideas, Cranmer appeared destined for a career of minor scholarship in the Fens until Henry VIII got to hear of his supportive suggestions for effecting divorce from Catherine of Aragon. Suddenly, Cranmer found himself conducting diplomatic business and, in 1533, was appointed to the see of Canterbury. Yet Henry was no Protestant, nor was he greatly excited by the prospect of his Church's liturgy being performed in the vernacular tongue. As a result, Cranmer had proceeded no further than an English-language processional litany when Henry died.

Thereafter, Cranmer got his chance. Surrounding the boy-king Edward VI were Protestant-leaning politicians who were determined to drive forward a liturgy in English. It was essentially a happy accident that Cranmer, to whom the task was entrusted, happened to possess an outstanding literary sensibility for the resonance of words. Eschewing contemporary humanist learning's sometimes mannered predilection for Greek and Latin vocabulary, Cranmer – like Tyndale – preferred words of English derivation. Indeed, he consciously used a slightly old-fashioned idiom and, in doing so, helped preserve this linguistic style for future generations. Besides Tyndale and Shakespeare, Cranmer must be rated among the most important shapers of the rhythm of English expression.

The first version of the Book of Common Prayer was introduced in 1547. The Church of England's task, as the state Church, was to hold a compromise position to which those of the old Catholic and new reformed faiths could equally adhere. Two areas of particular debate concerned transubstantiation and purgatory. Reformers disputed Rome's insistence that the sacramental wafer and wine truly became Christ's body and blood, nor could they find any scriptural justification for purgatory. They adjudged the latter to be a convenient invention, designed to maximize devotions and donations to the Church in return for speeding the path of the dead from purgatory to heaven. In both these matters, the wording of the 1547 version left sufficient scope to appease those who clung to Catholic interpretations.

Whatever their intention, such concessions failed to cool the anger of tradi-tionalists outraged by Cranmer's liturgical innovations. An anti-Prayer Book rebellion broke out in the South-West. Exeter was subjected to a thirty-five-day siege and several thousand people died before order was restored. There were also revolts in Oxfordshire, Buckinghamshire and – heightened by social and economic distress – in East Anglia. With the dissent suppressed, by 1552 the reformers felt sufficiently secure to bring out a revised version of the Prayer Book. This edition, also mostly by Cranmer, was far more overtly Protestant in tone. Even mention of the word 'Mass' had been replaced by 'Holy Communion' (the 1547 version had produced the wordy catch-all, 'Supper of the Lord and the Holy Communion, commonly called the Mass'). Indeed, one of Cranmer's great innovations was to make the laity's access to communion a regular feature of their worship. Previously they might have been called to take it as little as once a year.

Within months of this new version's introduction, Edward VI died of pneumonia and was followed on the throne by his devoutly Catholic half-sister, Mary. She immediately restored the Church to Rome, abolished the Book of Common Prayer and reintroduced the Latin rite. Accused of treason and heresy, Cranmer was burned at the stake.

The turning back of the theological tide lasted only as long as Mary survived. In 1558, the Protestant Elizabeth I succeeded her and the following year a new Act of Uniformity brought back a slightly modified version of the 1552 Book of Common Prayer. This remained in use after the royal house of Tudor gave way to the Stuarts. Indeed, it was Charles I's overzealous attempts to force the Prayer Book upon his Presbyterian-minded Scottish subjects in 1637 that prompted the signing of the Covenant, the defeat of the king's forces and a succession of events that resulted in the English Civil War. Gaining the upper hand in that conflict, English Puritans and their Scottish Presbyterian allies secured the Prayer Book's abolition in 1645.

Their victory, too, was short-lived. Along with the monarchy, it was duly reinstated in an updated version (still substantially in Cranmer's language) authorized in 1662. Despite the nineteenth-century battles between High and Low Church Anglicans over the use of ritual, this 1662 version continued to dictate the Established Church's liturgy into the twentieth century. An effort to produce a new version was voted down in the House of Commons in 1928 and during the century its uniform application varied across Anglican parishes. Finally, in 1980, a new version was approved. This, the not very self-confidently entitled *Alternative Service Book*, aimed at being more accessible for modern tastes. To those who preferred a less prosaic turn of phrase, it succeeded only in highlighting the sonorous superiority and commanding authority of Cranmer's original.

1555
THE ROYAL CHARTER OF THE MUSCOVY COMPANY

THE FIRST JOINT-STOCK COMPANY, FUNDING EXPLORATION AND THE EXPANSION OF TRADE

In 1555, a money-making venture was incorporated by royal charter with the title, 'The Merchants Adventurers of England for the discovery of Lands, Territories, Isles, Dominions and Seigniories Unknown'. It heralded a financial revolution. As the country's first major joint-stock company, it pointed the way to the stock market capitalism that shaped Britain's economic development in the nineteenth and twentieth centuries.

Its birth demonstrated that necessity can be the parent of invention. The textiles industries of the Low Countries had long been the most lucrative focus for English merchants. In the sixteenth century this trade faltered, forcing a search for alternative markets. The news that Portuguese ships were returning from the East Indies laden with highly valuable spices spurred a scramble for eastern riches. Unfortunately, without friendly ports along the route, English ships could scarcely hope to compete against Portugal's strategic advantages. So, in 1553, 240 London merchants pooled their investments to send an expedition with an extraordinarily daring goal: to reach China – then known as Cathay – by discovering a northern passage around the Arctic coasts of Scandinavia and Russia.

It was a trip into the unknown that failed utterly in its stated objectives. Two of the three ships were lost when their crews froze to death. However, one ship, the *Edward Bonaventure*, captained by Richard Chancellor, made it to the mouth of the Dvina and dropped anchor at Archangel. From there, Chancellor was invited to Moscow and was presented to the royal court. He made a favourable impression on Tsar Ivan the Terrible, who promised to open his northern domains to English traders.

Thus a scheme that intended to tap the wealth of the Far East was diverted into doing business with Russia. The royal charter of 1555 entitled the 'Merchant

From the royal charter of the Muscovy Company, 1555

That they by the Name of Merchants Adventurers of England for the discovery of Lands Territories Isles Dominions and Seigniories unknown and not before their late Adventure or Enterprise by Seas or Navigation commonly frequented as aforesaid shall be from henceforth one body and perpetual Fellowship and commonality of themselves both in Deed and in Name and them by the Names of Merchants Adventurers for the discovery of Lands Territories Isles and Seigniories unknown and not by the Seas and Navigations before their said late Adventure or Enterprise by Seas & Navigation commonly frequented. We do encorporate Name and Declare by these presents, And that the same Fellowship and commonalty from henceforth shall be and may have one Governour of the said Fellowship and Commonalty of Merchants Adventurers. And in consideration that the before named Sebastian Cabotto hath been the chiefest Setter forth of this Journey or Voyage therefore we make ordain and constitute him the said Sebastian to be the first and present Governour of the same Fellowship & Commonalty by these presents . . . Know ye therefore that We of our further Royal favour and munificence of our mere motion certain knowledge and especial Grace for as our Heirs and Successors have given and granted and by these presents do Give and Grant unto the same Governour Counsels Assistants Fellowship and Commonalty above named and to their Successors as much as in us is that all the Maynelands Isles Ports Havens Creeks and Rivers of the said Mighty Emperour of all Russia and Great Duke of Musky & c. And all singular other Lands Dominions Territories Isles Ports Havens Creeks Rivers arms of the Sea of all and every other Emperour King Prince Rulers or Governour whatsoever he or they be before the said late Adventure or Enterprise not knowen or by our foresaid Merchants and Subjects by the Seas not commonly frequented nor any part or parcel thereof and lying Northwards North Eastwards or North westwards as is aforesaid by Sea shall not be visited frequented nor haunted by any our Subjects other than of the said Company and Fellowship and their Successors without express License agreement and Consent of the Governour Consulls and assistants of the said Fellowship and Commonalty first above named.

Adventurers' to a trading monopoly with Russia and, as a result, they became commonly known as the Muscovy Company (and later, the Russia Company). The tsar also accorded the company privileges and it was soon exporting English cloth to Russia, while importing Russian furs, timber (for taller sailing masts), hemp, tar, wax and tallow to England.

In the sixteenth and seventeenth centuries, before the benefits of a competitive free market became accepted doctrine, state monopolies were granted to some expensive commercial enterprises as a means of protecting their initial investment. The monopoly that the English Crown gave to the Muscovy Company for Russian trade lasted until 1587 and was similar in intent to the monopolies granted to the Levant Company in 1581 to trade with the eastern Mediterranean (exporting cloth and bringing back raw silk and Turkish carpets), and to the Hudson Bay Company, which, in 1670, received a monopoly to trade in Canadian furs. The most significant monopoly was granted in 1600, to the East India Company.

The East India Company became the leading example of a joint-stock company, but it was the Muscovy Company that first demonstrated the effectiveness of this form of capitalist organization, effectively starting the tradition of share dealing in the City of London. Previously, investors were sought to sponsor individual ventures, like trade expeditions, receiving their cut of any profit upon the venture's completion. In this way, expeditions were financed one at a time. In contrast, those investing in a joint-stock company were buying share certificates, not in a one-off enterprise, but in an ongoing business concern that might use the money for any number of ventures, paying its shareholders a dividend from annual profits. This was the principle behind what became public limited companies with shares tradable on the stock exchange.

Share issues spread the risk, attracting the large sums of capital necessary for hazardous searches for new markets and subsequent business diversification. The Muscovy Company's investors included some of England's foremost names, including many of the leading politicians, as well as the financier and founder of the Royal Exchange, Thomas Gresham. The most striking name, however, is that of the investor who was appointed the company's governor – Sebastian Cabot.

It was Cabot's father, the Genoa-born John Cabot, who, in sailing out from Bristol in 1497 to the rich fishing shoals off Newfoundland, is often credited with starting England's interest in discovering new worlds. Yet it took more than half a century before the Muscovy Company, with his son at the helm, had the financial backing to mount a sustained campaign of exploration. Between the 1560s and the 1580s, the company sent its agents overland across Russia to meet the shah of Persia, who opened up his realm for the first time to direct trade with England. The company also renewed efforts to sail to China via the icy Siberian waters, battling the ice and fog to get as far as the Straits of Waigatz in 1556. It was the failure of a venture in 1580 to reach beyond the Kara Sea that suggested ultimate success was still some way off. Meanwhile, others were spurred to look for a route to the Pacific from the opposite direction, with Martin Frobisher and John Davis searching for the North-West Passage between North America and the Arctic.

These impulses to explore and to expand trade manifested themselves in the seventeenth century with the first settlements of what became the British Empire – paid for by joint-stock companies.

The original manuscript of the Muscovy Company's royal charter was destroyed by the Great Fire of London in 1666 but a transcript of it was made, which survives in the London Metropolitan Archives.

1563

FOXE'S *BOOK OF MARTYRS*

CREATING A NARRATIVE OF ENGLISH PROTESTANT IDENTITY UNDER THREAT FROM CATHOLICISM

No history book did more to establish Queen Mary I's posthumous reputation as 'Bloody Mary', to commemorate the martyrs she burned at the stake, or to entwine national identity with Protestantism, than John Foxe's *Acts and Monuments*, popularly known as 'Foxe's *Book of Martyrs*'.

It made its author Britain's first literary celebrity. The phenomenal sale of his work, which went into four extensively revised editions in his own lifetime and many more thereafter, was surprising for a book whose second edition ran to over 2,300 pages. Yet such was this edition's success that its production was temporarily imperilled because its publisher, John Day, ran out of paper.

Foxe's *Book of Martyrs* was the result of years of diligent – if one-sided – research by Foxe and his team of assistants. Its claims to historic authenticity were reinforced by its extensive recourse to archival material, in particular diocesan registers and the historic manuscripts collected by Matthew Parker, Queen Elizabeth I's first archbishop of Canterbury, many of which it reproduced. What helped to make it a popular sensation was its detailed and lurid woodcut illustrations of the torture and death meted out to Catholicism's opponents.

Most of all, the book's success can be attributed to a simple reality: whilst it was a work of propaganda, presenting only one side of the story, it related events that were at least true in outline, if not always in detail. Upon succeeding her Protestant brother Edward VI in 1553, Mary Tudor wasted little time in restoring the English Church to Rome and stamping out heresy with such vehemence that future generations – with Foxe's help – associated Catholic rule with unrestrained cruelty and despotism.

Edward VI had imprisoned senior prelates who refused to renounce their Catholic doctrine, but they were not put to death. In this respect, Mary's brief rule represented a return to previous measures against heretics, made worse by the swelling number of her subjects who fell into that category. In the space of three years, she committed 200 men and 60 women to the flames on account of their faith. Given her marriage to the deeply unpopular Philip II of Spain, the precariousness of her situation emboldened her brutality. Even on 17 November 1558, the day she died, she raised herself from a deathbed of considerable pain to confirm the death warrants of two more Protestants.

Some of those burned at the stake during her reign were the leaders of Protestant reform: John Hooper, bishop of Gloucester; Nicholas Ridley, bishop of London; Hugh Latimer, bishop of Worcester; and Thomas Cranmer, the former archbishop of Canterbury. However, most of her victims came from further down the social scale. Some, like the illiterate fisherman Rawlings White and the poor, blind Joan

This woodcut illustration from Foxe's Book of Martyrs shows a group of Protestants being burnt at Smithfield in 1546. Among them was Anne Askew, who was sentenced to death for refusing to name fellow believers. She had been so severely tortured on the rack that she had to be carried to the stake in a chair.

The order and manner of the burning of *Anne Askew*, *Iohn Lacels, Iohn Adams, Nicolas Belenian*, with certaine of the Counsell sitting in Smithfield.

Waist, were reduced to ashes merely for asking others to read the New Testament to them. Supplementing his archival research with potentially less accurate oral evidence, Foxe told all their stories.

Foxe himself had spent Mary's reign in exile. Born around 1516, he had formed his Protestant thinking while a student at Oxford and realized he was in danger when Mary restored the English Church to Rome. It was in 1559, while he was in Basel, Switzerland, that his first work on Protestant martyrs was published. Later that year he returned to England, secure in the knowledge that Elizabeth I's accession made it safe to do so. The first edition of *Acts and Monuments*, in a large folio format of 1,800 pages, was published in 1563. The second edition in 1570 came in two volumes, contained far more illustrations and greatly increased the first edition's scope with extensive coverage of the pre-Reformation Church and the treatment of heretics across Europe.

Despite an outlook made ever more austere by hard work, Foxe was known for his personal acts of charity towards the poor. No advocate of religious toleration, he supported imprisonment and punishment for, most notably, the Anabaptist sect; but because he believed everyone to be capable of personal redemption, he resolutely opposed the death sentence for those whose faiths he so actively denounced.

Revised editions of his *Book of Martyrs* continued to appear after his death in 1587, with contemporary detail added to bring Catholic cruelty up to date. In heightening the atmosphere of fear towards papist and High Church practices, its influence was perhaps greatest during the period of the English Civil War. Thereafter, heavily edited editions became increasingly sensationalist and ghoulish in their focus on the violence meted out to Protestant martyrs. In doing so, they hoped to keep sectarian animosities alive while in fact unintentionally undermining Foxe's reputation as a scholar.

It is arguable that the *Book of Martyrs* may have shaped popular and Low Church suspicion of Catholicism right up to the twentieth century.

THE THIRTY-NINE ARTICLES

THE DOCTRINE OF THE STATE CHURCH

Thomas Cranmer, archbishop of Canterbury, 1533–55.

The Thirty-Nine Articles were not just the defining statement on what constituted the doctrine of the Church of England; they became part of the test of who could play an active part in public life. Between 1672 and 1828, anyone wishing to hold civil office in England, Wales or Ireland had to adhere to them. In most cases, a refusal to subscribe excluded from office not just Catholics but also Nonconformists – those Protestants who were not Anglicans.

Like the Book of Common Prayer, the Articles were largely the work of Thomas Cranmer, who served both Henry VIII and Edward VI as archbishop of Canterbury. Under Henry VIII, the Church of England, although separated from Rome, remained Catholic in doctrine. This was made clear by the Six Articles of 1539. It was the succession of Edward VI that allowed Protestant sympathizers to move more firmly into positions where they could change matters. Cranmer was engaged to draw up Forty-Two Articles that would reposition the Church accordingly.

In 1553, Edward died before the new statement could be enforced. The succession of his Catholic half-sister, Mary, brought the reforms to an abrupt halt. The queen restored Church doctrine to where it had been before her father's break with Rome, and Cranmer, along with many of the other leading reforming theologians, was burned at the stake in Mary's campaign against 'heresy'.

With the accession of Elizabeth I, a Protestant again sat on the throne. The 1559 Act of Supremacy restored the monarch to the position of head of the Church of England, with the title 'supreme governor', but the doctrinal nature of her state Church remained to be determined. For political as well as personal reasons, Elizabeth wanted a compromise solution. She thought it important

THE REIGN OF ELIZABETH I

1558 Elizabeth succeeds her half-sister, Mary I.

1560 The Treaty of Edinburgh is signed between Scotland, England and France.

1568 Elizabeth puts her Catholic cousin, Mary, Queen of Scots, under house arrest.

1569 The Rising in the North by Catholics attempts to supplant Elizabeth with Mary.

1577–80 Francis Drake becomes the first Englishman to circumnavigate the globe.

1584 Sir Walter Raleigh establishes the English colony of Virginia in North America.

1586 The Babington plot to supplant Elizabeth with Mary is uncovered.

1587 Mary, Queen of Scots, is executed; Drake destroys a Spanish fleet at Cadiz.

1588 The Spanish Armada is defeated.

1597 A storm scatters the second Spanish Armada attempt.

1597–1601 Rebellion occurs in Ireland.

1601 The Earl of Essex stages an abortive rebellion.

1603 Elizabeth I dies and is succeeded by Mary, Queen of Scots' son, James VI of Scotland.

that the Church's practices should be generally familiar to covert Catholics while making sufficient acknowledgement of Protestant teaching to avoid creating an irretrievable rupture with Puritan adherents of the Geneva theologian John Calvin.

Producing this delicate balancing act was entrusted to Elizabeth's archbishop of Canterbury, Matthew Parker. A great scholar and archivist of historic documents, Parker nonetheless wanted to remain largely faithful to Thomas Cranmer's proposed Forty-Two Articles of 1553. In this he was successful, for the statement of doctrine approved by the Church Convocation in 1563 was little more than a minor revision of Cranmer's work.

The Convocation approved the Thirty-Nine Articles, thus upholding the central Protestant contention of justification by faith rather than merely through good works. Purgatory, the adoration of saints and the use of pardons were dismissed as Rome's inventions. No less contentiously, Article 17 affirmed support for the Calvinist belief in predestination – the premiss that God had secretly predetermined who would receive salvation and who damnation.

The greatest difference between the Thirty-Nine Articles adopted by Elizabeth I and Cranmer's original Forty-Two Articles for Edward VI concerned transubstantiation. The Catholic belief was reaffirmed that the sacrament of Eucharist converted bread and wine into Christ's body and blood. Nonetheless, Elizabeth still remained particularly apprehensive about needlessly offending her Catholic subjects. This fear motivated her rejection of Article 29, thereby reducing the total number of articles to thirty-eight.

Such appeasement proved short-lived, however, because in 1570 Pope Pius V excommunicated Elizabeth and called on English Catholics to rise up and overthrow her. The pope's pronouncement, an incitement to treason in the cause of Roman Catholic orthodoxy, was to have disastrous consequences for England's Catholics. The backlash was not long delayed. In 1571, Article 29 was reinserted, denying in the Eucharist the substance of the body and blood of

Article XXXVII: Of the Civil Magistrates

The Queen's Majesty hath the chief power in this realm of England and other her dominions, unto whom the chief government of all estates of this realm, whether they be ecclesiastical or civil, in all causes doth appertain, and is not nor ought to be subject to any foreign jurisdiction.

Where we attribute to the Queen's Majesty the chief government, by which titles we understand the minds of some slanderous folks to be offended, we give not to our princes the ministering either of God's word or of sacraments, the which thing the Injunctions also lately set forth by Elizabeth our Queen doth most plainly testify: but only that prerogative which we see to have been given always to all godly princes in Holy Scriptures by God himself, that is, that they should rule all estates and degrees committed to their charge by God, whether they be temporal, and restrain with the civil sword the stubborn and evil-doers.

The Bishop of Rome hath no jurisdiction in this realm of England.

The laws of the realm may punish Christian men with death for heinous and grievous offences.

It is lawful for Christian men at the commandment of the Magistrate to wear weapons and serve in the wars.

Christ to 'the wicked and such as be void of lively faith'. All Thirty-Nine Articles were given statutory authority by Parliament in 1571, making adherence from the clergy a legal requirement.

In Scotland, Protestant doctrine was enforced by a different route, being imposed upon a sovereign who remained Catholic. From 1557, Protestant nobles were in armed conflict with their nation's French regent, Mary of Guise (governing on behalf of the young Mary, Queen of Scots, who remained in France). Upon the regent's death in 1560, the Scottish Parliament was convened. It declared void Rome's jurisdiction over Scotland and banned the Catholic Mass. In its place, it drew up an equivalent version of the Thirty-Nine Articles, known as the Confession of Faith. Laying out the new state theology, it was heavily influenced by John Knox, an adherent of John Calvin. Thus the doctrine of the Church of Scotland became Presbyterian rather than Episcopalian.

1566–7
THE CASKET LETTERS

'PROOF' OF MARY, QUEEN OF SCOTS' COMPLICITY
IN MURDERING HER HUSBAND

Few documents in British history have caused more speculation than a cache of letters implicating Mary, Queen of Scots, in the murder of her husband. Successive generations have debated their authenticity. What has never been contested, however, is their role in sealing the fate of Scotland's most tragic monarch.

Mary Stuart was just six days old when she inherited the Scottish throne from her father, James V, in 1542. While her French mother acted as regent on her behalf, she was sent at the age of six to the French court in preparation for her marriage to the Dauphin, Francis. They wed in 1558 when Mary was fifteen and Francis fourteen. A year later, they ascended to the throne, the embodiment of the Franco-Scottish 'auld alliance', but the queen of Scots was not to remain the queen of France for long.

Francis died in 1560. Widowed, Mary returned to Scotland the following year to rule the country in her own right, only to discover that it had been politically transformed during her absence. Reformation theology had taken root and Parliament had renounced Scotland's adherence to Rome, abolished the Mass and drawn up an avowedly Protestant 'Confession of Faith'. Young, Catholic, and a woman – making her vulnerable on three counts – Mary thus found herself, precariously, head of state in a country being shaped by hard, unyielding Protestant men of whom the most powerful was her own half-brother, the earl of Moray.

The one concession made to her was that she was permitted Mass in her own chapel at the palace of Holyroodhouse in Edinburgh. This became simultaneously a focal point of irritation to Calvinist hardliners like John Knox as well as a magnet of hope for Scotland's Catholic adherents.

In 1565 she made a disastrous error, marrying her English cousin, Henry, Lord Darnley, a dissolute teenager of ill manners and opportunistic religious views. Too late, she realized her mistake. In March 1566, a mixture of personal jealousy and political calculation drove Darnley to join a faction that broke into his wife's privy chamber at Holyroodhouse and stabbed to death her unpopular Italian secretary, David Rizzio. Three months later, Mary gave birth to a son and heir, James.

Mary now had an heir, but unfortunately still a husband. Darnley was more than an embarrassment; seemingly deranged, he presented a clear danger. In February 1567, the house outside Edinburgh in which he was recovering (probably from syphilis) was mysteriously blown up with gunpowder. Having escaped from a window, Darnley was strangled in the grounds. Thus began a complicated whodunnit, which, given the number of his enemies, implicated many of Scotland's leading nobles and, some supposed, even Mary herself.

Nonetheless, from the first, the earl of Bothwell was the chief suspect. After the queen formally refused his hand, in April 1567 he abducted her, allegedly raped her and then, the following month, arranged for a marriage service to be conducted over them both. Scottish opinion quickly divided, between those appalled at Bothwell's apparent enslavement of the queen to his will, and those who deduced Mary was complicit and had planned with him both her 'abduction' and the murder of Darnley.

The scandal was too great for the Scottish nobility to bear. They raised forces to confront Bothwell and Mary and, after a brief confrontation at Carberry Hill, Mary was imprisoned in an island fortress on Loch Leven. Still only twenty-four years old, although thoroughly degraded by now, she was forced to abdicate in favour of her infant son, with his Protestant uncle, the earl of Moray, acting as regent.

In May 1568, Mary escaped confinement and raised an army, only to be defeated by Moray's forces. She duly fled to England. Although Queen Elizabeth was her cousin (Mary's great-grandfather was Henry VII), the closeness of their relationship contained as much threat as security. Catholics who had never accepted the validity of Henry VIII's divorce considered Elizabeth illegitimate. To them, Mary was therefore the rightful queen of England. Elizabeth had to decide how her own interests would be best served: by pressurizing the Scots to take back Mary, by keeping her indefinitely as an unwanted guest in England, or by finding a means of hastening her end.

Encouraging Scotland's government to accept Mary as their sovereign once more was seriously considered. To this end, an Anglo-Scots conference was convened at York in 1568, with the intention to discover whether Moray and Mary might

OVERLEAF: *A page from the longest of the 'casket letters', in a contemporary copy translated into English from the original French.*

103

for a surety gr mistanstite bee eschent that you know, & for gif this
But iij the end, after I gaue spoke fiue or thre good word to him
gi woue pory meam zorind. I haue not seen him this nigst for
ending yo thearlet, but I ray fynd no reasspee foryt. It is reddy
thereinto, und I feare last it should bring you yll happy, or tht
it should be knowey iff you word hurte. Send me word wetiger you
will haue it, und more monny, und wiay I shall return, And how
farre I may speak. now as farewill I greain I may do muts to you
this you weitiger I shall not be suspected. As for the rest, gr
me wood weiy gr geathe ofe Lodintoy, und of hat bayts
of yr brother gr suiyse nothiy, but of the Erle of Arguile gr els.
I am afraide of him to heare him talk, at the leaste gr assurity, him
self that gr hate no yll opiniey of hiij. gr speak iy nothing of thes
abroade, neiger god nor yll, but aboydite speaking of hiy. his
fates beinge his reinbeee. I haue not seen hiy. All the Hamiltons be
here, wgo acompany me pory honestly. All the freind of the els doo
stoy allwaie weiy I goe to deisitt hiy. Gr hate sent to me & prayeth me
to see hiy to morowe at his ryseing & he will ryse to morow iij ye
morning early. To be short, this bearer shall declare unto
you the rest And if I shall learne any thing, I will make anew
niyst & memoriall thereof. Gr shall tell you the tause of my stay.
Burne this let. for it is to dangerous, neyther is there any thing
well said iij it, for I think happy nothing and borry greife is you
be at Edinborough

Now if to pleasiry you my deere lyfe, I spare neiger hono consticiene
nor hazard, nor greatnes, tak it iy good hote, und not according to thes
interpretacy of yo false brother iy lawe, to wgo I pray you giue no credit
agaynst the most faytefull louer that euer you had or shall haue.
See not also ther weyse fayind feares you ouyst put more to regard the
the few travaile wh I indure to deserue the plear, for obtyning of
wt agaynst my owne nature I doo bettray those & I could lett me. for
forgiue me, und giue you my only freind the good luck & prosperitie that yo
humble & faytefull louer doth wiss the unto you, wgo hopith shortly to be
my oter thing unto you for the reward of my paynes. I haue not mad one
worde, And it is late, altho ugh I should neuer be wery & weryng to you. yet
will I end, after the hissing of yo hind. Excuse my ill wryting und reat it
ouer twise, Excuse also
I looke for your onswe neues
und ofsiry, Lou nor ally

Transcription of the longest of the 'casket letters'

To conclude, for surety, he mistruthith her of that that you know, and for his lyfe. But in the end, after I had spoken two or three good words to him, he was very merry and glad.

I have not seen him this night for ending you braceet, but I can find no clasps for yt; it is ready thereunto, and yet I fear lest it should bring you yll hap, or that shuld be known if you where hurt. Send me word whether you will have it, and more monney, and how farr I may speak. Now so farr as I perceive I may doo much without you; guesse you withir I shall not be suspected. As for the rest, he is mad when he hears of Ledinton, and of you, and my brother. Of your brother he says nothing, but of the Earl of Argile he doth; I am afraid of him to heare him talk, at the last he assurit himself that he hath no yll opinion of him. He speaketh bothing of these abrode, nither good nor yll, but avoid it speaking of him. His father keepith his chambre; I have not seen him.

All the Hamiltons be here who accompany me very honestly. All the friends of the others doo come allwais when I go visit him. He hath sent to me and prayeth me to see him rise in the morning early. To be short, this bearer shall declare unto you the rest; and if I learne anything, I will make every night a memorial thereof. He shall tell you the cause of my stay, Burn this letter, for it is too dangerous, neither is there anything well said in it, for I think upon nothing but upon grief if you be at Edinburgh.

Now if it please you, my deere lyfe, I spare neither hounour, conscience, nor hazard, nor greatness, take it in good part, and not according to the interpretation of your false brother-in-law, to whome I pray you, give no credit against the most faythfull lover that ever you had or shall have.

See not also her whose fayned tears you ought not more to regard than the true travails which I endure to deserve her place, for obtayning of which, against my own nature, I doo betray those that could lett me. God forgive me, and give you, my only friend, the good luck and prosperitie that your humble and fathyfull lover doth wisshe unto you, who hopith shortly to be another thing unto you, for the reward of my paynes.

I have not made one word and it is very late, although I shuld nver be weary in wryting to you, yet will I end, after kissing of your hands. Excuse my eviil wryting, and read it over twise. Excuse also that I scribbled, for I had yesternight no paper when I took the paper of a memorial. Pray remember your friend, and write unto her often; love me allwais as I shall love you.

be reconciled. It quickly turned into a trial in all but name, with Mary's role in Darnley's murder the central issue. The critical evidence was provided by the 'casket letters', which Moray laid before the conference and which had supposedly been found in a silver casket seized from Bothwell's servant, George Dalgliesh. They consisted of eight letters, written in French, and twelve love sonnets from Mary to Bothwell, along with a couple of draft marriage contracts. They dated from the period of Darnley's assassination and appeared to implicate Mary as Bothwell's lover and accessory to murder.

Even at the time there were questions over whether the letters were genuine and the conference broke up without coming to a formal conclusion. Nevertheless, whatever their provenance, the letters cast sufficient doubt to remove any likelihood of England forcing Mary back upon a reluctant Scottish nobility. So Moray returned as regent of Scotland, assisted with English funds, while Mary began eighteen years of imprisonment in England, confined under a house arrest that, although for the most part better than formal incarceration (she had forty servants), was nonetheless irksome. Her chance of reclaiming the Scottish throne through diplomacy had gone.

Still alive, however, was the possibility of her gaining the English Crown. Unfortunately for her, the pro-Catholic Northern Rebellion of 1569, together with the pope's call for Elizabeth's assassination the following year, hardened the hearts of those believing that the Protestant throne would be safer with Mary dead. Fatally, in 1586 Mary encouraged a conspiracy to kill Elizabeth and put herself on the throne with the help of a Spanish invasion. She did not realize that this 'Babington Plot' was being watched (and encouraged) by Elizabeth's spymaster, Sir Francis Walsingham, who had intercepted the damning correspondence. Having been thoroughly incriminated, Mary could finally be convicted of treason.

Reluctantly, Elizabeth was persuaded to bring her cousin to trial. Found guilty, Mary was beheaded at Fotheringhay Castle in Northamptonshire on 8 February 1587, almost exactly twenty years after Darnley's mysterious demise. However, she bequeathed England something that Elizabeth did not – an heir. In 1603, the English throne passed to James VI of Scotland who duly became King James I. He had done little to save his mother while she lived for fear of hampering his chance of this succession. Nonetheless, once established in England, he had her reinterred so that Mary, Queen of Scots, finally lay alongside the rulers of England in Westminster Abbey.

Meanwhile, the casket letters that had done so much to hinder her restoration to her own realm conveniently vanished. What is known is that after the 1568–9 conference they were brought back to Scotland to be placed in the earl of Morton's possession until his execution in 1581, then passing into the hands of the earl of Gowrie until he, too, was executed in 1584. They disappeared thereafter. One plausible theory is that James had them destroyed.

However, translated copies were made of them in Scots, English, Latin and French, from which successive historians drew differing conclusions. Some deductions can now be said to be erroneous. The French translations were wrongly assumed to be the original manuscripts until 1754. The sonnets can be dismissed as inauthentic. At least some of the letters are plausibly in Mary's style but betray signs of having been edited and altered to suit the prosecution's case. In particular, the most important letter, dated January 1567, clearly implies that Mary was preparing to do away with her husband. Supposedly written to Bothwell, certain passages suggest that it was actually intended for someone else entirely.

For 400 years after they were first produced, historians have attempted either to portray the letters as proof of the scheming and wanton nature of Scotland's last Catholic monarch or as evidence of Mary's personal tragedy, helplessly caught up by events and the machinations of devious men. The consensus is now that they are largely the work of forgery and malicious manipulation. Whether the attempt to frame her instead proves her innocence perhaps remains a matter best summarized by a uniquely Scottish verdict – not proven.

1591
MY LADYE NEVELLS BOOKE

WILLIAM BYRD'S WORKS FOR KEYBOARD

When the composer William Byrd died in 1623, the tributes paid to him went far beyond speaking respectfully of the dead. He was described as the 'parent' of British music or, as the records of the Chapel Royal put it, 'a father of musicke'. In life, he had been treated with scarcely less reverence. Despite making no effort to conceal his Roman Catholic faith at a time when it was dangerous to profess it, he escaped serious punishment. Queen Elizabeth I was among those who protected him from her own laws.

In truth, Byrd was not the first British composer to gain a reputation in his own lifetime, nor was he the progenitor of the country's distinct musical traditions, but rather the first Englishman to master the new sounds of Renaissance music. In doing so he produced music that bore comparison with the great continental composers of the period, Palestrina and Victoria, and influenced the sounds of native music-making in the century that followed.

England had already produced a musical genius of the previous generation in Thomas Tallis (c.1505–85). Tallis concentrated on liturgical music, most famously his *Lamentations of Jeremiah* for five voices and the forty-voice motet, *Spem in alium*, one of the masterpieces of polyphony, in which separate melodic lines are concurrently sounded by two groups of twenty singers. Born around 1543, Byrd was Tallis's pupil before joining him as joint organist of the Chapel Royal. As with so many subsequent British composers, this appointment within the royal household brought with it not only prestige but state favour. In 1575, Tallis and Byrd went into business together, gaining from Queen Elizabeth a twenty-one-year monopoly to publish all printed music in the realm. In the process, they virtually created the country's music publishing trade.

Nonetheless, it was for a hand-annotated manuscript that Byrd's finest works for keyboard were collated. The anthology, *My Ladye Nevells Booke*, was produced in 1591, probably for Elizabeth, the wife of a Berkshire landowner, Sir Henry

A GOLDEN AGE OF MUSIC

1499 Oxford University awards music degrees.

1560 Thomas Tallis composes the *Lamentations of Jeremiah*.

1568 The first primer for the lute is published.

1570 Tallis composes his forty-part motet, *Spem in alium*.

1575 Tallis and William Byrd jointly publish a motet collection, *Cantiones Sacrae*, and Elizabeth I grants them both a twenty-one-year monopoly on all music printing in England.

1580 The first mention of the ballad 'Greensleeves' appears.

1588 Nicholas Yonge's publication of *Musica Transalpina* popularizes Italian madrigals in Britain.

1588 Byrd publishes *Psalms, Sonnets and Songs of Sadness and Pietie*.

1589 Byrd publishes *Songs of Sundrie Natures*.

1591 Byrd publishes his anthology *My Ladye Nevells Booke*.

1594 Elizabeth I sends a Thomas Dallam organ to the Ottoman sultan.

1597 The publication of John Dowland's *First Book of Songes or Ayres* and Thomas Morley's *A Plaine and Easie Introduction to Practicall Musicke*.

1598 The twenty-one-year monopoly to publish music passes to Thomas Morley.

1600 Thomas Morley's *First Book of Ayres* is published.

c.1610 *The Fitzwilliam Virginal Book* is published, a treasure-trove of keyboard music.

1611–12 *Parthenia* is published, with keyboard works by John Bull, William Byrd and Orlando Gibbons.

1612–13 Orlando Gibbons's *First Set of Madrigals and Motets of Five Parts* is published.

1623 Gibbons is appointed organist of Westminster Abbey.

1649 The Welsh-born Thomas Tomkins writes the Royalist lament *Sad Pavan for These Distracted Times*.

Nevill. She may have been one of Byrd's patrons. However, as only two of the compositions are specifically dedicated to her, it is possible that she was one of his pupils and the anthology is a collection of her favourite pieces. Byrd wrote extensively for the virginal, a smaller version of the harpsichord, which was a particularly popular instrument among female players. In all, *My Ladye Nevells Booke* contains forty-two works. These include dances – most of them pavans and galliards – and variations based on such contemporary folk-tunes as 'The Carman's Whistle' and 'Will Yow Walke the Woods soe Wylde'. The manuscript was produced by John Baldwin of St George's Chapel, Windsor. The corrections, however, are believed to be in Byrd's hand.

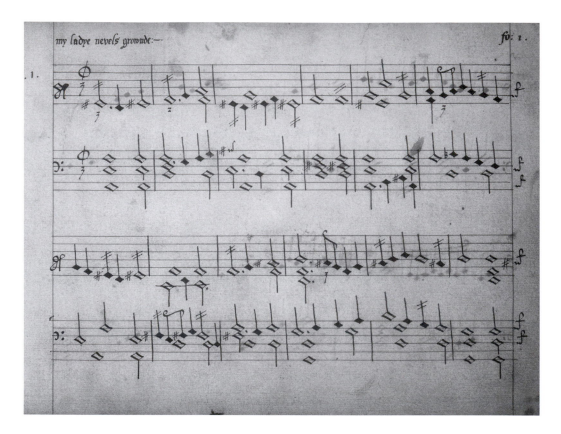

The music of 'My Ladye Nevell's Grownde', the opening piece of William Byrd's keyboard anthology My Ladye Nevells Booke.

Byrd's music stood out not only for its quality but for the versatility of the composer. Over the course of his life, he produced a huge corpus for virtually every major medium apart from the lute. He was as adept at writing popular songs as he was at producing sacred choral music and was an innovator of verse anthems as well as a master of contrapuntal composition. He described his own ability to match music for words: 'There is a certain hidden power in the thoughts underlying the words themselves, so that as one meditates upon the sacred words and constantly and seriously considers them, the right notes, in some inexplicable fashion, suggest themselves quite spontaneously.' He wrote Latin religious music for Catholics as well as English settings for the Prayer Book (despite his Roman beliefs), which proved highly influential, resonating throughout the Anglican liturgy long after his death. Perhaps, though, the most touching epitaph appears at the end of the fourth galliard in *My Ladye Nevells Booke*. There, John Baldwin, unable to contain his excitement appended a simple observation: *mr. w. birde. homo memorabilis.*

1600
THE ROYAL CHARTER OF THE EAST INDIA COMPANY

THE DEVELOPMENT OF BRITISH TRADE AND EMPIRE

The East India Company played the decisive role in establishing Britain's supremacy in India, generating wealth, commerce and industry back home. In doing so, it helped to prove the effectiveness of the joint-stock company as a motor of capitalist activity.

It was not preordained that Britain would be the European country that dominated India. For almost one hundred years after they bombarded Calicut in southern India in 1501, it was the Portuguese who led efforts to control trade, not only with the subcontinent but also with the spice islands of the East Indies (principally modern day-Indonesia and the Malaysian archipelago). By the end of the sixteenth century, however, the Dutch were financing highly lucrative voyages to the East Indies. In 1600, in the rush to grab a slice of this market before the Dutch controlled it all, a group of English merchants and investors founded the East India Company.

They started it with £30,000 raised in capital and a royal charter from Elizabeth I granting a fifteen-year monopoly (subsequently renewed and extended) on all English trading ventures to the East Indies. Given the Dutch competition, there was no time to waste and within months the first five ships were sailing from Torbay for Sumatra. In 1602, a trading base was established at Bantam on Java. Initially, the East India Company funded its voyages one at a time, unlike the rival Dutch East India Company – or Vereenigde Oost-indische Companie (VOC) – which was organized as a joint-stock company, a much more sensible vehicle for attracting long-term investment. By 1657, when Oliver Cromwell renewed the company's charter, it too had become a permanent joint-stock entity.

Copying the Dutch business model was not, of itself, enough to dislodge Holland's grip on the region. The maritime rivalry between the two powers intensified, three times breaking out into war between 1652 and 1674. It was not until the accession in 1688 of the Dutch *stadtholder*, William of Orange, to the British thrones that London conceded the ascendancy in the East Indies to the VOC, in return for which the East India Company became the dominant trading organization with India. This division of spoils proved highly advantageous for the British company. In 1700, India was producing about a quarter of world economic output at a time when Britain was responsible for only around 3 per cent of the total. During the eighteenth and nineteenth centuries, Indian textile exports in calicoes, raw cotton and silk proved much more valuable than the spice-orientated commerce with the East Indies.

The British had gained a foothold on the Indian subcontinent as early as 1613 at Surat and shortly thereafter Sir Thomas Roe established favourable diplomatic relations with India's Mughal emperor, Jahangir. Fortified trading posts were set up at Fort St George and Sutanuti, around which the cities of Madras and Calcutta would develop. The third of the East India Company's great entrepôts was Bombay (Mumbai), which the Portuguese ceded as part of Catherine of Braganza's wedding dowry to Charles II in 1661. During the eighteenth century, as Mughal rule fell apart and power fragmented across India, the East India Company increasingly enforced national security with its own private army, recruited from the Indian population as well as from Europeans. Besides threats from hostile native leaders, the company had to protect itself against the ambitions of India's other trade-settlers, in particular the French. The latter briefly seized Madras before seeing their colonial intentions dealt a shattering blow in the Seven Years War (1756–63).

The defeat of the French and the infighting between native rulers was ably exploited by the East India Company's man on the spot, Robert Clive. The victory of his 3,000 well-drilled soldiers against the Nawab of Bengal's force of 50,000 at Plassey in 1757 created an indelible impression. Following the Treaty of Allahabad in 1765, the Mughal emperor Shah Allam II ceded administrative and fiscal responsibility for Bengal to the East India Company. A private company had, in effect, become the government for 20 million Indians.

For its part, the British government had long supported the East India Company, viewing it as equal to taking the risks, yet whose profits could be creamed off by the Exchequer. Nonetheless, it drew the line at letting the company become a colonial law unto itself. In 1773, Warren Hastings, the Company's governor in Bengal, was given the elevated title of governor-general and, through his four-man council, was confirmed in his legislative powers there. In return, his appointment was made subject to the British government's approval, and law in Bengal was to be overseen by a judiciary appointed by the British Crown.

This arrangement proved insufficient to stop the East India Company's abuse of its position in India. Its wars of expansion were paid for by high taxation of the Bengalis (even during periods of famine) and much of the province's wealth was repatriated by the company's 'nabobs' to Britain. Eventually, Warren Hastings returned to London, where he was put on trial. After more than six years of legal debate, he was acquitted of the worst charges of malpractice but by then enough had been revealed to prompt drastic curtailment of the East India Company's power. In 1784, the government appointed its own department, the Board of Control for India, with ultimate authority over the East India Company's board of directors. In 1813, the company was stripped of most of its monopoly in India.

Thereafter, its trading activities were increasingly focused upon trafficking Bengali opium to China (sparking war with China and Britain's acquisition of Hong Kong), while using the money it earned there to buy tea, which it then shipped to Britain. Most of all, it had become a tax-raising body, since – through the fortunes of war and the submission of weakened local princes – it was the effective ruler not just of Bengal but of much of eastern and southern India as well. Despite these taps on Indian wealth, the company had

THE ORIGINS OF EMPIRE

1583 Sir Humphrey Gilbert claims Newfoundland for England.

1585 Sir Walter Raleigh's short-lived settlement at Roanoke is set up in modern-day North Carolina.

1600 The East India Company is founded.

1607 The Virginia Colony is established as the first permanent British settlement in the New World, at Jamestown.

1613 The East India Company's first trading settlement in India is established at Surat.

1625 Barbados is claimed for Britain.

1655 Admiral William Penn captures Jamaica from the Spanish.

1661 Bombay (Mumbai) is ceded by Portugal to Britain.

1670 A royal charter is granted to the Hudson Bay Company to exploit the Canadian fur trade.

1713 The Treaty of Utrecht grants Britain the Spanish possessions of Gibraltar and Minorca and the formerly French Canadian domains of Acadia, including Nova Scotia. France effectively gives up its attempt to compete with the Hudson Bay Company.

1757 Robert Clive wins the Battle of Plassey in Bengal.

1765 The Treaty of Allahabad grants the East India Company administrative and fiscal responsibility for Bengal.

1759 James Wolfe captures Quebec from the French.

1763 The Peace of Paris ends the Seven Years War; France cedes its remaining Canadian territories and its claims west of the Mississippi to Britain. Spain cedes Florida to Britain.

1768–71 James Cook undertakes voyages to Australia and New Zealand.

1776 The thirteen American colonies declare independence from the British Crown. The Revolutionary War follows.

1783 Britain acknowledges the independent United States of America.

1784 The British government sets up its Board of Control for India, curtailing the authority of the East India Company.

1788 The first convicts are transported to Botany Bay in Australia.

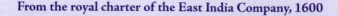

From the royal charter of the East India Company, 1600

Whereas our most dear and loving Cousin, George, Earl of Cumberland, and our well-beloved Subjects, Sir John Hart of London, Knight, Sir John Spencer of London, Knight, William Starkey, William Smith, John Ellecot, Robert Bailey, and Roger Cotton, have been Petitioners unto us for our Royal Assent and Licence to be granted unto them, that they, at their own Adventures, Costs, and Charges, as well as for the Honour of this our Realm of England, as for the Increase of our Navigation, and advancement of Trade of Merchandise, set forth one or more Voyages, with convenient Number of Ships and pannaces, by way of Traffick and Merchandise to the East-Indies, in the Countries and Parts of Asia and Africa, and to as many of the Islands, Ports and Cities, Towns and Places, thereabouts, as where Trade and Traffic may by all Likelihood be discovered, established or had; divers of which Countries, and many of the Islands, Cities and Ports thereof, have long been discovered by others of our Subjects, albeit not frequented in Trade or Merchandise.

developed a £40 million debt. It tried to raise much needed capital by simply issuing more shares, but in truth, it had over-reached itself. The cost of paying for a 150,000-strong army was prohibitive, a state of affairs that was the direct result of a long period in which the company's directors in Leadenhall Street had enjoyed little effective restraint over what their more ambitious employees were doing in a remote subcontinent where correspondence took months to arrive.

Finally in 1858, after the Indian Mutiny had been suppressed with tremendous barbarity on both sides, the British government assumed control of the East India Company's possessions. Its key assets having been nationalized, the company was wound up in 1874. British rule in India would continue for a further seventy-three years, but the age of informal, privatized empire was officially over.

1601

THE ELIZABETHAN POOR LAW

A NATIONAL SYSTEM OF POOR RELIEF

Throughout the Middle Ages there was no state system of welfare. Rather, providing alms to the poor was regarded as a religious obligation. It was in the reign of Elizabeth I that statutory measures made the treatment of her most needy subjects a matter of national policy.

During the sixteenth century, although the country was getting no poorer, contemporaries nonetheless believed that the problem of vagrancy was becoming more acute. Various reasons for this were put forward: the inflation of the period; the process of land enclosure, which denied the lowest peasants their means of subsistence; a supposed over-reliance on the textiles industry, whose trade went through regular cycles of boom and bust. To make matters worse, the religious upheavals of the Reformation and, in particular, the dissolution of the monasteries, had undermined some of the institutions upon which the destitute had previously relied.

The first laws to be enacted were more concerned with permitting than with enforcing measures of relief. What was to prove a long debate about the supposedly 'deserving' and 'undeserving' poor became a statutory concern when an Act of 1531 sought to draw a distinction between those who were indigent or homeless because of no fault of their own – such as illness or old age – and should thus be permitted to beg in their own parish, and those whose presumed fecklessness made them vagrants, who were therefore denied such rights.

Central government lacked the machinery to do much more than encourage other bodies to take the initiative. It fell to the major cities to innovate. In 1547, the City of London raised a mandatory poor rate from its citizens in order to fund poverty-alleviating schemes.

Implementing such reforms remained a matter for city and town councils until 1572 when parliamentary legislation forced local government throughout England and Wales to introduce compulsory poor rates. While punishments could still be visited upon those considered idle, the legislation relaxed the criteria by which some of the poor were deemed the agents of their own misfortune. Able-bodied paupers were to be found work to do.

In Scotland, legislation in the 1570s and 1590s firmly placed the onus of providing relief on the Church of Scotland. The 'Kirk' elders assessed those in need and entered their names upon parish lists. This was not quite the model adopted in England and Wales. There, the 1601 Poor Law brought together and codified the various pre-existing acts. As in Scotland, it recognized the parish as the confine of each administrating area, but in addition working alongside churchwardens were to be 'overseers of the poor', unpaid and appointed by justices of the peace. It was their task to assess the need and raise an appropriate poor rate from the community to cover the costs of providing for the old, to supervise work-creation schemes for the unemployed and to initiate apprenticeships for children in desperate circumstances.

Inevitably, some parishes took their statutory obligations more seriously than others. Following the letter of the law was less necessary where there was already considerable private charity or minimal poverty in the neighbourhood; and the disruptions of the Civil War weakened the state's role in ensuring the measures were uniformly applied. There was also an assumption that the levies raised by the parish were for the parish alone and were not freely available to any passing vagrant who happened to turn up in search of benefits. Thus the 1662 Law of Settlement and Removal tried to prevent those likely to become a burden from moving to more prosperous areas (which did not necessarily want to become the destination for large numbers of vagrants) by allowing for their repatriation if they could not demonstrate they had the means for long-term self-support. The extent to which individual parishes made use of this legislation varied according to how much they felt they needed an influx of labour.

Generating work to keep the unemployed occupied proved among the greatest problems. Outdoor relief continued, although some parishes opted to build work-houses, of varying quality and congeniality. Nonetheless, the cost of poor relief spiralled at the end of the eighteenth century. The introduction from 1795 of the Speenhamland system, which sought to guarantee the poor a minimum income, proved ruinously expensive and demonstrated that parishes were often too small in size to bear it. The cost of Poor Law administration in England and Wales rose from £619,000 in 1750 to £8 million in 1818, equivalent to a charge of 13s 3d per head of population.

From the Poor Law, 1601

Be it enacted by the Authority of this present Parliament, That the Churchwardens of every Parish, and four, three or two substantial Housholders there, as shall be thought meet, having respect to the Proportion and Greatness of the Same Parish and Parishes, to be nominated yearly in Easter Week, or within one Month after Easter, under the Hand and Seal of two or more Justices of the Peace in the same County, whereof one to be of the Quorum, dwelling in or near the same Parish or Division where the same Parish doth lie, shall be called Overseers of the Poor of the same Parish : And they, or the greater Part of them, shall take order from Time to Time, by, and with the Consent of two or more such Justices of Peace as is aforesaid, for setting to work the Children of all such whose Parents shall not by the said Churchwardens and Overseers, or the greater Part of them, be thought able to keep and maintain their Children: And also for setting to work all such Persons, married or unmarried, having no Means to maintain them, and use no ordinary and daily Trade of Life to get their Living by : And also to raise weekly or otherwise [by Taxation of every Inhabitant, Parson, Vicar and other, and of every Occupier of Lands, Houses, Tithes impropriate, Propriations of Tithes, Coal-Mines, or saleable Underwoods in the said Parish, in such competent Sum and Sums of Money as they shall think fit] a convenient Stock of Flax, Hemp, Wool, Thread, Iron, and other necessary Ware and Stuff, to set the Poor on Work : And also competent Sums of Money for and towards the necessary Relief of the Lame, Impotent, Old, Blind, and such other among them being Poor, and not able to work, and also for the putting out of such Children to be apprentices, to be gathered out of the same Parish, according to the Ability of the same Parish, and to do and execute all other Things as well for the disposing of the said Stock, as otherwise concerning the Premisses, as to them shall seem convenient.

As a result, the Elizabethan assistances of doles and outdoor relief codified in 1601 were finally replaced by the 1834 Poor Law Amendment Act, legislation motivated by a concern that a generation of urban welfare dependency was being created. Britain was fast becoming an industrial nation and the numbers of those who might opt to become a burden was beyond the means of the parish, with its bucolic notions and limited resources. Indeed, it was assumed that many unskilled people might find the old system far more appealing than working for a living in a factory. To disabuse them of this notion, the workhouse supposedly extended a

Aquatint of the St James's parish workhouse, from the Microcosm of London, *published in 1809. The figures were drawn by the famous caricaturist, Thomas Rowlandson (1756–1827). The background is by Augustus Pugin (1762–1832), father of the celebrated Gothic Revival architect.*

lifeline to them, on the understanding that it was a deliberate stigma, providing its inmates with an existence materially worse than that enjoyed by the struggling, but employed, poor.

These workhouses, to which the pauperized young, old, able-bodied and infirm were brought, were made purposefully disagreeable to an extent that initially went as far as banning inmates bringing – or being given – personal possessions. Although conditions improved in the second half of the nineteenth century, the workhouse remained the last resort for many until the beginning of the twentieth century, when those able to take advantage of the introduction of old-age pensions in 1908 and national insurance sickness and unemployment benefits in 1911 were in a position to avoid them. Further undermined in the 1920s, the last institutions of the Poor Law did not survive the Second World War.

IV

STUART BRITAIN

1605

THE 'MONTEAGLE LETTER' AND GUY FAWKES'S SIGNED CONFESSION

THE EXPOSURE OF THE GUNPOWDER PLOT

On 5 November 1605, King James I of England (James VI of Scotland) and most of his leading politicians, privy councillors, judges and bishops nearly lost their lives in an enormous explosion. The fact that this attempt at mass murder was thwarted can be largely attributed to an anonymous letter written to Lord Monteagle that warned the Catholic peer to stay away from Parliament that day.

The plan to blow up the House of Lords on the occasion of its state opening session was born of desperation. It was conceived by Robert Catesby, a Midlands squire who drew together a small group of fellow Catholic conspirators. Having concluded that Spain would not send another invasion armada and that the new king was not persuadable on the subject of toleration of Catholicism, they decided to dispose of him, together with the country's governing class, in a devastating fireball.

The plotters knew what they wanted but had only a blunt instrument to bring it about. They continued with the plan even after it became clear that the next in line to the throne, Prince Henry, would not be attending the state opening on 5 November. It seems they had, at best, hazy schemes for dealing with the other Protestant claimants to the throne in the aftermath of the carnage at Westminster. Even had they succeeded in taking hostage Princess Elizabeth as a precursor to persuading her to convert to Catholicism, they were hardly men of sufficient rank or influence to hold the country in thrall. Their best hope was perhaps to spark a period of anarchy that would be ended by a foreign invasion. The extraordinary magnitude of their wishful thinking did not make it any less diabolical. Ironically, their act of treason would be foiled by the patriotism of a fellow Catholic, and the legacy of the 'Gunpowder Plot' was to make life in Britain even more difficult for their co-religionists.

Initially, the plotters rented a house adjacent to the House of Lords and attempted to tunnel towards the chamber. When storage space became available to rent in the vaults under the Lords' chamber, they seized the opportunity, renting it in the name of one of their conspirators, Thomas Percy. Since he was the cousin of the earl of Northumberland, there was no reason for the authorities to be suspicious.

As the date drew near, Catesby was running short of funds to secure his *coup d'état*, so others were brought into the scheme, including Francis Tresham. On 26 October, an anonymous letter was sent to Tresham's brother-in-law, Lord Monteagle, warning him to keep away from the state opening of Parliament, which would receive a 'terrible blow'. Naturally suspicious, Monteagle informed the king's chief secretary, Robert Cecil, earl of Salisbury. Since threats and rumours were not unusual, Salisbury was not minded to take the matter too seriously. Nonetheless, just for good measure, on the afternoon of 4 November, Monteagle and the lord chamberlain, the earl of Suffolk, searched the House of Lords chamber and the vaults underneath. There they stumbled upon a large pile of firewood (concealing thirty-six barrels of gunpowder) and a man who claimed

A contemporary engraving of the gunpowder plotters by the Dutch engraver Crispin van de Passe.

121

to be called (somewhat unimaginatively) John Johnson. When questioned, he said the wood belonged to Thomas Percy.

This seemed to satisfy the inspectors. However, after they had left, Monteagle mentioned to Suffolk that he vaguely knew Percy, a Catholic with no obvious reason to be storing supplies in Westminster. Duly informed, the king insisted that the Palace of Westminster be properly searched again. Late on the night of 4 November, guards returned to the vaults. There, they discovered not only the barrels of gunpowder under the wood but also fire-lighting equipment and the man still purporting to be John Johnson. He was, in fact, the conspirator charged with igniting the fuse, Guy Fawkes.

While Fawkes was carted off for questioning, his colleagues were rounded up. Catesby and Percy died in a shoot-out at their safe house in Staffordshire. At first Fawkes would not yield his secrets until the level of torture was increased. The severity of pain inflicted on him may be gauged by the broken scrawl of his signature. Tried and found guilty, he was hanged, his heart ripped out and his body quartered. The heads of the conspirators eventually adorned the approach to the Palace of Westminster that they had hoped to reduce to rubble. By contrast, Monteagle was rewarded with a generous pension, which he used to invest in land in Virginia.

Bonfires were lit across London to celebrate national deliverance, a tradition that spread across the country, becoming a permanent feature when Parliament promptly responded to the popular clamour and made 5 November a day of annual thanksgiving. As early as the mid-seventeenth century, commemorative fireworks were being let off. The twin themes of anti-Catholicism and loyalty to parliamentary government were reinforced when, on 5 November 1688, William of Orange landed at Torbay and the Glorious Revolution began. Whilst the passage of time has blurred the more overtly sectarian overtones of 'Bonfire Night', it has not dimmed the nationwide desire to celebrate it.

There have been subsequent theories that the plotters were actually the dupes of a government conspiracy to frame Catholics, but they lack supporting evidence. Similarly, the suggestion has been dismissed that the amount of gunpowder used was either too degraded or insufficient to cause serious damage. Modern ballistics tests using comparable gunpowder strength have shown that if 'John Johnson' had detonated his near one ton of explosives, he would, indeed, have succeeded in blowing the king and the political class of his realm sky high.

1606
UNION JACK DESIGNS

THE UNION OF THE SCOTTISH AND ENGLISH CROWNS
AND THE SYMBOL OF A BRITISH IDENTITY

King James VI of Scotland also became James I of England when he succeeded the childless Queen Elizabeth in 1603. He wished, however, to consider himself not just the single head of state of two otherwise separate kingdoms but rather as the ruler of a united entity, as 'King of Great Britain'.

Preliminary designs for the Union flag are depicted in the second plate section.

In October 1607, James assured the Westminster Parliament that 'the benefits which do arise of that union which is made in my blood do redound to the whole island'. In this he was ahead of his time. Although the accompanying union treaty that he envisaged was passed by the Scottish Parliament, it got bogged down in Westminster and was clearly unlikely to be enacted in a form acceptable to His Majesty.

Yet the previous year the two realms had been given a unified emblem. In the succeeding centuries it was unfurled wherever Britons went: circumnavigating the globe with the world's largest navy; flying from barracks, schools, missions and embassies in the four corners of the earth; forming a rallying point for bloodied soldiers upon countless battlefields; rising with each Olympic gold medal won and falling with each colony set free. So far and wide did it journey that it was even the first man-made item to flutter from the world's highest mountain. This was the Union flag – more commonly referred to as the Union Jack – and it became inseparably entwined with the notion of Britishness.

It was brought into being by a royal proclamation of April 1606, 'declaring what Flags South and North Britains shall bear at Sea', which stipulated that all ships henceforth 'shall bear in their maintop the Red Cross, commonly called St George's Cross, and the White Cross, commonly called St Andrew's Cross, joined together, according to a form made by our Heralds and sent by Us to our Admiral to be published to our said Subjects'.

The design of the new flag, intended only for maritime use, was entrusted to the earl of Nottingham. The brief was to combine the crosses of Scotland and England's respective saints, St Andrew and St George. A traditional approach was to halve or quarter the flag between the two devices, but the problem was that whichever cross appeared nearer to the flagstaff, or on the top quarter, would be construed to enjoy a hierarchical precedence. Avoiding giving national offence was as important as coming up with an intelligible design.

Since 1604, Nottingham had toyed with various ideas, none of them satisfactory. These versions have survived although, sadly, not the original successful design, which was probably lost in a fire at Whitehall palace in 1618. Nonetheless, the solution was ingenious: the English cross would lie on top of the Scottish cross, but a section of the Scottish cross alone would appear in the canton – the top, left-hand quarter of the flag, which the laws of heraldry decreed was the most prestigious position.

It immediately became clear that this did not mollify the Scots. On 7 August 1606, the shipmasters of Scotland wrote to the king, protesting at the fact that 'the Scottis Croce, callit Sanctandrois Croce is twyse divydit, and the Inglishe Croce, callit Sanct George, haldin haill and drawne through the Scottis Croce, whiche is thairby obscurit and no takin nor merk to be seene of the Scottish Armes. This will breid some heit and discontentment betwixt your Majesteis subjectis.'

These gripes led to two versions of the Union flag. English ships flew it with the English cross imposed over the Scottish saltire (diagonal cross) while Scottish ships flew it with the Scottish saltire imposed over the English cross. After the 1707 Act of Union, the Scottish version became less evident and was abandoned altogether during the nineteenth century.

In the seventeenth century, officials busied themselves with controlling rather than promoting the Union flag's use. In 1634, instructions were issued that restricted flying the Union flag to ships of the Royal Navy. Henceforth, merchant ships were commanded to fly the St Andrew's cross if they were Scottish and the St George's cross if they were English, the latter being the first to be subsequently incorporated into the top canton of the red ensign. For warships, the Union flag was briefly abandoned with the execution of Charles I. The republican Commonwealth toyed with various versions before the previous design was reinstated for the restoration of the monarchy in 1660.

With the reign of Queen Anne and full legislative union, the Union flag's usage spread. During this period, the blue appears to have been somewhat lighter in hue than it subsequently became. The current version of the flag was first flown in 1801 to symbolize the Act of Union with Ireland and introduced the Irish diagonal red cross of St Patrick into the design, running it within the St Andrew's cross. In order not to obliterate the Scottish saltire, the Irish saltire was made less thick and was also 'counter-changed' – reversed in each half so that it is lower on the half nearer the flagpole (thereby ceding hierarchical priority to Scotland) but higher on the half more distant from the pole. This was another means of smoothing national sensibilities by ensuring that the precedence given to the Irish saltire – because it lay over the Scottish saltire – was balanced by the Scottish saltire having precedence in the more prestigious half of the design. It also allowed the flag to be flown upside down as a means of signalling distress.

By this time, the flag was ceasing to be purely a device flown by warships and regiments. During Queen Victoria's reign, it became ubiquitous. Occasionally, pedants attempted to assert that civilians had no right to fly it – until officialdom assured them otherwise. There also remained the debate over its name. Technically it was only the 'Union Jack' when flown from the jackstaff of a Royal Navy ship, which explains the origin of the name. The distinction has, however, long been a redundant one, as conceded by an Admiralty circular from 1902. Asked to settle definitively the matter of the flag's name during a House of Lords debate in 1908, the earl of Crewe announced the government's position on the subject, stating that 'the Union Jack should be regarded as the national flag, and may be flown on land by all His Majesty's subjects'.

1611
THE KING JAMES BIBLE

THE AUTHORIZED VERSION OF THE BIBLE IN ENGLISH

An extract from the King James Bible can be found on pages 62 and 63.

The union of the Scottish and English crowns appeared to safeguard the Protestant succession. Less immediately clear was the nature of the Protestantism to be promoted.

While Mary, Queen of Scots died adhering to the Catholic faith of her parents, her son James was brought up from the cradle without her and entrusted instead to the care of strict Presbyterians. He emerged into manhood as a serious, scholarly man, greatly interested in theological issues. With a strong sense of his divine right as monarch, he also rejoiced to be free of his Presbyterian schooling. Indeed, while ruling in Edinburgh, he had confronted its Presbyterian Establishment by trying to reintroduce bishops into the Church of Scotland.

Upon his becoming king in London and supreme governor of the Church of England, such episcopalianism more readily fitted in with the religious settlement of his predecessor, Elizabeth. Nonetheless, in the first years of James's reign, different factions looked for signs that he would accommodate their views. Puritans expected greater consideration from a monarch brought up in their culture. Catholics hoped that a king whose wife was widely assumed to have privately converted to their faith, and who had commenced his reign by making peace with Spain, could prove amenable to a restoration of Roman practices.

Instead, James continued a 'broad church' policy intended to ensure that Anglicanism was acceptable to the majority, but in reality displeasing the hardline disciples of both Geneva and Rome for whom compromise represented a retreat from truth. Besides the role of bishops and the issue of predestination, other contentious matters included the more elaborate ceremonies and the vestments worn by Anglican clergy, which were anathema to evangelical Puritans. Imbued with an egalitarian ethos bent on reducing symbols of hierarchy between clergy and laity, they sought simplicity.

It was in the largely vain hope of reaching a lasting settlement on these and other issues that in 1604 a conference was convened at Hampton Court by the king, his bishops and other prominent theologians. There, whilst making minor changes to the liturgy, they also agreed on something that was to prove a far more significant legacy: the need for a new translation of the Bible. After the failure to prevent Tyndale's translation of the New Testament being smuggled into Britain, a commission had been appointed charged with producing a legal version. Supervised by Miles Coverdale, this became the Great Bible of 1539. Yet neither it nor other versions, such as Archbishop Parker's 'Bishop's Bible', the Calvinist 'Geneva Bible' or – for underground Catholics – the 'Douai Bible', attracted overwhelming devotion. (The exception was in Scotland, where the Geneva Bible had become the standard text.)

Fifty-four revisers were appointed to produce the new version, among whom, at least forty-seven are known to have been actively engaged. Divided into sections, the work was undertaken by groups in Oxford, Cambridge and Westminster. The revisers were expected to follow most closely the Bishop's Bible; but it was Tyndale's style that remained the overwhelming influence. Nevertheless, some of his more controversial translations were reversed; for example, replacing 'congregation' by 'church' and 'love' by 'charity'.

The completed manuscript (subsequently lost) was bought by the king's printer for £3,500. Dedicated to King James I, it was published in 1611 in large bound folio volumes selling for 30 shillings, with the statement 'Appointed to be read in Churches' on its frontispiece. The copyright was held by the Crown, which in turn

The frontispiece of the first King James Bible features the twelve apostles at the top with Matthew, Mark, Luke and John occupying each of the four corners accompanied by their symbolic animals. In the centre, Moses (left) and Aaron (right) flank the title.

licensed other printers, although, independently, the university presses of Oxford and Cambridge were also given the right to print it. Its official imprimatur ensured its familiar description as the 'Authorized Version'. This is misleading as it never had statutory sanction. However, such was the scale of adoption that the previous versions ceased to be printed, giving it a scriptural monopoly in Protestant worship throughout the British Isles.

In its first year, two versions appeared that became known respectively as the 'He Bible' and the 'She Bible' because of the different gender usage in Ruth 3:15. Subsequent editions decided that the disputed passage should read 'and she went into the citie'. Of the approximately 200 surviving copies of the first edition, about 150 are 'She Bibles'. A far worse discrepancy followed in an edition of 1631, which inadvertently omitted the word 'not' from the seventh commandment, thereby inviting Christians to commit adultery. The edition became known as the 'Wicked Bible'. Other minor infelicities marked out future editions, including one of 1717 that contained the 'parable of the vinegar' instead of 'the vineyard'.

These printers' errors, while beloved of antiquarian book collectors, should not detract from the accomplishment of the King James Bible. More than any other English-language translation, this was the version that endured, perpetuating Tyndale's style and fixing the rhythm of spoken and written English for generations thereafter. It also travelled to the American colonies, helping to wed the New World to similar patterns of speech.

Such was the achievement that in Britain the King James Bible lasted without challenge for over 250 years. Only towards the end of the nineteenth century was there an attempt to tinker with revision. More comprehensive rewrites followed in the twentieth century. Whilst these latest efforts may make greater claims to biblical scholarship and easy accessibility, they have too frequently produced mundane and unmemorable prose, lacking the striking authority of the King James Bible's stirring language and synonym. It is difficult to imagine that they will find the same enduring place in the popular consciousness.

1623
SHAKESPEARE'S FIRST FOLIO

THE PLAYS OF WILLIAM SHAKESPEARE
ARE SAVED FOR POSTERITY

Few of the plays performed on the Elizabethan stage have survived for future generations to enjoy. Most did not make it into print, their scripts never circulating beyond the circle of actors who performed them. From this environment, the name of William Shakespeare could easily have faded to the point where it endured only in a few casual archival references, the titles of his work principally remembered by specialists in theatrical history. Generations of visitors to Holy Trinity church in Stratford-upon-Avon might have walked past his monument, glancing only fleetingly at what they took to be merely one more impressive tribute to a forgotten local worthy.

That Shakespeare is, instead, recalled as one of the transforming geniuses of Western civilization owes much to two of his colleagues in the King's Men, the theatrical company for which he acted, wrote plays and owned shares in its Globe theatre in Southwark. It was John Heminges (allegedly the first actor to play Falstaff) and Henry Condell who decided after Shakespeare's death in 1616 that his plays should be collected in an expensively produced edition in a 'folio' page size. In doing so, they preserved most of his work from the ravages of time and memory.

In the year of Shakespeare's death, a folio of Ben Jonson's dramas was published. This in itself was an innovation and it provided a model that Heminges and Condell determined to follow. No play in Shakespeare's hand still exists, but the compilers of his folio were still in a position to assemble primary material – essential evidence that has subsequently perished. In particular, they gathered documents then still in the King's Men's possession, including the prompt cards from which the actors had first learned their lines.

Access to such original, but sadly ephemeral, records was crucially important, given that much of what had been printed of Shakespeare's work in his own lifetime was of degraded quality. Shakespeare had been commissioned to write plays specifically for the King's Men and its predecessor, the Lord Chamberlain's Men. Without an effective dramatic copyright law, there had been little incentive to print and circulate his plays because doing so would have enabled rival companies to perform and benefit from his work, despite having not made the original investment in it. In consequence, most of the contemporary editions of his plays were unauthorized versions, badly printed, scarcely proof-read and put together either from notes or from the memories of those who had listened to them or had some hand in their production. Inevitably, they were far from accurate renditions. Errors ranged from garbled lines and serious misquotations to wholly fictitious efforts to fill gaps in lost recollection. Produced in cheap quarto (where the pages are created by twice-folding sheets of paper) paperback format, even

Title page of Shakespeare's First Folio. The note to the reader is by Shakespeare's fellow playwright Ben Jonson, and the engraving is by Martin Droeshout.

To the Reader.

This Figure, that thou here seest put,
   It was for gentle Shakespeare cut;
Wherein the Grauer had a strife
   with Nature, to out-doo the life:
O, could he but haue drawne his wit
   As well in brasse, as he hath hit
His face; the Print would then surpasse
   All, that was euer writ in brasse.
But, since he cannot, Reader, looke
   Not on his Picture, but his Booke.
                                    B. I.

Mr. WILLIAM
SHAKESPEARES
COMEDIES,
HISTORIES, &
TRAGEDIES.
Published according to the True Originall Copies.

LONDON
Printed by Isaac Iaggard, and Ed. Blount. 1623.

these versions might not have survived had the production of the folio not ensured Shakespeare's longevity of reputation and, thus, a recognition that even debased and crumbling quarto versions were worth preserving.

It is thanks to the folio compilers' patient scholarship and quest for original sources that we are able to discern the scale of error in these so-called 'bad' quartos. In their opening address 'To the Great Variety of Readers', Heminges and Condell stated that they aimed to reproduce Shakespeare's plays 'as he conceived them' and would not be repeating the quartos' 'divers stolen and surreptitious copies, maimed and deformed by the frauds and stealths of injurious imposters'. It may be argued that a truly authentic reproduction cannot exist because of Shakespeare's understandable tendency to make changes or cuts and to add additional material over the course of successive productions. Nonetheless, the folio's compilers did their best to put together what their own experience and knowledge of Shakespeare's methods taught them were the most polished versions of his art.

The First Folio was published in 1623 and was dedicated to two influential brothers, the earls of Pembroke and Montgomery. Heminges and Condell claimed to be motivated 'without ambition either of self-profit or fame, only to keep the memory of so worthy a friend and fellow alive as was our Shakespeare'. Around 1,000 copies of the First Folio were printed, of which approximately 230 are still in existence, most of the latter incomplete. While five are in the care of the British Library, the largest collection is to be found in

A GOLDEN AGE OF ENGLISH DRAMA

1567 London's first purpose-built playhouse, the Red Lion, opens: it fails within a year.

1576 The Theatre opens in Shoreditch.

1577 The Curtain theatre opens in Shoreditch.

1587 The Rose theatre opens on Bankside, south of the city.

c.1588 Christopher Marlowe's *Tamburlaine the Great* is produced.

c.1589 Marlowe's *Doctor Faustus* is performed.

c.1590 Marlowe's *The Jew of Malta* is performed.

1592 Thomas Kyd's revenge drama *The Spanish Tragedy* is produced, as is Marlowe's *Edward II*.

1593 Marlowe is killed in a brawl.

1594 The Lord Chamberlain's Men is formed.

1597 A 'bad' quarto of Shakespeare's *Romeo and Juliet* is published; a 'good' quarto appears in 1599.

1599 The Globe opens next to The Rose at Bankside.

c.1600 Shakespeare's *Hamlet* is first produced.

1603 The Lord Chamberlain's Men become the King's Men.

c.1606 Shakespeare's *King Lear* and Ben Jonson's *Volpone* are staged.

1613 John Webster's *The Duchess of Malfi* is performed.

c.1613 *The Two Noble Kinsmen* is produced, the last play attributed, at least in part, to Shakespeare.

1614 The fire-damaged Globe is rebuilt.

1616 Shakespeare dies. Ben Jonson's works are published in folio.

1623 Shakespeare's First Folio is published.

Washington, DC, where the Folger Shakespeare Library is the repository of seventy-nine copies. At over 900 pages, copies were initially priced at twenty shillings (£1), a luxurious expense at that time. However, there were buyers, and subsequent editions followed in 1632, 1663, 1664 and 1685.

The First Folio contained thirty-six plays, eighteen of which had never previously been published and might otherwise have vanished for ever. *Twelfth Night, Julius Caesar* and *Macbeth* are among those the Folio saved for posterity. It omitted four plays generally attributed, at least in part, to Shakespeare: *Pericles, The Two Noble Kinsmen, Love's Labour's Won* and *Cardenio*, seemingly on the grounds that they were not purely his own work but rather the result of his collaboration with other playwrights. This is a misfortune since *Love's Labour's Won* and *Cardenio* are now lost to the world.

The title page was illustrated with an engraving of the author by Martin Droeshout, which has proved the source of much debate among those searching for hidden meaning in its slight idiosyncrasies. It is unlikely that the young Droeshout knew Shakespeare at first hand, but that his image should be approved by those who did know him makes it probably a reasonable likeness. It was, however, the tribute published in the Folio by Ben Jonson to 'thou star of poets' and the 'Sweet swan of Avon' that gave the most fitting perspective on the dead playwright's legacy:

> Triumph, my Britain, thou hast one to show
> To whom all scenes of Europe homage owe.
> He was not of an age, but for all time.

1628
THE PETITION OF RIGHT

THE COMMON LAW VERSUS ROYAL ABSOLUTISM

How absolute was the monarch's power? According to the theory of the divine right of kings, their rule was absolute because they were anointed by God to whom, alone, they were answerable. James I of England (and VI of Scotland) was so certain that this was the case that he wrote philosophical discourses on the subject. The issue was no abstract debate, for it went to the heart of whether the constitution offered any effective checks against arbitrary rule.

James had a useful servant in Francis Bacon (1561–1626), successively attorney-general and lord chancellor. Bacon believed that the judiciary's role was to uphold the king's law – that judges were 'lions under the throne', but James also had a determined and equally erudite opponent in Sir Edward Coke (1552–1634). A great advocate of the common law and the independence of the judiciary, Coke argued that the Crown did not enjoy unlimited rights and that it was the judiciary's duty to see that the monarchy exercised its powers only within the law. According to Coke, the king could not issue proclamations that created new laws nor contradict what had already been established by the common law. The son of a Norfolk barrister, Coke had been appointed chief justice of the Court of Common Pleas in 1606 and chief justice of the King's Bench in 1613. Three years later he was dismissed for refusing to do the king's bidding.

Supporters of Coke's views had little reason to cheer when, in 1625, James was succeeded by his son, aged just twenty-four. Charles I, who had inherited his father's belief in the divine right of kings, warned his politicians in 1626 shortly before dissolving the legislature, 'Remember that parliaments are altogether in my power for their calling, sitting, and dissolution; therefore, as I find the fruits good or evil, they are to continue, or not to be.'

The difficulty with this view was that the precedent was well established that taxation could be raised only through parliamentary consent. In pursuing

OVERLEAF: The Petition of Right. Specifying liberties of the individual that the king may not infringe, the Petition is one of the most significant documents in British constitutional history.

Humbly shew vnto our Soveraigne Lord the King, The Lords Spirituall and
of the Raigne of King Edward the first comonly called *Statutum de Tallagio non concedendo*
Arch Bishopps, Bishopps, Earles, Barons, Knights, Burgesses, and other the free men of the Comona
of King Edward the third, it is declared and enacted, That from thenceforth noe person should
of the land.   And by other Lawes of this Realme it is provided, That none should be charged
other the good Lawes and Statute of this Realme, y᷎ Subiects haue inherited this freedome,
m Parliament.   Yet nevertheles of late divers Comissions directed to sondrie Comissioners
to lend certime somes of money vnto y᷎ Maiestie, And many of them vppon theire refusall
been constreyned to become bound to make apparence, and giue attendance before your
molested and disquieted. And divers other charges haue been layd and levyed vppon y᷎
others by Commando or direction from your Maiestie, or y᷎ Privy Councell against the
of England, It is declared, and enacted that, noe free man may be taken, or imprisoned,
but by the Lawfull Iudgement of his Peeres, or by the Lawe of the Land.   And in the
Parliament, That noe ... man of what estate or condition that he be, should be putt
to answer by due processe of Lawe.   Nevertheles against the tenor of the said Statute
imprisoned, without any cause shewed, And when for theire deliveraunce they were brought
order, and theire keepers comaunded to certifie the causes of theire detteyner, noe cause war
yet were returned back to severall prisons without being charged with any thing to which
Manners haue been dispersed into divers Counties of the Realme, And the inhabitants aga
Lawes and customes of this Realme, and to the greate greivance and vexation of the people
the third It is declared and enacted, That noe man should be forejudged of life, or lymbe aga
Statute of this y᷎ Realme, noe man ought to be adiudged to death, but by the Lawes establish
of what kind soever is exempted from the proceedinge to be vsed, and punishments to be inflicted by
Seale haue issued forth by which certeine persons haue been assigned and appointed Comi
Souldiers or Maryners, or other dissolute persons ioyning with them, as should comitt any mu
agreeable to Martiall Lawe, and as is vsed in Armyes in tyme of warr, to procede to the tryall
By pretext whereof some of y᷎ Maiesties Subiects haue been by some of the said Comissioners putt
Statuts also they might, and by noe other ought to haue been iudged and executed, And also
Lawes and Statute of this your Realme, by reason that divers of y᷎ officers and Ministers of
pretence that the said offenders were punishable onely by Martiall Lawe, and by authority of
Lawes, and Statuts of this your Realme

They doe therefore humbly pray y᷎ most excellent Maiestie, Tha
by Act of Parliament.   And that none be called to mak
for refusall thereof.   And that noe freeman in any such manner a
Maryners, And that your people may not be soe burdened in ty
hereafter noe Comissions of like nature may issue forth to any
or putt to death, contrary to the Lawes and franchise of the la
which they most humbly pray of y᷎ most excellent Maie
vouchsafe to declare, that the Awards doeinge and pro
And that your Maiestie would be alsoe gratiously pleased, for
and Ministers shall serue you according to the Lawes and Statut

Kings most Excellent Maiestie

...mons in Parliament assembled. That whereas it is declared and enacted by a Statute made in the tyme
...age, or Ayde should be layde, or levyed by the King or his heires in this Realme, without the good will and assent of the
...Realme. And by authoritie of Parliament, houlden in the five and twentith yeare of the raigne
...to make any Loanes to the King against his will, because such Loanes were against reason and the franchise
...ge, or imposition called a Benevolence, nor by such like charge. By which the Statutes before mencioned, and
...ould not be compelled to contribute to any Tax, Tallage, Ayde, or other like charge not sett by comon consent
...Counties, haue issued. By meanes whereof your people haue been in divers places assembled, and required
...had an oath administred vnto them not warrantable by the Lawes or Statute of this Realme, and haue
...d, and in other places, and others of them haue been therefore imprisoned, confined, and sundry other wayes
...verall Counties by Lord Lieutenante, Deputie Lieutenante, Comissioners for Musters, Justice of Peace and
...free customes of the Realme. And where also by the Statute called the Greate Charter of the liberties
...o of his freehould or liberties, or his free customes, or be outlawed, or exiled or in any manner destroyed
...twentith yeare of the raigne of King Edward the third, It was declared and enacted by authoritie of
...land, or tenements, nor taken nor imprisoned, nor disherited, nor putt to death without being brought
...the good Lawes and Statute of yo Realme to that end provided, divers of your Subiects haue of late been
...3 Justice, by yo Maiesties writts of Habeas corpus there to vndergoe and receiue as the Court should
...that they were deteyned by yo Maiesties speciall comaund signified by the Lords of yo Privy Councell, and
...ht make answere according to the Lawe. And whereas of late greate Companyes of Souldiers and
...will haue been compelled to receiue them into theire howses, and there to suffer them to soiourne against the
...and whereas also by authoritie of Parliament, in the five and twentith yeare of the raigne of King Edward
...ne of the Great Charter, and the Lawe of the land. And by the said Greate Charter and other the Lawes and
...yo Realme, either by the customes of the same Realme, or by Acts of Parliament. And whereas noe offender
...and Statute of this your Realme. Neuertheles of late tyme divers Comissions vnder yo Maiesties Greate
...th power, and authoritie to proceede within the land according to the Justice of Martiall Lawe against such &
...ry, felony, mutiny, or other outrage or misdemeanor whatsoeuer, and by such summary course and order as is
...onation of such offenders, and them to cause to be executed and putt to death according to the Lawe Martiall.
...chen, and where if by the Lawes and Statute of the land they had deserued death, by the same Lawes and
...doers offenders by culler thereof, clayming an exemption haue escaped the punishmente due to them by the
...onuistly refused, or forborne to proceed against such offenders according to the same Lawes and Statute, vpon
...ions as aforesaid. Which Comissions, and all other of like nature are wholly and directly contrary to the said

...hereafter be compelled to make or yeild any guifte, loane, benevolence, tax or such like charge without comon consent
...take such oath, or to giue attendance, or be confined, or otherwise molested, or disquieted concerning the same, or
...mencioned be imprisoned or deteyned. And that yo Maiestie would be pleased to remoue the said Souldiers, and
...And that the aforesaid Comissions for proceeding by Martiall Lawe may be revoked and annulled. And that
...persons whatsoeuer to be executed as aforesaid, least by culler of them any of yo Maiesties Subiects be destroyed
...ir rights and liberties according to the Lawes and Statutes of this Realme. And that yo Maiestie would allso
...e precedent of your people in any of the premisses, shall not be drawne hereafter into consequence or example
...comfort, and safety of yo people to declare yo royall will and pleasure That in the thing aforesaid all yo officers
...ustice, as they tender the honor of yo Maiestie, and the prosperity of this Kingdome.

From the Petition of Right, 1628

To the King's most excellent Majesty: Humbly shew unto our sovereign lord the king, the lords spiritual and temporal, and commons, in parliament assembled, that whereas it is declared and enacted by a statute made in the time of the reign of King Edward the First, commonly called *Statutum de tallagio non concedendo*, that no tallage or aid shall be laid or levied by the King or his heirs in this realm, without the goodwill and assent of the archbishops, bishops, earls, barons, knights, burgesses and other the freemen of the commonalty of this realm; and by the authority of parliament holden in the five and twentieth year of the reign of King Edward the Third, it is declared and enacted, that from thenceforth no person should be compelled to make any loans to the king against his will, because such loans were against reason and the franchise of the land; and by other laws of this realm it is provided, that none should be charged by any charge or imposition called a benevolence, nor by such like charge; by which the statutes before mentioned, and other the good laws and statutes of this realm, your subjects have inherited this freedom, that they should not be compelled to contribute to any tax, tallage, aid or other like charge not set by common consent in parliament. ...

And where also by the statute called *The Great Charter of the Liberties of England*, it is declared and enacted, that no freeman may be taken or imprisoned, or be disseised of his freehold or liberties, or his free customs, or be outlawed or exiled, or in any manner destroyed, but by the lawful judgment of his peers, or by the law of the land.

And in the eight and twentieth year of the reign of King Edward the Third, it was declared and enacted by authority of parliament, that no man of what estate or condition that he be, should be put out of his land or tenements, nor taken, nor imprisoned, nor disherited, nor put to death, without being brought to answer by due process of law.

Nevertheless against the tenor of the said statutes, and other the good laws and statutes of your realm to that end provided, divers of your subjects have of late been imprisoned without any cause shewed ...

They do therefore humbly pray your most excellent majesty, that no man hereafter be compelled to make or yield any gift, loan, benevolence, tax or such like charge, without common consent by act of parliament; and that none be called to make answer, or take such oath, or to give attendance, or be confined, or otherwise molested or disquieted concerning the same, or for refusal thereof; and that no freeman, in any such manner as is before mentioned, be imprisoned or detained; and that your majesty would be pleased to remove the said soldiers and mariners; and that your people may not be so burthened in time to come; and that the aforesaid Commissions for proceeding by martial law, may be revoked and annulled; and that hereafter no commissions of like nature may issue forth to any person or persons whatsoever to be executed as aforesaid, lest by colour of them any of your majesty's subjects be destroyed, or put to death contrary to the laws and franchise of the land.

an expensive and misbegotten war against Spain, Charles was badly in need of revenue. He therefore dreamed up an alternative means of getting hold of the money by demanding that a loan be forcibly extracted from taxpayers, equal to what he believed Parliament should have guaranteed. Those who refused to pay risked imprisonment. What was unclear was whether this kind of royal demand to pay up or be locked up was legal. Five detainees launched a test case by deploying a writ of habeas corpus, challenging the Crown's right to imprison them without due process, but the courts failed to uphold this most important provision of Magna Carta. Whatever might have been the case previously, it now seemed that Charles I did enjoy the right not only to detain his subjects without due legal process but also to raise revenue from them without the consent of their representatives in Parliament.

The 1628 general election made apparent voters' concerns at this apparent constitutional revolution. A House of Commons was returned that set about challenging untrammelled royal authority. The king's response was to try to bluff it out, claiming that because he observed existing statutes there was no need to have them restated in a new Act of Parliament. Unperturbed, Sir Edward Coke – by now MP for Buckinghamshire and seventy-six years old – proposed that both Houses of Parliament should unite in issuing a Petition of Right. This was an ancient device in which individuals could appeal to the king to reverse a perceived wrongdoing by him or his court. Parliament's petition aimed to make clear that its rights, as well as those of the people, needed defending. It asserted that no one should be forced to pay tax or make a loan without the explicit sanction of Parliament; that habeas corpus and Magna Carta still had legal force, which meant that no one should be detained without due cause having been demonstrated; that no one should have soldiers or sailors billeted in their property against their will; and that there should be no future commissions for proceeding by martial law.

Charles might have been tempted to ignore the opinion of the House of Commons, but the support lent to its petition by the House of Lords meant indifference was scarcely an option. Reluctantly, he signed his assent across the top of the document with the traditional French phrase used since Norman times, *Soit droit fait come est desire* (in English 'Let right be done as desired'). The petition's drafters, which included Coke, Sir John Eliot and John Pym, argued that they were not seeking new powers, merely clarifying ancient rights – a very English approach to justifying revolt. Charles played them at a similar game, in effect agreeing to the document because it claimed to change nothing. He addressed Parliament prior to proroguing it, in a speech that qualified his assent: 'The profession of both houses, in time of hammering this Petition, was no ways to intrench upon my prerogative, saying, they had neither intention nor power to hurt it. Therefore it must needs be conceived that I have granted no new, but only confirmed the ancient liberties of my subjects.'

Subsequent events soon demonstrated that Charles had no intention of abiding by the Petition of Right, regardless of whether it affirmed old wisdom or heralded new thinking. He prorogued Parliament in 1629 and did not call it again for another eleven years. Sir John Eliot, the leader of the opposition in the Commons, was sent to the Tower of London, where he languished until his death in 1632. Coke died in 1634, shortly after the king's officials had ransacked his home and removed manuscripts, including those he had been writing for his *Institutes of the Laws of England*, a magisterial exposition of the common law.

In the short term, the Petition of Right's only success was in putting an end to the innovation of forced loans. From a longer perspective however, it was a defining document in the history of Britain, drawing a line that monarchs crossed at the risk of being accused of acting unconstitutionally. By heedlessly crossing that line, Charles I proceeded down a path that plunged his kingdoms into civil war and brought about his own execution. When his son, James II, repeated the mistake, a second revolution ensued that dealt a death blow to royal absolutism in Britain.

1638
THE SCOTTISH NATIONAL COVENANT

SCOTLAND'S PLEDGE TO DEFEND PRESBYTERIANISM
AGAINST CHARLES I'S EFFORTS TO ANGLICIZE THE KIRK

D espite being born in Dunfermline, Charles I had little feeling for Scotland. Although he had succeeded to its throne, alongside that of England, in 1625, it took him eight years to venture north to Edinburgh for his coronation as the nation's king. Whilst his casual attitude did not go unnoticed, it was in the matter of his northern kingdom's religious traditions that he demonstrated the most fatal disregard.

Charles's father had imposed bishops upon the 'Kirk' (as the Church of Scotland was widely known), but had fallen short of forcing total religious uniformity across his politically disunited kingdoms. Charles, who had inherited his father's belief in royal 'divine right' without any of James's canny pragmatism, was determined to ensure that his will would be done throughout Scotland's churches. Moreover, he chose to do so at the very moment that his archbishop of Canterbury, William Laud, was taking Anglicanism along a path of increased 'High Church' ritualism, which to English Puritans and Scottish Presbyterians alike seemed indistinguishable from the Catholic Mass.

In 1637, Charles made a Scottish edition of the Book of Common Prayer mandatory across Scotland, without first securing the approval of the Kirk's General Assembly. It was an incendiary provocation. The new liturgy's introduction was met with a barrage of abuse and hurled stools, which was just the beginning. Charles, rather than beat a retreat, regarded the criticism as evidence of political treason.

The king's determination to press ahead met with one of the most extraordinary documents in Scottish history. Scotland's Calvinists were imbued with the notion that, like the Israelites, they had a bond with God and were his chosen people.

The Scottish National Covenant is depicted in the third plate section.

Consequently, a 'National Covenant' was signed on 28 February 1638 in a four-hour ceremony in front of the pulpit of Greyfriars church in Edinburgh. From there, it was taken to the Tailor's Hall in the Cowgate where it was signed by church ministers and town dignitaries. Then it was the turn of the townsfolk to sign, men and women, before copies were made and taken across the country. By the time the process was complete, a majority of the Scottish nobility and a third of the country's clergy had signed the covenant. Some did so in their own blood.

At first reading, the covenant's language appears conservatively worded, asserting its constitutionalism rather than revolutionary demands. This is at least partly misleading. Although it was largely drafted by the clergyman Alexander Hamilton in conjunction with Archibald Johnston of Wariston – a Calvinistic lawyer of the most unbending hue – it was designed to keep united all of the opponents of Charles's anglicizing policy. Given Presbyterianism's love of argument, this could not have been achieved if it had sought to prescribe a tightly defined doctrinal line beyond precedents already set. It nonetheless enshrined the central issue: that the Kirk's doctrine should be determined not by the monarch but by its own General Assembly and the Scottish Parliament.

In November 1638, the Kirk's General Assembly duly gathered in Glasgow without royal sanction. There it renounced both prayer book and bishops, and effectively declared ecclesiastic independence from royal interference. Protestant Scotland stood ready to defend the Calvinist settlement it had established in 1560. Charles would not tolerate such insubordination. 'So long as this Covenant is in force,' he had written five months previously, 'I have no more Power in Scotland than as a Duke of Venice.'

During 1639, the Covenanters raised a sizeable army, funded by two opposing factions – the Scots Kirk and the Scottish nobility – whom it had taken the king's monumental mishandling to finally bring together. In training as well as in morale, it was superior to the 18,000-strong force that Charles sent north to impose his theological will. A military stand-off ensued while Charles conceded the right of both the General Assembly and the Scottish Parliament to convene. The stalemate also granted him time to muster his resources. During the subsequent months, he took decisions that not only helped plunge his kingdoms into civil war but also ultimately sealed his own fate.

Since 1629, Charles had ruled without Parliament at Westminster but in 1640 the need to raise the taxes necessary to prosecute his Scottish campaign forced him to summon it again. When it proved hostile and unwilling to do his business, he quickly suspended it once more. Defeat soon turned to disaster when the Royalists lost a skirmish at Newburn, allowing the Scots Covenanter army to occupy Newcastle, from where they could block coal supplies. Charles was compelled to offer humiliating terms.

His authority was now crumbling in all three kingdoms. Conflict in Ireland and a second failure to receive parliamentary support at Westminster proved to be the prelude to the outbreak of the Civil War in 1642. The following year, the English Parliamentarians and the Scots Covenanters formed an alliance, called the 'Solemn League and Covenant'. In return for Scottish military assistance, Parliament promised to abolish episcopacy and reform the church in England and Ireland along Presbyterian lines. This assistance proved of great value, particularly at the Battle of Marston Moor in 1644. With Parliament's victory on the battlefield, its pledge to introduce Presbyterian reforms across Britain was honoured.

Although the Covenanters may not have recognized Charles I's right to guide their Church, they were opposed to his execution. With his death, they speedily endorsed his son, Charles II, as king of Scotland, provoking invasion and defeat at the hands of Oliver Cromwell's well-drilled soldiers. Further disappointment ensued. Upon his restoration, Charles II quickly showed himself no friend of Presbyterianism. In 1662, he re-established episcopalianism in Scotland as well as in England, and 300 ministers of the Kirk were removed. Barred from their churches, Covenanter clergy took to meeting clandestinely in outdoor 'Conventicles', risking prosecution and transportation.

In 1679, Greyfriars church again became the Covenanters' meeting ground when 1,200 of them were imprisoned in its kirkyard, pending trial. What ultimately saved their cause was William of Orange's victory in the Glorious Revolution. In 1690, Parliament finally re-established Presbyterianism as the governing theology of Scotland's Established Church.

1647
THE RECORD OF
THE PUTNEY DEBATES

THE NEW MODEL ARMY DEBATES UNIVERSAL
MANHOOD SUFFRAGE

Should all men by given the vote? Is property theft? These were the issues that shaped the ideologies of the nineteenth and twentieth centuries, but they were debated at a senior level long before they became the rallying calls of Victorian radicals or revolutionary Marxists. In 1647 they were seriously considered at Putney, when the New Model Army met to decide what to do with its victory in the Civil War.

The fact that power was by then in the hands of army officers demonstrated how far five years of warfare had undermined the traditional institutions of Crown and Parliament. Although civil war between King Charles I and his parliamentary opponents had broken out in 1642, it was not until the early, indifferent leadership of the earls of Essex and Manchester gave way to the more skilful generalship of Sir Thomas Fairfax and Oliver Cromwell that the Parliamentarians gained the upper hand. The highly trained New Model Army that Fairfax and Cromwell created proved to be far more than just a disciplined fighting force. Up from its ranks came a new cadre of men, often from artisan backgrounds, who were literate, sure of themselves and motivated by religious and political radicalism.

Parliamentarians whose war aims were limited to a mere clipping of royal excesses began wondering whether they had created a monster they could no longer control. In April 1645, the Self-Denying Ordinance was passed, preventing any MP or peer from holding command in the New Model Army. Oliver Cromwell, the MP for Cambridge, was one of the few politicians exempted from this prohibition on account of his obvious military ability. The stated intention was to prevent the squabbling of politicians from impairing the performance of the armed forces, but it also helped to sever the bond between Parliament and its soldiers. Civil war had transferred power to the barrel of the musket.

In June 1645, the New Model Army proved its effectiveness by crushing the Royalist forces at the Battle of Naseby. Bristol, England's second city, fell in September. Trapped at Oxford, Charles weighed his diminishing options and opted to surrender himself to the Scottish Covenanter forces at Newark in May 1646. In January 1647, the Scots handed him over to Parliament in return for £400,000. It was now up to the politicians to decide how far to take the revolution that the army had won for them. They soon found this prerogative questioned. Suspicious of the politicians' intentions, and angry at the arrears in their pay, the army set up its own General Council, composed of officers and 'agitators' elected from the ranks of common soldiers. Radicals in this General Council believed that they had a better mandate to shape the revolution settlement than those who sat, by grace of a limited franchise, at Westminster.

Frightened, Parliament tried to disband the army only to find it refusing to disperse. Indeed it made clear, ominously, that it was not 'a mere mercenary army, hired to serve an arbitrary power of state'. Seizing custody of the king, it marched on London. With these moves, the army appeared to hold all the cards: it had the weapons, the king, the capital and, with London, the funds. The issue was now what it should do with this power.

The circulation of rival demands indicated the gulf of opinion. The gentry members in the high command had taken up arms to prevent Charles I's destruction of what they viewed as the ancient constitution. They were not interested in the sweeping social and political reforms insisted upon by the more egalitarian-minded agitators, the Levellers. The latter claimed they had fought not merely to free the gentry from the constraints of royal power but for their own rights too. They wanted democracy, demanding that all men (women were not discussed) over the age of twenty-one should be given the vote to elect a new Parliament every two years.

In October and November 1647 the two sides slogged it out – with words rather than swords – when the Army Council met at St Mary's church in Putney, in today's South London. Fortunately, stenographers, led by William Clarke, were engaged to take the minutes and their transcripts (subsequently lost until being found at Worcester College, Oxford, in 1890) provide a detailed account of one of the most fundamental debates in British history.

The Levellers' argument was most eloquently put by Colonel Thomas Rainsborough, who insisted, 'I think that the poorest he that is in England hath a

From the Putney Debates, 1647

John Wildman

Our case is to be considered thus, that we have been under slavery. That's acknowledged by all. Our very laws were made by our conquerors; and whereas it's spoken much of chronicles, I conceive there is no credit to be given to any of them; and the reason is because those that were our lords, and made us their vassals, would suffer nothing else to be chronicled. We are now engaged for our freedom. That's the end of Parliaments: not to constitute what is already [established, but to act] according to the just rules of government. Every person in England hath as clear a right to elect his representative as the greatest person in England. I conceive that's the undeniable maxim of government: that all government is in the free consent of the people. If [so], then upon that account there is no person that is under a just government, or hath justly his own, unless he by his own free consent be put under that government. This he cannot be unless he be consenting to it, and therefore, according to this maxim, there is never a person in England [but ought to have a voice in elections]. If [this], as that gentleman says, be true, there are no laws that in this strictness and rigour of justice [any man is bound to], that are not made by those who[m] he doth consent to. And therefore I should humbly move, that if the question be stated — which would soonest bring things to an issue — it might rather be thus: Whether any person can justly be bound by law, who doth not give his consent that such persons shall make laws for him?

Commissary-General Henry Ireton

Let the question be so: Whether a man can be bound to any law that he doth not consent to? And I shall tell you, that he may and ought to be [bound to a law] that he doth not give a consent to, nor doth not choose any [to consent to]; and I will make it clear. If a foreigner come within this kingdom, if that stranger will have liberty [to dwell here] who hath no local interest here, he, as a man, it's true, hath air, [the passage of highways, the protection of laws, and all] that by nature; we must not expel [him from] our coasts, give him no being amongst us, nor kill him because he comes upon our land, comes up our stream, arrives at our shore. It is a piece of hospitality, of humanity, to receive that man amongst us. But if that man be received to a being amongst us, I think that man may very well be content to submit himself to the law of the land; that is, the law that is made by those people that have a property, a fixed property, in the land. I think, if any man will receive protection from this people though [neither] he nor his ancestors, not any betwixt him and

Adam, did ever give concurrence to this constitution, I think this man ought to be subject to those laws, and to be bound by those laws, so long as he continues amongst them. That is my opinion. A man ought to be subject to a law, that did not give his consent, but with this reservation, that if this man do think himself unsatisfied to be subject to this law he may go into another kingdom. And so the same reason doth extend, in my understanding, [to] that man that hath no permanent interest in the kingdom. If he hath money, his money is as good in another place as here; he hath nothing that doth locally fix him to this kingdom. If that man will live in this kingdom, or trade amongst us, that man ought to subject himself to the law made by the people who have the interest of this kingdom in them. And yet I do acknowledge that which you take to be so general a maxim, that in every kingdom, within every land, the original of power of making laws, of determining what shall be law in the land, does lie in the people — [but by the people is meant those] that are possessed of the permanent interest in the land. But whoever is extraneous to this, that is, as good a man in another land, that man ought to give such a respect to the property of men that live in the land. They do not determine [that I shall live in this land]. Why should I have any interest in determining what shall be the law of this land?

Major William Rainsborough

I think if it can be made to appear that it is a just and reasonable thing, and that it is for the preservation of all the [native] freeborn men, [that they should have an equal voice in election] — I think it ought to be made good unto them. And the reason is: that the chief end of this government is to preserve persons as well as estates, and if any law shall take hold of my person it is more dear than my estate.

Colonel Thomas Rainsborough

I do very well remember that the gentleman in the window [Colonel Rich] [said] that, if it were so, there were no propriety to be had, because five parts of [the nation], the poor people, are now excluded and would then come in. So one on the other side said [that], if [it were] otherwise, then rich men [only] shall be chosen. Then, I say, the one part shall make hewers of wood and drawers of water of the other five, and so the greatest part of the nation be enslaved. Truly I think we are still where we were; and I do not hear any argument given but only that it is the present law of the kingdom. I say still, what shall become of those many [men] that have laid out themselves for the Parliament of England in this present war, that have ruined themselves by fighting, by hazarding all they had? They are Englishmen. They have now nothing to say for themselves.

life to live, as the greatest he; and therefore truly, sir, I think it's clear, that every man that is to live under a government ought first by his own consent to put himself under that government.' The notion was anathema to Cromwell and his son-in-law, General Henry Ireton, who did not see why those without what Ireton called 'an interest or share' (in other words, property and commerce) should frame the laws of those who did have such a stake. Here was the crux of what became – 200 years later – the defining issue of parliamentary reform in the nineteenth century: was the franchise a universal right or a trust placed in those responsible for business and property?

Rainsborough denied Ireton's assertion that he intended anarchy. However, the Utopian, proto-communist statements of some of the Levellers were sufficient to convince moderates that a society of complete equality was their aim. Indeed, an extreme Leveller movement, 'the Diggers', was poised to begin occupying enclosed land and claiming it as the common property of all. It was a fate that Colonel Nathaniel Rich foresaw if Rainsborough's demands for democracy were met, since, he said, in an electorate in which servants greatly outnumbered masters, 'It may happen, that the majority may by law, not in a confusion, destroy property; there may be a law enacted, that there shall be an equality of goods and estates.'

Cromwell tired of a discussion that seemed to be extending the scope for future division rather than solving the immediate concerns – not least what to do with the king, whose brief escape from custody provided a timely reason to bring the conference to a close before it had reached agreement. The Putney Debates were duly postponed and although the Army Council met again in January 1648, the experiment in army democracy was ended – although the arguments raised continued to resonate for centuries to come.

During 1648, the gentry officers remained in control and Rainsborough was killed while besieging Pontefract. In May 1649, an attempted mutiny by army agitators was put down at Burford. However, by then, one of their most arresting demands had been realized: England was a republic.

1649

THE DEATH WARRANT
OF KING CHARLES I

THE EXECUTION OF THE KING

Victorious in the Second Civil War, the Parliamentarian forces took Charles I captive. Whatever hopes may have been entertained that he could be prevailed upon to accept terms for an enduring peace were undermined by his duplicity and efforts to escape. Furthermore, some of his more war-weary opponents were now suspected of being over-ready to compromise. New divisions had opened up because the war had made the army, not Parliament, the greatest power in the land. Influential army officers were concerned that Westminster's politicians might negotiate away the rights that the soldiers believed they had won with their swords. Beheading the king seemed the surest way of avoiding defeat being snatched from the jaws of victory.

Creating the enabling legal process proved difficult, as insufficient support existed for it in Parliament. Thus, to get the necessary numbers, soldiers were posted at Westminster to forcibly exclude those MPs assumed to be hostile. Shorn of the vast majority of its members, the resulting 'Rump Parliament' duly passed an ordinance bringing the king to trial. The opposition of the House of Lords was overcome by ignoring it altogether. In this way, those who had championed the rights of Parliament got their own way by subverting the laws of Parliament.

Trial proceedings began on 20 January 1649 in Westminster Hall. The charges against the king – now ominously described as 'Charles Stuart' – included that he 'hath traitorously and maliciously levied war against the present Parliament, and the people therein represented'. The case was to be heard by 135 commissioners, sitting as a High Court of Justice, although less than half of them had agreed to serve. The verdict was scarcely in doubt. The trial lasted for seven days during which Charles refused to recognize the court's legitimacy and, in turn, was not permitted to address it at length.

Charles I's death warrant is depicted in the third plate section.

THE CIVIL WARS

The First Civil War

1642

22 August Charles I raises his standard at Nottingham, declaring war on Parliament.
23 October The first major battle at Edgehill in Warwickshire ends in a stalemate.

1643

26 July Royalists take England's second city, Bristol.
20 September Parliamentary forces under the earl of Essex win the first Battle of Newbury.
25 September The Solemn League and Covenant creates an alliance between Parliament and the Scots Covenanters.

1644

2 July At Marston Moor, west of York, the Royalist forces are heavily defeated by a combined Scots and Parliamentarian force and Oliver Cromwell demonstrates his ability as a cavalry commander.
22 October The second Battle of Newbury ends in a draw.

1645

6 January Parliament creates a full-time professional force, the New Model Army, under the command of Sir Thomas Fairfax.
14 June The decisive battle of the war is fought at Naseby in Northamptonshire, where Royalist forces are crushed.
11 September Parliamentarian forces retake Bristol.
13 September The marquess of Montrose's Royalist army in Scotland is defeated at the Battle of Philiphaugh.

1646

6 May Charles I hands himself over to the Scots at Newark.
24 June Oxford, the Royalist capital, surrenders.

1647

30 January The Scots hand Charles I over to Parliament. He escapes in November to the Isle of Wight.

The Second Civil War

1648

17 August Cromwell defeats a joint Scots–Royalist invading force at Preston.
19 December Charles I is arrested by the army and returned to London.

1649

30 January Following a swift trial, Charles I is executed.

The Third Civil War

11 September During his Irish campaign, Cromwell's forces massacre the garrison at Drogheda.

1650

3 September Cromwell routs, at Dunbar, the Scottish army loyal to Prince Charles.

1651

3 September Royalist and Scottish forces are defeated by Cromwell at Worcester.
13 October Prince Charles flees to France.

He was sentenced on 27 January. It remains a point of dispute among historians whether the warrant for his execution had been drawn up shortly before or immediately after the sentencing. Certainly, blanks were left for the date and place of execution to be filled in later, and the names of two of the three army officers to whom the warrant was issued had to be changed. It has been speculated that this was because two of the original choices refused to be involved, although authoritative evidence is lacking that the regicides had already begun signing their names even before sentence was passed. Nonetheless, not all the signatures (which were accompanied by individual seals in red wax) were written in a single session. There was a short delay after the first twenty-eight had been added and it was subsequently suggested that some of the second batch of regicides appended their names under duress. It would certainly be convenient for them to later make this claim.

Fifty-nine of the commissioners who had pronounced Charles guilty signed the warrant. The first to sign was John Bradshaw, the presiding judge at the trial. Oliver Cromwell signed third. Other notable Parliamentarian commanders who followed

Contemporary engraving of Charles I's execution outside his Banqueting Hall in Whitehall.

included Henry Ireton (who was Cromwell's son-in-law), John Hutchinson and Thomas Harrison. Noticeable absentees included the army's commander-in-chief, Sir Thomas Fairfax, who had fought to uphold the rights of Parliament, not to kill the king.

On 30 January, Charles duly stepped out through a window of the Banqueting House at Whitehall onto a specially erected scaffold. He was allowed a farewell statement to the public spectators, although his voice did not carry far enough beyond the deep ranks of soldiers encircling the stage. He assured them of his innocence without reneging on the belief in divine right that had got him and his realm into much of the trouble in the first place. 'A subject and a sovereign are clean different things,' he maintained, before announcing that 'I go from a corruptible to an incorruptible Crown.' When the axe severed his head, the crowd responded not with a cheer but a groan. It was an early sign that his enemies had succeeded only in making a martyr out of him.

Within eleven years the republic that replaced Charles's kingship had foundered. At the monarchy's restoration in 1660, the Convention Parliament passed an Act of Indemnity and Oblivion, offering a general pardon to those who had taken up arms against the late king. The exceptions were the regicides. Of the fifty-nine who had signed the death warrant, thirty-nine were still alive. Some sensibly fled, either to the continent or to the American colonies. Those the state could get its hands on were all either executed or imprisoned for life, save for Richard Ingoldsby. Alone of the captured regicides, he escaped punishment when his claim to have signed under duress was accepted.

After execution, Charles I's remains had been interred next to those of Henry VIII in the vault of St George's Chapel at Windsor Castle. With the Restoration, however, the bodies of Cromwell and Ireton were disinterred from Westminster Abbey and, along with the remains of Bradshaw, were publicly hanged and desecrated. Like that of Charles I, Cromwell's head was severed from its body. It was placed on a pike outside Westminster Hall, where it remained for over twenty years, not finding a final resting place until 1960 when it was laid to rest at his old college, Sidney Sussex, Cambridge. Even then, over 300 years after the Civil War, it was deemed safest if the sole identifiable remains of the great regicide should lie in an unmarked grave.

1653

THE INSTRUMENT
OF GOVERNMENT

BRITAIN'S FIRST – AND SHORT-LIVED –
WRITTEN CONSTITUTION

On 4 January 1649, the House of Commons adopted a revolutionary philosophy, voting:

> That the people are, under God, the original of all just power: ... that the commons of England, in parliament assembled, being chosen by, and representing, the people, have the supreme power in this nation: ... that whatsoever is enacted, or declared for law, by the commons, in parliament assembled, hath the force of law; and all the people of this nation are concluded thereby, although the consent and concurrence of king, or house of peers be not had thereunto.

Within weeks, the king had been executed and the Commons had moved 'that the house of peers in parliament is useless and dangerous, and ought to be abolished'. This assertion was carried into law on 19 March, two days after the legislation was passed formally created a republic.

The reality fell short of what was implied by these highly democratic proclamations. The House of Commons may have gained untrammelled legislative power, but its claim to represent 'the people' was a nonsense. It merely consisted of those MPs whose perceived ideological purity to the revolution meant the army had permitted them to attend. Rather than submit themselves to the popular will, the surviving MPs contrived every means possible to prevent the calling of a general election. Eventually, Oliver Cromwell, tiring of their self-serving ways, marched his troops into the Commons chamber on 20 April 1653 and closed Parliament down.

From the Instrument of Government, 1653

The government of the Commonwealth of England, Scotland, and Ireland, and the dominions thereunto belonging.

I. That the supreme legislative authority of the Commonwealth of England, Scotland, and Ireland, and the dominions thereunto belonging, shall be and reside in one person, and the people assembled in Parliament; the style of which person shall be the Lord Protector of the Commonwealth of England, Scotland, and Ireland.

II. That the exercise of the chief magistracy and the administration of the government over the said countries and dominions, and the people thereof, shall be in the Lord Protector, assisted with a council, the number whereof shall not exceed twenty-one, nor be less than thirteen.

III. That all writs, processes, commissions, patents, grants, and other things, which now run in the name and style of the keepers of the liberty of England by authority of Parliament, shall run in the name and style of the Lord Protector, from whom, for the future, shall be derived all magistracy and honours in these three nations; and have the power of pardons (except in case of murders and treason) and benefit of all forfeitures for the public use; and shall govern the said countries and dominions in all things by the advice of the council, and according to these presents and the laws.

IV. That the Lord Protector, the Parliament sitting, shall dispose and order the militia and forces, both by sea and land, for the peace and good of the three nations, by consent of Parliament; and that the Lord Protector, with the advice and consent of the major part of the council, shall dispose and order the militia for the ends aforesaid in the intervals of Parliament.

V. That the Lord Protector, by the advice aforesaid, shall direct in all things concerning the keeping and holding of a good correspondency with foreign kings, princes, and states; and also, with the consent of the major part of the council, have the power of war and peace.

VI. That the laws shall not be altered, suspended, abrogated, or repealed, nor any new law made, nor any tax, charge, or imposition laid upon the people, but by common consent in Parliament, save only as is expressed in the thirtieth article.

VII. That there shall be a Parliament summoned to meet at Westminster upon the third day of September, 1654, and that successively a Parliament shall be summoned once in every third year, to be accounted from the dissolution of the present Parliament.

VIII. That neither the Parliament to be next summoned, nor any successive Parliaments, shall, during the time of five months, to be accounted from the day of their first meeting, be adjourned, prorogued, or dissolved, without their own consent. . . .

XIII. That the Sheriff, who shall wittingly and willingly make any false return, or neglect his duty, shall incur the penalty of 2000 marks of lawful English money; the one moiety to the Lord Protector, and the other moiety to such person as will sue for the same.

XIV. That all and every person and persons, who have aided, advised, assisted, or abetted in any war against the Parliament, since the first day of January, 1641 (unless they have been since in the service of the Parliament, and given signal testimony of their good affection thereunto) shall be disabled and incapable to be elected, or to give any vote in the election of any members to serve in the next Parliament, or in the three succeeding Triennial Parliaments.

XV. That all such, who have advised, assisted, or abetted the rebellion of Ireland, shall be disabled and incapable for ever to be elected, or give any vote in the election of any member to serve in Parliament; as also all such who do or shall profess the Roman Catholic religion.

XVI. That all votes and elections given or made contrary, or not according to these qualifications, shall be null and void; and if any person, who is hereby made incapable, shall give his vote for election of members to serve in Parliament, such person shall lose and forfeit one full year's value of his real estate, and one full third part of his personal estate; one moiety thereof to the Lord Protector, and the other moiety to him or them who shall sue for the same.

XVII. That the persons who shall be elected to serve in Parliament, shall be such (and no other than such) as are persons of known integrity, fearing God, and of good conversation, and being of the age of twenty-one years.

XVIII. That all and every person and persons seised or possessed to his own use, of any estate, real or personal, to the value of £200, and not within the aforesaid exceptions, shall be capable to elect members to serve in Parliament for counties.

In its place, the army selected 140 persons it deemed sufficiently 'fearing God and of approved fidelity and honesty' to sit as a wholly nominated Parliament. The resulting assembly was a peculiar mixture of religious zealots, unworldly dreamers and traditional landed gentry. A legislature thus contrived was unlikely to hold firm in the turbulent climate of post-Civil War Britain. Nine months later, on 12 December 1653, this Parliament of nominees recognized that it was already out of its very limited depth and resigned.

Four days later, Cromwell endorsed the Instrument of Government, Britain's first written constitution. Drawn up by Major-General John Lambert and a small group of army officers, it vested power in Cromwell as head of state with the title of 'Lord Protector'. He would lead a Council of State, whose first fifteen members were named in the instrument. Both Lord Protector and council were vested with executive authority and also given the power to make legislation, except when Parliament was called. For its part, Parliament should meet for at least five months following general elections, which were to be held every three years. The old suffrage requirements remained in the boroughs but in the counties a new uniform prerequisite was created, with the vote given to persons (men) with property valued at £200 or more. The vote, however, would be denied, for the next four general elections, to those who had fought for the Royalists, and to Catholics eternally. Toleration was shown to all religions 'provided this liberty be not extended to Popery or Prelacy'.

The Instrument of Government created not just a reformed English Parliament but one that for the first time represented the whole British Isles. Sitting with the 400 English and Welsh MPs were to be thirty Irish and thirty Scottish MPs. The (as it transpired, premature) parliamentary union of England, Scotland and Ireland was accompanied by other measures to break down the barriers between the formerly separate nations, including the introduction of free trade between them. Such benefits, however, did not compensate for the grievances felt by Scots towards the new regime being imposed upon them, nor to the native Irish, most of whose land had been confiscated and their Catholic religion proscribed.

The instrument aimed to create rule by a head of state working through a unicameral Parliament or, for those times when the Commons were not sitting, the Council of State. Parliament retained tax-approving powers and the Lord Protector could only briefly delay, not veto, legislation. As part of the intended checks and balances, neither the executive nor the legislature was given total control of the armed forces. However, compared to the democratic and socialist demands heard at the Putney Debates and from the Levellers, it was a conservative document. The vote was entrusted to gentlemen with sufficient wealth. It was by no means the right of all.

What was more, the state would brook no dissent. In 1655, England and Wales was divided into eleven cantons, each administered by a major-general. In this way, military government was established in peacetime, with the army being used not merely to help maintain civil order and collect taxes but to impose Puritan dictates on private behaviour – shutting down theatres and other places of entertainment and punishing not just lewdness but even minor, harmless, levity among the populace. When in the 1656 general election the country protested by returning MPs opposed to this new order, the Council of State disallowed about one hundred members whom it considered particularly hostile from taking their seats. A further sixty MPs refused to attend in protest at this travesty of democracy.

Like the rule of the major-generals, the Instrument of Government did not last long. It was replaced in May 1657 by the Humble Petition and Advice. This new constitution sought to re-create some of the familiar institutions of the past without reinstalling the Stuarts and their supporters to run them. Most controversially, it proposed reviving the monarchy, offering the Crown to Cromwell. He refused it but accepted the right to choose his eventual successor (who, with kingly assumption, proved to be his son, Richard). The document revived the House of Lords and recast the Council of State as the Privy Council, personnel for which were to be chosen by Cromwell and subject to ratification by MPs. The forty-one men who were sworn into the new House of Lords were largely country gentry and army officers, plus seven members of Cromwell's own family.

These developments simultaneously infuriated genuine revolutionaries while lacking the sort of tradition-conferring legitimacy that appealed to admirers of the pre-Civil War institutions. In reality, the regime was more truly held together by the unique personality of its head of state than had been the case with any previous crowned monarch. Consequently when Cromwell died in September 1658, the republican experiment – or rather experiments – quickly fell apart, succumbing to the restored royal house of Stuart without a fight.

1656

MENASSEH BEN ISRAEL'S HUMBLE PETITION TO THE LORD PROTECTOR

THE READMISSION OF JEWS TO BRITAIN

The Jews were a small but important community in early medieval England. They dominated finance because the Church's stance on usury – charging interest on credit – effectively prohibited Christians from being moneylenders, a position that lasted, with various qualifications and exceptions, until the Reformation. This made Jews both indispensable sources of credit and easy targets for abuse from those struggling to pay their debts. Subject to increasing restrictions and periodic violence, Jews were banned from practising usury by King Edward I in 1275. Worse was to follow. In 1290, having first granted them a compensatory pay-out, the king expelled them from the kingdom.

During the following 350 years, there were officially no Jews in England or Wales. (They were never formally banned from Scotland, although there is scant evidence of them residing there in any numbers.) In truth, a few Sephardic (Spanish and Portuguese) Jews were, unofficially, living and working in seventeenth-century London. The pretence was maintained that they were 'Marrano' Jews, those who had converted to Christianity, but the reality was that in 1657 they opened a secret synagogue in Creechurch Lane. Nonetheless, their numbers were tiny and their status precarious.

This might have remained the situation had not a strand of Puritan thought, British economic self-interest and the theological views of a Dutch rabbi coincided in 1655. With the title 'Lord Protector', the British republic's head of state was Oliver Cromwell. The government executive was the Council of State with John Thurloe as its secretary. Both Cromwell and Thurloe favoured readmitting the Jews, partly as an issue of religious toleration and also as a means of tapping into the financial acumen that Amsterdam's Jews were providing for the Dutch Republic.

Believing it imminent, Puritan millenarians eagerly anticipated the Second Coming which they thought would be prefaced by the conversion of the Jews and their return to Zion. Their arrival, first, in Britain would be a step along this path. Meanwhile, Menasseh Ben Israel (1604–57), an Amsterdam rabbi and publisher, believed that the Messiah would come when Jewish populations could be found in every country of the world. Thus he too wanted them to settle in Britain (he was already under the impression that some American Indians were, in fact, the lost ten tribes of Israel).

THE JEWISH POPULATION IN BRITAIN 1070–1900

1070 William the Conqueror invites Jewish merchants from Rouen to lend money and settle in England.

1144 In Norwich, the first 'blood libel' charge is made against Jews for ritual sacrifice.

1194 Richard the Lionheart orders the Ordinance of the Jewry, a record of all Jewish money transactions.

1218 Pope Innocent III's instruction that all Jews should wear identifying badges is instituted.

1253 Jews are prevented from moving to towns where they are not already established.

1255 The 'Hugh of Lincoln' blood libel gains popular credence.

1264 York's Jewish community is massacred by a mob.

1265 The Crown starts transferring its financial business from Jewish to Italian bankers.

1269 Jews are denied the right to hold property or inherit money.

1275 Edward I's *Statutum de Judaismo* forbids Jews to loan money with interest.

1290 Edward I expels Jews from England in perpetuity. Between 4,000 and 16,000 are forced into exile.

1494 There is evidence of small numbers of Portuguese Jews, nominally converted Christians, privately practising their true faith in England.

1655 The readmission of Jews is debated by the Whitehall Conference.

1657 A synagogue is opened in Creechurch Lane in the City of London.

1664 Charles II promises his protection to English Jews.

1698 The Act of Suppressing Blasphemy confirms that practising the Jewish faith is legal. There are believed to be about 400 Jews in Britain.

1701 Bevis Marks Synagogue is opened in the City of London.

1809 George III's sons, the dukes of Cambridge, Cumberland and Sussex attend a service in the Great Synagogue in Duke's Place, London.

1858 Jews are permitted to take their seats in the Houses of Parliament.

1881 The Jewish population of 48,000 swells to 250,000 by 1914, due largely to Ashkenazi Jews emigrating from Russia and Eastern Europe.

In 1655, Menasseh Ben Israel arrived in London and was granted an audience with Cromwell. Sympathetic to his cause, Cromwell convened the Whitehall Conference, made up of lawyers, theologians and merchants, to discuss Jewish readmittance. In December, the conference broke up without agreement. The theologians were divided and the merchants – fearful of competition – hostile. The legal opinion, however, was favourable. John Glynne, lord chief justice of the Upper Bench, and William Steele, chief baron of the Exchequer, maintained that Edward I's royal edict of expulsion not only had no legislative force but had never been ratified by Parliament. Historians are unclear as to exactly what was agreed. John Evelyn was certain that it meant Jews had legal protection to settle, writing in his diary for 14 December 1655, 'Now were the Jews admitted.'

The following year, Britain went to war with Spain. One of those whose goods were impounded as a result was the Jewish merchant Antonio Rodrigues Robles. Actually of Portuguese descent, he took the matter to court, claiming he was Jewish not Spanish. For some of London's covert Jewish community, the case was a source of unwelcome publicity. There was, however, no further hiding place when, in March 1656, Menasseh headed a list of Jewish signatories in a formal petition, requesting protection and a place to bury their dead. While Cromwell referred the petition to the Council of State, the court delivered an ambiguous verdict that, nevertheless, returned Robles's possessions to him.

The combined effect of these developments was to demonstrate that London's Jewish community openly existed and was not prosecuted for doing so. No formal statement of readmittance was issued and Menasseh returned to Amsterdam, believing that his mission had been a failure (he was so poor that he had to beg Cromwell for the money to travel home with the body of his son who had passed away in London). He was given an annual £100 state pension but died on his way back to Amsterdam. The legality of Jewish settlement in Britain was affirmed by Charles II. Turning down appeals to have them formally banished again, he promised them his protection. They began worshipping openly, in 1701 opening the Bevis Marks synagogue. Nor were they slow in demonstrating their loyalty to their adopted home. During both the American War of Independence and the Napoleonic Wars, London's Jewish community fasted for British victory.

They also assisted Britain in more practical ways, making an incalculable contribution towards establishing the dominance of the City of London as the world's financial centre. In the panic of 1745, London's Jews enlisted for the capital's military defence against the expected Jacobite attack and Samson Gideon provided valuable funds to shore up Hanoverian rule. Adopting his mother's Christian religion, his son became an MP and in 1789 was rewarded with an Irish peerage.

Despite these services to the state, the path to full acceptance was not a smooth one. In 1754 popular disapproval forced Parliament to scrap new legislation allowing Jews to seek British naturalization. Many Jewish fathers opted to have their children

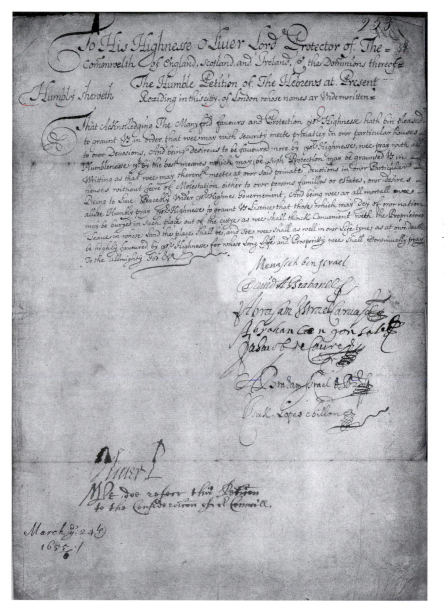

Ben Israel's humble petition on behalf of his fellow Jews. Cromwell has signed it 'Oliver P', the initial standing for his title, 'Protector'.

christened, among them the twelve-year-old Benjamin Disraeli, subsequently leader of the Conservative Party and prime minister in 1868 and 1874–80.

The first practising Jew to be given a baronetcy was the financier and promoter of University College London, Isaac Lyon Goldsmid, in 1841. David Salomons became lord mayor of London in 1855. Despite the election of Lionel Rothschild in 1847 and David Salomons in 1851, the parliamentary oath required members to profess the Christian faith and therefore prevented Jews from taking up their seats in the House of Commons. They were finally allowed to do so in 1858. The first practising Jewish government minister was appointed in 1871 and the first judge in 1873.

By this time, the Jewish population of Britain was around 50,000 and heavily concentrated in London. Eight years later there began the wide-scale migration of Ashkenazi Jews, fleeing the poverty and pogroms of Eastern Europe and Russia. Between 1881 and 1914, about 150,000 of them arrived in Britain, soon forming a distinctive community in Stepney in the capital's East End, where a disproportionate number worked as tailors.

This influx quickly became contentious, not only among anti-Semites but also among many settled Jews who looked down upon the far poorer Lithuanian, Polish or Russian new arrivals. Legislation in 1905 barred a right of entry to immigrants with criminal records or a history of destitution, while further measures in 1919 and 1920 prevented them settling if they could not prove they had the means of support. Some who did not want Jewish immigration in large numbers in Britain made common cause with the Zionist movement in hoping Jews would instead settle in Palestine. However, by the end of the 1930s the British government (which held the League of Nations Mandate to administer Palestine) curtailed the flow of settlers there in the face of mounting Arab opposition.

Meanwhile, the Cabinet had responded to Hitler's rise to power in 1933 by a gentle relaxation of the rules governing entry to Britain after the leaders of the Jewish community agreed to shoulder the financial responsibility of those arriving without jobs. About 30,000 came from Central and Eastern Europe over the following five years. Neville Chamberlain's government loosened the criteria again in 1938, to the particular benefit of those aged under seventeen who were allowed to enter the country without visas or parents. Even with these concessions in place, only a further 25,000 Jews (9,000 of them, children) were able to flee to Britain in 1939, before the outbreak of the calamitous war that annihilated around 6 million of those they had left behind.

1660
MEMORANDUM FOR THE ROYAL SOCIETY

THE ADVANCEMENT OF SCIENCE IN THE AGE OF BOYLE, HOOKE AND NEWTON

The Royal Society of London for the Improvement of Natural Knowledge is the oldest scientific society in the world to have enjoyed a continuous existence. Since its foundation in 1660, it has been Britain's premier academy of sciences, promoting research, bringing together leading minds and facilitating the cross-fertilization of ideas that have shaped scientific understanding. It was through the Royal Society that many of Robert Boyle's chemical discoveries and Isaac Newton's universal laws were first disseminated.

Its founding members had met regularly, if informally, in Oxford and London since the 1640s. On 28 November 1660, they gathered at Gresham College to hear a lecture by Christopher Wren, an astronomer as well as a pre-eminent architect. At the meeting's conclusion, twelve of them – including Wren and Boyle, Sir Robert Moray and John Wilkins – decided to found a 'Colledge for the promoting of Physico-Mathematicall Experimentall Learning'. With the patronage of King Charles II, it was incorporated as the Royal Society in 1662. A second charter extended its privileges in 1663 and a third charter of 1669 granted it land. Always independent, it benefited from royal patronage without coming under state control. It essentially started as a forum for thinkers to meet, confer and crystallize ideas at a moment when Britain found itself blessed by a generation of pioneering geniuses whose interests ranged widely across what would subsequently come to be regarded as distinctly separate academic disciplines.

No less important than bringing together Britain's eminent men (women became Fellows only in 1945), the Royal Society also fostered correspondence between the leading scientists in Europe and beyond. This began to be published in March 1665 as *Philosophical Transactions: Giving Some Account of the Present Undertakings,*

THE SCIENTIFIC REVOLUTION

1614 John Napier publishes his work on logarithms for calculation.

1628 William Harvey's *De Moto Cordis* explains the circulation of the blood.

1659 Robert Boyle and Robert Hooke test the properties of air with their 'pneumatical engine' air pump.

1660 The Royal Society is founded in London.

1661 Robert Boyle's *Sceptical Chymist* is published.

1662 Boyle produces his law of ideal gas, showing the inverse proportionality of pressure and volume.

1665 *Philosophical Transactions of the Royal Society*, the world's first 'peer-reviewed' scientific journal, is published.

1665 Robert Hooke's *Micrographia* is published, detailing his observations through microscopy.

1666 Isaac Newton begins work on the development of the Calculus.

1668 Newton builds the first practical reflecting telescope.

1676–8 Hooke elaborates his law of elasticity.

1687 Newton's *Principia Mathematica* explains his laws of motion and universal gravitation.

1704 Newton's *Optiks* is published, popularizing his experiments in colour and light diffraction.

Studies and Labours of the Ingenious in Many Considerable Parts of the World. In the process the Royal Society effectively created modern notions of scientific publishing and peer review, making English rather than Latin the primary language in which science and mathematics were promoted and discussed. The *Philosophical Transactions* remains a publication of international renown to this day, divided since the 1880s into two series, one concerning mathematics, physics and engineering sciences and the other biology.

Many of the Royal Society's early weekly meetings were devoted to performing and discussing experiments. Robert Hooke (1635–1702), the polymath inventor and researcher into optics and gravitation, was appointed 'Curator of Experiments'. At the time, not everyone appreciated the significance of what was being examined. For all King Charles's support of the society, the diarist Samuel Pepys (1633–1703; he was its president from 1684 to 1686) noted that His Majesty 'mightily laughed' at it 'for spending time only in weighing of ayre, and doing nothing else since they sat'. In fact, the investigations being made into atmospheric pressure had considerable value as, in time, the power of steam to transform the world would show.

Besides creating a celebrated library for its members' consultation, the Royal Society published, or paid for the printing of, important contributions to learning. It began by publishing John Evelyn's *Sylva* (a treatise on forest management) and Hooke's *Micrographia*, an extraordinary work of microscopic observations. In 1672, Isaac Newton (1642–1727), Professor of Mathematics at Cambridge, was elected a Fellow and in April 1686 he presented the first part of his *Philosophiae Naturalis Principia Mathematica* to the Royal Society. With its explanation of the basic laws governing physical forces, the *Principia* was immediately recognized as a seminal

From the first journal book of the Royal Society, 1660

Memorandum that Novemb[er] 28 1660. These persons following according to the usuall Custome of most of them, mett together at Gresham Colledge to hear Mr Wrens Lecture, viz The Lord Brouncker, Mr Boyle, Mr Bruce, Sir Robert Moray, Sir Paul Neile, Dr Wilkins, Dr Goddard, Dr Petty, Mr Ball, Mr Rooke, Mr Wren, Mr Hill. And after the Lecture was ended they did according to the usuall Manner, withdrawe for mutuall converse. Where amongst other matters that were discoursed of, Something was offered about a designe of founding a Colledge for the Promoting of Physico-Mathematicall Experimentall Learning.

And because they had these frequent occasions of meeting wth one another, it was proposed that some course might be thought of to improve this meeting to a more regular way of debating things, & according to the Manner in other Countries, where there were voluntary associations of men into Academies for the advancement of various parts of learning, So they might doe something answerable here for the promoting of Experimentall Philosophy.

In order to which it was agreed, that this Company would continue their weekly meetings on wensday at 3 of the clock in the Tearme time at Mr Rookes Chamber at Gresham Colledge. In the vacation at Mr Balls Chamber in the Temple. And towards the defraying of occasionall expenses, every one should at his first admission, pay downe ten shillings, & besides engage to pay one shilling weekly, whether present or absent, whilest he shall please to keep his relation to this company.

contribution and the Society's council declared that 'Mr Newton's work should be printed forthwith.' Embarrassingly, the funds allocated for publishing had already been spent for the year – on a history of fish – so it fell to another Fellow of the Society, the astronomer Edmund Halley (1656–1742), to defray the cost of bringing out one of the greatest opuses in the history of science. Given its author's hesitancy to put his observations into print, this support and encouragement was important. Newton served as the Royal Society's president from 1703 until his death.

THE CLARENDON CODE

THE PENALTIES FOR DISSENTING FROM
THE ESTABLISHED CHURCH

The Clarendon Code was a series of statutes passed by Parliament in the immediate aftermath of the monarchy's restoration. The aim was to exclude Puritans from playing an active part in religious and public life. During the 1650s Anglicanism had suffered a similar fate as befell its supreme governor, Charles I. In alliance with Scottish Presbyterians, Parliament had abolished episcopacy during the Civil War. Meanwhile, toleration of most Protestant sects was introduced. Paradoxically, this widening of religious liberty often had the consequence of emboldening the more intolerant forms of Puritanism. The repression of essentially harmless activities and traditions that were not explicitly condoned in the Bible (including, in some cities, the celebration of Christmas) did much to give the name Puritan its pejorative, killjoy connotations.

During the life of the English republic, about 2,000 of the 9,000 church benefices were held by Puritans. In many cases, they had gained their benefices from traditional Anglican clergy who had been forced into hiding or exile.

With the Crown's restoration in 1660, one of the first tasks was to decide the Church of England's future form. Not all Puritans were necessarily opposed to a state Church so long as it either followed Presbyterian principles or readopted bishops only in a heavily modified role acceptable to moderate Puritan opinion. The talks broke down without agreement, and in consequence episcopacy was revived. With Parliament devising means to restore the displaced Anglican clergy to their former benefices, the incumbent Puritans were faced with a stark choice: accept the readoption of the old Anglican doctrine and liturgy, or get out.

The new king, Charles II, was not personally devout and had no reason to indulge a narrow view of Anglican triumphalism. After all, he owed his life to English Catholic sympizers and foreign Catholic powers. Like Elizabeth I at her accession just over one hundred years previously, Charles II's instincts were

From the Corporation Act, 1661

III. That all persons who upon the four and twentieth day of December one thousand six hundred sixty and one shall be mayors, aldermen, recorders, bailiffs, town clerks, common council men and other persons then bearing any office or offices of magistracy, or places or trust or other employment relating to or concerning the government of the said respective cities, corporations and boroughs, and cinque ports and their members and other port towns, shall, at any time before the five and twentieth day of March one thousand six hundred and sixty and three, when they shall be thereunto required by the said respective commissioners or any three or more of them, take the oath of allegiance and supremacy and this oath following:

I, A. B., do declare and believe that it is not lawful upon any pretence whatsoever to take arms against the king, and that I do abhor that traitorous position of taking arms by his authority against his person, or against those that are commissioned by him. So help me God.

And also at the same time shall publicly subscribe before the said commissioners or any three of them this following declaration:

I, A. B., do declare that I hold that there lies no obligation upon me or any other person from the oath commonly called the Solemn League and Covenant, and that the same was in itself an unlawful oath, and imposed upon the subjects of this realm against the known laws and liberties of the kingdom. . . .

IX. Provided also, and be it enacted . . . that from and after the expiration of the said commissions no person or persons shall forever hereafter be placed, elected or chosen in or to any the offices or places aforesaid that shall not have within one year next before such election or choice taken the sacrament of the Lord's Supper according to the rites of the Church of England, and that every such person and persons so placed, elected or chosen shall likewise take the aforesaid three oaths and subscribe the said declaration at the same time when the oath for the due execution of the said places and offices respectively shall be administered; and in default hereof every such placing, election and choice is hereby enacted and declared to be void.

*Edward Hyde,
earl of Clarendon
(1609–74).*

for a doctrinally broad-based Established Church. In this, he had the support of his lord chancellor, Edward Hyde, earl of Clarendon. In contrast, Parliament – bent upon punishing past Puritan excesses – was less prepared to be so accommodating and wanted a Church settlement that divided and ruled. Clarendon duly found himself lending his name to laws that went further than either he or his royal master intended.

The 1661 Corporation Act forced town officials to swear an oath of allegiance to the king. This was to be expected, but it also required them to take Anglican communion. What was more, the Act of Uniformity the following year instilled a form of Anglicanism noxious to most Puritans. Having been banned during the republic, the Book of Common Prayer was reintroduced as the only Church liturgy. All clergy had to be ordained by a bishop and subscribe to the Thirty-Nine Articles. Rather than comply, about 2,000 clergymen, mostly Baptists, Presbyterians and independents, resigned their livings. Initially referred to as Dissenters, they were later known as Nonconformists.

Not content to drive them out of the Established Church, the Clarendon Code was also determined to prevent them publicly practising their beliefs at all. Although the Dissenters' faith was acknowledged as lawful, it was to be conducted in private. The 1664 and 1670 Conventicle Acts made it an offence (punishable by a fine or imprisonment) to attend a service of worship that did not use the Book of Common Prayer. The 1665 Five Mile Act prevented dissenting ministers from living within five miles of either their former parish or of any corporate town, unless they first swore an oath of non-resistance. A separate statute, the 1662 Quaker Act, imprisoned more than 1,000 Quakers for their beliefs.

What the Clarendon Code did to Dissenters, the 1673 and 1678 Test Acts did to Roman Catholics. The Test Acts barred Catholics from accepting military or civil office and prevented them from sitting in Parliament. An exception was made for James, duke of York, the heir presumptive to the throne, who had converted to Catholicism. He survived a protracted 'Exclusion Crisis' in which 'Tory' politicians upheld his right and 'Whigs' unsuccessfully tried to block his right to succeed. This dividing issue is often seen as one of the milestones in the creation of Westminster's two-party system.

Taken together, these measures aimed at ending the strife and upheavals of the Civil War period by creating an Anglican state for an Anglican people. Not only were the official churches only for Anglicans, so were the schools and the two universities. Undoubtedly, the legislation had some success in quelling the scale and visibility of dissent, but it also produced unintended consequences. Unable to enter public life or take part in formal education, the Protestant Dissenters did their own thing and found more profitable avenues to explore. Disproportionate to their numbers, they provided the next generations of bankers, inventors and manufacturers. In any case, far from withering on the vine, by the end of the eighteenth century the number of Nonconformists had swelled thanks to the decision of John Wesley's Methodist followers to break away from the Church of England.

By then, the Clarendon Code had proved less successful than its zealous sponsors hoped and was being largely discarded. The Conventicle Acts were difficult to administer and fell into disuse. Following the Glorious Revolution, Dissenters were allowed, by the 1689 Toleration Act, to form their own congregations. The Five Mile Act had fallen into abeyance long before it was taken off the statute book in 1812. Imprisonment of Quakers ended with the 1672 Declaration of Indulgence. True, measures were passed during the devoutly Anglican Queen Anne's reign to close up the 'occasional conformity' loopholes through which non-Anglicans had come to hold office and to prevent them opening their own schools. However, the crackdown did not long outlast the arrival of the Hanoverian monarchy and was scrapped in 1719. From 1727, annual indemnity acts allowed many non-Anglicans to hold local office.

Finally, in 1828 the Test and Corporation Acts were repealed, making Nonconformists free to hold municipal and state office. Catholics were similarly emancipated the following year. The dismantling of the Restoration's Anglican supremacy was effectively completed between 1868, when mandatory Church rates were abolished, and 1871, with the removal of the last restrictions to non-Anglicans at Oxford and Cambridge universities.

1688

THE IMMORTAL SEVEN'S INVITATION TO WILLIAM OF ORANGE

THE GLORIOUS REVOLUTION

The last successful invasion of England took place not in 1066 but in 1688. In November of that year William of Orange, the hereditary *stadtholder* of the Dutch Republic, landed at Torbay with his 15,000-strong army of Dutch, Swedish, German, Swiss and Huguenot as well as Scottish and English troops. Within seven weeks he was ensconced in London's Whitehall Palace. Yet his actions were widely seen not as those of a hostile occupier and usurper but rather as a welcome liberation from the arbitrary rule of James II. That this was so owed much to the invitation dispatched by the 'Immortal Seven'.

Having survived parliamentary attempts to exclude him from the succession, James II (he was James VII in Scotland) became king upon the death of his brother, Charles II, in 1685. Although he easily defeated a rebellion led by his illegitimate half-brother, the duke of Monmouth (whom he executed), James's position remained a difficult one. He was a devout Roman Catholic ruling three kingdoms of which only Ireland had a majority of his co-religionists. His faith was also at odds with his role as supreme governor of the Church of England.

James had two interlinked objectives: to increase royal authority, and to circumvent the laws that persecuted Catholics. After dispensing with Parliament, he exploited legal loopholes to promote Catholics to key civil and military posts, sacking most of his ministers and preferring to govern with a council of fellow Catholics. The traditions of ancient corporations, the Inns of Court and the college fellowships of Oxford and Cambridge were all overridden as part of James's imposition of religious positive discrimination. Maintaining a standing army in peacetime, he also hoped to dispense with habeas corpus in order to make arbitrary

BRITAIN'S LAST SUCCESSFUL REVOLUTION

1678–81 'The Exclusion Crisis' sees a succession of foiled parliamentary efforts to prevent the Catholic James, duke of York, succeeding his brother, King Charles II.

1685 Charles II dies and is succeeded by James II (James VII in Scotland).

1685 Rebellion by James's illegitimate half-brother and the Protestant pretender to the throne, the duke of Monmouth, ends with Monmouth's execution.

1687 James's Declaration of Indulgence creates religious freedom.

8 June 1688 Seven bishops are imprisoned for refusing to read out James's second Declaration of Indulgence.

10 June James's wife, Mary of Modena, gives birth to a Catholic heir, James Francis Edward.

30 June The seven bishops are acquitted by the courts, and the 'Immortal Seven', powerful figures of church and state, write to William of Orange asking him to invade Britain.

5 November William of Orange lands with his force at Torbay.

21 December James flees London for the continent.

22 January 1689 The Convention Parliament convenes.

13 February William and Mary accept the offer of the English throne as co-regents and accept the Declaration of Rights.

4 April The Scottish Parliament meets in Edinburgh and proceeds to pass the Claim of Right, offering the crown of Scotland to William and Mary.

11 April William and Mary are crowned in Westminster Abbey.

24 May The Toleration Act grants freedom of worship to Protestant Dissenters.

27 July A rising of pro-James Scottish Highlanders loses momentum when its leader, James Graham, Viscount Dundee, is killed at the Battle of Killiecrankie.

1690 James's efforts to hold onto Ireland are crushed at the Battle of the Boyne.

1694 The Triennial Act necessitates the calling of a general election every three years.

1701 The Act of Settlement confirms the Protestant line of succession; James dies in exile.

arrest easier. These initiatives coincided with Louis XIV's persecution of France's Protestant Huguenot minority, a development that James did not condemn. British Protestants began to fear that their monarch was poised to become a second 'Bloody Mary'.

Anglican fears for their Church did not extend as far as protecting the faiths of others. It was in fact James's 1687 Declaration of Indulgence that created religious freedom for all his subjects. He intended to recall Parliament to ratify the declaration but not before he had rigged a general election to make it compliant to his will. When seven bishops – including the archbishop of Canterbury – refused to read a second Declaration of Indulgence from their pulpits because they believed the king's dispensing authority to be illegal, he had them arrested and committed to the Tower of London. Two days later, on 10 June 1688, James's wife, Mary of Modena, gave birth to a son. Whilst the news delighted James, it sent Protestants into deeper despair – they would have not just one Catholic ruler but a whole succession of them.

On 30 June, the trial of the bishops ended – sensationally – with their acquittal. The courts were openly defying the king. That night, as celebratory bonfires were lit across London and the shires, a group of senior peers of the realm, together with Henry Compton, the bishop of London, wrote to William of Orange asking him to invade. The signatories became known as the 'Immortal Seven'. Besides Compton, they comprised: two leading Whig politicians, Henry Sidney (who drafted the letter) and Edward Russell; the earl of Danby (a Tory who had helped organize William's marriage to James's daughter, Mary, in 1677); the earl of Shrewsbury; the earl of Devonshire; and Lord Lumley, whose troops had been responsible for capturing the fugitive duke of Monmouth during the latter's abortive uprising of 1685.

The letter is truly remarkable. In plain and almost matter-of-fact language, it solicited a war to safeguard the future of Britain. It also perpetuated the widely held but erroneous, allegation that James's infant son was an impostor, smuggled into the royal bedchamber in a bedpan. The signatories risked being beheaded for treason, so, fearing the letter might be intercepted, they signed their names by numbered code. The incriminating epistle was carried to The Hague by Arthur Herbert, an admiral cashiered by James for refusing to serve under Catholic officers. Herbert went disguised as a common sailor and would return to England at the head of the invasion fleet.

For William, the letter from the Immortal Seven was not merely convenient; he had in fact actively solicited it. Plans for assembling his invasion force were already under way, but he needed the letter of invitation from some of Britain's leading figures – Tory, Whig and clergy – before agreeing to proceed. Not only did it grant him a pretext for intervention, it was also evidence that he would enjoy political and Church backing on his arrival. It was, after all, a risky endeavour and William was not only James's son-in-law, as a grandson of Charles I, he was also his nephew. Without the letter, he made clear he would go no further.

William's motivations went beyond restoring political stability to Britain. He wanted British help in containing Louis XIV on the continent. Nonetheless,

From the letter of the Immortal Seven, 1688

These considerations make us of opinion that this is a season in which we may more probably contribute to our own safeties than hereafter (although we must own to your Highness there are some judgments differing from ours in this particular), insomuch that if the circumstances stand so with your Highness that you believe you can get here time enough, in a condition to give assistances this year sufficient for a relief under these circumstances which have been now represented, we who subscribe this will not fail to attend your Highness upon your landing and to do all that lies in our power to prepare others to be in as much readiness as such an action is capable of, where there is so much danger in communicating an affair of such a nature till it be near the time of its being made public. But, as we have already told your Highness, we must also lay our difficulties before your Highness, which are chiefly, that we know not what alarm your preparations for this expedition may give, or what notice it will be necessary for you to give the States beforehand, by either of which means their intelligence or suspicions here may be such as may cause us to be secured before your landing. And we must presume to inform your Highness that your compliment upon the birth of the child (which not one in a thousand here believes to be the queen's) hath done you some injury, the false imposing of that upon the princess and the nation being not only an infinite exasperation of people's minds here, but being certainly one of the chief causes upon which the declaration of your entering the kingdom in a hostile manner must be founded on your part, although many other reasons are to be given on ours.

when issuing his declaration he was careful not to lay his own claim to the throne, preferring to focus on his determination to safeguard the country's liberties by calling a Parliament uncontaminated by James's election rigging.

Dodging James's fleet, William's armada of 49 warships and 2,000 troop transport vessels, borne by 'a Protestant wind', landed at Torbay on 5 November (fittingly, Guy Fawkes Night). A chain of small risings announced popular support. James advanced as far as Salisbury before taking fright. Key commanders, including John Churchill, the future duke of Marlborough, defected to William's camp. Returning to London, James weighed his options and, on 21 December, fled.

In February 1689, William and Mary jointly accepted Parliament's offer of the English throne. On 4 April, the Scottish Convention of Estates renounced its loyalty to James, who had disobeyed 'the fundamental constitution of this Kingdom' and altered it 'from a legal limited monarchy to an arbitrary despotic power'. On the day that they were crowned in Westminster Abbey, William and Mary were also proclaimed Scotland's new king and queen. A Scottish Jacobite rising led by Viscount Dundee was defeated. In Catholic Ireland, however, James found broader loyalty and convened a supportive Parliament there. This Irish power base did not last long. In June 1690, James's forces were decisively defeated by William at the Battle of the Boyne.

From this defeat until his death in 1701, James ran a shadow court in exile from the royal château of Saint-Germain-en-Laye, west of Paris. He still intrigued at reclaiming his throne, turning down Louis XIV's offer to make him king of Poland in case it reduced his chances in Britain. The opportunity never came. After visiting him at St Germain, it was the celebrated novelist, Madame de Lafayette, who delivered the damning verdict: 'As one listens to him, one realises why he is here.'

1689
THE BILL OF RIGHTS

THE CONSTITUTIONAL MONARCHY

The Glorious Revolution did more than replace a Catholic king with his Protestant daughter and son-in-law. It did so on terms, laid out in the Bill of Rights, that fundamentally altered the relationship between the Crown and Parliament. Henceforth, the monarchy's power would be determined by Parliament. If the Bill of Rights did not create a constitutional monarchy, it nonetheless provided the clearest indication that this was the prevailing nature of government in Britain.

Parliament had not sat for three years when James II fled, ahead of William of Orange's entry into London. One of the first actions of the interim authorities was to hold a general election. This returned the 'Convention' Parliament, which met in January 1689. On 13 February 1689 it offered the Crown, jointly, to William and Mary, with conditions attached. The new co-rulers would have to agree to terms drawn up in a document called the Declaration of Rights. Its intent was to limit royal power and enhance the freedom of Parliament. Instead of the occasional summons favoured by past Stuart monarchs, the Declaration stipulated that Parliament should meet regularly, and that the freedom of its members' speech as well as its proceedings must be guaranteed. It would be illegal to levy taxes, or to make or suspend laws, without the explicit endorsement of Parliament.

The Declaration of Rights was passed by the Convention Parliament and put on the statute books as the Bill of Rights. The Scottish Parliament passed it as the Claim of Right. Its primary aim was to deny the Crown the means by which it could descend into despotism. A standing army could not be maintained in peacetime except through parliamentary consent. James II's attempts to disarm his Protestant subjects were thus reversed. The bill specified that Protestants had the right to bear arms for their self-defence. Stripped of its sectarian condition, this clause would form the basis of the Second Amendment of the United States' Constitution over a hundred years later.

Die Martis 12° ffebruary 1688

The Declaration of the Lords Spirituall &
Temporall and Comons Assembled at Westm[inster]

Whereas the late King James the second by the
assistance of diverse evill councellors Iudges and
Ministers imployed by him did endeavour to
subvert and extirpate the Protestant Religion
and the Lawes and Libertyes of this Kingdome.

By assumeing and excercisseing a Power of dis:
pencing and suspending of Lawes and the execution
of Lawes without consent of Parliament:

By committing and prosecuteing diverse worthy
Prelates for humbly petitioning to be excused from
concurring to the said assumed Power

By issueing a Commission under the Great Seale
for erecting a Court called the Comissioners for
Ecclesiasticall Causes.

By levying money for and to the use of the Crowne
by pretence of Prerogative for other time and in
other manner then the same was granted by Parliament.

By raiseing and keeping a standing Army within
this Kingdom in time of Peace without consent of
Parliament. and quartering Souldiers contrary to Law

By causeing severall good subjects being —
Protestants to be disarmed at the same time when
Papists were both armed and

By violating the free
members to serve in Par[liament]

By causeing

and prosecuted in the

for matters and causes

ascent and by diverse other

illegall courses. By Prosecu

of Kings Bench for matters

cognizable only in Parliament and by diverse

other arbitrary or illegall

7
8

12

21

23

26

From the Bill of Rights, 1689

That the pretended power of suspending the laws or the execution of laws by regal authority without consent of Parliament is illegal;

That the pretended power of dispensing with laws or the execution of laws by regal authority, as it hath been assumed and exercised of late, is illegal;

That the commission for erecting the late Court of Commissioners for Ecclesiastical Causes, and all other commissions and courts of like nature, are illegal and pernicious;

That levying money for or to the use of the Crown by pretence of prerogative, without grant of Parliament, for longer time, or in other manner than the same is or shall be granted, is illegal;

That it is the right of the subjects to petition the king, and all commitments and prosecutions for such petitioning are illegal;

That the raising or keeping a standing army within the kingdom in time of peace, unless it be with consent of Parliament, is against law;

That the subjects which are Protestants may have arms for their defence suitable to their conditions and as allowed by law;

That election of members of Parliament ought to be free;

That the freedom of speech and debates or proceedings in Parliament ought not to be impeached or questioned in any court or place out of Parliament;

That excessive bail ought not to be required, nor excessive fines imposed, nor cruel and unusual punishments inflicted;

That jurors ought to be duly impanelled and returned, and jurors which pass upon men in trials for high treason ought to be freeholders;

That all grants and promises of fines and forfeitures of particular persons before conviction are illegal and void;

And that for redress of all grievances, and for the amending, strengthening and preserving of the laws, Parliaments ought to be held frequently.

The bill also dealt with the royal succession. The convenient fiction was perpetrated that James II's flight from his kingdoms meant that he had abdicated. However, the reality was now that the new monarchs owed their power not to the ancient rights of inheritance or to some mystical notion of divine right, but to the say-so of Parliament. The Bill of Rights decreed that the subsequent succession would pass down through Mary's heirs, or, if she had none, those of her sister, Anne. In fact, neither had surviving children, forcing the succession issue to be

Opposite: The Declaration of Rights was presented by the Convention Parliament to William and Mary in February 1689 and put on the statute books as the Bill of Rights ten months later.

readdressed in the 1701 Act of Settlement. Members of the royal family who converted to Catholicism or who married Catholics were debarred from the succession.

The Bill of Rights was only the most important of a series of laws that established the Revolution Settlement. The 1689 Toleration Act lifted the anti-Dissenter penal laws on all Protestant Nonconformists who took the oaths of allegiance and supremacy. The Catholic disabilities remained. The timescale for calling regular parliaments was set by the 1694 Triennial Act, which ensured a general election at least once every three years (this was extended to seven years in 1716 and cut to five years in 1911). William's expensive wars against France entailed extensive debate about taxation at Westminster and the creation of the Bank of England in 1694. The Bill of Rights was modified in 1698 when the maintenance of a standing army was permitted during what proved a temporary period of peace.

The Bill of Rights did not set out with precision which powers belonged to the Crown, which to the legislature and which to the executive. These were shaped by subsequent events, for which the Bill of Rights established part of the constitutional framework, particularly with regard to what the Crown could *not* do. The bill's success could, however, be assessed by one important measure. Arbitrary rule was henceforth consigned to history.

1689–90

JOHN LOCKE'S *TWO TREATISES OF GOVERNMENT*

THE REFUTATION OF DIVINE RIGHT AND ADVOCACY OF GOVERNMENT BY POPULAR CONSENT

John Locke had more influence upon the world than any other British philosopher. Not only did he provide the Glorious Revolution with its philosophical legitimacy, but his thinking was central to the development of liberalism, influencing the arguments against absolutism in Europe and, more directly, inspiring the Founding Fathers of the United States.

Locke was born in 1632 into a minor Somerset gentry family. His father fought for the Parliamentarians during the Civil War. Locke was educated at Westminster School and Christ Church, Oxford, during the period of the republican Commonwealth. Awarded a college studentship, he demonstrated wide academic curiosity in subjects ranging from theology and philosophy to Greek, medicine, meteorology and chemistry. His breadth of interests brought him into contact with such eminent scientists as Isaac Newton and Robert Boyle.

It was his friendship with Anthony Ashley Cooper, later earl of Shaftesbury, the emerging leader of the Country – or 'Whig' – faction in Parliament, that ensured he was also at the forefront of political controversy. Doubling as the earl's secretary and physician, Locke lodged at his mentor's London mansion, Exeter House. Like Shaftesbury, he suffered recurring ill health and it was partly to escape London's polluted air, as well as to extract himself from an increasingly precarious political situation, that he spent the years between 1675 and 1679 in France. There he made the acquaintance of many of Europe's leading Enlightenment thinkers.

He returned to England but his stay there was soon interrupted. Shaftesbury's attempts to exclude the future James II from the throne collapsed and, fearing incarceration, the earl fled in 1682 to Amsterdam, dying there the following year. Locke departed hurriedly, first to Rotterdam and then to Amsterdam. There, he dodged English warrants sent to the Dutch to have him arrested by living under the assumed identity of 'Dr Van der Linden'. It was 1688's Glorious Revolution that gave him his chance to go home once more. During his exile he met William of Orange and in February 1689 sailed for England on the ship carrying the future Queen Mary II.

Locke maintained that his *Two Treatises of Government*, finished later that year (but post-dated to 1690 as its year of publication), was his means of defending philosophically the British revolution to the world. In fact, he had begun writing it around 1680–2 and had left the manuscript behind when fleeing to the Dutch Republic. The elapse of time between conception and publication made Locke less the prophet and more the legitimizer of events.

The first treatise kicked away the main prop of the House of Stuart's claim to autocratic power – the divine right of kings. Locke demolished the justification put forward by the political writer Sir Robert Filmer that subjects were to sovereigns as children were to parents because sovereigns, like fathers, were descended from Adam. Giving short shrift to such notions was the easier part of Locke's task. In the second treatise, his implicit target was the view expressed in Thomas Hobbes's 1651 work *Leviathan*, that in order to curb the anarchic rule of Nature that would otherwise make their lives unendurable, the people entered into a contract with the sovereign power. By it, they surrendered their rights in return for being provided with security. In this way the sovereign (whether a monarch or some other form of government) was entitled to exercise absolute power for the greater good of law and order, without which human existence would be 'nasty, brutish, and short'.

Hobbes had done his thinking (in exile) at a time when England had descended into the near anarchy of civil war. His philosophy did not necessarily advocate the despotic wielding of power, but by imagining that the state and society were one and the same he nonetheless provided absolutist regimes with a justification for expecting their subjects' unequivocal submission.

Locke rejected the notion that mankind was faced only with the stark options of anarchy or capitulation to absolute power. On the contrary, he suggested that certain God-given and inalienable rights existed beyond the give or take of the state, among them freedom of action and the ownership of private property. Since these rights were natural, not a retractable gift from government, the latter could remove them only with the consent of those to whom they belonged.

This was the nature of the 'social contract' that Locke believed defined the relationship between government and the governed. The loyalty that the people

1440–6 – HENRY VI'S CHARTERS FOR ETON COLLEGE AND KING'S COLLEGE, CAMBRIDGE

Charter of King's College, Cambridge, 16 March 1446. In the top left-hand corner members of the House of Lords (led by the Lord Chancellor, Archbishop Stafford) with members of the House of Commons below them, are illustrated petitioning King Henry VI, who prays for his foundation. The college's patron saints, St Nicholas and the Virgin Mary, are depicted to the right of the royal coat of arms. The calligraphy is by John Broke, the clerk of the chancery, and the illuminations are by the London artist, William Abell.

1546 – THE ANTHONY ROLL

The Anthony Roll provides the only surviving contemporary depiction of the Mary Rose.

my lord out of the loue i beare to some of youer frends
i haue a caer of youer preseruacion therfor i would
aduyse yowe as yowe tender youer lyf to deuyse some
excuse to shift of youer attendance at this parleament
for god and man hathe concurred to punishe the wickednes
of this tyme and think not slightlye of this aduertisment
but retyere youre self into youre contri wheare yowe
maye expect the euent in safti for thowghe theare be no
apparance of anni stir yet i saye they shall receyue a terrible
blowe this parleament and yet they shall not seie who
hurts them this cowncel is not to be contemned because
it maye do yowe good and can do yowe no harme for the
dangere is passed as soon as yowe haue burnt the letter
and i hope god will giue yowe the grace to mak good
use of it to whose holy proteccion i comend yowe

1605 – THE 'MONTEAGLE LETTER'
An anonymous correspondent warns Lord Monteagle to stay away from the state opening of Parliament.

1605 – GUY FAWKES'S SIGNED CONFESSION
Worn down by torture, Fawkes's scrawl 'Guido' can only just be made out on his confession document beneath the words 'good stead', towards the bottom right of the document.

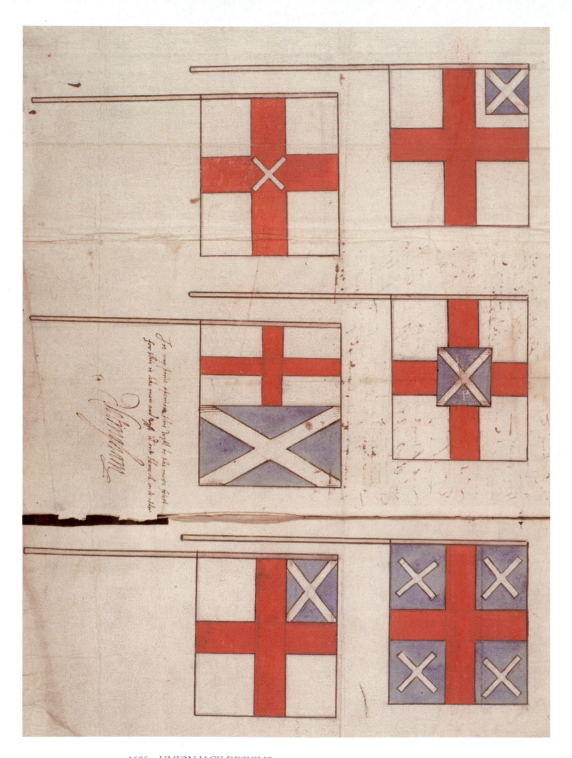

1606 – UNION JACK DESIGNS

Wrestling with the problem of how to give the crosses of St George and St Andrew equal esteem in these preliminary designs for the Union Flag, the Earl of Nottingham inserted his hand-written recommendation below the lower middle design, noting it was 'like man and wife.'

From the Second Treatise, Chapter 18: 'Of Tyranny'

Wherever law ends, tyranny begins, if the law be transgressed to another's harm; and whosoever in authority exceeds the power given him by the law, and makes use of the force he has under his command, to compass that upon the subject, which the law allows not, ceases in that to be a magistrate; and, acting without authority, may be opposed, as any other man, who by force invades the right of another. This is acknowledged in subordinate magistrates. He that hath authority to seize my person in the street, may be opposed as a thief and a robber, if he endeavours to break into my house to execute a writ, notwithstanding that I know he has such a warrant, and such a legal authority, as will impower him to arrest me abroad. And why this should not hold in the highest, as well as in the most inferior magistrate, I would gladly be informed. Is it reasonable, that the eldest brother, because he has the greatest part of his father's estate, should thereby have a right to take away any of his younger brothers portions? or that a rich man, who possessed a whole country, should from thence have a right to seize, when he pleased, the cottage and garden of his poor neighbour? The being rightfully possessed of great power and riches, exceedingly beyond the greatest part of the sons of Adam, is so far from being an excuse, much less a reason, for rapine and oppression, which the endamaging another without authority is, that it is a great aggravation of it: for the exceeding the bounds of authority is no more a right in a great, than in a petty officer; no more justifiable in a king than a constable; but is so much the worse in him, in that he has more trust put in him, has already a much greater share than the rest of his brethren, and is supposed, from the advantages of his education, employment, and counsellors, to be more knowing in the measures of right and wrong.

owed to the state existed on the presumption that the state sought to pursue their best interest. If it wilfully failed to do so, then the people had the right to remove that government.

Ultimate sovereignty thus lay with the people. This was, in effect, an argument for representative democracy. Believing that constitutional restraint made for better government, Locke suggested that government was less likely to tend towards oppression if there was a separation of powers between the legislature and the executive: the former elected, the latter residing in the person of a head of state.

Nor was this the only separation he advocated. Theologically, Locke was a moderate Anglican who set out his attitude in his *Letter on Toleration*. He believed that the state and religion were fundamentally different, the latter being a voluntary matter unrelated to civil promotion or disabilities so long as a Church did not promulgate doctrine at odds with the principles of civil society or force allegiance to a foreign overlord. He also wrote on education and monetary policy (some of his arguments preshadowing the free-trade advocacy of Adam Smith) and, in his *Essay Concerning Human Understanding*, he contradicted Descartes' view that ideas were innate and that universal truths could therefore be deduced by purely rational deduction alone. Rather than such philosophical abstractions, he believed in empirical research, garnered through experience and reflection.

Although the *Two Treatises of Government* was originally published anonymously, it burnished Locke's reputation as an exponent of freedom in the decades after his death in 1704. Locke, the defender of the Glorious Revolution, had created an intelligible theory of limited government as the servant of the people. His thinking infused Whig arguments during the eighteenth century and influenced nineteenth-century liberalism, in particular that of John Stuart Mill. Outside Britain, his legacy was perhaps even more apparent. In 1669 he had helped draft the constitution of the colony of Carolina, and the first American printed edition of his *Two Treatises* was published in Boston in 1773. Its timing was perfect, providing arguments that American colonists would use against what they considered the overweening and unrepresentative authority of George III. No document better conveys Locke's arguments for the separation of powers than the constitution of the United States of America.

1694

THE ROYAL CHARTER OF THE BANK OF ENGLAND

FINANCE AND THE BANKER OF LAST RESORT

Until the beginning of the seventeenth century, Britain had no major financial sector. There was nothing to compare with the credit revolution taking place in the Dutch Republic, where the Bank of Amsterdam was founded in 1609. The goldsmiths were the nearest London came to a coherent banking community. Providing strongrooms for merchants to deposit their treasure, the goldsmiths brought together the main functions of modern banking, offering deposit and lending facilities and issuing notes redeemable for the valuables in their safe keeping.

However, they were not geared to meet the mounting credit demands of late seventeenth-century government. These became acute following the Glorious Revolution of 1688 because of William III's determination to fight France in a war he could ill afford. Between 1690 and 1697, the state managed to raise around £28 million in revenue but spent £40 million prosecuting the war. Expedients such as the £1 million lottery loan, which offered huge cash prizes, were less a sign of the state's ingenuity than of its failure to develop the institutions necessary to provide long-term security.

The answer to England's financial problems was provided by a Scotsman. William Paterson (1658–1719), an adventurer who had done business in the West Indies and Holland, proposed Britain's first incorporated joint-stock bank, to be called the Bank of England. It would solicit £1.2 million from the public, which would be lent to the government at a rate of 8 per cent interest guaranteed by Parliament. Investors of more than £500 would also get to vote for the bank's board of management.

Investors were attracted not just by the rate of interest but also by the absence of a time limit for repayment. Potentially (and in reality), interest would continue to accrue indefinitely, becoming the National Debt. The state of its finances made

A Short History of British Banking

1546 Henry VIII repeals the usury laws, making lending with interest legal.

1640 Confidence in the Royal Mint is shattered by Charles I's seizure of its gold. Growing use of the private quasi-banking facilities is offered by the goldsmiths – who fund the Parliamentarian war effort.

1659 The first surviving example of a cheque dates from this time.

1690 John Freame and Thomas Gould begin trading as Goldsmith bankers. Their firm eventually becomes Barclays Bank.

1692 Coutts & Co. is founded.

1694 The Bank of England receives its royal charter.

1695 The Bank of Scotland is founded, and the Scottish Parliament grants it a twenty-one year monopoly of public banking in Scotland.

1727 The Royal Bank of Scotland is founded.

1759 The Bank of England issues the first £10 note. The £5 note follows in 1793.

1804–9 The number of 'country banks' outside London increases from 470 to 800.

1811 N. M. Rothschild & Sons established as a bank in London and helps finance the war effort of Britain and her allies during the Napoleonic Wars. For much of the 19th century, Rothschild dominates the international bond market.

1821 The gold standard makes Bank of England notes convertible at a fixed weight of gold. (The gold standard was suspended in 1914 and briefly reintroduced between 1925 and 1931.)

1866 There are 154 joint-stock banks with 850 branches, and 246 private banks with 376 branches.

1870 The Bank of England assumes the right to set interest rates.

1900 There are seventy-seven joint-stock banks and only nineteen private banks left with branches. Consolidation during the Edwardian period creates the domination of the 'Big Five' clearing banks during the 1920s (Barclays, Lloyds, Midland, National Provincial, Westminster).

1946 The Bank of England is nationalized; sterling's exchange rate is fixed relative to the dollar. The system breaks down in 1971, after which sterling's exchange rate floats.

1966 Barclaycard, the first credit card, is introduced in Britain.

1968 The merger of National Provincial and Westminster banks to create 'NatWest' reduces the 'Big Five' to the 'Big Four'.

1971 The coinage is decimalized.

1980s–90s A spate of demutualization of building societies effectively creates a string of new banks.

1986 The 'Big Bang' deregulation of finance markets ushers in a series of mergers and take-overs of British brokerages and merchant banks by foreign banks and restores the City of London's financial supremacy over New York. Banking sector assets increase sevenfold between 1986 and 2006.

1995 Barings Banks – the oldest merchant bank in London – collapses after one of its derivatives traders, Nick Leeson, loses over £800 million in unauthorized speculation.

1997 The Bank of England regains operational independence but loses financial regulatory powers.

2007 £2.15 trillion of capital flows into UK financial institutions.

2008–9 The financial crisis leads to the government nationalizing some banks and taking large shares in others. Lloyds TSB rescues the debt-laden Halifax–Bank of Scotland (HBOS), but then itself needs government support.

the government ill placed to haggle. Among the influential persons won over by Paterson was Charles Montagu, a commissioner of the Treasury. Overcoming the opposition of the goldsmiths and other vested interests, Montagu steered the government towards supporting the legislation and the royal charter that created the Bank of England in 1694.

The bank began in a rented hall in Cheapside with a staff of nineteen. Despite these modest beginnings, its attractiveness to investors was evident from the first. It was launched on 27 July 1694, and eleven days later had successfully raised the required £1.2 million. Initially, there were nearly 1,300 shareholders. Paterson, however, soon fell out with the other directors and quit. Returning to the land of his birth, he conceived and promoted the ill-fated Darien scheme to establish a colony in Central America, which wrecked the Scottish economy and humbled its leaders into seeking full economic, political and monetary union with England. Paterson then helped draw up the terms of the Treaty of Union.

This late-eighteenth-century engraving of Threadneedle Street shows the Bank of England building shortly before its expansion – which resulted in the demolition of its neighbour, the Church of St Christopher-Le-Stocks.

Extract from The Charter of the Corporation of the Governor and Company of the Bank of England, 1694

WILLIAM and MARY, by the Grace of God, King and Queen of England, Scotland, France and Ireland, Defenders of the Faith, &c. To all to whom these Presents shall come, Greeting.

... And all and every Person and Persons, Natives or Foreigners, Bodies Politick and Corporate, who, either as original Subscribers of the said Sum of Twelve Hundred Thousand Pounds so subscribed, and not having parted with their Interests in their Subscriptions, or as Heirs, Successors, or Assignees, or by any other lawful Title derived, or to be derived from, by, or under the said original Subscribers of the said Sum of Twelve Hundred Thousand Pounds so subscribed, or any of them now have, or at any Time or Times hereafter shall have, or be entituled to any Part, Share, or Interest of or in the Principal or Capital Stock of the said Corporation, or the said yearly Fond of One Hundred Thousand Pounds, granted by the said Act of Parliament, or any Part thereof, so long as they respectively shall have any such Part, Share, or Interest therein, shall be, and be called one Body Politick and Corporate, of themselves, in Deed and in Name, by the Name of The Governor and Company of the Bank of England; and them by that Name, one Body Politick and Corporate, in Deed and in Name, We do, for Us, our Heirs, and Successors, make, create, erect, establish, and confirm for ever, by these Presents, and by the same Name, they and their Successors shall have perpetual Succession, and shall and may have and use a Common Seal, for the Use, Business, or Affairs of the said Body Politick and Corporate, and their Successors, with Power to break, alter, and to make anew their Seal from Time to Time, at their Pleasure, and as they shall see Cause. And by the same Name, they and their Successors in all Times coming, shall be able and capable in Law, to have, take, purchase, receive, hold, keep, possess, enjoy, and retain to them and their Successors, any Manors, Messuages, Lands, Rents, Tenements, Liberties, Privileges, Franchises, Hereditaments, and Possessions whatsoever, and of what Kind, Nature, or Quality soever; ... And we do hereby for Us, our Heirs and Successors, declare, limit, direct and appoint, that the aforesaid Sum of Twelve Hundred Thousand Pounds so subscribed as aforesaid, shall be, and be called, accepted, esteemed, reputed and taken, The Common Capital and Principal Stock of the Corporation hereby constituted.

Rivals like the Land Bank were quickly seen off and while small provincial private banks issued their own notes, the Bank of England's notes were subsequently given a monopoly in the London area where their promise to pay the 'bearer' (not just the original depositor) made them easily exchangeable units of currency. By the 1930s the Bank of England had gained a monopoly on producing all England's banknotes (Scottish and Northern Irish banks continued to print notes north of the border and in Ulster). Successive notes bore the image of Britannia. The decision to follow the ancient practice of the coinage and put the monarch's face on the notes began only as late as 1960.

Although the Bank of England was not created as the state's central bank, this is what it became. During the eighteenth century, four-fifths of its business was government-related. It looked after government department accounts and managed a National Debt that increased from £12 million in 1700 to £850 million by 1815. As early as 1781, the prime minister, Lord North, described the bank as 'from long habit and usage of many years . . . a part of the constitution'. The bank's reputation for financial security was acknowledged in a popular catchphrase, 'as safe as the Bank of England', while currency stability created in between the end of the Napoleonic Wars and the onset of the First World War (by a gold standard that valued the pound sterling to a fixed quantity of gold) also helped London emerge as the world's financial centre.

It was as this age was passing, during the inter-war period, that the Bank of England completed its long process of becoming Britain's central bank and lender of last resort. It had been setting the country's interest rates since 1870. How little difference its nationalization in 1946 initially made may be judged by the fact that the same board was retained after the state formally took control. The collapse of an international system of fixed currency exchanges in 1971, and a belief that Treasury interference in interest-rate policy involved more political than economic calculation, led to the bank regaining operational independence in 1997. At the same time, it lost its regulatory role over the City to a new Financial Services Authority. This proved controversial and following the financial crisis of 2008–9, the incoming coalition government in 2010 set about restoring some of the FSA's regulatory powers to the bank.

1701
THE ACT OF SETTLEMENT

ESTABLISHING THE ROYAL SUCCESSION

The Glorious Revolution removed the Catholic James II and replaced him on the throne with William III and Mary II, his Protestant son-in-law and daughter. The Bill of Rights stipulated the subsequent terms of the succession: the children of William and Mary, followed by the children of Mary's sister Anne, followed by any children William might have by a second marriage. Catholics were debarred. Events confounded this careful order. In 1694, Mary died of smallpox, aged only thirty-two and without issue. William continued to rule but as a widower with no interest in remarriage. The next in line, Anne, endured seventeen pregnancies, all of which ended in miscarriage or children who died in infancy. In 1700, her one remaining son died shortly after his eleventh birthday. With his demise passed the last real prospect of the beneficiaries of the Glorious Revolution securing the throne for their descendants.

The monarchy appeared to be heading towards a crisis. The Bill of Rights' prohibition of a Catholic ought to have ruled out any possibility of the Crown being returned to the deposed James II or his son, James Francis Edward Stuart, who were both languishing in French exile as the guests of Louis XIV. However, unless Parliament made clear who the next rightful monarch ought to be after Anne, the scope for dispute and revolt would create a void in which the seizure of power by the exiled Stuarts' supporters could not be discounted.

It was to remove any ambiguity that in 1701 Parliament passed the Act of Settlement. It established that, in the event of Anne dying childless, the throne would pass to the nearest surviving Protestant Stuart relation. This was Sophia, Electress of Hanover, who was James I's granddaughter. Recently widowed from the German state's ruler, the Elector Ernest Augustus, Sophia also had Protestant offspring who could inherit on her death. In the event, she died only weeks before Anne in 1714, whereupon the British throne passed to Sophia's son, George I. A Jacobite rebellion in favour of James Francis Edward was defeated the following year.

ROYAL FAMILY TREE: FROM THE STUARTS TO THE HANOVERIANS

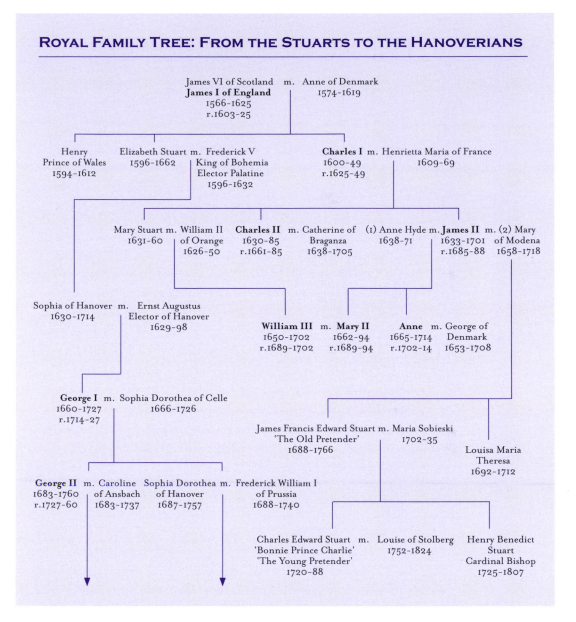

Scotland's response to the passage of the Act of Settlement made clear how real the prospect was of the throne passing on Anne's death to the disinherited Catholic wing of the Stuart family. Rather than endorse Westminster's statute, the Scottish Parliament pointedly refused to follow suit, raising the possibility that on Anne's death, Scotland might declare James Francis Edward the new King of

From the Act of Settlement, 1701

That the most excellent Princess Sophia, Electress and Duchess Dowager of Hanover, daughter of the most excellent Princess Elizabeth, late Queen of Bohemia, daughter of our late sovereign lord King James the First, of happy memory, be and is hereby declared to be the next in succession, in the Protestant line, to the imperial Crown and dignity of the said Realms of England, France, and Ireland, with the dominions and territories thereunto belonging, after His Majesty, and the Princess Anne of Denmark, and in default of issue of the said Princess Anne, and of His Majesty respectively: and that from and after the deceases of His said Majesty, our now sovereign lord, and of Her Royal Highness the Princess Anne of Denmark, and for default of issue of the said Princess Anne, and of His Majesty respectively, the Crown and regal government of the said Kingdoms of England, France, and Ireland, and of the dominions thereunto belonging, with the royal state and dignity of the said Realms, and all honours, styles, titles, regalities, prerogatives, powers, jurisdictions and authorities, to the same belonging and appertaining, shall be, remain, and continue to the said most excellent Princess Sophia, and the heirs of her body, being Protestants: and thereunto the said Lords Spiritual and Temporal, and Commons, shall and will in the name of all the people of this Realm, most humbly and faithfully submit themselves, their heirs and posterities: and do faithfully promise, that after the deceases of His Majesty, and Her Royal Highness, and the failure of the heirs of their respective bodies, to stand to, maintain, and defend the said Princess Sophia, and the heirs of her body, being Protestants, according to the limitation and succession of the Crown in this act specified and contained, to the utmost of their powers, with their lives and estates, against all persons whatsoever that shall attempt anything to the contrary.

Scots. In 1704, the Scottish Parliament passed an Act of Security that asserted its right to choose a different monarch from that chosen by England unless London signed a free-trade agreement. The legislation restricted the choice to Protestant claimants although the likely consequential division clearly created opportunities for Jacobites to exploit. Unwilling to risk the security of the English realm by tolerating a pro-French Scottish king who believed himself entitled to the English throne as well, Westminster quickly began coercing the Scots towards full political union. The resulting 1707 Act of Union made the Act of Settlement applicable in Scotland.

Thus the Act of Settlement's legacy was profound: it established the succession of all subsequent monarchs of Great Britain and, subsequently, the United Kingdom – entities that it was instrumental in bringing into being. The act also modified the Bill of Rights by stipulating that the monarch had to be not only Protestant but also Anglican. Judicial independence was strengthened by the clause that prevented judges being removed by the monarch. A royal pardon could not block an impeachment by Parliament. However, a measure to prevent Parliament being packed with royal 'placemen', holding government positions or pensions would have separated the legislature from the executive, thereby injuring the development of parliamentary government. It was largely scrapped in 1706 when MPs who accepted office had to fight a by-election to confirm their appointment.

While securing the British monarchy for the house of Hanover, the Act of Settlement sought to bar its sovereigns from putting German considerations before British ones. They could not bestow offices and Crown lands on foreigners, nor could they leave Britain without parliamentary approval. The first of these clauses was later replaced by legislation permitting the naturalization of foreigners, while George I managed to have his travel restrictions lifted within two years of becoming king. Nonetheless, the framers of the 1701 legislation were particularly alive to the potential conflict of national interests with a monarch who was also ruler of Hanover. To prevent Britain being drawn into Hanover's wars, the Act of Settlement established that no fighting on the behalf of foreign countries would be legal without first securing parliamentary assent.

All four Hanoverian Georges as well as William IV combined being king of Britain with ruling Hanover, although only George I spent much time in his German domain. This connection was severed in 1837. Hanover's rules of succession precluded a woman inheriting in her own right, so Queen Victoria ascended the throne in Britain, leaving Hanover to her uncle.

1707
THE ACT OF UNION

THE UNITED KINGDOM OF GREAT BRITAIN

The Act of Union is depicted in the third plate section.

On 11 August 1607, the Scottish Parliament had voted in favour of full political union with England. Less enamoured by the prospect of marriage, Westminster's politicians had jilted the bride at the altar.

One hundred years later, it was England's politicians who came courting. The change of heart was a result of Scotland's determination to choose its own monarch on the death of Queen Anne. It seemed possible that while the house of Hanover would succeed to the English throne, the Scots – despite explicitly legislating for a Protestant succession – might end up restoring the Catholic branch of the Stuart family. The thought of James II's son ruling as James VIII in Edinburgh, perhaps supported by French troops and still claiming to be England's rightful ruler, posed a real threat to the English realm, especially since the country was again engaged in continental warfare against France. Suddenly, the political settlement of the Glorious Revolution looked altogether less secure.

Scotland had not prospered during the century in which its royal family moved to London. In 1700, her widely dispersed population of around 1 million equated to one-fifth of England's size. In terms of prosperity however, the chasm was far greater. At the end of the seventeenth century, famine and emigration conspired to reduce the Scottish population by 15 per cent. It was during these 'Lean Years' that the country gambled much of its remaining wealth in an intrepid scheme to start a colonial trading empire, only to learn a humiliating lesson in the dangers of going it alone.

In 1698, the attempt to establish a Scottish colony at Darien, on the isthmus of Panama, collapsed in ruin. The expedition to colonize a strip of central America that had the potential to become the Atlantic–Pacific trading gateway between Europe and Asia looked strategically shrewd on a map of the world. In reality, establishing 'New Caledonia' in a humid, fever-ridden swamp was ill-conceived from the first. Most of the settlers died in appalling conditions. In the search for scapegoats, England's callously obstructionist attitude to the scheme made it a target for Scottish blame. Nonetheless, the financial consequences were such that Scotland had to consider going cap in hand to its southern neighbour. Darien had consumed nearly a quarter of the country's liquid capital.

Thus while English supporters of union were guided by security fears, Scottish unionist objectives were primarily economic. After all, Scotland's failure to become a colonial power in a world of protectionist tariffs restricted its access to markets. Threatening to install a rival claimant on its throne was one means of trying to force the English into commercial concessions. The 1704 Act of Security that asserted Scotland's right to choose its own monarch came with the rider that it would not do so if England signed a free-trade agreement.

Westminster was not so easily cajoled. Raising the stakes, it passed an Alien Act that threatened not only to block key Scottish imports but to treat all Scots as foreigners unless the Scottish Parliament either declared for the Hanoverian succession or agreed full political union. Reluctantly, Edinburgh's politicians conceded among themselves that their alternative options were narrowing while each month their financial outlook darkened.

With the blessing of Queen Anne, negotiations began in April 1706. England's lord treasurer, Sidney Godolphin, and the Scottish dukes of Queensberry and Argyll were the driving forces. Commissioners from both nations were appointed to meet in separate rooms and haggle over the details. In July, agreement was reached on the twenty-five articles of the Treaty of Union. These provided the substance of the subsequent Act of Union, which the English Parliament endorsed by 274 votes to 116 and the Scottish Parliament by 110 to 67.

The new nation created would be called the United Kingdom of Great Britain. The house of Hanover would succeed to its throne after Queen Anne's death. The parliament in Edinburgh would be abolished and, instead, forty-five Scottish MPs would join the existing 513 English and Welsh MPs at Westminster, with equal legislative powers. In the upper house, sixteen peers, elected by the far larger old Scottish nobility, would represent the Scots aristocracy in the House of Lords. Although these ratios were less than Scotland was entitled to in terms of comparative population size, they were deemed appropriate to its far smaller fiscal contribution. Scotland would retain its own legal system and the (Presbyterian) Church of Scotland would remain the Established Church north of the border.

In economic matters, the Scots got most of what they wanted. Free trade was established and Scots were given equal access to the colonies of the English – now

British – Empire. Monetary union, as well as common weights and measures were adopted, along with English usage. A financial calculation called The Equivalent compensated Darien shareholders for their losses and offset Scotland's share of the assumption of England's National Debt.

The sum of £20,000 was dispersed among those affected by the changes: financial sweeteners to ensure that the Scottish Parliament voted itself out of existence. While some of the money may have represented legitimate expenses, it looked suspiciously like bribery and encouraged the presumption that the nation had been sold out by those whom the poet Robert Burns later called a 'Parcel of Rogues'. There was widespread protest in Scotland as the prospect of agreement drew near. The public rejoicing in London that marked the Union coming into force on 1 May 1707 found no echo in Edinburgh. There, the bells of St Giles tolled the melody 'Why should I be sad on my wedding day?'

In the short term, the Union delivered neither security for the English nor prosperity to the Scots. Jacobite risings sprang up in Scotland in 1715 and 1745 in an attempt to restore the Catholic house of Stuart on both sides of the border. It was not until Jacobitism was comprehensively crushed at the Battle of Culloden in 1746 that tensions abated. Thereafter, Scotland began to benefit more evidently from the trading opportunities now within its grasp as part of a larger market. Having failed so catastrophically at going it alone in the swamps of Panama, the Scots proceeded to distinguish themselves as fervent colonists under the Union flag. As soldiers, traders, financiers, engineers, politicians and missionaries, Scots were pre-eminent in pushing the perimeters of the British Empire to their furthest extents.

Thus a nation that had been one of Europe's poorest at the beginning of the eighteenth century became one of its richest by the late nineteenth century. The retention of a separate Scottish legal system, as well as the 'Kirk' and long-standing traditions in education acknowledged – and preserved – Scotland's own identity. These separate institutions did not, however, prevent the Scots from also occupying many of the most important offices in London.

For a marriage driven more by contrasting necessities than genuine affection, the Anglo-Scottish union proved remarkably enduring, surviving over 300 years while so many of Europe's other multinational countries fragmented and split. During the nineteenth and twentieth centuries there remained periodic irritation and the natural difficulties created by a union of two nations of vastly different size and power, but no blood was spilled in trying to keep it together. Elsewhere, history during that period offers few comparable examples.

V

HANOVERIAN BRITAIN

1745

THE MUSIC AND LYRICS OF 'GOD SAVE THE KING'

THE ORIGINS OF THE NATIONAL ANTHEM

In July 1745, James II's grandson, Prince Charles Edward Stuart – 'Bonnie Prince Charlie' – landed at Moidart on the west coast of Scotland and the following month raised his standard at Glenfinnan. His intention was to overthrow Hanoverian rule, to revoke the 1701 Act of Settlement and to assert the right of his father, James Francis Edward Stuart, then aged fifty-seven, to the throne for which he had been born.

Many of the Highland Scottish clans were reluctant subjects of the Hanoverian monarchy and quickly pledged allegiance to the Stuart cause. With this swelling band of 'Jacobite' followers, Prince Charles Edward marched into Edinburgh in September, holding court there and defeating government forces outside the city at Prestonpans.

In London there was good reason to panic. With much of the British army engaged on the European continent, fighting in the War of the Austrian Succession, the capital was defended only by a numerically inferior detachment of Guards and a ragbag militia ineffectually blocking the road at Finchley. The capital, it seemed, was on the brink of falling into the hands of a rabble Scottish army, while the country stood in danger of being ruled by a pro-French Roman Catholic with tendencies favourable to absolute monarchy.

It was in this fevered atmosphere that a song was struck up in the theatres at Drury Lane and Covent Garden. Its composer and lyricist remain unclear, the first published form of the tune having appeared, without attribution, the previous year. It may have been a reworking of an earlier tune, bearing some similarities to works by John Bull (1562–1628) and Henry Purcell (1659–95). Whatever its origins, it was perfect for the moment in 1745. It immediately caught on, being sung in the theatres night after night with increasing vehemence and defiance as the crisis deepened. Indeed, its choruses were echoed across the capital, its popularity fuelled by the publication of the words and music in the *Gentleman's Magazine* and similar newspapers.

The song was 'God Save the King' and it was arranged for performance at Drury Lane by Thomas Arne, who was at that time second only to George Frideric Handel as London's most celebrated composer. Despite being himself a Catholic, Arne was a supporter of the Hanoverian cause. Five years previously, he had composed the song 'Rule Britannia!' (whose lyrics were by the Scottish poet, James Thomson) as the centrepiece of *Alfred: A Masque*, which he performed for the Prince of Wales at Cliveden in Buckinghamshire. 'God Save the King' was intended to rally anti-Jacobite sentiment rather than become a defining declaration of Britishness (there was no concept of a national anthem at that time). Therefore, the lines 'Confound their politics/ Frustrate their knavish tricks' referred to Jacobite sympathizers rather than foreign countries. Various alternative versions soon flourished, one of which included a fourth verse expressing the hope:

> Lord, grant that Marshal Wade
> May by thy mighty aid
> Victory bring
> May he sedition hush
> And like a torrent rush
> Rebellious Scots to crush
> God save the King.

THE JACOBITE RISINGS

1708 Admiral Byng thwarts an attempt by the Old Pretender (James Francis Edward Stuart) to land with French troops in the Firth of Forth.

The 1715 Rising

8 March 1715 The Earl of Mar raises the Scottish clans to the Jacobite cause.

13 November The Jacobite advance is halted at the Battle of Sheriffmuir in Perthshire.

14 November A Jacobite force surrenders at Preston.

23 December The Old Pretender lands at Peterhead with the intention of being crowned King James VIII of Scots at Scone. Instead, he finds the Jacobite forces already demoralized and returns to France on 4 February 1716.

1719 Storms disrupt a pro-Jacobite Spanish invasion fleet. A small landing party surrenders at Glen Shiel.

The 1745 Rising

1744 A storm wrecks a pro-Jacobite French invasion fleet intending to land in Essex.

19 August 1745 Prince Charles Edward Stuart raises his standard at Glenfinnan and claims the Scottish and English thrones for his father.

21 September The Hanoverian camp is overwhelmed at Prestonpans, east of Edinburgh.

4 December Prince Charles's army reaches as far as Derby before retreating to Scotland to raise more support.

17 January 1746 The Jacobites are victorious at the Battle of Falkirk.

16 April The Jacobites are routed at Culloden Moor, near Inverness.

20 September Prince Charles is rescued by a French ship, which takes him back into exile.

1759 A French invasion plan to foment a new Jacobite rebellion is called off.

The words and music for what became the national anthem were published in The Gentleman's Magazine *in October 1745.*

552   *A Song for two Voices. As sung at both Playhouses.*

God save great GEORGE our king, Long live our noble king.

God save great GEORGE our king, Long live our noble king.

God save the king. Send him vic‑to‑ri‑ous, Happy and glo‑ri‑ous,

God save the king. Send him vic‑to‑ri‑ous, Happy and glo‑ri‑ous,

Long to reign o‑ver us, God save the king.

Long to reign o‑ver us. God save the king.

2.
O Lord our God arise,
Scatter his enemies,
   And make them fall;
Confound their politics,
Fruftrate their knavifh tricks,
On him our hopes we fix,
   O fave us all.

3.
Thy choiceft gifts in ftore
On *George* be pleas'd to pour,
   Long may he reign;
May he defend our laws,
And ever give us caufe,
To fay with heart and voice
   God fave the king.

A SOLILOQUY.

——*From evil ftill educing good.*   Thomfon.

SHALL FREEDOM, now, her care for *Britain*
   o'er,   [fhore!
Spread her white wings, and fpurn her long‑lov'd
Our weeping *maids* fhall lawlefs ruffians ftain!
To fpare the *babe* our *mothers* kneel in vain?
Infulted, vanquifh'd, in unequal ftrife
Shall the fond hufband ftabb'd refign the wife?
Shall hungry robbers plunder *Englifh* wealth?
And fkulking *Britons* eat their bread by ftealth?
  With thee, O GODDESS! ev'ry *filial art,*
Peace, plenty, fcience, fhall at once depart;
Incumbent o'er us *Ign'rance* fhall difplay
Her leathern wings, and intercept the day;
Blind Zeal's red torch alone, with hateful light,
Shall juft difclofe the terrors of the night,
While *Superftition,* raving, fhakes the blade,
That fmokes ☿ blood, and glitters thro' ỹ fhade;
What once were men grow brutes at her controul,
Debas'd, enflav'd—in *body* and in *foul!*
  But whence thefe doubts, and whence the fears
   I feel?
Can rebel outlaws fhake the publick weal?
Slaves—by a beardlefs, hot‑brain'd bigot led!——
My indignation burns, my fears are fled;

They come to bid our fleeping virtues rife,
By thefe our Genius fpeaks;—his words are wife?
' Hear me, ye fons of *Eafe,* whom *Sloth* difarms,
' And *Pleafure* captivates, with tinfel charms,
' Yours is the finewy nerve that taught fo late
' *France,* conquer'd *France,* to tremble for her fate.
' You fmil'd, contemptuous, at the tyrant's nods,
' And drew the fword for *Liberty* and GOD,
' Each man an hero,—*Glory* all his pay;
' And yet you fleep in *Lux'ry's* lap to‑day.
' The foe's at hand!—there's ruin at the door;!
' Wake now *for Liberty,* or wake no more!'
Rouz'd at the call, our heroes fhine again,
Old Englifh courage beats in ev'ry vein,
With honeft blufhes ev'ry cheek is dy'd,
And ev'ry hand is to the fword apply'd;
Rome's hoft of fculptur'd faints neglect her pray'r,
And all her curfes are difpers'd in air:
Still, as of old, the cords fhe weaves we break,
Our ftrength returning with the rowzing fhake.
  So *Sampfon,* flumb'ring on an harlot's knee,
With eafe was fetter'd, dreaming he was free;
But—*The Philiftines come!*—he heard and rofe,
Lord of himfelf, the terror of his foes;
Refumes his might, their various arts difdains,
Looks up, and fmiling breaks the facile chains.

                        BRITANNICUS.

Field Marshal George Wade was in charge of the army in the north during the Jacobite invasion. This verse was not in Arne's arrangement, did not outlive the crisis and was never a part of the version adopted as the national anthem.

The crisis passed because Prince Charles Edward flunked his chance. Rather than pressing on to take the lightly defended London, he was persuaded at Derby to turn back to gather more support in Scotland. This gave the Hanoverian forces time to muster and, in April 1746, on Culloden Moor near Inverness, the bedraggled and half-starving Jacobite party, wielding swords and uttering ancient battle-cries, was shot to pieces by a modern, well-drilled army commanded by the king's younger son, William, duke of Cumberland. Those who escaped the slaughter were hunted down, often with excessive savagery, and the 'Bonnie Prince' went on the run before escaping to France. This great hope of all those who wanted to restore a Stuart and a Catholic to the British throne died in Rome in 1788, a debauched and broken figure.

By then, 'God Save the King' was becoming recognized as the national anthem, in an innovation that other European countries rushed to follow. Initially, Prussia and Russia copied it to the extent of retaining the same tune, and for most of the nineteenth century it was also the Swedish royal family's anthem. Even the infant United States held on to it, although substituting the loyalist sentiments with new words: 'My country, 'tis of thee'. With the help of the British Empire, it was a tune that travelled the world.

1755
SAMUEL JOHNSON'S
DICTIONARY

THE CELEBRATED ENGLISH-LANGUAGE DICTIONARY

When Samuel Johnson published *A Dictionary of the English Language* in 1755, he was not breaking new ground. There had been Latin–English dictionaries since the fifteenth century, while the first to offer definitions of English words without Latin equivalents was Robert Cawdrey's *A Table Alphabeticall* in 1604. Thus Johnson's work was neither the first nor – despite its 42,773 entries – even the one with the greatest number of words defined. However, it was the one that caught the popular imagination. In its various versions, it remained the most commonly used dictionary until the completion of the *Oxford English Dictionary* in 1928.

Remarkably, it was the product not of a team of lexicographers but of one man's erudition and labour, aided only by five or six copyists working in the garret of his house off Fleet Street. It was not surprising that, denied the support of a patron or an institution, it took Johnson almost nine years to compile. Whilst many of his predecessors had devoted excessive space to Latin and Greek terms, Johnson paid particular attention to everyday language. Furthermore, his compilation was revolutionary in a second respect, because it contained around 114,000 quotations, providing polished literary examples of usage. The result was a dictionary that also strove to be the most significant anthology of English literary quotation then in existence.

Unquestionably, this facet was part of its enduring appeal. Even a critic of Johnson's skills as an etymologist – the writer and politician Thomas Babington Macaulay (1800–59) – readily conceded that it was 'the first dictionary which could be read with pleasure. The definitions show so much acuteness of thought and command of language, and the passages quoted from poets, divines and philosophers are so skilfully selected, that a leisure hour may always be very agreeably spent in turning over the pages.'

Naturally, as the work of one man, it contained some idiosyncrasies, although this was also part of its charm. The famous disdain for Scotland with which he later teased his friend and biographer, James Boswell, was apparent in, for example:

> **Oats** n.s. [*aten*, Saxon] A grain, which in England is generally given to horses, but in Scotland supports the people.

Nor could Johnson resist mockery in matters close to his own experience. His definition of 'Lexicographer' was 'a writer of dictionaries; a harmless drudge', while the entry for 'patron' started, 'One who countenances, supports or protects' before continuing, 'Commonly a wretch who supports with insolence, and is paid with flattery.' He was also honest enough to admit when he did not know the meaning and etymology of some words, whilst also decrying some usages of which he disapproved. He was prepared to include crude terms but drew the line at obscenities.

Samuel Johnson, portrayed at the age of sixty-seven by Sir Joshua Reynolds.

Two thousand copies were printed of the first edition, which appeared in two volumes on 15 April 1755. At £4 10s, the price was far beyond the average means of most and sales were initially sluggish. The following year, Johnson brought out a two-volume abridged version, shorn of quotations, which proved far more popular. He produced a considerably revised edition in 1773, a process that other editors continued, in his name, after his death in 1784, by which time the dictionary was established as a classic work.

He was born the son of a Lichfield bookshop owner in 1709 and was educated at the local grammar school. Little in Samuel Johnson's early years suggested he would become one of the most eminent men of his age. Tall, clumsy, short-sighted and deaf in one ear, as well as subject to involuntary convulsions, he endured poor health throughout his life. Bracing himself for the financial hardship involved, he went up to Pembroke College, Oxford, but dropped out without a degree. (Oxford subsequently conferred upon him an MA in recognition of his dictionary; it is thanks to an honorary doctorate from Trinity College, Dublin, in 1765 that he became known as 'Dr Johnson'.) From 1740 he lived in London,

A SHORT LIST OF ENGLISH DICTIONARIES

1604 Robert Cawdrey's *A Table Alphabeticall* (contains definitions for 2,500 words).

1676 Elisha Coles's *An English Dictionary*.

1702 John Kersey's *New English Dictionary*.

1721 and 1727 Nathan Bailey's *Universal Etymological English Dictionary*.

1730 Nathan Bailey's *Dictionarium Britannicum*.

1755 Samuel Johnson's *Dictionary of the English Language*.

1881 The first volume (A–Ant) of what will be the *Oxford English Dictionary*.

1928 Complete edition of the *Oxford English Dictionary*.

scraping a precarious living as a journalist, a reporter of parliamentary debates and a biographer. He was down on his luck when, in 1746, the offer came from a consortium of publishers to write the dictionary in return for 1,500 guineas, minus expenses.

The work took three times longer than was budgeted for and brought its author no great wealth. However, it did establish his reputation and helped bring him further into the circle of many of the most noted literary and political figures of the age as well as the young James Boswell, with whom he travelled to the Hebrides. The resulting *A Journey to the Western Islands of Scotland* offered a poignant depiction of a pre-Enlightenment world. Always a loyal friend, Boswell's post-humous life of Johnson – detailing his Tory irascibility together with his great compassion and humanity, his struggles with disappointment and physical pain, and recording for posterity his many aphorisms – came to be recognized as one of the foremost examples of the biographical genre.

Johnson also wrote many fine poems, sermons, political essays and produced an edition of Shakespeare's plays, but it was his dictionary that endured. Although the *Oxford English Dictionary* finally and comprehensively superseded his masterpiece, its editors could not escape reproducing over 1,700 of his definitions, duly acknowledged under the letter 'J'.

1766
THE DECLARATORY ACT

WESTMINSTER ASSERTS ITS RIGHT TO TAX AND
LEGISLATE IN THE AMERICAN COLONIES

British politicians did not squander George III's North American colonies in one foolish act, but in several. It is doubtful whether even the most considered understanding of the colonists' desires and aspirations would have prevented an eventual breach, but possibly some loose relationship under the British Crown might have endured, as it did, for instance, in Canada. While the causes of the American War of Independence (known in the United States as the Revolutionary War) were many, they mostly touched upon one overarching question: should a parliament in Westminster enjoy the legal right to tax and order the affairs of distant Americans who had no direct representation in it? This was the substantive issue that the 1766 Declaratory Act sought to settle.

Laws in all thirteen British colonies in America were enacted by their own legislatures. Their lower houses were elected and their rights codified in written constitutions. Nine were classified as 'Crown colonies' where the executive, in the guise of the governor and his council (the upper house of the legislature), were appointed by the king in London. Thus, Britain's principal relationship with these American colonies was via the monarch, not the Westminster Parliament. Some eminent Americans, like Benjamin Franklin, were originally keen to keep this distinction, lamenting how 'Every man in England seems to consider himself as a piece of a sovereign over America; seems to jostle himself into the throne with the king, and talks of our subjects in the Colonies.'

Two problems had emerged by the mid-eighteenth century to trouble this arrangement. The first concerned the constitutional balance in Britain, which had tilted during the previous one hundred years towards viewing the monarch as ruling through, and not over, Parliament. The second issue was that the defence and security of the American colonies imposed costs upon the British taxpayer

201

The Declaratory Act, 1766

Whereas several of the houses of representatives in his Majesty's colonies and plantations in America, have of late, against law, claimed to themselves, or to the general assemblies of the same, the sole and exclusive right of imposing duties and taxes upon his Majesty's subjects in the said colonies and plantations; and have, in pursuance of such claim, passed certain votes, resolutions, and orders derogatory to the legislative authority of Parliament, and inconsistent with the dependency of the said colonies and plantations upon the Crown of Great Britain: may it therefore please our most excellent Majesty that it may be declared; and be it declared by the King's most excellent Majesty, by and with advice and consent of the Lords Spiritual and Temporal, and Commons, in this present Parliament assembled, and by the authority of the same, that the said colonies and plantations in America have been, are, and of right ought to be, subordinate unto, and dependent upon the imperial Crown and Parliament of Great Britain; and that the King's Majesty, by and with advice and consent of the Lords Spiritual and Temporal, and Commons of Great Britain, in Parliament assembled, had, hath, and of right ought to have, full power and authority to make laws and statutes of sufficient force and validity to bind the colonies and people of America, subjects of the Crown of Great Britain, in all cases whatsoever.

II. And be it further declared and enacted by the authority aforesaid, that all resolutions, votes, orders, and proceedings, in any of the said colonies or plantations, whereby the power and authority of the Parliament of Great Britain, to make laws and statutes as aforesaid, is denied, or drawn into question, are, are hereby declared to be, utterly null and void to all intents and purposes whatsoever.

that the colonists themselves were reluctant to help shoulder. And in Britain, levying taxes was firmly the prerogative of Parliament.

By its end in 1763, the Seven Years War had tilted Anglo-French rivalry, in North America and India, decisively in Britain's favour, but the victory was won at a cost. The National Debt exceeded £129 million with the annual interest charged running at £4.6 million. At a time when the average British male was paying 26 shillings a year in tax, his American cousin was being levied just 1 shilling. His Majesty's subjects in Bristol were not slow to ask why His Majesty's subjects in Boston were let off

THE AMERICAN REVOLUTION

1763 American colonists bristle at George III's proclamation ordering them not to settle Native American land west of the Appalachian Mountains.

1765 The Stamp Act is imposed on all printed matter.

1766 The Stamp Act is abolished, but the right to tax the colonists is asserted by the Declaratory Act.

1767 New 'Townshend duties' are imposed on everyday items including lead, paper and tea.

1770 All Townshend duties repealed except on tea. The Boston 'Massacre' occurs, in which British troops kill five members of a hostile mob.

1773 The 'Boston Tea Party': colonists protest against the East India Company's monopoly of the tea trade.

1774 Coercive Acts are introduced to bring the Boston boycotts to an end. The first Continental Congress meets in Philadelphia with representatives of all thirteen colonies except Georgia to discuss common action.

1775 The first skirmishes of the rebellion take place at Lexington and Concord. The second Continental Congress in Philadelphia puts George Washington in charge of a 'Patriot' army. The indecisive Battle of Bunker Hill is fought near Boston. George III refuses negotiations.

1776 The Continental Congress approves the Declaration of Independence. George Washington proves unable to take New York and abandons Philadelphia.

1777 General Burgoyne's British force surrenders at Saratoga. Washington's army endures a harsh winter at Valley Forge.

1778 France enters the war on the American rebels' side.

1779 Spain declares war on Britain. The British win a victory at Savannah.

1780 The British are victorious at Charleston.

1781 A Franco-American force receives the British General Cornwallis's surrender at Yorktown.

1782 The British Parliament votes to end the war.

1783 Britain acknowledges the independence of the United States at the Treaty of Paris. About 100,000 pro-British loyalists flee the new nation, many going north. George Washington resigns his commission.

so lightly, despite enjoying the personal and commercial protection of the British army and navy. Indeed, it was a costly business to station troops in the colonies to safeguard them against Native American tribes and the French.

Seeking to cover part of the expense, the government in London, led by the prime minister, George Grenville, caused outrage across the Atlantic by imposing upon colonists a Stamp Act that taxed official papers, newspapers and pamphlets, playing cards and dice. The measure was unpopular not just because that is the nature of new taxes but because it was felt to exceed Westminster's remit.

Facing howls of colonial outrage and boycotts of British goods, in July 1765 a new administration was formed under the Marquess of Rockingham that began the process of backing down. The Stamp Act's repeal was accompanied by what, at first, looked merely like a statement designed to save London's face. The Declaratory Act, which passed through both Houses of Parliament with minimal dissent, insisted that Westminster 'had, hath and of right ought to have, full power and authority to make laws and statutes of sufficient force and validity to bind the colonies and people of America'.

What did this mean in practice? Benjamin Franklin at first thought it tolerable only in the sense that it could be considered 'in the same Light with the Claim of the Spanish Monarch to the Title of King of Jerusalem'. Yet it was clear that British politicians – despite lacking an elected mandate from across the Atlantic – were not content to treat Americans with benign neglect. Although nominal, the tax on tea was kept. Also retained was legislation designed to maintain good relations with the Native American tribes by restricting further colonial expansion beyond the Appalachian mountains, which conflicted with the colonists' desire to 'go west'. The escalating disorder and disobedience in radical port cities like Boston all but invited a heavy-handed response, a trap into which the British fell.

There were belated attempts by both sides to stave off outright rebellion. Indeed, the first Continental Congress meeting in Philadelphia in 1774 on the eve of the revolution rejected by just one vote a proposal by the Pennsylvanian politician Joseph Galloway that would have given the thirteen colonies the right to collectively veto Westminster legislation while keeping them within the British Empire. Meanwhile, Lord North's government was reluctant to concede the basis upon which the Declaratory Act rested. It was this that provided the rebel colonists with their most persuasive battle-cry, 'No taxation without representation!'

The result was a bitter conflict that divided the loyalties and sympathies of Britons and colonists alike. The intervention of the French eventually tilted the campaign in the rebel colonists' favour. After British defeat at Yorktown in 1781, London decided to cut its losses. After all, on the eve of war the value of the American colonies' exports to Britain was still worth only a fifth of what was being traded from Jamaica. In 1783 Britain duly recognized the independent United States of America. So ended one phase in Britain's colonial expansion: with the emergence of an English-speaking power that would eventually eclipse the United Kingdom.

1767

JAMES CRAIG'S PLAN FOR EDINBURGH'S NEW TOWN

❧

GEORGIAN URBAN PLANNING AND THE 'SCOTTISH ENLIGHTENMENT'

In the half-century following the monarchy's restoration in 1660, British architecture was transformed by four men of genius: Sir Christopher Wren, Nicholas Hawksmoor, Sir John Vanbrugh and James Gibbs. Their buildings exemplified the dramatic tension and exuberance of the Baroque style that was already so prevalent across Europe. However, after 1715, a new architectural movement in Britain rejected the fussy ornamentation and dramatic artifices of the Baroque. Instead, design was to be more pure, seeking inspiration from a closer study of classical antiquity and the work of the sixteenth-century Italian scholar-architect, Andrea Palladio.

This Classical Revival became the style associated with Whig politics, rationalism and the philosophical principles of the Enlightenment. It found its most sublime expression in the latest 'neo-Palladian' country houses of the Whig aristocracy and the urban planning of a city that was the intellectual capital of Britain's 'Age of Reason' – Edinburgh.

Despite losing its national parliament in 1707, Edinburgh remained the capital of Scotland's separate legal and Church establishments. In addition, while Oxford and Cambridge universities were temporarily descending into intellectual torpor, Edinburgh University was experiencing its golden age. The economist Adam Smith, the philosopher David Hume and the sociologist Adam Ferguson were among the leaders of this Scottish Enlightenment, elevating Edinburgh into a 'Capital of the Mind'.

The city's problem was that it had been built on the volcanic ridge leading from the palace of Holyroodhouse at one end up to the castle at the other. The location of this, the Old Town, and its main artery, the Royal Mile, was a confined site, with

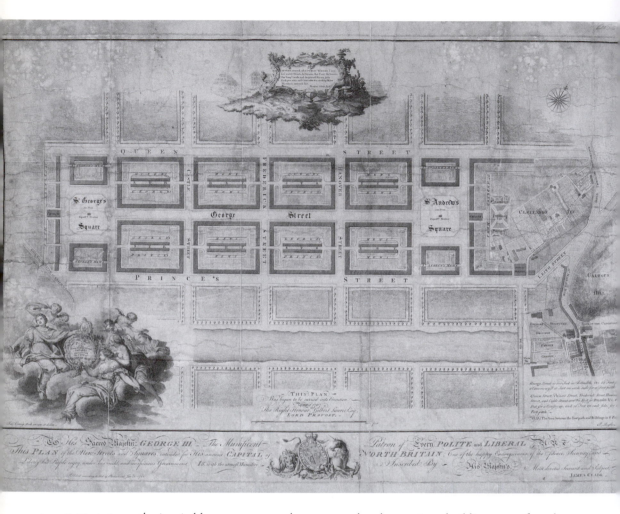

James Craig's winning plan for Edinburgh's New Town, complete with street names exalting both the union of Scotland with England and the Hanoverian succession.

the inevitable consequences that congested and unsanitary buildings were forced precariously upwards rather than outwards. Finally, the city council decided to sponsor the drainage of the land to the north and to build a bridge, beyond which it was proposed to construct an entirely new residential district far more worthy of Edinburgh's moneyed and cultured citizens.

In 1766, a competition to design what became known as the New Town was won by James Craig, a native of the city, aged just twenty-seven, whose uncle was James Thomson, the poet and librettist of 'Rule, Britannia!' Craig envisaged a grid street plan of straight boulevards. After some revisions were made by others, Craig showed his plan to King George III.

The king's approval was never in doubt. He was presented not just with a scheme of urban planning but with a document that wiped clean the Scottish capital's previous taints of Jacobitism and separatism. Rather, with names like Hanover Street, George Street and Frederick Street, the projected stately avenues boldly proclaimed allegiance to the Hanoverian succession. The west and east ends were to be marked by two grand spaces symbolizing the union of Scotland and England: St George's Square and St Andrew's Square.

Upon completion in 1791, St George's was in fact named Charlotte Square after George III's queen, Charlotte of Mecklenburg. Its buildings were the work of Robert Adam (1728–92). A Scot who had travelled to Rome and worked extensively in London, Robert Adam was among the foremost architects of the period, through his combination of neo-Palladian elegance with exquisite interior decoration inspired by his deep classical knowledge. His work even intruded into the Old Town, where the university quadrangle received his elegant classical treatment.

Craig, however, proved unable to win fresh commissions and died in obscurity in 1795. His debts mounting, he had been forced to pawn his competition winner's gold medal, and he was buried in an unmarked grave. Less than a mile away, his New Town was finally taking shape, however, lined by the stone-fronted townhouses of Adam and others, achieving a harmonious unity by their fashionable emphasis on order and symmetry, the ordered monotony of their layout broken by spacious squares and sweeping crescents.

In England during the 1830s, a reaction set in against classical architecture, manifesting itself in the Gothic Revival. It was this neo-medieval aesthetic that became the most recognizable style of the Victorian age. Yet perhaps because of its connotations of High Church ritualism, Gothic Revival fared less well in Presbyterian Scotland, where classicism's simple austerity continued to marry philosophy with architectural principles. There, study turned from Roman to Hellenic classicism in the work of the architects Thomas Hamilton (1784–1858) and W. H. Playfair (1790–1857), expanding and enhancing the Georgian city with grand Greek Revival buildings. Calton Hill was turned into a Scottish Acropolis and the phrase of the artist Hugh William Williams stuck: Edinburgh was truly the 'Athens of the North'.

1769

ARKWRIGHT'S
WATER FRAME PATENT

TEXTILES AND THE INDUSTRIAL REVOLUTION

In 1760, Britain's textile industry consisted of men and women who sat in their cottages working their own spinning wheels to make thread, which was passed on to weavers. The market for fine muslins was provided by importing quality cloth from India. The smallness of the British enterprise can be measured by how little raw cotton was imported – only around 3 million pounds, which came mostly from South America and the West Indies. By 1789, the situation was transformed. Imports of raw cotton exceeded 32 million pounds, a figure that by 1802 had passed 60 million. The cottage-dweller working away between periodic tendings of the pot over the fire had been replaced by hundreds of employees in huge mills, churning out finished textiles for both the home and export markets at a fraction of the previous price.

Inventions drove this Industrial Revolution, among which Richard Arkwright's water frame heralded the most fundamental change in the scale and organization of manufacturing in Britain.

In 1764, James Hargreaves (c.1720–78), an illiterate carpenter and weaver from Lancashire, was credited with devising the 'spinning jenny'. It represented a significant advance on the traditional tools of the trade because it featured a mobile carriage that allowed multiple spindles to be worked, thereby greatly increasing output. However, it produced brittle thread.

The spinning machine that Richard Arkwright patented in 1769 was different in several respects. It consisted of three sets of rollers that ran parallel to each other and turned the yarn at different speeds, with the fibres twisted and tightened together by a set of spindles. The result was a much stronger thread, which successfully made good-quality cloth from pure cotton.

Other factors were more broadly significant. Hargreaves' jenny was hand-

DRIVING FORCES OF THE INDUSTRIAL REVOLUTION

1700 Total national coal output is estimated at 2,612,000 tons.

1709 Abraham Darby uses coke, rather than wood or charcoal, to smelt iron ore.

1712 Thomas Newcomen's steam engine is used to pump out water from mines.

1733 John Kay patents his flying shuttle.

1742 The publisher, Edward Cave, buys Marvel's Mill in Northamptonshire and converts it into Britain's first water-powered cotton mill. It soon has over a hundred employees.

1761 The Bridgewater Canal opens, the first canal in Britain to be constructed that did not follow an existing watercourse. Originally connecting Worsley to Manchester, it was extended to the Mersey, at Runcorn, in 1766.

1764 James Hargreaves creates the spinning jenny.

1769 Richard Arkwright patents his water frame.

1772 Manchester and Salford have a combined population of about 25,000.

1773 The first factory-produced all-cotton textiles are made.

1775/6 James Watt's steam engine greatly improves upon Newcomen's pump.

1777 The Grand Trunk Canal links the Midlands with the major ports.

1779 Samuel Crompton invents the spinning mule.

1784 Henry Cort patents the puddling process for refining iron ore which, with his steel rolling mill, proves a superior way of producing bar iron from pig iron.

1785 Edmund Cartwright patents his power loom.

1789 The Thames–Severn Canal opens.

1790 The Forth and Clyde Canal opens, allowing vessels to pass through Scotland from the west coast to the east coast.

c.1792 William Murdoch invents gas lighting (but fails to patent it). In 1805 the Philips and Lee cotton mill in Manchester becomes the first to be entirely lit by gaslight.

1800 Manchester and Salford have a combined population of about 95,000.

1815 Sir Humphry Davy invents his safety lamp, permitting deep seams to be mined without igniting flammable gases.

1816 Total national coal output estimated at 15,635,000 tonnes.

powered, which made it compatible with the cottage as the place of work. Arkwright's machine, in contrast, was powered by water and was intended not for the humble home but for large mills yoking the power of rivers. It therefore involved a shift in industrial organization, creating mass-production techniques in factories worked by unskilled labour.

The mill that Arkwright opened at Cromford on the River Derwent in Derbyshire in 1771 emphasised the shift in scale. Within a decade it had 5,000 employees. It exemplified the industrial future and, as such, was a disaster for traditional weavers. Work that had previously been undertaken by skilled labourers could now be done, far more quickly and cheaply, by children as young as six. Unable to compete with this new invention, the response of many whose livelihoods it removed was to try to smash it up. A mob broke into Hargreaves' house and destroyed his working models; in 1779, rioters sacked Arkwright's mill in Chorley in Lancashire. At Cromford, which already resembled a forbidding fortress, he kept a cannon loaded and ready to fire grapeshot against a similar assault. Innovation in working practices came at the price of an abrasive attitude to labour relations.

The long hours, the tough conditions, the dehumanizing nature of the unskilled work and the reality that so many of the employees were children symbolized all that was least attractive about this fresh way of making profits for factory owners.

One of the copies made of Arkwright's water frame patent.

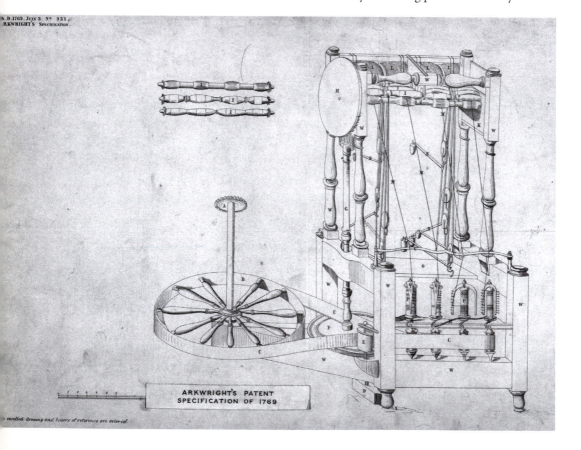

ARKWRIGHT'S PATENT
SPECIFICATION OF 1769

The poet William Blake encapsulated this in his indelible phrase when he wrote of 'dark Satanic Mills'. The description was fair but, on the other hand, factories also brought gains. The wages paid were low, yet sufficiently higher than those often paid to farm labourers, prompting them to leave the fields and make instead for the new northern towns and cities growing up around these novel sources of employment. There were knock-on benefits: the factories produced garments at a fraction of their previous price to the purchaser. The cost of living came down and the mass consumer society was born.

The process also, of course, made the likes of Arkwright extremely rich. His story illustrates the social mobility that the Industrial Revolution brought in its wake. He had been born in Preston in 1732, the youngest of thirteen children. His parents could not afford to send him to school and the only education he received was from a cousin who taught him to read and write. He became a wigmaker before turning his mind from hair to thread, although the water frame with which he made his fortune was not, for the most part, his invention. It has always been disputed exactly how much input he contributed to the design – so much so that he lost the patent for it in 1785. It was probably largely the work of John Kay, a former clockmaker from Warrington whom Arkwright engaged. Kay, in turn, developed a design originally made by Thomas Highs, who has also been credited with the prototype for Hargreaves' jenny.

Whoever came up with the model, it was Arkwright who saw the possibilities for maximizing its potential. He and others like him represented something sufficiently new in England that a French word had to be conscripted: Arkwright was an *entrepreneur*. He died in 1792 in conditions far removed from the circumstances of his birth – having been awarded a knighthood by King George III and having amassed a fortune estimated at £500,000. The machine that had made his success possible was superseded first by Samuel Crompton's 'spinning mule' and thereafter by other developments as water gave way to steam power, an advance that Arkwright had embraced at his factory in Nottingham. He had, nonetheless, lived long enough to see the economy and society of Britain embark on an extraordinary transformation that set the country on course to becoming the workshop of the world.

1772
THE SOMERSET JUDGMENT

SLAVERY IN ENGLAND IS RULED ILLEGAL

Slavery had long been common throughout much of Africa, but it was from the sixteenth century onwards that Britons saw great opportunities for personal gain by joining the trade in human cargo. In this, they were hoping to exploit a market that the Portuguese had already opened up and which other nations, including the French, were also keen to exploit. From ports across Britain, ships sailed out, bound for the West African coast, there to buy slaves from a network of Arab and African traders. During the eighteenth century, when the transatlantic slave trade reached its peak, around 3 million slaves were shipped in horrific conditions across the Atlantic to be worked to death in the British plantations of North America and the sugar-growing islands of the Caribbean. Such were the slaves' importance to the vast profits being generated for their masters that the Westminster Parliament did not think to overrule the colonial legislatures that permitted such exploitation. What, however, was slavery's legal status on the British mainland?

Serfdom, a form of quasi-slavery, had for centuries been part of the feudal structure of medieval England. Tying the lowest class of peasants (and their offspring) to manors, it obliged them to work at least part of the week for their lord in return for shelter, protection and the lease of a plot for personal cultivation. The practice declined rapidly in the fourteenth century when the Black Death created a scarcity of labour, thereby improving the working conditions of those who survived. By the end of the fourteenth century serfdom was all but extinct.

Whether slaves could be legally imported from abroad was disputed. The fact that there was no law on the statute books explicitly endorsing chattel slavery in England did not, of itself, make it illegal. The position of the common law on the subject was not clear-cut, since various judgments had been contradictory. A 1569 judgment on the use of a Russian slave allegedly declared that 'England was too pure an air for slaves to breathe in', although this had not prevented imported slaves being a continuing presence in Britain nor even the periodic existence of slave markets in cities like Bristol and Liverpool. In 1729 the attorney-general and the solicitor-general both gave their opinions that slaves were not accorded their freedom merely by setting foot on English soil nor through receiving baptism and that, therefore, they could be legally transported from England to plantations.

Modern estimates suggest that in the 1770s there were between 3,000 and 15,000 black people in Britain. Some were free; some were in servitude akin to, or actually involving, slavery. It was during the second half of the eighteenth century that slavery became a far more contentious issue, rousing the Nonconformist conscience and drawing Quakers to the fore in exposing its evils. However, it also disgusted many Anglicans, opening up a division that cut right across the religious and political Establishment.

It was in this changing environment that the campaigner Granville Sharp led a group of abolitionists determined to bring before the courts a new test case on the legality of slaveholding. In James Somerset they found someone they hoped would prove the perfect cause. Somerset was an African-born slave from Virginia who had been brought to England by his master, a Boston customs officer. While in England, Somerset had seized his moment to escape, only to be recaptured. Chained, he was about to be shipped to Jamaica, where he was to be resold, when Sharp's friends managed to serve a writ of habeas corpus that prevented his departure.

BRITAIN AND THE SLAVE TRADE

1562 England's first slave trader, Sir John Hawkins, picks up 500 Africans and sells them to Spanish and Portuguese traders.

1660 The Royal Adventurers into Africa (subsequently the Royal African Company) is granted a monopoly to trade in slaves. Its governor is James, duke of York (later James II).

1698 With the end of the Royal African Company's monopoly, the slave trade is opened up to competition.

1727 The London Meeting of the Society of Friends (the Quakers) condemns the slave trade and prohibits Quakers from trading in or owning slaves.

1729 The Yorke–Talbot ruling by the attorney-general and the solicitor-general states that baptism does not free slaves from their servitude.

1765–69 Sir William Blackstone's *Commentaries on the Laws of England* argues that when a negro arrives in England he 'becomes a freeman'.

1772 Lord Mansfield delivers the Somerset Judgment in *Rex v. Knowles, ex parte Somersett*.

1774 John Wesley's *Thoughts upon Slavery* condemns the practice.

1775 A Royal Commission is established to investigate the slave trade.

1778 *Knight vs Wedderburn* establishes the legal precedent that slavery is illegal in Scotland.

1781 There is popular outrage at the throwing overboard of shackled slaves by the captain of the *Zong*.

1787 The Society for the Abolition of the Slave Trade is launched by Granville Sharp and Thomas Clarkson. By 1792 it has gathered half a million signatures.

1792 The House of Commons passes a bill to abolish the slave trade in four years' time, but it fails to pass in the House of Lords.

1807 The slave trade is abolished.

1833 The Abolition of Slavery Act makes slavery illegal throughout the British Empire (with final anomalies removed by 1843).

Lord Mansfield's judgment: from *Howell's State Trials*, vol. 20

So high an act of dominion must be recognised by the law of the country where it is used. The power of a master over his slave has been extremely different, in different countries. The state of slavery is of such a nature, that it is incapable of being introduced on any reasons, moral or political, but only by positive law, which preserves its force long after the reasons, occasion, and time itself from whence it was created, is erased from memory. It is so odious, that nothing can be suffered to support it, but positive law. Whatever inconveniences, therefore, may follow from the decision, I cannot say this case is allowed or approved by the law of England; and therefore the black must be discharged.

The case was heard by the Court of King's Bench in Westminster Hall. Sitting in judgment was the Scottish jurist, Lord Chief Justice William Murray, earl of Mansfield. Despite his private sympathy, there was little in Mansfield's previous pronouncements to give the abolitionists grounds for excessive optimism. As proceedings unfolded, it was clear that he wanted to keep to the specifics of the case while avoiding making sweeping declarations of general emancipation. Finally, after a lengthy period of deliberation he delivered his judgment on 22 June 1772. No exact record of it exists, only the newspaper reports of what he said. While varying in the exact choice of words, they broadly concurred that what he stated was to the effect that slavery was 'so odious that nothing can be suffered to support it but positive law. Whatever inconveniences, therefore, may follow from the decision, I cannot say this case is allowed or approved by the law of England; and therefore the black must be discharged.' For good measure, he reportedly repeated the dictum he had expressed in a previous case: *Fiat justitia, ruat coelum* ('Let justice be done, though the heavens fall').

In view of Mansfield's reluctance to create a new legal principle, his judgment was specific to the case rather than an absolute statement of emancipation. However, the work of the newspapers in printing and circulating his opinion ensured that the public understood the underlying principle underpinning his ruling – that the holding of slaves was illegal anywhere in England and Wales. In 1777, a judgment by the Court of Session in Edinburgh made explicit that the same applied in Scotland and, indeed, that slavery was incompatible with Scots law.

The Somerset Judgment thus became both a landmark ruling and evidence of the growing power of newspapers in quickly disseminating news and influencing opinion. When the news reached America, it was seen as an ominous sign by some slave-owning colonists, many of whom were soon to fight for independence from Britain. Nevertheless, Mansfield's verdict did not affect the transatlantic trade. It took the untiring work of many campaigners – in particular, by the evangelical Anglicans Thomas Clarkson and William Wilberforce, the latter the Tory MP for Hull – to finally bring the trade's abolition on to the statute book in 1807. As a result the British navy was to be actively deployed thereafter in liberating slaves wherever they were discovered on the seas. In 1833, Westminster finally grasped the nettle and overruled the practices tolerated overseas in its colonies by abolishing slavery throughout the British Empire.

It is not known what became of the freed James Somerset.

———•◦•———

<h1>1776</h1>

<h1>ADAM SMITH'S
THE WEALTH OF NATIONS</h1>

<h2>THE PHILOSOPHY OF FREE-MARKET ECONOMICS</h2>

Adam Smith's *An Inquiry into the Nature and Causes of the Wealth of Nations* provided the first truly comprehensive critique of what, until that moment, had been the prevailing economic consensus governing all Western thought. In its place, it promoted a new philosophy: the free market.

The received wisdom that Smith overturned was called mercantilism, which held that trade benefited the seller, who made money from the transaction, rather than the buyer, who had to pay for the purchase. Therefore, the government's role was to encourage exports and discourage imports through various interventions, ranging from prohibition or restriction of certain imports, to the imposition of protective tariffs that made them more expensive and less of a threat to domestic traders. Similarly, guilds and other regulatory bodies protected their members from being undercut. At the core of this mercantilist approach was the belief that trade was a zero-sum game because the wealth of the nation existed in the worth of its commerce and property – which meant that activities diverting that wealth abroad harmed the national wealth.

Published in 1776, when the Industrial Revolution had scarcely begun its transforming role, Smith's *Wealth of Nations* argued that the great assumption upon which mercantilist theory rested was mistaken. Trade was not a one-way transaction that benefited only the seller. His position was that imports could be good for business because they allowed the buyer to purchase what he wanted at a price lower than if he either had to make it himself or rely on an artificially restricted range of suppliers. The resulting saving could be invested more profitably elsewhere. Trade was therefore *mutually* beneficial.

At heart, the argument was expressed by Smith's insistence that 'Consumption is the sole end and purpose of all production.' This observation, at variance with the traditional favour shown to producers, implied that trade barriers and other protective regulations were, in reality, a means of distorting the true relationship. They stifled competition, creativity and innovation, all of which were in fact motors for increasing the variety and reducing the price of goods. 'People of the same trade seldom meet, even for merriment and diversion,' he claimed, 'but the conversation ends in a conspiracy against the public, or in some contrivance to raise prices.' The role of government was to remove the market-rigging mechanisms whereby producers created cartels or monopolistic restrictive practices.

Smith never actually used the term *laissez-faire*, subsequently applied to his views. Whilst he took the view that it was dangerously presumptuous of any government to think it could better direct the use of resources than multitudes of individuals interacting in a free market, he did believe that government was necessary to administer impartial justice, organize national defence, build essential public works and support public provision in areas like schooling where private enterprise could not do the job alone. He supported the notion of an income tax – which, needless to say, was one of the first of his proposals to be taken up by government.

Adam Smith (1723–90) was a reluctant sitter for portraits, but he did sit for his fellow Scot, James Tassie (1735–99), who made a white enamel medallion of his profile from which this popular engraving was made.

Some of the *Wealth of Nations'* most famous passages deal with its author's attempts to show that self-interest and natural liberty go hand in hand to produce the common good. The virtuous end may not be perceived by the individual searching for the most profitable return for an investment, yet this was the result as if 'led by an invisible hand to promote an end which was no part of his intention'. Indeed, by looking after themselves, those engaged in trade did everyone else a favour too: 'It is not from the benevolence of the butcher, the brewer, or the baker that we expect our dinner, but from their regard of their own interest. We address ourselves not to their humanity, but to their self-love, and never talk to them of our own necessities, but of their advantage.'

The *Wealth of Nations* sold out its first print run within six months, which is somewhat surprising for a two-volume, 900-page work on political economy.

From *The Wealth of Nations*, Book IV, Chapter 2

The general industry of the society never can exceed what the capital of the society can employ. As the number of workmen that can be kept in employment by any particular person must bear a certain proportion to his capital, so the number of those that can be continually employed by all the members of a great society, must bear a certain proportion to the whole capital of that society, and never can exceed that proportion. No regulation of commerce can increase the quantity of industry in any society beyond what its capital can maintain. It can only divert a part of it into a direction into which it might not otherwise have gone; and it is by no means certain that this artificial direction is likely to be more advantageous to the society than that into which it would have gone of its own accord.

Every individual is continually exerting himself to find out the most advantageous employment for whatever capital he can command. It is his own advantage, indeed, and not that of the society, which he has in view. But the study of his own advantage naturally, or rather necessarily leads him to prefer that employment which is most advantageous to the society.

Its author was a shy man, well liked by those who knew him, who was given to wrestling with ideas during long walks, often with such intensity that he found himself miles out of his way. On one occasion he was so distracted from where he was walking that he fell down into a pit of tar.

Smith was born in 1723 in the small Scottish port of Kirkcaldy, where his father was a customs collector. At the age of four he was stolen by gypsies and no more might ever have been heard of him, had he not been quickly rescued. As one of his biographers put it, 'He would have made, I fear, a poor gypsy.' Instead he went at the age of fourteen to study at Glasgow University and then, less profitably, to Balliol College, Oxford, before becoming an academic at Glasgow where his popularly attended lectures provided the basis for his *Theory of Moral Sentiments* in 1759. He began working on the *Wealth of Nations* while travelling through France as the tutor of the young duke of Buccleuch. The tour gave him the opportunity to converse with many of the continent's leading thinkers, including several meetings with Voltaire in Geneva. A slow writer, he completed his masterpiece in London and at his aged mother's house in Kirkcaldy.

Even before Smith's death in 1790, his arguments had found a receptive audience in the government of William Pitt the Younger. However, further progress towards the abolition of tariffs and the adoption of free trade was checked by events at home and abroad: the dislocations of the Napoleonic Wars and the imposition of the Corn Laws in 1815, which increased the price of bread in order to support the profitability of land ownership. Smith's arguments prevailed nevertheless. Many manufacturing tariffs were scrapped during the 1820s, and the age of free trade was explicitly embraced with the repeal of the Corn Laws by Sir Robert Peel in 1846. On the centenary of the *Wealth of Nations'* publication in 1876, the economist and journalist Walter Bagehot proclaimed that its arguments 'have settled down into the common sense of the nation and have become irreversible'.

In fact, Smith's economic theories were about to be threatened by Marxism and the re-emergence of a faith in the positive effects of state intervention. By the 1930s the world had retreated into protectionism, national self-sufficiency planning and rival versions of totalitarianism. With the 1980s and increasing globalization, the *Wealth of Nations'* time appeared to have come again.

> Little else is required to carry a state to the highest degree of opulence from the lowest barbarism, [Smith wrote] but peace, easy taxes, and a tolerable administration of justice: all the rest being brought about by a natural course of things. All governments which thwart the natural course, which force things into another channel, or which endeavour to arrest the progress of society at a particular point, are unnatural, and to support themselves are obliged to be oppressive and tyrannical.

1785
FIRST EDITION OF *THE TIMES*

THE 'THUNDERER' OF THE FREE PRESS

O n New Year's Day 1785, a newspaper was launched that established a new benchmark in British journalism. The first edition was called *The Daily Universal Register*, but three years later it changed its name to *The Times*. As such, it achieved extraordinary eminence across the English-speaking world and beyond. This was evident in the decision of so many foreign newspapers to launch with titles that consciously paid it homage: the *New York Times*, the *Irish Times*, the *Times of India*, the *New Straits Times*. Even France's foremost newspaper began in 1861 as *Le Temps* (although following Paris's liberation in 1944, Charles de Gaulle instigated its rebirth as *Le Monde*).

There was nothing to suggest that this newspaper would prove so influential when it started from offices in Printing House Square, an alleyway off Fleet Street to the west of St Paul's Cathedral. The area had been the centre of the printing trade since the time of Caxton and many journals had already been launched there in the eighteenth century, among them Britain's first daily newspaper, the *Daily Courant*, between 1702 and 1735, and the *Morning Post* from 1772. The primary motivation of John Walter, *The Times*'s founder, was less about improving the quality of national journalism than using his paper as a vehicle to advertise a new printing technique for which he held the patent. Keen to recoup money lost as a Lloyd's underwriter in the insurance markets, he was inspired by the profit motive and, like many of his newspaper rivals, was amenable to taking government bribes in return for favourable editorial comment.

Success was not instant. Walter found himself sent to Newgate prison, first for libelling the dukes of Clarence and Cumberland, and then for libelling the Prince of Wales as well. Although his 'logographical' printing technique proved a technological dead end, by the beginning of the nineteenth century his newspaper was gaining ground on its rivals. Under the direction of his son, John Walter II, it innovated and became something deemed unusual for the time – independent and incorruptible. Between 1817 and 1877, it had just two editors, Thomas Barnes and John Thadeus Delane, who between them established its reputation as the most trusted source of information in the country.

Perhaps its greatest merit was its ability to break foreign news before its competitors, a particular benefit to readers whose finances might rest on getting in ahead of other investors. On 22 June 1815, it reproduced the duke of Wellington's dispatch from the battlefield of Waterloo, only four days after it had been written. In 1854, its war correspondent (a post it innovated), William Howard Russell, sent eyewitness reports from the Crimean War so shocking that they ultimately helped bring down the government of the earl of Aberdeen. By the mid-nineteenth century, *The Times* had full-time correspondents posted not just across Europe but in Constantinople and Cairo, and later in Alexandria and Peking. During the Franco-Prussian War of 1870–71, a miniature version of *The Times* was sent by pigeon into the besieged city of Paris. In 1878, during the Congress of Berlin, the German chancellor, Otto von Bismarck, gave a five-hour interview to the *Times* correspondent Henri de Blowitz, who subsequently got a text of the Treaty of Berlin printed in the paper in London even before it was signed in Berlin. For international reputation, it had no rival anywhere in the world.

Although never a radical force in domestic politics, *The Times* championed the cause of parliamentary reform in 1832, gaining a reputation as a paper 'that thundered out' on various subjects. Naturally, it also made enemies. Its attack on Queen Victoria's withdrawal from public life in 1862 spurred even Her Majesty to write to the paper a letter in her defence intended for publication. In 1856, the Whigs' leader,

THE GROWTH OF THE PRESS

1621 *The Courante* is published in London. It contains only foreign news.

1665 The oldest surviving English-language journal, the *Oxford Gazette* (subsequently the *London Gazette*), an official government publication, is launched.

1690 The first edition of *Berrow's Worcester Journal* appears. Along with the *Stamford Mercury*, it claims to be Britain's oldest surviving (non-official) newspaper.

1702 The *Daily Courant* is launched in Fleet Street as the first daily newspaper. It merges with the *Daily Gazetteer* in 1735.

1737 The Belfast *News Letter* is founded. It is the world's oldest surviving English-language daily newspaper.

1748 The *Aberdeen Journal* (subsequently *Press and Journal*) becomes Scotland's first daily newspaper.

1772 The *Morning Post* is founded. It lasts until 1937 when it is subsumed by the *Daily Telegraph*.

1785 John Walter launches the *The Daily Universal Register* which he renames *The Times* in 1788.

1791 The *Observer* becomes the world's first Sunday newspaper.

1821 The *Manchester Guardian* is founded. It becomes the *Guardian* in 1959 and relocates to London in 1964.

1842 The *Illustrated London News* is published, the first weekly to print pictures.

1851 Reuters news agency is established.

1855 The abolition of stamp duties on newspapers reduces their cost and encourages their proliferation.

1855 The *Daily Telegraph* is launched and quickly becomes the market leader.

1896 Lord Northcliffe's *Daily Mail* begins the new age of mass-market journalism.

OVERLEAF: The front and back pages of the first edition of The Daily Universal Register, *which was to be renamed* The Times.

THE Universal DAILY Register,

Printed Logographically — DIEU ET MON DROIT — By His Majesty's Patent.

NUMB. 1.] SATURDAY, JANUARY 1, 1785. [Price Two-pence Halfpenny.

The SIXTH NIGHT.
By His MAJESTY's Company

AT the THEATRE ROYAL in DRURY-LANE, this present SATURDAY, will be performed

A New COMEDY, called
The NATURAL SON.

The characters by Mr. King, Mr. Parsons, Mr. Bensley, Mr. Moody, Mr. Baddeley, Mr. Wrighten, and Mr. Palmer. Miss Pope, Miss Tidswell, and Miss Farren.
With new Scenes and Dresses.
The Prologue to be spoken by Mr. Bannister, jun.
And the Epilogue by Miss Farren.
After which will be performed the last New Pantomime Entertainment, in two Parts, called
HARLEQUIN JUNIOR;
Or, The MAGIC CESTUS.
The Characters of the Pantomime, by
Mr. Wright, Mr. Williamson, Mr. Burton, Mr. Staunton, Mr. Williames, Mr. Palmer, Mr. Waldron, Mr. Fawcett, Mr. Chaplin, Mr. Phillimore, Mr. Wilson, Mr. Alfred, Mr. Spencer, Mr. Chapman, and Mr. Grimaldi. Mrs. Burnet, Miss Burnett, Miss Tidswell, Miss Barnes, Miss Cranford, and Miss Stageldoir.
To conclude with the Repulse of the Spaniards before
The ROCK of GIBRALTAR.

To-morrow, by particular desire, (for the 4th time) the revived Comedy of the DOUBLE DEALER, with the favorite Masque of ARTHUR and EMMELINE.

On Tuesday the Tragedy of VENICE PRESERVED: Jaffier by Mr. Brereton, Pierre by Mr. Bensley, and Belvidera, by Mrs. Siddons: And on Friday the Carmelite. Massinger's Play of the MAID of HONOUR, (with alterations and Additions) is in Rehearsal and will soon be produced.

NINTH NIGHT. FOR THE AUTHOR.

AT the THEATRE-ROYAL, COVENT-GARDEN, this present SATURDAY, January 1, 1785, will be performed, a New Comedy, called
The FOLLIES of a DAY,
Or, The Marriage of Figaro.
With new Dresses, Decorations, &c.

The principal characters by Mr. Lewis, Mr. Quick, Mr. Edwin, Mr. Wilson, Mr. Wewitzer, Mr. Bonnor, Mr. Thompson, and Mrs. Martyr; Mrs. Bates, Mrs. Webb, Miss Wewitzer, and Miss Younge.
With a new Prologue, to be spoken by Mr. Davies.
To which will be added, for the the sixth time,
A new Pantomime, called,
The MAGIC CAVERN,
Or, VIRTUE's TRIUMPH.
With new Scenery, Machinery, Music, Dresses, and Decorations.
The Scenes chiefly designed by Mr. Richards, and executed by him, Mr. Carver, Mr. Hodgins, and Assistants.
The Overture, Songs, Chorusses, and the Music of the new Pantomime, and composed by Mr. Shield.
Nothing under full Price will be taken.
The Words of the Songs, &c. to be had at the Theatre.

MR. WALTER returns his thanks to his Friends and the Public for the great encouragement and generous support he has already received from them to his new improvement in Printing, by the readiness with which they have subscribed to his intended publication of the works of some eminent Authors; and whilst he solicits a continuance of their favours, begs leave to acquaint them that by

The middle of January will be published,
In One Volume 12mo,
MISCELLANIES IN VERSE AND PROSE,
Intended as a Specimen of his Printing Types at the Logographic Office, Printing-House Square, Blackfriars.—And by the beginning of February, his first volume, containing Watts's Improvement of the Mind, with an Introduction written on the occasion, will be ready to be delivered to the subscribers.

This Day is published, Price 6d.

PLAN of the CHAMBER of COMMERCE, King's-Arms Buildings, Cornhill, London: which is open every day, for Consultation, Opinion, and Advice (verbal or in Writing) Mediation, Assistance, Arbitration, &c. in all *Commercial, Maritime,* and *Insurance* Affairs, and matters of *Trade* in general; and the *Laws* and *Usages* relating thereto.——The Address is, To the Director of the Chamber of Commerce, as above.

To be had of Richardson and Urquhart, Royal Exchange; J. Sewell, Cornhill; T. Whieldon, Fleet-street; W. Flexney, Holborn; and at the aforesaid Chamber.

Where may also be had, in one Volume Folio,
Mr. Weskett's COMPLETE DIGEST of the THEORY, LAWS and PRACTICE of INSURANCE; an entire new and comprehensive work, including all the adjudged Cases extant, with several never before printed; Extracts from the Statutes, foreign Ordinances, and marine Treaties; accounts of all the Insurance Companies the Maritime Courts, the commercial and maritime Laws, the Law of Nations, &c. the whole forming (alphabetically) a new *Lex Mercatoria.*

☞ "This Work has been compiled with great Care and Industry, by one who is evidently a Master of the Subject. It abounds with Proofs of extensive Reading, as well as mature Reflection, and judicious Remarks; and if the completest System of Insurance that has hitherto been composed be entitled to Praise, the present useful Digest must meet with the Approbation of the commercial World." Crit. Rev. Vol. 52, p. 443.—All the other Literary Journals speak in similar Terms of this Book; which had already been translated abroad.

This Day is published, in 3 Vols. Price 9s. sewed.
By the LITERARY SOCIETY,

MODERN TIMES: or The ADVENTURES of GABRIEL OUTCAST. A Novel, in Imitation of Gil Blas.
"Qui capit ille facit."

Printed for the Author, and sold by J. Walter, Printing-house Square, Black-friars; where may be had, gratis, the Plan of this Society, associated for the Encouragement of Literature, who propose to print and publish at their own Risk and Expence such original Works as they may approve of, and give their Authors all Profits arising from the same.

MRS. KING begs leave to acquaint her Friends she opens her SCHOOL at CHIGWELL in ESSEX, on Monday, the 10th of January, for the EDUCATION of YOUNG LADIES: as she has always been accustomed to watch and improve the opening mind, hopes to give satisfaction to those who trust her with so important a charge.

Till the 10th of January Mrs. King may be spoke with at Mr. Kerr's, Bitt-maker to his Majesty, in the Mews, Charing-cross.

N. B. Wanted an Apprentice and Half-boarder.

SHIPPING ADVERTISEMENTS

For NICE, GENOA, and LEGHORN,
(With Liberty to touch at One Port in the Channel,)
The NANCY.
THOMAS WHITE, Commander,

BURTHEN 160 Tons; Guns and Men answerable. Lying off the Tower, and will absolutely depart on Saturday the 8th instant.

The said Commander to be spoken with every morning at Sam's Coffee-house, near the Custom-house; at Will's Coffee-house, in Cornhill; and at Exchange hours on the French and Italian Walk, or
WILLIAM ELYARD, for the said Commander,
No. 16, Savage-Gardens.

Direct for LISBON,
The NANCY.
JOHN RACKHAM, Commander,

BURTHEN 300 Tons, Men answerable. Lying off Horslydown Chain; Seven-eighths of her Cargo absolutely engaged, and is obliged by Charter-party to depart on Saturday the 8th instant.

The said Commander to be spoken with every morning at Sam's Coffee-house, near the Custom-house; at Will's Coffee-house, in Cornhill; and in Exchange hours in the French and Italian Walk; or
WILLIAM ELYARD, for the said Commander,
No. 16, Savage-Gardens.

For NICE, GENOA, and LEGHORN.
(With Liberty to Touch at One Port in the Channel.)
The LIVELY,
ROBERT BRINE, Commander,

BURTHEN 209 Tons, Guns and Men answerable. Lying off Iron Gate.

The said Commander to be spoke with every Morning at Sam's Coffee-house, near the Custom-house; at Will's Coffee-house in Cornhill; and in Exchange Hours in the French and Italian Walk; or
WILLIAM ELYARD, for the said Commander,
No. 16, Savage-Gardens.

For CONSTANTINOPLE and SMYRNA, or SMYRNA and CONSTANTINOPLE,
(With Liberty to Touch at One Port in the Channel,)
The BETSEY,
ROBERT LANCASTER, Commander,

BURTHEN 200 Tons, Men answerable. Lying at Iron-Gate. Two-thirds of her Cargo engaged, and is obliged to depart by Charterparty, in all the present Month of January.

The said Commander to be spoke with every Morning at Sam's Coffee-house, near the Custom-house; at Will's Coffee-house in Cornhill; and in Exchange Hours in the French and Italian Walk; or
WILLIAM ELYARD, for the said Commender,
No. 16, Savage-Gardens.

N. B. No Goods to be taken on Board the Vessel without an Order from the Broker.

NEW NOVELS.

This Day are published, (in two Volumes, price 5s. sewed,)

THE YOUNG WIDOW; or, the HISTORY of Mrs. LEDWICH.

The HISTORY of Lord BELFORD and Miss SOPHIA WOODLEY, 3 vol. 9s. bound.

Printed for the Editor, and sold by F. Noble, in Holborn;
Where may be had lately published,
St. Ruthin's Abbey, a Novel, 3 vols. 9s. bound.
The Woman of Letters; or, History of Fanny Belton, 2 vol. 7s. bound.
A Lesson for Lovers; or, History of Col. Melville and Lady Richly, 2 vols. 7s. bound.
Literary Amusements; or, Evening Entertainer, 2 vol. 7s. bound.
Adventures of a Cavalier, by Daniel Defoe, 3 vols. 9s bound.

T. RICKABY, PRINTER,
No. 15, Duke's Court, Drury Lane;

REspectfully informs his Friends and the Public in general, that the Partnership between him and Mr. Moore being entirely dissolved, he now intends to carry on every branch of the PRINTING BUSINESS upon his own account;—and having purchased a complete assortment of the neatest and best materials, is determined to pursue a Mode of Printing which he hopes will meet with the approbation of his employers.

N.B. Cards, Hand-Bills, Circular Letters, and all articles of the kind, accurately printed at a few hours notice, in a manner particularly neat, and at the lowest prices.

⁎ An Apprentice wanted.

To the Readers of the London Medical Journal.
This day is first published, price 1s.

SYMPATHY DEFENDED; or, the State MEDICAL CRITICISM in London; written to improve the Principles and Manners of the Editor of the London Medical Journal: To which are added the Contents of the Treatise on Medical Sympathy, and a Postscript, on account of a premature Review in a late Number of the London Medical Journal.

By a Society of Faculties;
Friends to the Public and Enemies to Imposition.
"Cum tua non edas, carpis mea carmina, Laeli,
"Carpere vel noli nostra, ede tua."
MART. Epig.

This pamphlet has been hitherto distributed gratuitously. The repeated applications for them, particularly from the country, have become so numerous, that the Society feel themselves under the necessity of putting them into the hands of a publisher.

Sold by J. Murray, Bookseller, Fleet-street.

Nondum lingua silet dextra, peregit opus.
MART.

SHORT-HAND, on the latest and most approved Principles taught by J. LARKHAM, No 11, Rose Alley, Bishopsgate Street.

It would exceed the limits of an advertisement merely to mention the various errors either in the *plan* or the *execution* of the different schemes of Short-hand hitherto made public, or to point out the peculiarities and excellencies of the present: Mr. L. therefore only begs leave to observe, that the approbation of many gentlemen well known in the literary world, and well versed in the *Theory* and *Practice* of Short-hand, expressed in stronger terms than delicacy will permit him to repeat, warrants him in saying *his* will be found a system of short and swift writing; more *easy* to acquire and retain, more *expeditiously*, more *legible* and more *regular* than any ever yet offered to the Public.

The terms of teaching *one* Guinea, the *usual* time of learning *seven* lessons.

To the Public.

TO bring out a New Paper at the present day; when so many others are already established and confirmed in the public opinion, is certainly an arduous undertaking; and no one can be more fully aware of its difficulties than I am: I, nevertheless, entertain very sanguine hopes, that the nature of the plan on which this paper will be conducted, will ensure it a moderate share at least of public favour; but my pretensions to encouragement, however strong they may appear in my own eyes, must be tried before a tribunal not liable to be blinded by *self-opinion*: to that tribunal I shall now, as I am bound to do, submit these pretensions with deference, and the public will judge whether they are well or ill founded.

It is very far from my intention to detract from the acknowledged merit of the Daily Papers now in existence; it is sufficient that they please the class of readers whose approbation their conductors are ambitious to deserve; nevertheless it is certain some of the best, some of the most respectable, and some of the most useful members of the community, have frequently complained (and the causes of their complaints still exist) that by radical defects in the plans of the present established papers, they were deprived of many advantages, which ought naturally to result from daily publications. Of these some build their fame on the length and accuracy of parliamentary reports, which unquestionably are given with great ability, and with a laudable zeal to please those, who can spare time to read ten or twelve columns of debates. *Others are principally attentive to the politics of* the day, and make it their study to give satisfaction to the numerous class of politicians, who, blessed with easy circumstances, have nothing better to do, than to amuse themselves with watching the motions of ministers both at home and abroad; and endeavouring to find out the secret springs that set in motion the great machine of government in every state and empire in the world. There is one paper which in no degree interferes with the pursuits of its cotemporaries; it looks upon parliamentary debates as sacred mysteries, that cannot be submitted to vulgar eyes without profanation; political investigations it apprehends to be little short of treason, and therefore *loyally* abstains from them; it deals almost solely in advertisements; and consequently, though a very useful, it is by no means an entertaining paper. Thus it would seem that every News-Paper published in London is calculated for a particular set of readers only; so that if each set were to change its favourite publication for another, the commutation would produce disgust, and dissatisfaction to all; the politician would then find nothing to amuse him but long accounts of petty squabbles about trifles in Parliament, or panegyrics on the men and measures that he most disliked; or libels on those whom he most revered. The person to whom parliamentary debates afford unspeakable delight, would find himself bored with political speculations about the measures that the different courts in Europe might probably adopt; or disgusted with whole pages of advertisements, in which he felt no concern;—whilst the plain shop-keeper who wanted to find a convenient house for his business, and the servant who purchased his paper in hopes of seeing in it an advertisement directing where he might find a place to suit him, would have their labour for their pains, in perusing publications, filled with senatorial debates, or political essays and remarks, which would direct them to nothing less than the house or place they wanted.—A News-Paper, conducted on the true and natural principles of such a publication, ought to be the Register of the times, and faithful recorder of every species of intelligence; it ought not to be engrossed by any particular object; but, like a well covered table, it should contain something suited to every palate: observations on the dispositions of our own and of foreign courts should be provided for the political reader; debates should be reported for the amusement or information of those who may be particularly fond of them; and a due attention should be paid to the interests of trade, which are so greatly promoted by advertisements.—A paper that should blend all these advantages, and by steering clear of extremes, hit the happy medium, has long been expected by the public.—Such, it is intended, shall be the UNIVERSAL REGISTER, the great objects of which will be to facilitate the *commercial* intercourse between the different parts of the community, through the channel of *Advertisements*; to record the principal occurrences of the times; and to abridge the account of debates during the sitting of Parliament.

It is no less the interest of the proprietors of News-Papers, than of the public, that every encouragement should be given to advertising correspondents; yet this private interest of the proprietors is frequently sacrificed to the rage for parliamentary debates, to the great injury of trade; for the extreme length of these debates so greatly retards the publication of the New-Papers which are noted for detailed accounts of them, that the advantages arising from this species of intelligence, though highly acceptable in itself, are frequently over-balanced by the inconvienences occasioned to people in business by the delay. These inconveniences are great and many; it generally happens, that when either House of Parliament has been engaged in the discussion of an important question till after midnight, the papers in which the speeches of the Members are reported at large, cannot be published before noon; nay, they sometimes are not even sent to press so soon; consequently parties interested in *sales* are essentially injured, as the advertisements, inviting the public to attend them at *ten* or *twelve* o'clock, do not appear, on account of a late publication, till some hours after.—From the same source flows another inconvenience; it is sometimes found necessary to *defer* sales, after they have been advertised for a particular day; but the notice of putting them off not appearing early enough, on account of the late hour at which the papers containing it are published, numbers of people, acting under the impression of former advertisements, are unnecessarily put to the trouble of attending.—It will be the object of the *Universal Register* to guard against these great inconveniences, without depriving its readers of the pleasure of learning what passes in Parliament.—It is intended, then, that the debates shall be regularly reported in it; but on the other hand, that the publication may not be delayed to the prejudice of people in trade, the speeches will not be given on a large scale; the *substance* shall be faithfully preserved; but all the uninteresting parts will be omitted. I shall thus be enabled to publish this paper at an early hour; and I propose to bring it out *regularly* every morning at *six* o'clock. The *Universal Register* will therefore have this advantage over the *Daily Advertiser*, that, though published as early, it will contain a substantial account of the proceedings in Parliament the preceding night, which is never to be found in that paper; and compared with the other morning papers it will be found to have the merit of containing in substance, what they give in long detail (which men in business cannot well spare time to read) and, nevertheless, of being published much sooner. These circumstances, it is hoped, will give the *Universal Register* at least an *equal* claim to public favour with the parliamentary papers, and the *trading* part of the metropolis, it is presumed, will find it their advantage to give it the preference.

An essential part of the plan of this new paper is, that, for the convenience of advertising correspondents, their favours shall, *to a certainty*, be inserted on the very day that they shall direct; provided they deliver them at the office in due time. For the *strict* observance of this rule, the credit of the paper shall stand pledged; and its pretensions to public countenance will be renounced, if this fundamental principle in its institution shall ever be violated, except in cases of absolute necessity, which human prudence cannot prevent.—And here I beg it may be understood that I do not make use of the word *necessity* as a reserve, under colour of which, I may, whenever I think fit, be released from my engagements; I mean by that word a necessity arising from accidents that sometimes happen in the printing business, and from which, the most careful man cannot, at all times, be secure. But so far from wishing to shrink from my engagements, I intend, whenever the length of the Gazette, Parliamentary Debates, &c. shall render it impossible for me to insert all the advertisements promised for the day, in *one* sheet, to print an additional half sheet, and publish it with the ordinary paper without any additional charge to my customers.—From the difficulty that people experience in procuring the insertion of their advertisements even in the *Daily Advertiser*; and particularly from the impossibility of obtaining an *early* insertion at some periods of the year, it may be presumed that this regulation will greatly recommend the UNIVERSAL REGISTER to public notice, and procure it support.

These, though in my opinion good, are not the *only* grounds on which I build my hopes of success. I flatter myself, I have some claim to public encouragement, on account of a great improvement which I have made in the art of printing. The inconveniences attending the old and tedious mode of composing with letters taken up *singly*, first suggested the idea of devising some more expeditious method. The cementing of several letters together, so as that the type of a *whole word* might be taken up in as short a time as that of a *single letter*, was the result of much reflection on that subject. But the bare idea of cementing was merely the opening, not the accomplishment or perfection of the improvement. The fount consisting of types of words, and not of letters, was to be so arranged, as that a compositor should be able to find the former with as much facility as he can the latter. This was a work of inconceivable difficulty. I undertook it however, and was fortunate enough, after an infinite number of experiments, and great labour, to bring it to a happy conclusion. The whole English language is now methodically and systematically arranged at my fount: so that printing can now be performed with greater dispatch, and at less expence, than according to the mode hitherto in use.

In bringing this work to perfection, I had not my own advantage solely in view; I wished to be useful to the community; and it is with pleasure I see that the public will derive considerable benefit from my industry; for I have resolved to sell the REGISTER *One halfpenny* UNDER the price paid for seven out of eight of the morning papers; however I indulge a hope that this ſacrifice which I make of the uſual profits of printing, will be felt by a generous public; and that they will ſo far favour me with advertiſements, as to enable me to defray the heavy expences attending the literary departments in the paper, and to make a livelihood for myſelf and my family.—The favour that I now earneſtly ſolicit, I ſhall diligently labour to preſerve, without entertaining a preſumptuous wiſh that I may enjoy it one moment longer, than I ſhall be found to deſerve it.

The *Regiſter*, in its politics, will be of no party: weakened as the country is by a long and expenſive war, and rent by inteſtine diviſions, nothing but the union of all parties can ſave it from deſtruction. Moderate men, therefore, I truſt, will countenance a paper, which has for one of its objects to cool the animoſities, ſtifle the reſentments' manage the perſonal honour, and reconcile the principals of contending parties; while the favours of thoſe will be courted, who ſupport principles, by fair *argument*, and think that a good cauſe may be injured by perſonalities, and low invective, the correſpondence of ſuch as deſcend to illiberal abuſe, and attack the *man* rather than the *meaſure*, will always be diſregarded. The *Regiſter*, inſtead of dealing in ſcurrilities and abuſing the great men in power, or the great men out of power; or, inſtead of deifying the one or the other, will reſerve to itſelf a right of cenſuring or applauding either, as their conduct may occaſionally appear proper or improper.

If cenſure ſhould be thought neceſſary, it ſhall be conveyed in language ſuited to the reſpect that is due to the public, before whoſe tribunal the individual is arraigned; and no provocation ſhall be deemed an excuſe for illiberal abuſe, or perſonality.

Nothing ſhall ever find a place in the *Univerſal Regiſter*, that can tend to wound the ear of delicacy, or corrupt the heart: vice ſhall never be ſuffered there to wear the garb of virtue: To hold out the former in alluring colours, would ſtrike at the very root of morality; and, concealing the native deformity of vice, might ſeduce unſuſpecting innocence from the paths of virtue.

As a News-Paper ought to be at the ſervice of the Public, by whom it is ſupported, I ſhall not hold myſelf excuſeable, through the example of others, in opening the *Regiſter* to one kind of advertiſers, and partially ſhutting it againſt others: I hold that I have a right to conſider only whether the advertiſements offered for inſertion contain any thing contrary to law or morality; and that, if they do not, I ſhould violate my duty to the public, in refuſing to inſert them when paid for. A News-Paper in this particular ought to reſemble an *Inn*, where the proprietor is *obliged* to give the uſe of his houſe to all travellers, who are ready to pay for it, and againſt whoſe perſons there is no legal or moral objection.

The miſcellaneous articles of intelligence will be regularly arranged under the heads of *Theatres, Trials, Ship News, Market Prices, Bills of Entry, Prices Courant, Stocks, Promotions, Marriages, Deaths, &c.* Though it is intended that faithful accounts ſhall be given of all remarkable trials at law, ſtill thoſe will be more particularly attended to, in which the mercantile world may be moſt intereſted. In a word, no pains or expence will be ſpared, that can render the *Univerſal Regiſter* of utility to the public.

The miſcellaneous articles of intelligence will be regularly arranged under the heads of *Theatres, Trials, Ship News, Market Prices, Bills of Entry, Prices Courant, Stocks, Promotions, Marriages, Deaths, &c.* Though it is intended that faithful accounts ſhall be given of all remarkable trials at law, ſtill thoſe will be more particularly attended to, in which the mercantile world may be moſt intereſted. In a word, no pains or expence will be ſpared, that can render the UNIVERSAL REGISTER of utility to the public.

Such is the plan that Mr. WALTER has laid down for the conduct of his paper: he now ſends it forth into the world, in hopes that it will appear to the public deſerving of their encouragement. For his own part, he will no longer expect their countenance and favour, than he ſhall be found ſtrictly to adhere to the engagements into which he now enters, in this ſketch that he humbly begs leave to lay before them.

J. WALTER.

*** Advertiſements, Eſſays, real Articles of Intelligence, &c. to which great attention will be paid, will be taken in at the OFFICE in *Printing-houſe Square*; and for the greater convenience of the diſtant parts of the town, at Mr. SEARLE's, Grocer, No. 55, *Oxford-ſtreet*; Mr. THRALE's, Paſtry Cook, *oppoſite the Admiralty*; M. WILSON's LIBRARY, No. 45, *Lombard-ſtreet*; Mr. PRATT's, Green Grocer, No. 84, *Wapping*; and Mr. STERNEY, No. 156, *oppoſite St. George's Church, Borough.*

‡§‡ The Ladies and Gentlemen who may be pleaſed to take in this Paper, may be ſupplied with it by any of the NEWSMEN.

FOREIGN INTELLIGENCE.

Yeſterday arrived the Mails from France *and* Flanders, *which brought the following news.*

Nuremberg, Nov. 25, 1784.

THE agreement concluded between the Emperor's commiſſaries and thoſe of the Circle of Franconia, with regard to the neceſſary ſupply of proviſions of every kind for the Imperial troops during their march through the Circle, to the Low Countries, is in ſubſtance as follows: 1ſt, each ſoldier and non-commiſſioned officer ſhall receive at their lodgings, half a pound of fleſh, two pounds of bread, roots and a pot of beer, or a bottle of wine, at the rate of 8 kreutzers; 2d, each horſe ſhall have 8 pounds of oats, 10 pounds of hay, and half a truſs of ſtraw, at 30 kreutzers; 3d, waggons drawn by four horſes or ſix oxen, may be paid at the rate of 2 florins per head; 4th, nothing more than what is contained in the firſt article ſhall be exacted from thoſe who quarter the troops, and whatever ſurplus they may give ſhall be paid for in ready money; 5th, officers and all perſons following the army, muſt pay ready money for whatever they contract for.

We are aſſured that the commiſſaries of the Circle have requeſted of thoſe of the Emperor, to inſert in this converſation, that, in conſequence of the dearth of grain, and particularly of forage, it would be impoſſible for the Circle, in caſe of another march through their State, to furniſh the troops with ſupplies; and that they intended addreſſing his Imperial Majeſty on this point.

Francfort, Dec. 16. The military cheſt is to be eſtabliſhed in this city, and to be guarded by the regiment of Prieſs, which will remain here during the winter. It ſeems our town will be the rendezvous of a conſiderable part of the Auſtrian army, for within theſe few days we have had 85 commiſſaries for proviſions. Enliſting is carried on with the greateſt ſucceſs in this city and neighbourhood.

On the 7th 300 of Wormſer's huſſars paſſed through Hof; 13,019 of the Imperial troops, with 721 horſes, were expected in the environs of Landibus, on the 17th current.

The Swiſs have refuſed granting troops to the Dutch.

Cologne, Dec. 21. We learn from Baruth, that on the morning of the 11th inſtant, the regiment of Coubourg paſſed through there on their way to Luxembourg.

By letters from Nuremberg of the 13th, we learn, that 25 poſtilions preceded by an officer, two gentlemen, eight Imperial chaſſeurs, leading fifty-two ſaddle horſes, belonging to the Emperor, arrived the 6th current at Ratiſbonne, and that they are to be followed by two waggons loaded with his Majeſty's kitchen furniture.

Orders are given to prepare quarters for the Emperor, at the White Lamb at Nuremberg, and on the 12th and on the 13th at night, the whole of the above mentioned cavalcade entered this city. On the 13th, a large body of Imperial troops paſſed through Neuſtadt-An-der-hard, which is to be followed by many other corps, all deſtined for the Low Countries.

Prince Kaunitz Ritſbourg, Chancellor of State, has diſappeared for ſome days; his place is filled by Vice Chancellor, Count de Cobentzel. On the 3d, diſpatches were received from the Imperial Ambaſſador, at Paris, which employed his Imperial Majeſty the whole afternoon; he was the entire evening in his cloſet, and not at leiſure to aſſiſt at the opera, as he intended. His Majeſty has abſolutely rejected the laſt propoſitions for a reconciliation from the Court of France, and inſiſts upon the free and unlimited navigation of the Scheld. The declared oppoſition of France would not change this reſolution, as his Majeſty's dignity is at ſtake. The Emperor has often made known theſe diſpoſitions; he has even been heard to ſay, that he might forgive an attack from a crowned head, but that he could never forgive the injury done to by the Dutch. According to the declaration of the French Court, although conceived in general, yet friendly terms, it is not imagined that it will openly oppoſe the Auſtrians. Who is unacquainted with the powerful influence which the Count de Vergennes and his party have, to inſpire the King with other counſels, when fully convinced of his Majeſty's invincible reſolution? Mean time we ſee innumerable couriers, and the diſpatches are ſealed by the Chancellor in perſon. On the other hand, the King of France's letter, ſo emphatically mentioned, has exiſted only in the brains of newsmongers. The truth is, the miniſtry of Verſailles, on the 20th of November, ſent a ſufficiently energetic memoir to our Cabinet; it was delivered on the 27th of the ſame month, by the Marquis de Noailles: it is certain no anſwer was made to it on the 4th current.

Antwerp, Dec. 23. Although the Emperor has accepted the mediation of France, his reſolution is, let the reſult be what it may, to maintain conſtantly 40,000 men in the Low Countries, to be ready on any emergency. Lodgings are ſtill preparing here for the army; a body of waggoners arrived here, with 100 horſes from Luxembourg, for the Emperor's ſervice.

Leige, Dec. 19. His Highneſs our gracious Prince was this morning conſecrated Biſhop, by the Marquis of Hoenſbroek, Biſhop of Ruremonde, aſſiſted by the Abbots of St. Lawrence and St. Giles. This auguſt ceremony was performed in the chapel of the palace, with the uſual formalities, and with the moſt edifying dvotions without any oſtentatious preparation. To-morow being theday appointed for inaguration, there will be no illuminations. His Highneſs wiſhes they may be ſuppreſſed, and in conformity to his paternal views the expences attending them will be converted to objects more uſeful, and more pleaſing to his beneficent heart.

Letters from Sicily inform, that a 24 gun ſhip, belonging to Chevalier Emo's ſquadron, ſunk in a ſtorm, and that the ſecond in command of her, died in a wound he had received at the bombardment of Suje.

Paris, Dec. 20. We are informed of an anſwer made by the King of Pruſſia to the Commandant of Cleves, who wanted to know of his Majeſty how he was to act if the Auſtrian troops ſhould attempt to paſs through his territories—The anſwer was, "That if the Auſtrian troops marched towards the Dutchy of Cleves, he ſhould tell them they had miſtaken the way; if they perſiſted, he ſhould make priſoners of them; and if they reſiſted, kill them."

"Signed, *Frederick.*"

L O N D O N.

Yeſterday their Majeſties came from Windſor, and laſt night honoured the Theatre with their preſence.

This day being New-Year's Day, their Majeſties will appear in the drawing room at St. James's, and receive the compliments of the nobility, gentry, and foreign miniſters on the occaſion of the day. The following Ode, compoſed by Paul Whitehead, Eſq. Poet Laureat, will be ſung in the great Council Chamber.

ODE FOR THE NEW YEAR.

Jan. 1ſt, 1785.

DELUSIVE is the poet's dream,
Or does prophetic truth inſpire
The zeal which prompts the glowing theme
And animates th' according Lyre?
Truſt the Muſe: her eye commands
Diſtant times, and diſtant lands
Thro' burſting clouds in opening ſkies,
Sees from diſcord union riſe,
And friendſhip bind unwilling foes
In firmer ties than duty knows.
Torn rudely from its parent tree
Yon Scion, riſing in the Weſt,
Will ſoon its genuine glory ſee,
And court again the foſtering breaſt
Whoſe paſture gave its powers to ſpread
And feel their force, and lift an alien head.
The parent tree, when ſtorms impend,
Shall own affection's warmth again,
Again its foſtering aid ſhall lend
Nor hear the ſuppliant plead in vain,
Shall ſtretch protecting branches round,
Extend the ſhelter, and forget the wound.
Two Britons thro' the admiring world,
Shall wing their way with ſails unfurl'd;
Each from the other kindred ſtate,
Avert by turns the bolts of fate,
And acts of mutual amity endear
The Tyre and Carthage of a wider ſphere.
When Rome's divided eagles flew,
And different thrones her Empire knew,
The varying language ſoon disjoin'd
The boaſted maſters of mankind.
But here no ills like thoſe we fear,
No varying language threatens here
Congenial worth, congenial flame,
Their manners and their arts the ſame;
To the ſame tongue ſhall glowing themes afford,
And Britiſh heroes act, and Britiſh bards record.
Fly ſwift ye years, ye minutes haſte,
And in the future loſe the paſt.
O'er many a thought-afflicting tale,
Oblivion, caſt thy friendly veil,
Let not memory breathe a ſigh,
Or backward turn th' indignant eye;
Nor the inſidious arts of foes
Enlarge the breach that longs to cloſe,
But acts of amity alone inſpire
Firm truth, and cordial love, and wake the willing lyre.

The buſineſs which brought Mr. Secretary Orde and Mr. Foſter, Chancellor of the Exchequer, from Ireland, was finally determined on Tueſday in a cabinet council, held for that purpoſe. This buſineſs was relative to the *Protecting Duties*, ſo generally called for in Ireland, and an adjuſtment of ſeveral difficulties that occurred in the commercial intercourſe between that country and this. The friends of the Iriſh adminiſtration ſay, that the terms Mr. Orde has obtained from the miniſter, will give general ſatisfaction in Ireland: but without fearing the danger of being found falſe prophets, we do not heſitate to ſay that theſe terms, ſo far from giving general ſatisfaction, will be received by the Iriſh as an inſult to their underſtanding, if it be true, as it is reported, that the miniſter has bound himſelf to no more than this—"That he "will adviſe his Majeſty to give his royal aſſent "to a bill or bills ſent to him from Ireland, "for impoſing certain duties on woollen cloths, "&c. *of an inferior quality*, imported into that "kingdom from Great Britain." Duties, amounting even to a prohibition, on *ſuch* cloths, will never give ſatisfaction to the Iriſh, for this reaſon—very little of ſuch cloths, if any, is imported by them; for the manufacture of lower priced woollens is carried to much greater perfection in Ireland than in England; and even whilſt the prohibition to export Iriſh woollens exiſted, Ireland, by a ſmuggled trade, ſupplied the Americans with coarſe cloths, and greatly under-ſold the Engliſh manufacturer. It is in the making of *ſuperfine* cloths that the Engliſh ſurpaſs the Iriſh; it was on *ſuperfine* Britiſh woollens that Ireland called for duties, which ſhould operate as a *protection* and encouragement to her own manufacture of *firſt* cloths; and theſe duties being refuſed, nothing in fact is granted.

Three days before Chriſtmas day, a meſſenger extraordinary from the Court of Peterſburgh arrived at the hotel of his Excellency Monſ. Kalitchoff, the Ruſſian Miniſter at the Hague, with the following memorial, which his Excellency, by order of his Sovereign, immediately delivered to the Preſident of the States General: we are happy to lay before our readers the contents of a memorial, which has for object the preventing of a war, and the preſervation of public tranquillity.

"Her Majeſty the Empreſs of all the Ruſſias "never loſt ſight for a moment ſince the beginning "of her reign, of the happineſs and tranquillity of "Europe in general: it was therefore with the "moſt lively concern, the received intelligence "that the negociations between the States General and the Emperor, her friend and ally, "had been interrupted by acts of hoſtility, which "would ſeem to put it out of the power of "his Imperial Majeſty to take any other ſteps, "than ſuch as the care of his dignity, which "ſtands committed in the face of Europe, ſhould "ſuggeſt. Her Majeſty the Empreſs has given "too many marks of the intereſt ſhe takes in "the peace and proſperity of the Republic, not "to be confident that their High Mightineſſes "will conſider the invitation which ſhe new "ſends them, to deviſe means for opening again "the way to accommodation, as the fruits of "the moſt pure and laudable deſire to reſtore "tranquillity, and prevent hoſtilities, that might "end in open war, and diſturb the peace of all "Europe. Her Majeſty then requeſts their "High Mightineſſes will think of the means "that their wiſdom may ſuggeſt, to bring the diſpute to an amicable concluſion, a conſummation as ſalutary as it is uſeful to both "parties."

This memorial has given an alarm in Amſterdam; for though the Empreſs ſeems to breathe nothing but peace; though magnanimity is manifeſted in it, to a great degree; yet, ſtill it is feared that her connexions with the Emperor may have great influence on her mind, when acting as a mediatrix between the Dutch, and a monarch whom ſhe emphatically calls her *friend* and *ally*.

Lord Grantham arrived in Town on Thurſday night: a particular mandate or meſſage from a Great Perſonage, it is ſaid, was the occaſion of his Lordſhip's haſte. A return to official buſineſs in Cleveland Row, is ſuppoſed to be the object of his Lordſhip's call from his rural retreat.

GUILDHALL INTELLIGENCE.

The adjourned examination of Mr. Turner, a bankrupt, was reſumed yeſterday.—The nature of the caſe was this.—Meſſrs. Turner and Smith, Linendrapers in Oxford-Road, had failed ſome time ago, and a commiſſion of bankruptcy iſſued againſt them. On their examination, the commiſſioners were ſo diſſatisfied with their anſwers, that they committed them both to Newgate. On Thurſday they were exemaned again, and Mr. Smith was diſcharged from his confinement; but his partner, Mr. Turner, not appearing to deſerve the ſame indulgence, was again committed. The commiſſioners ſeemed to be of opinion at firſt, that his examination ſhould be cloſed; and that he ſhould be made to abide by the anſwers he had already given: but his creditors wiſhing that this unhappy man ſhould not periſh on this occaſion, begged that he might be indulged with another examination, in which he might at laſt tell the truth, and ſave his life. The commiſſioners then gave him three hours more to reflect upon his ſituation; but the creditors ſtill deſirous that he might have time to ſleep upon the buſineſs, they prolonged the indulgence to yeſterday at noon. The creditors had great reaſon to believe that concealments of property to a conſiderable ammount, had been made by the bankrupt; and the anſwers given by him, confirmed them in this opinion, though they were intended by him to remove it. The commiſſioners met yeſterday purſuant to adjournment, and the priſoner having been brought before them, Mr. Morgan, his counſel, opened the buſineſs with a written ſtring of interrogatories, which he put to the bankrupt; this mode of proceeding was objected to by Mr. Garrow, counſel for the creditors; he grounded his objection on that, firſt, ſuch a method would neceſſarily protract the buſineſs of the day to an uſeleſs length; ſecond, that it was ſhewing too great an indulgence to the priſoner, whom he ſuppoſed to be previouſly inſtructed in his anſwers, he therefore did not heſitate to prefer a narrative from the priſoner to an interrogatory from his counſel.

Mr. Morgan roſe and entered into a ſhort, though intereſting detail of the many inconveniences and loſſes to which people in trade are daily liable to, he did not at all doubt but there were many among the priſoner's creditors, there preſent, who had ſome time or other, experienced the truth of his aſſertion, and who would wiſh in their misfortunes to have met with indulgence; his argument went to prove that a perſon in the unhappy circumſtances of Mr. Turner, whom poverty with its concomitant diſadvantages ſtared in the face, had the ſhadow of an excuſe to ſequeſter ſome of his good, to be able thereby in ſome time, with œconomy and prudent regulation, to ſatisfy all his creditors; he however by no means approved the conduct of thoſe who concealed their goods to deceive the merchants who truſted them; on the contrary he reprobated it, and thought no puniſhment too great for the offence; but he contended that the bankrupt then in court was by no means in the predicament alluded to, and conſequently was intitled to the indulgence due to innocence, he concluded by mentioning the ſeverity of the laws with reſpect to bankrupts. Here Mr. Garrow ſtood up, and was of opinion that poverty or any other wordly inconvenience could not lead an honeſt man from the paths of probity; if there ever was an example of the kind, the priſoner in queſtion could not plead his right to be excepted; he had given proofs of his diſhoneſt intentions, and he, (Mr. Garrow,) was in poſſeſſion of a letter which would every way tend to diſcloſe his ſecret manœuvres; he further aſſerted that Mr. Turner had been treated with unexampled lenity and favour, he had many advantages allowed him to give him every opportunity of exculpating himſelf from the crime he was accuſed of, he feared that his indulgence to the priſoner would draw on him the diſpleaſure of his clients: he owned that the laws were very ſevere with reſpect to bankrupts, but he inſiſted that they were only ſo for the fair trader, the honeſt merchant, whoſe loſſes were the effects of the capricious deity, rather than thoſe that reſult from diſſipation and extravagance.

The priſoner being aſked whether the court was in poſſeſſion of all the papers notifying all the debts due to him and owing to others, he anſwered in the affirmative, but being forewarned by his counſel of the fatal conſequences of any ſecret embezzlement, he owned that a Mr. Fairborne, broker, had a bill of his for 18 guineas, that he had given a note of 179l. to Mrs. Wright, (with whom he had lived,) and alſo ſeventy odd pounds for having lodged with her. The priſoner anſwers on the whole were evaſive and nugatory. The Commiſſioners adjourned to a Coffee Houſe, in order to examine him ſtill further in private.

Extract of a letter from Vienna, Dec. 4.

"We are ſending off the heavy artillery from this city, which is alſo to furniſh two thouſand recruits for the army of the Low Countries. They are raiſing in Galicia a body of Uhlans, who are to aſſemble at Brinn."

TO CORRESPONDENTS.

We would with pleaſure have inſerted gratis *all the Advertiſements that were ſent to us, had we not received an intimation from the Stamp-Office, that the King's duty muſt be paid for every advertiſement that ſhould appear in our firſt day's paper; we were therefore obliged to leave out all the favours of our advertiſing friends, who, unappriſed of this circumſtance, did not ſend the ſtamp-duty with each advertiſement.*

TO PARENTS AND GUARDIANS.

A YOUTH properly qualified, may be placed out an Apprentice in a wholeſale and retail tea and grocery warehouſe in the city, where he will be properly qualified in a genteel lucrative line of buſineſs; and at the expiration of his engagement, an opportunity of eſtabliſhing himſelf on the ſpot: a circumſtance which ſeldom happens. As every requiſite ſatisfaction will be given his friends, a liberal premium is expected.——Addreſs a line to Mr. Pugh, at Baker's Coffee-houſe, Change-Alley,

Lord John Russell, moaned that 'If England is ever to be England again, this vile tyranny of *The Times* must be cut off', but those at a greater distance saw the value of its independent spirit. '*The Times* is one of the greatest powers in the world,' pronounced Abraham Lincoln, 'in fact, I don't know anything which has more power, except perhaps the Mississippi.' Nonetheless, the quality of its writing and its generally unsensationalist tone were not always matched by the perspicacity of its analysis: it supported the appeasement of Hitler in the 1930s, upheld rapprochement with Stalin in the 1940s and backed the Franco-British occupation of the Suez Canal in 1956. Generally, however, its editorial policy looked favourably on the cause of moderate reform, advocating liberal Conservatism and eschewing campaigning journalism.

Thus *The Times* has always been an influential rather than a popular or profitable paper. It was still selling fewer than 60,000 copies a day when in 1855 the abolition of stamp duty on newspapers created new and competitive domestic rivals like the cheaper *Daily Telegraph*. Even during the twentieth century – until its circulation figures improved in the 1980s – the paper's daily sales were often under a quarter of a million copies, and in the 1950s it even marketed itself with the somewhat exclusive advertising slogan 'Top People Take *The Times*.' Ironically, the paper of choice for the British Establishment had several times to be rescued: first in 1908 by Lord Northcliffe, the innovator of mid-market journalism, before being bought successively by the Anglo-American Astor family, in 1966 by the Canadian Thomson family and, in 1981, by the Australian-born Rupert Murdoch.

The improving authority of rivals, the expanding sources of alternative media information, including radio, television and internet, and a desire to broaden its previously limited readership base all conspired to end *The Times*'s claims to preeminence. Despite this, it retained, in at least some aspects, its claim to be Britain's foremost 'newspaper of record'. Its law reports are without equal in the press, its letters page continues to provide a national forum of interaction between the powerful and the general public, and the court and social page is a noticeboard for events and announcements. Its crossword, instigated in 1930, still provides one of the most recognized daily tests of mental dexterity. Most of all, a longevity of over 220 years at the forefront of national and international discourse has earned its central place in the history of Britain's fourth estate.

1788
MARYLEBONE CRICKET CLUB'S CODE OF LAWS

CODIFYING CRICKET

Bat-and-ball games have been played in England since at least the Middle Ages and almost certainly since the Dark Ages. Indeed, cricket's etymology may come from 'cryce', the Old English word for stick. The distance between wickets is still twenty-two yards: the traditional dimension of an Anglo-Saxon farmer's strip-holding.

Surviving early references to cricket proliferate from the seventeenth century and something resembling the modern game dates from that period. The first eleven-a-side match for which there is an authoritative record was played in Sussex in 1697. By 1709, Kent were facing Surrey and the following year undergraduates at Cambridge University began forming teams.

During the eighteenth century, the sport was particularly popular in the southern counties of England, its appeal crossing social divides. In the thirty years after 1767, the acknowledged centre of cricketing talent was, improbably, the small Hampshire village of Hambledon. There, a winning team was marshalled by Richard Nyren, who was the landlord of the Bat & Ball inn. In 1777, the Hambledon Club even humiliated a side drawn up of England's supposed best cricketers by an innings and 168 runs.

Yet despite cricket's rustic roots, its adoption by gentlemen in London facilitated its transformation into the modern game. Matches were played on the commons at Chelsea and Clapham, as well as at the artillery ground in Finsbury. In common with the other leading sports of the day, considerable stakes often awaited the winners, attracting professional promoters, serious betting and even occasional crowd trouble.

As much to regulate the terms for fair gambling as to establish the legality of actions on the field, in 1744 the first cricket rules were drawn up by the London

CRICKET'S EARLY HISTORY

*c.*1550 'Creckett' is played at the Royal Grammar School, Guildford, according to a court testimony of 1598.

1598 Giovanni Florio's English–Italian dictionary mentions 'to play cricket-a-wicket' (there is some debate over whether this is a sport or a sexual act).

1646 The oldest surviving record of a match being played that can be properly authenticated as cricket takes place at Coxheath in Kent.

1697 An eleven-men-a-side game is first mentioned.

1709 Kent v. Surrey is the first recorded county match.

1722 The London Cricket Club is in existence.

1744 The oldest surviving laws are drawn up by the London Cricket Club.

*c.*1767 The Hambledon Club is established in Hampshire and soon fields the most successful side in the country.

1769 John Minshull of the duke of Dorset's XI scores the first recorded century.

1774 The Star and Garter Club of London publishes its Laws of Cricket; the leg before wicket law is established.

1787 Marylebone Cricket Club is founded.

1788 MCC's Code of Laws is laid down.

1794 The oldest recorded interschool match occurs: Charterhouse v. Westminster.

1806 The tradition of the Gentlemen v. Players match begins at Thomas Lord's ground.

1807 Round-arm bowling is first mentioned.

1811 The first women's match at county level, Surrey v. Hampshire, is played.

1814 Thomas Lord selects his third, and final, site for MCC's ground.

1827 The first Oxford v. Cambridge match at Lord's ends in a draw.

Club of which Frederick, Prince of Wales, was president. Other versions followed, with none gaining definitive acceptance.

In 1787 a club was founded that quickly asserted its authority, with its roots in the aristocratic White Conduit Club, whose ground had been swallowed up by urban developers. Two of its luminaries, the earl of Winchelsea and the future duke of Richmond, helped a business-savvy bowler, Thomas Lord, find them a new ground in Marylebone. With this move, Marylebone Cricket Club (MCC) was founded. When the lease expired and the ground was built over to become Dorset Square, Lord found fresh premises in St John's Wood and, taking the original turf with him, he settled on a third – and final – site for the club in 1814. This ground is still called Lord's and remains the headquarters of MCC to this day.

Within a year of its establishment, MCC drew up its own Code of Laws (as the rules were grandly styled). This code quickly gained acceptance throughout the rest of the country while MCC, although no more than a private club, assumed responsibility as the sport's governing body. While other bodies were later set up to administer English Test and county cricket, MCC retained its lead role in setting the guidelines for, and administering, Test cricket throughout the world until 1993, when the International Cricket Council took over. Despite encroachment from the ICC, MCC still owns and retains the right to frame the Laws.

Inevitably, over the past two centuries or more, the Laws have been subject to revision during a period that saw sheep-grazed fields give way to pitches carefully prepared with a heavy roller and in which the game spread throughout the British Empire. The number of balls bowled in an innings, for instance, was increased from four to five in 1889 and again to six in 1900. The parameters for a Leg Before Wicket (LBW) decision generated considerable debate. Concerned by excessive 'padding away' by batsmen, in 1934 MCC introduced a new law, allowing not just balls pitched in a straight line between the two wickets but even those pitched outside off stump to be capable of producing a LBW verdict. It was on the legality of various bowling actions that the hottest controversy raged. Bowling was delivered underarm during the eighteenth century. However, bowlers increasingly tested the latitude offered by umpires, progressively raising the point at which they released the ball with round-arm deliveries. MCC attempted to end this upward creep by specifically outlawing it in an 1816 law clarification. Unable to make the judgment stick, MCC kept redefining upwards the height at which a delivery could be made, until finally legalizing round-arm in 1835 and overarm in 1864, when the bowler was permitted freedom of delivery so long as he did not throw the ball (i.e. deliver it with a bent arm).

Some of the greatest changes of format have come more recently. Limited-overs competitions were introduced at county level in 1963 and at international level in 1971, the format adopted four years later with the first World Cup. A new limited-overs format, Twenty20 – involving two innings of twenty overs apiece rather than the fifty that had become standard in one-day cricket – was introduced in 2003 and rapidly became popular, especially in India. Despite these innovations, the five-day Test match retains its prestige as the most demanding form of the game, with the 'Ashes' series between England against Australia among the most celebrated contests in world sport.

For all its successful transplantation from Marylebone to Melbourne and its centrality to life in places from Hyderabad to Kingston, Jamaica, cricket has been mythologized as a sport particularly emblematic of the country of its birth. Certainly, the language of cricket has become part of everyday English usage. Whatever the sharper, competitively charged reality on the field, its cultural association with fair play, patience and good sportsmanship remain among qualities that the English fondly imagine are most representative of their own national character traits. Even in spheres far removed from bat and ball, anything resembling sharp practice or underhand behaviour remains decidedly 'just not cricket'. Few other codes of laws have given the world such an ethos without anything stronger than a private members' club to ensure their enforcement.

The Laws Of Cricket, 1788
As revised by The Cricket Club at St Mary-le-bone

THE BALL
Must weigh not less than 5 ounces and a half, nor more than 5 ounces and three-quarters; it cannot be changed during the game but by the consent of both parties.

THE BAT
Must not exceed four inches and one quarter in the widest part.

THE STUMPS
Must be twenty-two inches out of the ground, the bails six inches in length.

THE PARTY
Which goes from home shall have the choice of innings and the pitching of the wickets, which shall be pitched within thirty yards of a centre fixed by the adversaries.

When the parties meet at a third place, the bowlers shall toss for the pitching of the wickets and the choice of going in.

It shall not be lawful for either party during a match, without the consent of the other, to alter the ground by rolling, watering, covering, mowing or beating. This rule is not meant to prevent a striker from beating the ground with his bat near where he stands, during the innings, or to prevent the bowler from filling up holes, watering his ground, or using sawdust, etc., when the ground is wet.

THE BOWLER
Shall deliver the ball with one foot behind the bowling crease, and within the return crease; and shall bowl four balls before he changes wickets, which he shall do but once in the same innings. He may order the striker at his wicket to stand on which side of it he pleases.

THE STRIKER
Is out if the bail is bowled off or the stump bowled out of the ground.

Or, if the ball, from a stroke over or under his bat, or upon his hand (but not his wrists), is held before it touches the ground, although it be hugged to the body of the catcher.

Or, if in striking, or at any time while the ball is in play, both his feet are over the popping-crease, and his wicket is put down, except his bat is grounded within it.

Or, if in striking at the ball, he hits down his wicket.

Or, if under pretence or running a notch or otherwise, either of the strikers prevents a ball from being caught, the striker of the ball is out.

Or, if the ball is struck up and he wilfully strikes it again.

Or, if in running a notch, the wicket is struck down by a throw, or with the ball in hand, before his foot, hand or bat is grounded over the popping-crease; but if the bail is off the stump must be struck out of the ground.

Or, if the striker touches or takes up the ball while in play, unless at the request of the opposite party.

Or, if with his foot or leg he stops the ball, which the bowler, in the opinion of the umpire at the bowler's wicket, shall have pitched in straight line to the wicket and would have hit it.

If the players have crossed each other, he that runs for the wicket which is put down is out; if they are not crossed, he that has left the wicket which is put down, is out.

When a ball is caught, no notch to be reckoned. When a striker is run out, the notch they were running for is not to be reckoned.

When the ball has been in the bowler's or the wicket-keeper's hands, it is considered as no longer in play, and the strikers need not keep within the ground until the umpire has called PLAY; but if the player goes out of ground with an intent to run before the ball is delivered, the bowler may put him out.

If the ball is struck up the striker may guard his wicket either with his bat or his body.

In single wicket matches, if the striker moves out of his ground to strike at the ball, he shall be allowed no notch for such stroke.

THE WICKET-KEEPER

Shall stand at a reasonable distance behind the wicket, and shall not move until the ball is out of the bowler's hand, and shall not by any noise incommode the striker; and if his hands, knees, feet or head, be over or before the wicket, though the ball hit it, it shall not be out.

THE UMPIRES

Are the sole judges of fair and unfair play, and all disputes shall be determined by them; each at his own wicket. But in the case of a catch, which the umpire at the wicket cannot see sufficiently to decide upon, he may apply to the other umpire, whose opinion is conclusive.

They shall allow two minutes for each man to come in, and fifteen minutes between each innings, when the umpire shall call PLAY, the party refusing to play shall lose the match.

When a striker is hurt they are to permit another to come in, and the person hurt shall have his hands in any part of that innings.

They are not to order a player out unless appealed to by the adversaries.

But, if the bowler's foot us not behind the bowling-crease, when he delivers the ball, they must, unasked, call NO BALL.

If the strikers run a short notch the umpire must call NO NOTCH.

That the umpire at the bowler's wicket shall be first applied to, to decide on all catches.

BETS

If the notches of one player are laid against another, the bets depend on the first innings, unless otherwise specified.

If the bets are made on both innings, and one party beats the other in one innings, the notches in the first innings shall determine the bet.

But if the party goes in a second time, then the bet must be determined by the number of the score.

VI

THE YEARS OF REFORM

1792
MARY WOLLSTONECRAFT'S
A VINDICATION OF THE RIGHTS OF WOMAN

THE BIRTH OF FEMINISM

In the period immediately after its publication, *A Vindication of the Rights of Woman* made its author, Mary Wollstonecraft, Europe's most famous female political writer. Although that reputation ebbed in the succeeding decades, her status was restored during the twentieth century with the embrace of much of her feminist philosophy.

Born in 1759, Wollstonecraft was unhappy in her youth. The family wealth was squandered by a bullying and incompetent father, while her mother openly favoured her eldest son. 'What was called spirit and wit in him,' his sister later summarized, 'was cruelly repressed as forwardness in me.' She received only brief schooling, a shortcoming for which she subsequently compensated by vociferous reading and teaching herself several foreign languages.

A propitious marriage – as a recurring theme in Jane Austen's novels emphasized – was the primary means by which middle-class women retained or enhanced their social station. With a minimal dowry, Mary Wollstonecraft's chances were blighted by her father's financial ineptitude. She embarked instead upon a career as a teacher and governess, whose rewards were meagre. Women's education, which had been a feature of Tudor gentry society, had still not fully recovered from the disruptions of the seventeenth century. To make matters worse, Wollstonecraft's efforts were not greatly appreciated by those who employed her.

In two areas, however, women were established in their own right. Since the Restoration, the stage had offered opportunities to women prepared to risk moral compromise. During the eighteenth century, a second, safer market developed in literature written by – and usually for – women. Wollstonecraft determined to become a writer. In 1787, Joseph Johnson, a sympathetic publisher, brought out her book, *Thoughts on the Education of Daughters*.

The transforming event was the outbreak of the French Revolution. Britons were divided between those like the Whig politician-turned-Tory philosopher Edmund Burke, who preferred the orderly society of the *ancien régime* to the bloody anarchy unleashed by the mob, and radicals like Thomas Paine, the author of *The Rights of Man* (1791), who interpreted events in France as the birth of a new liberty.

Wollstonecraft firmly endorsed the latter view and sought to broaden its message to her own sex. In 1792, Johnson published her *A Vindication of the Rights of Woman*. An instant best-seller, it was soon translated into French and German and was also brought out in an American edition. It argued that a male-ordered society obsessed by rank and position had confined and stunted female development and self-expression. Furthermore, women had connived in their own disadvantage. Upon attaining their goal of marriage they had proceeded to behave as 'weak beings . . . fit only for a seraglio!' Society was constructed so that even 'civilised women of the present century, with a few exceptions are only anxious to inspire love, when they ought to cherish a nobler ambition, and by their abilities and virtues exact respect'.

M.^{RS} WOLLSTONECRAFT.

Mary Wollstonecraft (1759–97).

Her own private life exemplified the struggles of women to gain esteem beyond the parameters of conformity. She fell in love with a bisexual married man, but the relationship was broken off when she suggested to his wife cohabiting with them in a *ménage à trois*. In 1792 she travelled to Paris and there began an affair with an American officer. To protect her from the murderous vengeance of the anti-British French revolutionaries, he registered her at the American Embassy as his wife. However, despite her being pregnant with his child, he largely deserted her to follow his own commercial ventures, and other lovers, before sending her to Scandinavia to conduct his business. Made miserable by his treatment, she twice tried to commit suicide. Rescued once by her maid from an opium overdose and a second time by rowers from drowning under Putney Bridge, she survived, working off some of her pain by using the experience as the basis for an epistolary novel, *A Short Residence in Sweden, Norway and Denmark* (1796). In the radical philosopher

From *A Vindication of the Rights of Woman*, Chapter 2

Women ought to endeavour to purify their heart; but can they do so when their uncultivated understandings make them entirely dependent on their senses for employment and amusement, when no noble pursuits set them above the little vanities of the day, or enables them to curb the wild emotions that agitate a reed, over which every passing breeze has power? To gain the affections of a virtuous man, is affectation necessary? Nature has given woman a weaker frame than man; but, to ensure her husband's affections, must a wife, who, by the exercise of her mind and body whilst she was discharging the duties of a daughter, wife, and mother, has allowed her constitution to retain its natural strength, and her nerves a healthy tone, – is she, I say, to condescend to use art, and feign a sickly delicacy, in order to secure her husband's affection? Weakness may excite tenderness, and gratify the arrogant pride of man; but the lordly caresses of a protector will not gratify a noble mind that pants for and deserves to be respected. Fondness is a poor substitute for friendship!

In a seraglio, I grant, that all these arts are necessary; the epicure must have his palate tickled, or he will sink into apathy; but have women so little ambition as to be satisfied with such a condition? Can they supinely dream life away in the lap of pleasure, or the languor of weariness, rather than assert their claim to pursue reasonable pleasures, and render themselves conspicuous by practising the virtues which dignify mankind? Surely she has not an immortal soul who can loiter life away merely employed to adorn her person, that she may amuse the languid hours, and soften the cares of a fellow-creature who is willing to be enlivened by her smiles and tricks, when the serious business of life is over.

Besides, the woman who strengthens her body and exercises her mind will, by managing her family and practising various virtues, become the friend, and not the humble dependent of her husband; and if she, by possessing such substantial qualities, merit his regard, she will not find it necessary to conceal her affection, nor to pretend to an unnatural coldness of constitution to excite her husband's passions. In fact, if we revert to history, we shall find that the women who have distinguished themselves have neither been the most beautiful nor the most gentle of their sex.

William Godwin she finally met a like-minded man who treated her with respect. Overcoming their mutual opposition to the idea of marriage, they exchanged vows when she discovered she was pregnant by him; but lasting happiness eluded her. In September 1797, aged thirty-eight, she died following complications in giving birth. The child survived and grew up to become the novelist Mary Shelley.

Godwin was heartbroken, but when he published his memoirs he unintentionally severely damaged her posthumous reputation by detailing her bohemian life. As a consequence, she quickly plummeted from her position as the most read and discussed exponent of women's rights, while the personal details Godwin had revealed provided ammunition for her political opponents. It did not help that her deeply sexual and largely unhappy odyssey did not sit easily with the high moral tone adopted by the female Victorian campaigners. Nevertheless, while her writing produced little discernible gain in the short term, she benefited from a reassessment by the women's suffrage movement at the end of the nineteenth century. From then on, her standing continued to recover. The liberal attitudes expressed in *A Vindication of the Rights of Woman* have made the book a central text not only of twentieth-century feminism but of equality itself.

1800

THE ANGLO-IRISH
ACT OF UNION

THE CREATION OF THE UNITED KINGDOM'S PARLIAMENT

B ack in 1171, Henry II had launched a full-scale invasion of Ireland. In doing so, he cited papal sanction (Rome was concerned about Ireland's Celtic ecclesiastical traditions); but he was chiefly motivated by greed and the fear that other rivals might establish too strong a foothold there if he did not assert his own authority. Disunited by its competing regional chieftains, the country was taken over piecemeal, with Anglo-Norman barons seizing land predominantly in the south-east. Parliaments were called from 1264. Yet, despite successive campaigns in the fourteenth century, English forces failed to subdue the rest of the island. Indeed, by the fifteenth century, English influence had contracted to the area of the Pale around Dublin. The realization that the whole island could not readily be brought under centralized control ensured its division between the native Gaelic chiefs, the semi-autonomous Anglo-Irish lords and the centre of anglicized leadership in Dublin.

It was Henry VIII who adopted new strategies, seeking to strengthen his own authority while pursuing measures that avoided costly formal colonization. The Dublin Parliament had recognized successive English monarchs as 'Lord of Ireland', but in 1541 this title was upgraded to 'King of Ireland'. In return for acknowledging their royal overlord and English law, the Gaelic chiefs were guaranteed retention of their possessions. Peerages were also conferred upon them in the belief that this would foster their integration and collaboration. However, the adoption of Protestantism and the 'plantation' of (largely Scots Presbyterian) settlers in Ulster succeeded only in widening the divide between the colonists and the colonized. Successive uprisings in the last years of Elizabeth I's reign were put down only at considerable cost.

In the seventeenth century the plight of the Catholic Irish majority worsened significantly. On the eve of the English Civil War, 60 per cent of Ireland was still in Catholic ownership. Atrocities by both sides in the 1640s were followed in 1649 by Oliver Cromwell's invasion and the ruthless imposition of a new settlement.

Cromwell's experiment in uniting the Irish and English Parliaments, with (Protestant) Irish MPs sitting at Westminster, was undone upon the Restoration. The Anglican Church of Ireland was given statutory authority as the Established Church. Largely left in place was the Protestant land grab, which engulfed 80 per cent of the country. Except in parts of Ulster where Scottish migration created a Presbyterian culture that was both anti-Catholic and anti-Establishment, the imposition of Anglican landowners without a corresponding Anglican yeomanry defined the class division along a clearly delineated religious faultline. Controlled by the all-powerful Anglican landed gentry, the revived Parliament in Dublin proceeded to pass penal laws that stripped Catholics of most of their remaining rights.

Yet Dublin's Protestant 'Ascendancy' politicians also resented interference from the mainland. In 1720, Westminster restated its legal right to legislate on Ireland's behalf, a reality made especially evident when rival economic interests clashed. In Dublin, this battle for ultimate authority found in Henry Grattan a leader gifted with the unusual combination of eloquence and moderation. He appeared victorious when, in 1782–3, Westminster – not wanting a repetition of the American War of Independence closer to home – formally renounced its own legislative powers over Ireland. What Britain retained was executive authority through its appointment of a lord lieutenant based at Dublin Castle.

IRELAND 1169–1800

1169 A Norman army occupies Wexford at the request of Dermot MacMurrough, the ousted king of Leinster.

1171 Henry II of England invades Ireland.

1366 The Statutes of Kilkenny attempt to stop the descendants of English settlers adopting Gaelic Irish customs.

1494 The so-called Poyning's Law asserts that the Irish Parliament is subservient to Westminster.

1541 The Irish Parliament recognizes Henry VIII as king of Ireland.

1560 The Irish Parliament acknowledges the Elizabethan supremacy and Anglicanism as the Established Church.

1592–1603 Rebellion in Ireland is finally suppressed with the surrender of Hugh O'Neill and the assertion of English rule throughout the island.

1608 The plantation of Ulster brings large-scale settlement in the North by Scottish Presbyterians.

1641 A bloody insurrection by Catholics breaks out, in an attempt to regain confiscated lands.

1649 Oliver Cromwell's forces massacre garrisons at Wexford and Drogheda.

1654 The 'Cromwellian Plantation' effectively further curtails Catholic land ownership.

1689 Protestants in Londonderry withstand a 105-day siege by Jacobites loyal to the ousted James II.

1690 At the Battle of the Boyne Protestant forces of William of Orange defeat Catholics loyal to James II.

1695 Penal Laws persecuting Catholics are introduced (by 1714 Catholics own a mere 7 per cent of the land).

1782 The Irish Parliament wins legislative independence from Westminster.

1793 The Catholic Relief Act grants Catholics right to vote on same terms as Protestants.

1798 The United Irishmen's rebellion is crushed.

1800 The Irish Parliament votes itself out of existence by passing the Act of Union, effective from 1801.

From the Act of Union, 1800

Article First. That it be the first Article of the Union of the Kingdoms of Great Britain and Ireland, that the said Kingdoms of Great Britain and Ireland shall, upon the 1st day of January which shall be in the year of our Lord 1801, and for ever after, be united into one Kingdom, by the name The United Kingdom of Great Britain and Ireland; and that the royal style and titles appertaining to the Imperial Crown of the said United Kingdom and its dependencies; and also the ensigns, armorial flags and banners thereof shall be such as H.M., by his royal Proclamation under the Great Seal of the United Kingdom, shall be pleased to appoint.

Article Second. That it be the second Article of Union, that the succession to the Imperial Crown of the said United Kingdom, and of the dominions thereunto belonging, shall continue limited and settled . . . according to the existing laws, and to the terms of union between England and Scotland.

Article Third. That it be the third Article of Union that the said United Kingdom be represented in one and the same Parliament, to be styled The Parliament of the United Kingdom of Great Britain and Ireland.

Article Fourth. That it be the fourth Article of Union that four Lords Spiritual of Ireland by rotation of sessions, and 28 Lords Temporal of Ireland elected for life by the peers of Ireland, shall be the number to sit and vote on the part of Ireland in the House of Lords of the Parliament of the United Kingdom; and 100 commoners (two for each County of Ireland, two for the City of Dublin, two for the City of Cork, one for the University of Trinity College, and one for each of the 31 most considerable Cities, Town and Boroughs) be the number to sit and vote on the part of Ireland in the House of Commons of the Parliament of the United Kingdom.

It was the French Revolution that provoked London into rethinking legislative devolution. The fear was that Ireland might prove susceptible to the republican spirit emanating from Paris or, worse still, become the launching ground for a French invasion of the British mainland. There were also worries that the Dublin Parliament would seek to pass economic policies injurious to Britain. Such fears were well founded. Although a minor French invasion attempt in 1796 ended ignominiously, two years later the 'United Irishmen' launched a major republican uprising. It was defeated. Yet, the scale of the loss of life – perhaps as many as 20,000 lives – underlined the magnitude of the discontent.

How Ireland's greater political liberty and religious toleration might be achieved without threatening the security of the rest of the British Isles now exercised the government of William Pitt the Younger. London nudged the Dublin Parliament into passing the 1793 Catholic Relief Act, permitting Irish Catholics to bear arms, to serve commissions in the army and (for those with 40-shilling freeholds) to vote. There had, in the previous decade, already been some easing in the restrictions on Catholics in terms of property, law, religion and education. The remaining injustices meted out to the Catholic majority – including their inability to sit in Parliament – still needed to be addressed. The problem was that doing so threatened to destroy the Protestant Ascendancy's hold on Irish politics and could expect rough treatment in the Dublin Parliament. William Pitt's solution was to incorporate Irish representation into a United Kingdom-wide Parliament. Thus Catholic emancipation could be granted without those enfranchised becoming more than a small minority at Westminster.

The first attempt was defeated in 1799. But the scheme's advocates persevered. Where argument and persuasion failed, bribery – the tactic that overcame opposition to union in the Scottish Parliament – was successfully deployed in the Irish Parliament. Money and promises of titles proved sufficient inducement to convince waverers and hard bargainers. The Irish Parliament voted itself out of existence by 158 votes to 115.

The Act of Irish Union was passed in August 1800 and came into force on New Year's Day 1801. Dublin's 300-member House of Commons was abolished and in its place, 100 Irish seats were created in the new United Kingdom House of Commons. The Irish peerage also got to vote on which twenty-eight of them would take their seats in the enlarged House of Lords at Westminster. This arrangement resembled that introduced by the 1707 Act of Union for the Scottish peers, except that the Irish representative peers would sit for life. And, unlike the leaders of the

Dublin Castle, from where the lord-lieutenant as viceroy and the chief secretary administered Ireland for the British Crown.

Church of Scotland, four Church of Ireland bishops, serving in rotation, were also admitted to the House of Lords.

Catholic acquiescence in the Anglo-Irish Union had been bought on the pledge of full religious emancipation. Pitt resigned when the intransigence of George III prevented him delivering on his promise. Britain's side of this bargain was thus granted only in 1829 when the Catholic Emancipation Act finally became law. The scarcely tenable situation in which the Established Church in Ireland was Anglican – despite the Presbyterianism of Ulster and overwhelming Catholicism of the rest of the country – endured until its disestablishment finally came in 1869. Although as early as 1832 there were thrity-nine Irish MPs at Westminster opposed to the Act of Union, the long and tortuous path to repeal the legislation of 1800 would take 120 years.

THE GENERAL ENCLOSURE ACT

LAND RIGHTS AND THE AGRARIAN REVOLUTION

The enclosure of land transformed the English countryside, fundamentally altering the nature of farming and creating a patchwork of hedgerow-bordered fields that became the familiar face of the landscape for most of the nineteenth and twentieth centuries.

Traditionally, the countryside was farmed in open fields in which villagers grew produce in their own, often widely dispersed, strips, which allowed cottagers to engage in subsistence farming. All tenants enjoyed the right to graze whatever livestock they might have on common pasture. In consequence, herds intermingled.

This was an inefficient form of farming. Indeed, the survival of mixed-use land, subject to the rights of so many individuals, undermined any return on investment a landowner might seek to make by improving its quality. Small cultivators were far less likely to have the resources necessary to drain land. Tellingly, much land was left uncultivated. In an effort to extract better value from the soil, enclosure involved withdrawing community rights to common pasture and consolidating strips into single ownership fields that could be hedged or fenced off for private use.

When the first enclosures of common land took place in the thirteenth century, there was still sufficient common pasture to satisfy the needs of the whole village. Indeed, legislation sought to ensure that enclosure did not go so far as to wipe out access to communal grazing. A far greater assault on traditional methods came in the fifteenth century, when manors, keen to meet the growing demand for wool, pushed on with the enclosure of large-scale fields for sheep pasture. Depleting common pasture created unrest and an increasing numbers of dispossessed vagrants. Legislation followed no consistent path during this period, sometimes supporting, at other times hindering, the process according to the perceived economic circumstances of the moment. Nonetheless, there was a tendency towards trying to limit enclosure and soften the consequences for its victims, especially in areas of traditional mixed husbandry. During the seventeenth century, however, Parliament effectively gave up trying to prevent the process.

Nonetheless, open fields were still prevalent during much of the eighteenth century. It was mostly in the enclosed areas, however, that improvements became viable and where land drainage and strict crop rotation heralded an agrarian revolution. The increasing cultivation of root crops such as turnip provided forage for the hardier and heavier livestock being produced by selective stock-breeding. New breeds of sheep became worth eating, as well as merely shearing.

Across England the pace of enclosure slowed during the first half of the eighteenth century before picking up again after 1750. In seeking to prevent disputes, Parliament was asked to legislate approval for each application for enclosure. This was generally granted when the proposal had the support of three-quarters of the landholders affected. Commissioners duly surveyed and apportioned the land in a manner they deemed equitable, and the dispossessed were compensated. To this approach, there were two major objections – that the process was costly and that the compensation received by those deprived of their common rights was often inadequate.

By the end of the eighteenth century, the movement for 'improvement' was again in full swing, burdening Parliament with a surge of applications for legislation. Westminster passed almost four thousand enclosure acts between 1750 and 1810, covering about 20 per cent of the land of England and Wales, with the Midlands a particularly intense area of activity. It was to simplify the procedure, reduce costs and speed the process that in 1801 the General Enclosure Act – then known as the 'Inclosure (Consolidation) Act') – was passed. It established a template for the drafting of suitable legislation. In this it was successful, and the transformation was largely complete by the time a further General Enclosure Act in 1845 drew together all the individual grants in an annual act. By comparison, enclosure was still in its relatively early stages in the rest of Western Europe and had scarcely begun in Eastern Europe.

The overall social and economic consequences of enclosure were hotly contested at the time and continue to divide historians now. It would be surprising if such a change, carried out over so long a period and over such varied terrain, produced consistent results. Generally though, it suited the interests of landowners. Yet the nature of land redistribution can be misunderstood. The average farm in the

OPPOSITE: 1801 'inclosure map' of the Northamptonshire parish of Wilby. The area is now on the outskirts of Wellingborough.

early nineteenth century was still relatively small. Even the effects on the cottager, dispossessed of his common grazing rights, were mixed.

In the short term, though, it was cottagers who appeared to have lost out. They were faced with the choice of either staying on, reduced to the status of hired hands, or turning their backs on the land in search of work in the towns and cities. But these were not invariably unfortunate consequences. Enclosure – married to other agricultural improvements – improved yields. It made food more plentiful and cheaper. In this light, the declining numbers engaged in subsistence farming may be viewed as a positive consequence rather than a sign of harmful effects. The surge in agricultural productivity freed labourers to seek more remunerative work in the towns and cities, providing, in turn, the workforce that made the Industrial Revolution possible and Britain the 'workshop of the world', a status that ultimately raised living standards far beyond what previous generations could have imagined possible.

1805

JAMES GILLRAY'S
THE PLUM-PUDDING IN DANGER

PRESS FREEDOM AND POLITICAL SATIRE

ew men better tested the eighteenth century's limits of the freedom of the press than the caricaturist James Gillray. Viewing his work, foreigners were astonished that his decidedly undeferential lampooning of Britain's royal family and political leaders did not land him in jail. Yet, not only did Gillray remain at liberty, but George III and the Prince of Wales were among those who bought his work.

The Plum-Pudding in Danger is depicted in the third plate section.

In Britain, the freedom of the press was created not by a statute but rather by the failure to renew a statute. In 1695 the Licensing of the Press Act of 1662 – 'for preventing the frequent Abuses in printing seditious treasonable and unlicensed Bookes' – lapsed. The House of Commons refused to extend its life with fresh legislation. Thus a new age of literary liberty began, freed from state censorship. Treason, seditious libel and blasphemy remained on the statute books as the main restraints and, anomalously, between 1737 and 1968 the lord chamberlain's department censored the theatre, largely to cut out perceived obscenity, but initially also because of perceived dangers inherent in spectators excited by potentially subversive politics. But compared to anywhere else in Europe, Britain's writers, polemicists and caricaturists enjoyed unparalleled freedom of expression, held in check only by the risk of being sued for libel.

Pamphlets and cheeky, often vulgar, cartoons were churned out lambasting the chicanery and corruption of British politics, particularly between 1721 and 1742 when Sir Robert Walpole was the country's first prime minister. This was the golden age of 'Grub Street', which took its name from the Moorfields neighbourhood of London where many of the hack writers and down-at-heel controversialists eked out their living by chipping away at the pretensions of the rich and powerful.

245

BRITAIN IN THE AGE OF REVOLUTION

1790 Edmund Burke's *Reflections on the Revolution in France* becomes the classic argument against revolutionary change.

1791 Thomas Paine's *Rights of Man* defends revolutionary change.

1792 The London Corresponding Society is founded to promote radical reform; the Libel Act hands to juries the right to determine libel cases.

1793 Revolutionary France declares war on Britain.

1794–5 The Habeas Corpus Act is suspended.

1795 The size of public meetings is legally restricted to fifty persons.

1796 Edward Jenner injects an eight-year-old boy with his inoculation against smallpox.

1797 A French force lands at Fishguard, Pembrokeshire: the last such incursion on British soil.

1798 Income tax is announced as an emergency measure.

1801 Habeas Corpus is again suspended.

1802 The Treaty of Amiens ends war with France. The Factory Act restricts the working hours of children and improves their conditions. William Cobbett launches his *Political Register*.

1803 Conflict with France is renewed. Lord Ellenborough's Act tightens the common law restrictions on abortion, imposing the death penalty for those performing abortions after a foetus's 'quickening' (about 18–21 weeks).

1805 Nelson's victory at Trafalgar effectively removes the likelihood of Britain being invaded.

1806 Napoleon's imposition of his Continental System tightens economic warfare against Britain.

1808 British troops are dispatched to the (Iberian) Peninsular War: victory is achieved in 1813.

1811 Luddite riots against modern machinery break out. The Regency Act places royal authority in the hands of the Prince Regent during George III's 'madness.'

1812 War breaks out between the United States and Britain and lasts until 1814. Prime Minister Spencer Perceval is assassinated.

1813 Jane Austen's *Pride and Prejudice* is published.

1815 The Battle of Waterloo ends the Napoleonic Wars. Corn Laws introduced to protect domestic agriculture.

1817–18 Habeas Corpus is suspended for the third time.

1819 A radical meeting is violently broken up in Manchester: the so-called Peterloo Massacre. 'Six Acts' are passed to restrict the size of meetings and curtail alleged seditious activities.

1820 The 'Cato Street Conspiracy' to murder the Cabinet is exposed. There is unrest in Scotland.

Among caricaturists, none equalled James Gillray (1756–1815) in fame or skill. His upbringing in the strict Protestant beliefs of the Moravian sect could hardly have provided an early environment less given to levity and vulgarity. It was his apprenticeship with a Holborn letter engraver and his subsequent training at the

Royal Academy School that ensured his skills as a draughtsman were developed and recognized. The market for his subsequent work was already established. William Hogarth (1697–1764) had been the dominant artist-as-satirist from the 1730s to the 1750s. While much of Hogarth's work concerned cautionary tales with moral lessons, Gillray increasingly concerned himself with savaging those in authority. Huge crowds pressed around the shop window of his publisher, Hannah Humphrey (at 18 Old Bond Street until 1798; thereafter at 27 St James's Street), to view his latest lampoons and to buy copies, many of which were colour-tinted by hand.

No man, woman, cause or party was off limits to Gillray. His cynicism was impartial. Furthermore, he supplemented traditional humour with wit, often employing wordplay and providing his characters with speech bubbles – subsequently the standard device of illustrated 'comics' around the world. The carryings-on at court, especially George III's bouts of insanity and the Prince of Wales's debauchery, provided a rich seam of scandal for his satire. He was no less sparing with Westminster politics, which was dominated by two men: the corpulent, easygoing gambler and Whig leader, Charles James Fox; and the lean, boyish and physically fragile Tory prime minister, William Pitt the Younger.

A popular engraving of James Gillray's self-portrait.

After the excitement of the fall of the Bastille had subsided, the increasingly frightening news coming from across the Channel fundamentally recast British politics. While Fox and his fellow radicals continued to applaud what they took to be the victory of liberty, much of Britain recoiled at the accompanying brutality. The outbreak of war with revolutionary France in 1793 made these divisions ever more stark, prompting Gillray to cease being the impartial denigrator of both parties. Never a Francophile (his father had lost an arm fighting the French at the Battle of Fontenoy in 1745), he allied himself – rarely without equivocation – with Pitt's Tories and British patriotism.

It was during this period that Gillray's depiction of John Bull took full shape. The national stereotype had been created by James Arbuthnot in 1712 and, in the hands of later *Punch* cartoonists John Leech and John Tenniel, would appear as a stocky, mostly amiable, figure. Gillray's version was an argumentative and often uncomprehending rustic whom the vicissitudes of life and politics regularly pushed to the verge of fury, but never beyond the point at which he ceased to be a patriot.

Gillray's work also popularized the image of Napoleon Bonaparte – 'Little Boney' – as a scrawny, crazed midget. In *The Plum-Pudding in Danger*, published in February 1805, Gillray anticipated a decisive moment in the Napoleonic Wars. Admiral Horatio Nelson's destruction of the French and Spanish fleets at Trafalgar in October that year removed the threat of invasion. An armed stalemate followed in which Napoleon was master of Europe while the success of the Royal Navy gave Britain mastery of the seas. It is this emerging reality that Gillray depicted, with slices of plum pudding being simultaneously carved by Pitt the Younger (who would die the following year) and Napoleon.

Gillray's powers declined soon thereafter. His eyesight began to fail, then he suffered a breakdown, bouts of madness, and he attempted suicide. He was last seen through his shop window, wandering around disorientated, naked and unshaven, like a grotesque from one of his own cartoons. He died later that day, 1 June 1815, without living to hear of the final defeat of Napoleon at Waterloo seventeen days later. Nonetheless, he left behind a tradition of caricature, satire and lack of deference to those in authority that was continued in the years after his death by his protégé George Cruikshank. The baton has been passed on, through the twentieth century and beyond, by newspaper cartoonists from David Low and Philip Zec to Gerald Scarfe, Steve Bell and Peter Brookes.

1829

STEPHENSON'S DESIGN
FOR *ROCKET*

THE BIRTH OF THE RAILWAY AGE

The success of his *Rocket* at the Rainhill trials in 1829 did more than win £500 prize money for its inventor, George Stephenson: it established that steam locomotives represented the future of travel. As far as covering distances was concerned, it was the single most revolutionary advance since antiquity.

Despite being the child of illiterate parents, George Stephenson's early circumstances were in fact propitious for his subsequent career. He was born in 1781 in the Tyneside mining village of Wylam near a wooden rail track, along which coal wagons were pulled by horse. He spent his childhood not in school, but instead found himself deputed to shoo cows off the track.

It was from mining that the railway age would emerge. Atmospheric steam engines using pistons and cylinders had been invented by Thomas Newcomen to pump water out of mines in 1712. Stephenson's father operated a mine engine until it blinded him. Stationary steam engines were also developed to pull coal wagons along rails, although most of the work was still done by horses.

It was the Cornish engineer, Richard Trevithick, who in 1804 designed the first locomotive that could successfully run a significant distance, pulling both freight and customers on rail track. However, the unreliability of such early locomotives was compounded by their weight. They were too heavy for the rails – whether wooden or iron – to carry them without splitting. Most investors, believing the problem intractable, withdrew finance. At best, it was assumed the engines would never serve more than short lines connecting collieries to canals and ports, with the long-distance travel still done by water.

Having largely taught himself to read and write, Stephenson began designing colliery engines; but his real success came when he was appointed engineer for a line to run the twenty-six miles from Stockton to Darlington. Opened in 1825, it was the first freight- and passenger-carrying public railway to use steam traction. Leased to whoever wanted to pay to use them, its lines were intended for both horse- and engine-drawn traffic. Championing the latter, Stephenson designed his *Locomotion No. 1*, which caused a stir by pulling thirty-six wagons at an average speed of 4 mph.

Stephenson's success at Darlington led to his being asked to survey a route for a proposed rail track to be operated by the Liverpool and Manchester Railway Company. The company's directors had not decided whether moving locomotives or fixed engines using chains represented the best future for pulling coaches along the line. To test the practicality of the former, they offered a prize to the inventor who could design a locomotive that worked.

Sketch of Rocket's *boiler made on 5 October 1829 by John Urpeth Rastrick (1780–1856). Rastrick was one of the three judges who awarded* Rocket *first prize at the Rainhill Trials.*

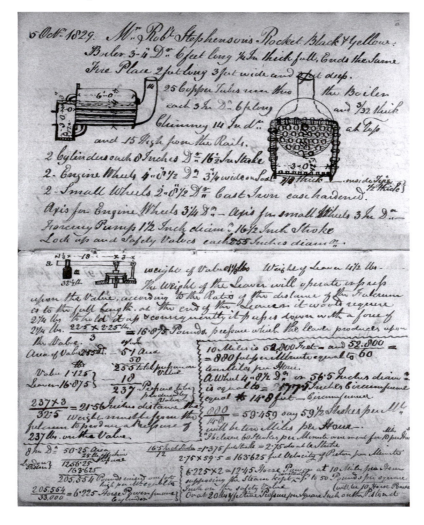

Five entries got as far as the trials, held at Rainhill, east of Liverpool, in October 1829. Such was the curiosity and excitement that crowds in their thousands gathered to watch. At various stages, four of the engines developed teething problems. In the case of one entry, *The Cycloped*, there was a total loss of power when the horse trotting on its drive-belt fell through the locomotive's floor. The clear winner was George Stephenson's *Rocket*. It travelled untroubled for seventy miles, during which it recorded a top speed of 29 mph. The quality of its performance settled the argument. Henceforth, the future of distance travel was by steam locomotive.

The world-changing moment was recognized at the time. Such was the celebration the following year at the official opening of the Liverpool and Manchester Railway that the prime minister, the duke of Wellington, attended. Failing to get out of the way of the fast-approaching *Rocket*, William Huskisson, the duke's parliamentary colleague and a senior Tory politician, fell under its wheels to achieve fame as the first fatality of the railway age.

Much of the credit for *Rocket*'s design actually lay with George Stephenson's son, Robert (1803–59). It contained several innovations that, taken together, ensured its superiority. It more effectively transferred heat from the firebox gases into the boiler water because it ran twenty-five copper tubes through the boiler rather than the customary single cylinder. The steam exhaust created a far more powerful air draught thanks to a blast pipe. Connection and stability were improved through direct coupling, with connecting rods and pistons set at a slanting angle rather than vertically. With amendments and improvements, these remained the principles that guided all steam-train design until the technology's replacement in the 1960s.

Thus with *Rocket*, travel by train moved swiftly from impractical novelty to the driving force of the modern world. In the locomotive's first full year of operation,

THE GROWTH OF THE RAILWAYS

1781 James Watt patents the 'sun and planet gear', which allows a piston to drive a wheel by an off-centre connection.

1783 The invention of the rolling and puddling process creates much stronger iron.

1804 Richard Trevithick's steam locomotive is the first to be able to travel any significant distance by rail.

1825 The Stockton–Darlington Railway opens; George and Robert Stephenson's *Locomotion No. 1* runs on it.

1829 George and Robert Stephenson's *Rocket* sets a world speed record of 29 mph at the Rainhill Trials.

1830 The Liverpool and Manchester Railway opens; there are now ninety-five miles of rail track in Britain.

1837 The first electric locomotive is designed by Robert Davidson.

1840 There are by now 1,500 miles of rail track in Britain.

1841 Isambard Kingdom Brunel's line opens between London and Bristol.

1850 There are 6,000 miles of rail track in Britain.

1857 Steel rails are introduced.

1863 The first section of the London Underground railway is opened, from Paddington to Farringdon Street.

1870 The rail network amounts to 13,400 miles of track.

1900 There are now 18,100 miles of rail track in Britain.

in 1830, parliamentary approval was given for the construction of 375 miles of public track. A decade later, there were nearly 1,500 miles of track. By 1852, lines connected different parts of both Wales and Scotland to London. By 1870, there were 13,400 miles of track. This expansion made travel practical for Britons who had previously struggled to find the time or money to wander far from their home county. The effect in breaking down parochial attitudes was incalculable. The need for consistent timetabling nationwide led to the abolition of local 'parish time' and its replacement by a uniform Greenwich Mean Time throughout Britain.

Arguments that so important a vehicle for social change should be brought under the auspices of the state were trumped by those who feared the resulting monopoly. For this reason, the construction of competing companies' lines going to the same places was seen not as wasteful but as a sign of healthy competition. The government neither financed nor directed where new lines should go. Parliament merely gave legislative permission to construct lines, to ensure compulsory land purchase and to regulate the terms of use. Nonetheless, an Act of 1844 reserved the future right to take lines into public ownership if necessary and, in the meantime, forced the railway companies to offer at least one daily service for which passengers would be charged no more than a penny a mile.

The speed at which goods – foodstuffs as well as manufactures – could be transported long distances delocalized trade, enhancing markets for producers and driving down costs for consumers. The way in which this rapid expansion was funded had profound consequences, in that joint-stock companies appeared more attractive investment opportunities than government securities. Although subject to spurts of unsustainable boom followed by some inevitable collapses, this transformed capitalism, creating – unusually at that time – a huge sector of the economy in which ownership and control were not one and the same. Nor was the investment confined to Britain. The development of the rail network around the globe was often the work of British companies, underwritten from London.

It was such an outstanding achievement that the growing centrality of rail travel to Britain's economic success in the nineteenth century might be measured by how three successive generations of its innovators ended their days. Richard Trevithick died a pauper in 1833; George Stephenson passed away at his sizeable Derbyshire country house in 1848; his son Robert went on to construct lines and bridges as well as locomotives, became Conservative MP for Whitby, and following his death, in 1859, was buried in Westminster Abbey. It was not just in travel that the railways brought social mobility.

1829
THE CATHOLIC EMANCIPATION ACT

GROWING RELIGIOUS LIBERTY

In the popular consciousness, the link between Roman Catholicism and continental despotism was the single greatest barrier to the acceptance of Rome's adherents in British society. At its most virulent, this animosity lasted for as long as there remained a plausible likelihood of a successful, French-aided, Jacobite invasion bent on undoing the work of the Glorious Revolution. The threat was finally removed by the crushing defeat of Prince Charles Edward's Jacobite forces at Culloden in 1746. In any case, the number of Catholics had by then shrivelled to a tiny proportion, mostly confined to pockets in the countryside where a few aristocrats (presumed eccentric) retained the faith of their forebears. Despite its being the dominant faith in Ireland, perhaps no more than 2 per cent of the population of England and Wales were Catholic.

However, the sense of security of the Hanoverian settlement after 1746 meant that Catholics found themselves increasingly unmolested when opening schools and chapels, even though such activities were still illegal. Their numbers, particularly among the artisan class, began to swell in towns and cities, but they remained a distinct minority, at the mercy of events and sporadic demagoguery. In 1778, following the passage of the Catholic Relief Act, 'No Popery' riots in Edinburgh and Glasgow greeted the readmittance of Catholics to the armed forces and the removal of restrictions on their purchasing property, scaring the government into scrapping plans to make the law applicable in Scotland. London was convulsed in ten days of fighting when, two years later, Parliament refused to bow to the demands of the Protestant Association, led by Lord George Gordon, to repeal the 1778 legislation for the rest of Britain. The houses of Catholics were burned down and Newgate prison and other buildings were ransacked. George III felt compelled to call up 12,000 troops to fire on the mob and restore order. In all,

RELIGIOUS LIBERTY IN BRITAIN

1661 The Corporation Act restricts the holding of government and town office in England and Wales to those taking the Anglican Communion.

1678 The Test Act forces all MPs and peers to deny transubstantiation.

1689 The Toleration Act grants religious liberty to Protestant Dissenters.

1698 The Popery Act gives financial rewards to those who expose clandestine Catholic worship and makes Catholic teachers liable to serve a life prison sentence.

1714 The Schism Act requires all school headmasters in England to be licensed by an Anglican bishop. The Occasional Conformity Act removes a loophole through which Catholics and Dissenters can evade the Test and Corporation Acts. Both acts are repealed in 1718.

1723 State grants are introduced to support Dissenting ministers.

1766 The papacy finally recognizes the house of Hanover as the legitimate monarchy in Britain.

1778 The Catholic Relief Act removes semi-redundant statutes that placed Catholic priests at risk of arrest for felony and restricted Catholics' rights in passing on and acquiring property. Catholics are permitted to join the armed forces.

1780 The Gordon riots in London witness mob violence against extending Catholic rights.

1791 The Catholic Relief Act guarantees Catholic freedom of worship and education, as well as admission to the legal profession. Catholic property owners gain the right to vote.

1813 Unitarians are included in the terms of the Toleration Act.

1821 The Catholic Relief Bill is passed in the Commons but later defeated in the Lords.

1828 The repeal of the Test and Corporation acts opens public office to Dissenters.

1829 The Catholic Emancipation Act removes the remaining legal barriers confronting Catholics, including the right to sit in Parliament.

the anarchy of the Gordon riots caused around 500 casualties. Although acquitted on treason charges, Lord George Gordon was ruined. He later converted to Judaism, was imprisoned for libelling Marie Antoinette and died in Newgate.

Moderate opinion was horrified not just by the anti-Catholic rabble on the streets of London but also by the anti-clericalism of the Terror in France. The sanctuary given to French Catholic royalty, aristocrats and priests fleeing the atheist ideologues of the French Revolution did much to temper previous attitudes. Unusually, Britain found itself in alliance with Bourbon absolutists, by which time native Catholics had made a statement on where their primary loyalties lay. In 1788, the four Catholic 'Vicars Apostolic', together with 240 priests and 1,500 laymen, issued a protestation renouncing the Vatican's temporal authority. The government responded to this overture in 1791 with legislation removing Catholic religious disabilities and making them free to worship without the threat of having their chapels or schools closed down. Catholics owning property with an annual rental of £2 or more were granted the right to vote. However, one major cause of emancipation remained beyond their grasp: the right to sit in Parliament and hold civic or state office.

Seeking to address the discontent of Ireland's Catholic majority, William Pitt the Younger had in 1800 attempted to link the union of the British and Irish Parliaments with full Catholic emancipation. George III, however, remained obstinate, fearful of triggering another Gordon riot and insisting that approving such rights breached his coronation oaths. Without

From the Catholic Emancipation Act, 1829

Whereas by various Acts of Parliament certain restraints and disabilities are imposed on the Roman Catholic subjects of H.M., to which other subjects of H.M. are not liable; and whereas by various Acts certain oaths and declarations, commonly called the declaration against transubstantiation, and the declaration against transubstantiation and the invocation of Saints and the sacrifice of the Mass, as practised in the Church of Rome, are or may be required to be taken, made, and subscribed by the subjects of H.M., as qualifications for sitting and voting in parliament, and for the enjoyment of certain offices, franchise, and civil rights: be it enacted . . . that . . . all such parts of the said Acts as require the said declarations, as a qualification for sitting and voting in Parliament, or for the exercise or enjoyment of any office, franchise or civil right are (save as hereinafter provided and excepted) hereby repealed.

sufficient Cabinet support to face down his monarch, Pitt felt compelled to resign on the matter. Yet the Irish problem would not go away. In 1823, Daniel O'Connell founded the Catholic Association, a pressure group demanding full emancipation. At the County Clare by-election in 1828 he was returned as the MP but was unable to take his seat at Westminster on account of his religious faith.

As the Irish-born scion of a Protestant Ascendancy landowning family, the prime minister, the duke of Wellington, was not naturally sympathetic to O'Connell's cause. Nevertheless, when faced with the possibility of serious disorder in Ireland, he felt compelled to act against his instincts. In pushing through Catholic emancipation he staved off the possibility of civil war in his native land, but at a cost. The issue divided his Tory Party, ensuring that it would be out of office for most of the following decade of reform.

When the act passed into law on 13 April 1829, Catholics were finally allowed to sit in Parliament as well as on lay corporations. Only a small number of restrictions were placed on their admittance to the highest offices of state: they could not become lord chancellor, keeper of the great seal, lord-lieutenant of Ireland or high commissioner of the Church of Scotland. The case for allowing the head of state to become Catholic was not seriously considered. It was unthinkable that the monarch, as supreme governor of the Church of England, would be (or

Field Marshal Arthur Wellesley, 1st duke of Wellington (1769–1852), Anglo-Irish soldier and statesman. As prime minister from 1828 to 1830, the hero of Waterloo was compelled to act against his instincts in pushing through Catholic emancipation. In doing so, however, he staved off the possibility of civil war in Ireland.

would marry) a Catholic; allowing even the possibility would have involved tearing up the whole Glorious Revolution settlement. A nod to Protestant sensibilities also prevented Catholic clergy standing as MPs or wearing their vestments outside church.

The Catholic Emancipation Act had considerable constitutional implications. The rights of the Established Church could be determined by legislation passed by politicians who were not its communicants. The admission to Parliament of Jews in 1858 and atheists in 1886 meant that MPs did not even have to be Christian. The inclusion of the atheists particularly outraged the leaders of Britain's Catholic community. By then, massive Irish emigration had transformed the visibility of the Catholic faith across the mainland's great cities on a scale that few involved in the 1829 legislation could have foreseen.

1832

THE GREAT REFORM ACT

THE SPREAD OF DEMOCRACY

The 'Great' Reform Act of 1832 increased the number of men who could vote in general elections by 50 per cent, from 435,000 to 652,000. In doing so, it brought many middle-class voters within the democratic process. Whilst it meant that about one in five men had the vote, it did little to extend the franchise to the labouring man and did nothing at all for women, regardless of their class. Nevertheless, it signified the first comprehensive attempt to create a more equitably distributed pattern of constituencies across the United Kingdom, initiating a process that within a hundred years would result in universal franchise.

The 1832 legislation created uniform criteria for who was entitled to vote. Prior to its enactment, some constituencies enjoyed something close to universal male suffrage. In other boroughs the vote lay solely in the possession of the members of the town corporation. Those with small electorates often found themselves 'in the pocket' of the local landowner. An 1827 study estimated that of the 658 parliamentary constituencies, the choice in 276 of them was essentially determined by the influence, direct or indirect, of the local grandee. Furthermore, the distribution of seats had ceased to bear much relationship to the shifting population patterns of an industrializing country. Seaside boroughs were massively over-represented, yet northern towns were hugely under-represented. Cornwall and Wiltshire had more borough constituencies than in all eight northern counties. In Scotland, the nature of the franchise was particularly arcane: 4,000 electors returned all the Scottish burgh and county MPs. The member for the capital, Edinburgh, was determined by a mere thirty-three voters.

It was to address the worst anomalies of voting practice and regional distribution that the Whig government of Earl Grey determined to reform the system. The legislation, largely drafted by Lord John Russell (1792–1878), made uniform the

257

From the Great Reform Act, 1832

Schedule A. [fifty-six boroughs ceasing to return any MPs]

Amersham, Wendover, Bossiney, Callington, Camelford, East Looe, Fowey, Lostwithiel, Newport, St Germans, St Mawes, St Michael (Midshall), Saltash, Tregony, West Looe, Beeralston, Okehampton, Plymouth, Corfe Castle, Stockbridge, Whitchurch, Newtown, Yarmouth, Weobly, Queenborough, New Romney, Newton, Castle Rising, Higham Ferrers, Brackley, Bishop's Castle, Ilchester, Milborne Port, Minehead, Aldeburgh, Dunwich, Orford, Blechingley, Gatton, Haslemere, Bramber, East Grinstead, Seaford, Steyning, Winchelsea, Appleby, Great Bedwin, Dowmton, Heytesbury, Hindon, Ludgershall, Old Sarum, Wootton Bassett, Aldborough, Boroughbridge, Hedon.

Schedule B [Thirty boroughs to return one MP only]

Wallingford, Helston, Launceston, Liskeard, St Ives, Ashburton, Dartmouth, Lyme Regis, Shaftesbury, Wareham, Christchurch, Petersfield, Hythe, Clitheroe, Great Grimsby, Morpeth, Woodstock, Eye, Reigate, Arundel, Horsham, Midhurst, Rye, Calne, Malmesbury, Westbury, Wilton, Droitwich, Northallerton, Thirsk.

Schedule C [Twenty-two new boroughs to return two MPs each]

Macclesfield, Stockport, Devonport, Sunderland, Stroud, Greenwich, Bolton, Blackburn, Manchester, Oldham, Finsbury, Marylebone, Tower Hamlets, Stoke-upon-Trent, Wolverhampton, Lambeth, Brighton, Birmingham, Bradford, Halifax, Leeds, Sheffield.

Schedule D [Twenty new boroughs to return one MP each]

Whitehaven, Gateshead, South Shields, Merthyr Tydvil, Cheltenham, Chatham, Ashton-under-Lyne, Bury, Rochdale, Salford, Warrington, Tynemouth, Frome, Walsall, Kendal, Dudley, Kidderminster, Huddersfield, Wakefield, Whitby.

criteria for voting: in the boroughs, this meant those owning or occupying properties valued above £10 a year and, in the counties, £10 'copyholders' (referring to an archaic, long-term and low-rent tenancy agreement) and £50 leaseholders. Those previously enfranchised because they had 40-shilling freeholds retained their vote. Over-represented parts of the country lost constituencies, while under-represented areas gained new ones.

In March 1831, the proposals passed their second reading in the House of Commons by just one vote. When the bill was defeated at the committee stage a general election was called, which returned a decisive majority for reform. A second attempt was defeated in the House of Lord, provoking anger in many parts of the country at the hereditary chamber's veto. Riots broke out in Bristol. Minor concessions were attached to the third attempt to pass the bill and pressure was put on the king, William IV, to create a dozen pro-

Charles, Earl Grey, prime minister from 1830 to 1834 and one of the architects of the Great Reform Act of 1832.

reform peerages if the Lords voted it down again. Aware of this threat, the Lords passed the bill on its second reading, only to seek to hold it up on procedural grounds. The government resigned but was reinstalled within the week. It then became known that the king was prepared to go further, creating as many new peerages as were needed to pass the legislation. This time the Lords bowed and, on 4 June 1832, passed the Reform Bill on its third reading. Accompanying reform bills for Scotland and Ireland also became law.

Although the immediate effect of the Reform Act was to create an extra 217,000 voters, its provisions brought in a further 400,000 electors during the following thirty years. It abolished many of the most flagrantly 'rotten' boroughs, where MPs had been returned by very few voters, yet it changed the social composition of the House of Commons only marginally. In 1833, 217 MPs were the sons of peers or baronets. By 1865, the figure had fallen merely to 180. Constituencies that had been won through blatant corruption became the subject of parliamentary inquiry, with the worst offenders stripped of their victory; but it was not until 1872 that the replacement of open voting with the secret ballot really stamped upon electoral intimidation and vote buying.

THE RIGHT TO VOTE

1832 The Great Reform Act enfranchises about 20 per cent of the adult male population.

1867 The vote is extended to all male urban householders and to lodgers paying more than £10 rent. About 30 per cent of the adult male population is enfranchised. The legislation is extended to Scotland and Ireland in 1868.

1869 Women ratepayers gain the right to vote in local government elections.

1872 The Secret Ballot Act ends 'open' voting in all local and parliamentary elections.

1884 Equal qualification in town and country means that men paying £10 rent or owning property with a £10 value are granted the vote. Over 60 per cent of the adult male population is now enfranchised.

1918 Universal franchise (apart from minor anomalies) applies to all men over twenty-one and all women over thirty.

1928 Men and women have the vote on equal terms at the age of twenty-one.

1948 The abolition of university seats and the end of registration in both home and business constituencies end plural voting.

1969 The voting age is lowered to eighteen.

In one respect the Reform Act's opponents were correct. The Whigs had promised that it represented 'finality'. Indeed, such was Lord Russell's determination in making this claim that he acquired the nickname 'Finality Jack'. Tories like Sir Robert Peel disputed this, arguing that, on the contrary, it created a dangerously precise division of who could vote, based on property and wealth, where previously the criteria had been less overt. Such an explicit class-delineated measure could not endure without further revision. And so it proved, with the numbers enfranchised increased by subsequent Reform Acts in 1867, 1884 and 1918, by which time all men over twenty-one and all women over thirty had the vote. Both sexes got the vote equally at twenty-one in 1928, with the voting age lowered to eighteen in 1969.

1834
THE TAMWORTH MANIFESTO

THE BIRTH OF THE MODERN CONSERVATIVE PARTY

Across Europe in the nineteenth and twentieth centuries, right-wing parties emerged with an uncompromisingly hostile response to the onslaught of liberalism and secularism. By contrast, the forces of Conservatism in Britain adopted a more measured stance, generally seeking to moderate and adapt social change in the hope of reducing destabilizing tendencies rather than to oppose all change outright.

There were many reasons why British Conservatism moved away from the more extreme manifestations of continental 'throne and altar' assertiveness. The first, most obviously, was the relative moderation of British radicalism, which was less determinedly republican or atheist than many European left-wing movements. After the seventeenth century, the British monarchy was rarely threatened by bloody revolution, precisely because it generally kept within its constitutional limits. If British Tories were less extreme than continental 'Ultras', then it was because the institutions they sought to defend drew back from the sort of provocations that caused uprisings and revolutions across Europe in 1848. Security bred moderation. The same was true in religion. For all its defence of its own rights and presumptions, nineteenth-century Anglicanism did not turn its back on the modern world. Unlike the papacy, it did not wholeheartedly denounce the ideals of democracy.

Yet there was no predestined path towards moderation. The Tory Party was born in the 1670s around a group of politicians bent on preserving the constitutional right of the future James II to inherit the throne regardless of his Catholicism. It was their Whig opponents who first taunted them as 'Tories' (an abusive term connotative of Irish Catholic rebels). This taint of Jacobitism was mostly an exaggeration, although Tories did tend to be 'High Church' Anglicans, determined to defend the political supremacy of the Established Church. In the succeeding one

To the Electors of the Borough of Tamworth, 1834

. . . With respect to the Reform Bill itself, I will repeat now the declaration I made when I entered the House of Commons as a member of the Reformed Parliament – that I consider the Reform Bill a final and irrevocable settlement of a great constitutional question – a settlement which no friend to the peace and welfare of this country would attempt to disturb, either by direct or by insidious means.

Then, as to the spirit of the Reform Bill, and the willingness to adopt and enforce it as a rule of government: if, by adopting the spirit of the Reform Bill, it be meant that we are to live in a perpetual vortex of agitation; that public men can only support themselves in public estimation by adopting every popular impression of the day – by promising the instant redress of anything which anybody may call an abuse, by abandoning altogether that great aid of government, more powerful than either law or reason, the respect for ancient rights, and the deference to prescriptive authority – if this be the spirit of the Reform Bill, I will not undertake to adopt it. But if the spirit of the Reform Bill implies merely a careful review of institutions, civil and ecclesiastical, undertaken in a friendly temper combining, with the firm maintenance of established rights, the correction of proved abuses and the redress of real grievances, – in that case, I can for myself and colleagues undertake to act in such a spirit and with such intentions.

hundred years, they fought several general elections on the slogan 'The Church in Danger'.

The social and political discontent that followed the end of the Napoleonic Wars in 1815 brought out the authoritarian side of Tory administrations and it was necessity rather than enthusiasm that prompted the conversion of the prime minister, the duke of Wellington, to the cause of Catholic emancipation. Industrialization and urbanization were transforming the country in ways that traditional Toryism had difficulty comprehending. The party's opposition to the franchise extension of the Great Reform Act placed it decisively on the losing side of the argument. The immediate political price was obvious. In the 1832 general election, only 185 Tory MPs were returned to Parliament. Their opponents numbered 473.

It fell to the new Tory leader, Sir Robert Peel (1788–1850), to decide how Conservatism should respond to its marginalization. A decision to reject the legitimacy of the increasingly democratic temper of the times could either have gifted the future to Whig and Radical administrations or, indeed, begun a process in which normal party politics disintegrated, bringing down the edifice of constitutional parliamentary government. As home secretary, Peel had shown himself a capable administrator who created the Metropolitan Police in 1829. His early political philosophy, however, suggested that he was still, in sentiment, a traditionalist.

More accurately, Peel was a man of contradictions. He inherited a baronetcy, was educated at Eton and Oxford, and became an MP at the age of twenty-one. Far from coming from the landed elite, his father had been one of the pioneering generation of northern industrialists. Peel's background was thus entrepreneurial. He was not only 'new money' but was perceptive enough to recognize when an old nostrum had had its day.

It was this quality that shone through his address to the 586 electors in his Tamworth constituency, in December 1834, at the outset of the 1835 general election campaign. In the narrow sense, his proclamation was scarcely necessary. With no opponent being put up to run against him at Tamworth, Peel's re-election was a foregone conclusion. In reality, his argument was addressed to the wider, national electorate. His manifesto laid out not a specific set of legislative proposals but a new philosophical path for the Tories, realigning the party as one of moderation

FROM TORYISM TO CONSERVATISM

1678–81 The Tories are identified as a parliamentary group loyal to the hereditary right of the Catholic James, duke of York, to succeed to the throne. The term is derived from *Tóraidhe*, the Irish word for 'outlaw'. Their opponents are labelled 'Whigs' from the Scots' word *Whiggamor* or 'cattle drover'.

1715 The flight of the Tory leader, Lord Bolingbroke, to the Old Pretender's court allows the Whigs to taint the Tories with Jacobite treason.

1714–60 During the so-called 'Whig Oligarchy', the Tories are continuously out of government.

1762–3 Lord Bute serves as the first Tory prime minister. The Tories are viewed as the defenders of King George III's royal prerogatives.

1794 The Whig unity fractures over its response to the French Revolution and domestic radicalism. Whig conservatives support the administration of William Pitt the Younger, which is retrospectively categorized as Tory. The realignment ensures that Toryism comes to be associated with patriotism and the philosophy of Edmund Burke.

1783–1806 and 1807–30 The Pittites/Tories are continuously in power.

1812–27 The Tory leader, Lord Liverpool, becomes Britain's longest-serving prime minister.

1829 The Tory Party splits over the decision of its leader, the duke of Wellington, to support Catholic emancipation.

1834 Sir Robert Peel's Tamworth Manifesto realigns Conservatism with moderate reform.

1841 The Conservatives win the general election.

1846 The Conservative Party splits over Peel's repeal of the Corn Laws.

1852 Benjamin Disraeli, the Conservative leader in the Commons, abandons protectionist economics and endorses free trade.

1859 Peel's adherents, including William Ewart Gladstone, join with Whig and Radical factions to found the Liberal Party.

and open-mindedness to reform, rather than as a force of instinctive reaction. Reported and published nationwide, the Tamworth Manifesto became, in effect, the founding charter of the modern Conservative Party.

The manifesto accepted the widened democracy created in 1832 as a settled reality. Instead of opposing change on principle, it pledged the party to a more pragmatic and empirical response, still committed to 'the firm maintenance of established rights' but also wedded to 'the correction of proved abuses and the redress of real grievances'. Even the entitlements of the Church of England were not sacrosanct where there was a case to answer. To some, this looked like an opportunistic sell-out of time-honoured Tory principles.

For Peel, the Tamworth Manifesto was not just about finding a new direction for his party; it was also about asserting his own role as its policy-maker. In aiming to marginalize dissent within its fractious ranks, he helped restore the party to power. One hundred seats were gained in the ensuing general election, enough to demonstrate recovering Tory fortunes.

Peel proceeded to win a working majority in the 1841 election, serving as a reforming prime minister until 1846. It was at that point that he tried to take his supporters further than their adherence to landed interests would allow. Having been converted to the cause of free trade, and conscious of the urgent need to tackle the Irish potato famine, he repealed the agriculture protection measures of the Corn Laws, ushering in an age of cheaper food but also ensuring a division in his own party that forced him from office.

During the succeeding twenty years, the Conservatives were mostly out of power. Some of Peel's followers – including William Ewart Gladstone – drifted towards the Liberal Party. However, the central tenets laid out in the Tamworth Manifesto were eventually revived as the guiding principles of Conservatism. In 1867, a Conservative government passed a second Reform Act that began the enfranchisement of urban working men. Social reform followed in the 1870s. In its attitude to domestic politics, the party spent the twentieth century as a centre-right group, far removed from the sort of right-wing factions that did so much to destabilize liberal Europe between the two world wars.

1838

THE PEOPLE'S CHARTER

DEMANDS FOR POPULAR DEMOCRACY

The 1832 Reform Act scarcely touched the labouring classes. Indeed, the insistence of Whig politicians that their legislation concluded – rather than commenced – the process of widening political representation suggested that the working classes faced permanent exclusion from the political process.

Not satisfied that their interests were taken into account by those in authority, a Co-operative storekeeper, William Lovett (1800–77), and his associates founded the London Working Man's Association in 1836. Run by the working class *for* the working class, it was a pressure group that aimed to secure for labourers the same rights as the middle and upper classes enjoyed.

The association's political objectives were drawn up by Lovett, assisted by the Radical MP Francis Place, in a document entitled the 'People's Charter'. Published in May 1838, it consisted of six demands: universal suffrage for all males (Lovett was dissuaded from including women); annually elected parliaments; voting by secret ballot; abolition of the property qualification for MPs; the payment of MPs; and equally sized constituencies. The common thread uniting these demands was the social broadening and greater accountability of parliamentary government. It could be decided later what policies the resulting democracy might adopt.

The People's Charter became the common ground bringing together otherwise geographically and ideologically disparate radical and working men's organizations. Support was strong and especially vocal in the mill towns of Lancashire, although the waxing and waning of the Chartist campaigns closely followed the trade cycle's consequences for these communities. Many of the leading activists were skilled artisans, literate figures who were well versed in radical publications. Their views on other issues ranged from protectionism to advocacy of free trade and from pro-industrialization to a Luddite desire to return to cottage industries supplying an agrarian-based economy.

The Six Points
OF THE
PEOPLE'S
CHARTER.

1. A VOTE for every man twenty-one years of age, of sound mind, and not undergoing punishment for crime.

2. THE BALLOT.—To protect the elector in the exercise of his vote.

3. NO PROPERTY QUALIFICATION for Members of Parliament —thus enabling the constituencies to return the man of their choice, be he rich or poor.

4. PAYMENT OF MEMBERS, thus enabling an honest trades-man, working man, or other person, to serve a constituency, when taken from his business to attend to the interests of the country.

5. EQUAL CONSTITUENCIES, securing the same amount of representation for the same number of electors, instead of allowing small constituencies to swamp the votes of large ones.

6. ANNUAL PARLIAMENTS, thus presenting the most effectual check to bribery and intimidation, since though a constituency might be bought once in seven years (even with the ballot), no purse could buy a constituency (under a system of universal suffrage) in each ensuing twelvemonth; and since members, when elected for a year only, would not be able to defy and betray their constituents as now.

It was Chartism's mixed blessing to attract the energy and attention-grabbing skills of Feargus O'Connor (1794–1855). An Irish MP who had lost his County Cork constituency in 1835, O'Connor began campaigning across the British mainland on the Chartist programme with a mixture of oratorical zeal and scarcely concealed menace, assisted by the newspaper he controlled, the *Northern Star*. For all his passion, his personality was a divisive factor in the movement and helped its opponents characterize it as the dangerous instrument of an aspiring demagogue.

The 'People's Charter' became tied to a parallel innovation in working-class agitation. This was the Convention of the Industrious Classes, a shadow parliament that aimed to set the political agenda. Its delegates met in London in February 1839 and began debating what to do if the real Parliament did not bow to the Charter's demands. Despite the many divisions of opinion, agreement was reached that in this eventuality a general strike would be called to bring the politicians to their senses.

Westminster was not so easily intimidated. When, in July 1839, a copy of the Charter was presented to Parliament with the endorsement of 1,200,000 signatures, the Commons divided, 235 votes to 46, against bothering to discuss its demands. Having moved to Birmingham the Convention was becoming increasingly fractious and broke up in September. With little sign of a nationwide appetite for a general strike, plans for direct action were scaled back. Some hotheads called for a rising, which resulted in November in an ill-conceived skirmish between Chartists and soldiers at Newport, in Wales. The instigators were sentenced to transportation (but pardoned in 1854) while more moderate activists received short jail sentences.

OPPOSITE: The six demands of the People's Charter, published in 1838.

It was during this period that Lovett and O'Connor's paths diverged. Lovett concluded that a movement confined to working-class membership was doomed and that the only hope lay in alliance with the middle classes. The problem with this was that much of the middle class viewed uneducated labourers as the very people with whom they did not wish to share the franchise. Keen to remain the leader of his own movement, O'Connor, by contrast, hoped to lead the National Charter Association, founded in July 1840, on the twin delusions that centralization could be achieved and victory delivered.

A second petition to Parliament in 1842 attracted 3,317,752 signatures. Parliament did not hide its lack of interest, again rejecting considering the Charter by 287 votes to 49. In 1848, while Europe was convulsed by revolutions, a third and final petition was organized. What was intended as a mass rally on Kennington Common proved smaller than anticipated and dispersed in the rain, having been prevented from marching towards Parliament by the police (back-up troops were on standby). Bathetically, the petition was delivered in three cabs instead. The large number of genuine signatures were discredited by the smaller number of autographs purporting to be those of the duke of Wellington or Mr Punch.

The damp squib of 1848 was a sign of Chartism's terminal decline and it ceased to be a significant force after 1854. O'Connor's reputation was ruined by the collapse of a subscriber-driven scheme that he had devised for small landholders, and in 1852 he became insane, dying three years later. Improving economic conditions did much to quell political unrest. Ex-Chartists increasingly turned to other causes, particularly those that motivated Protestant Nonconformists: educational reform and temperance campaigns against the 'demon drink'.

However, the Great Charter was not a failure, merely a false dawn. A successful working-class political movement did eventually emerge in the guise of the Labour Party, and, ultimately, five of the Charter's six demands were adopted. The MPs' property qualification was scrapped in 1858; the secret ballot was introduced in 1872; legislation in 1876, 1884 and 1918 helped create nearly equal-sized constituencies; in 1911 the payment of MPs came in; universal male suffrage was achieved in 1918. Only the least sensible of the Chartists' demands – annual general elections – has never reached the statute books.

VII

THE VICTORIAN AGE

1839–43
BRUNEL'S DESIGN FOR THE SS *GREAT BRITAIN*

THE WORLD'S FIRST SCREW-PROPELLED,
IRON-HULLED OCEAN LINER

F̲ew Victorians better expressed their age's restless energy and the desire to find practical solutions to physical problems than Isambard Kingdom Brunel (1806–59). Almost any of his major engineering triumphs – from the Clifton suspension bridge to the Great Western Railway to the ambitious, if ill-fated SS *Great Eastern* – could be taken as representative of his genius, drive and vision. It was with the SS *Great Britain*, however, that he most demonstrably revolutionized travel and shrank the world.

Steam-powered vessels came into operation at the end of the eighteenth century. The first of these to cross the Atlantic was the American *Savannah*, which in 1819 made the journey from Savannah to Liverpool in twenty-nine days – although it had sufficient steam power for only a small proportion of the trip and relied mostly on its sails. A further fourteen years passed before a British steam-and-sail ship crossed the ocean in the other direction. These were achievements that had uncertain practical application. Sail still remained the only realistic means of transporting large cargos of goods or passengers by sea. It was believed that the amount of fuel necessary to cross the Atlantic purely by steam would take up so much room on board that there would not be space to take sufficient passengers or goods. Therefore, the current wisdom concluded, transatlantic steam travel could never be commercially viable.

Isambard Kingdom Brunel proved otherwise. In 1833, when he was still just twenty-six, he was commissioned by the Great Western Railway to survey, design and engineer their route from London to Bristol. Employing a mixture of impressive bridges, tunnels and viaducts, he proposed taking the London–Bristol line one stop further, crossing the Atlantic by steam to New York. Undaunted by having no experience as a ship designer, Brunel came up with his solution: the SS *Great Western*, a wooden-hulled paddle steamer which, in the water, displaced 2,300 tons. On her maiden voyage in 1838, she proved that the Atlantic could be crossed by steam power. The rival and smaller *Sirius* beat her into port at New York by a matter of hours (having been forced to burn its own cabin furniture in the effort) but it was the *Great Western* whose design and performance illustrated how the crossing could prove viable.

Temperamentally ill-suited to resting on his laurels, Brunel, when he came to build the *Great Western*'s sister ship, proved himself an even greater driver of innovation. At over 3,000 tons displacement, the SS *Great Britain* was at the time of her launching in 1844 by far the largest vessel in the world. More importantly, she represented a first in two breakthrough technologies: she was not only the world's first large iron craft, with a hull made of wrought-iron plates riveted together, but also the first major screw-propelled ship. Driven by a colossal 1,000-horsepower engine, the single sixteen-foot screw propeller was a late design change, but one

Sectional line drawing with wash of the oscillating paddle engines made by Maudslay Sons & Field for Brunel's SS Great Britain. Following an early modification, the engines achieved 1,663 horsepower (ihp).

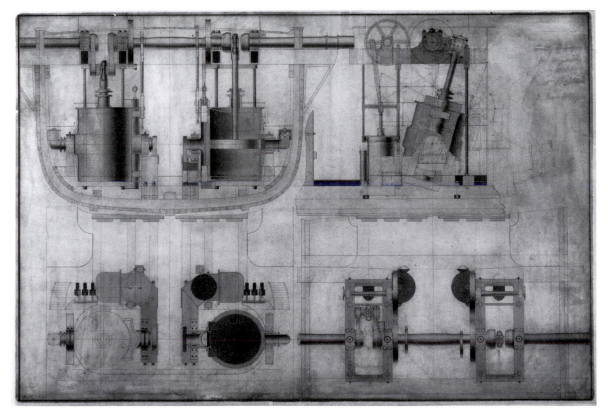

that proved revolutionary. The superiority of her iron hull was demonstrated when in 1846 she ran aground and was stuck off the Irish coast for eleven months before being pulled free, undamaged.

She could carry over 250 passengers (a figure later increased to 750), thereby demonstrating the future possibilities of ocean-going passenger liners. She broke the steam-powered transatlantic speed record on her maiden voyage, reaching America in fourteen days and twenty-one hours. After seeing service as a troopship during the Crimean War and the Indian Mutiny, she switched routes and became an Australia-bound liner, carrying the first 'All England' cricket team to tour in the Antipodes in 1861. By the time her active service ended in 1886, she had travelled nearly 1 million miles. Left as a storage hulk in the Falkland Islands, and subsequently abandoned there in 1937, she was rescued in a state of sad dilapidation in 1970 and brought home to Bristol. Her original iron hull still held together sufficiently for her to float serenely up the River Avon, passing under Brunel's magnificent suspension bridge, before ending her journey back in the same dock from which she had been launched 127 years earlier. There, she was meticulously restored and opened to the public, and can be seen to this day.

1843

CHARLES DICKENS'S
A CHRISTMAS CAROL

POPULAR NOVELS, THE VICTORIAN SOCIAL CONSCIENCE AND THE REVIVAL OF THE CHRISTMAS SPIRIT

Dismissed by some critics as a mere creator of caricatures and mawkish sentimentality, Charles Dickens (1812–70) was, by most popular measures, the greatest novelist in British history and, without question, the most influential.

The fact that the term 'Dickensian' is still used, even by those who have not read his books 150 years after they were written, confirms his centrality to the British psyche. In Dickens's lifetime and thereafter, his audience was never confined to the refined tastes of polite society nor to the ranks of light popular entertainment. Rather, his novels crossed social boundaries, appealing to all classes of reader and both sexes. That was part of their power. Few, if any, politicians, philosophers or artists gained broader acknowledgement or wider appreciation for doing what Dickens did best: holding a mirror up to Victorian Britain and exposing its blemishes.

The social evils were too great and too entrenched to be expunged by any single social reformer, but Dickens influenced movements that attacked some of the most degrading aspects of nineteenth-century life. His novels highlighted the cruelty of the Poor Law of 1834 and, in particular, the workhouse. Many of his works, most memorably *Oliver Twist*, laid bare the brutal treatment of children. His depiction of the Marshalsea prison in *Little Dorrit* helped spur the eventual scrapping of imprisonment for debt in 1869. *Bleak House* painted an uninspiring portrait of the self-serving aspects of the legal system, in particular, Chancery.

A recurring theme in Dickens's work is the fragility of comfort and the sudden reversal of fortune, where wealth may be either won or lost. Of this he had direct experience. The son of a navy pay-office clerk who fell into debt and was sent to the Marshalsea, at the age of twelve Dickens was wrenched out of a comfortable, middle-class existence and put to work in a warehouse, labelling blacking pots. Eventually, the family fortunes recovered so that he was able to complete his schooling, becoming first a solicitor's clerk and then launching his career in journalism, as a parliamentary reporter. Nevertheless, his truest vocation was to be a novelist and he made his name in 1836 with *The Pickwick Papers*.

In this greatly loved work, Dickens constructed a cosy, snow-bound image of Christmas. Prior to the mid-seventeenth century, the twelve days of Christmas had been a time of nationwide conviviality, charity, gluttony, intoxication and neighbourliness. However, although the prohibitions and censure of Puritans did not outlive the English republic of the 1650s, the festival's spirit of bonhomie had become critically dampened, until by the 1820s it was a shadow of its former self. Disheartened by this, Dickens painted a nostalgic picture of Christmas's old, generous-hearted traditions that very effectively reminded readers what they were missing.

The Pickwick Papers was just the beginning. It was *A Christmas Carol* that forever imprinted itself upon our notions of the festive season. The idea came to him suddenly in October 1843, when he was still only thirty-one. He worked on the manuscript at high speed over a six-week period, adding and crossing out as he went along. *A Christmas Carol* was ready for publication on 19 December in a small bound volume, with four illustrations by the *Punch* cartoonist John Leech. Copies were priced at 5 shillings.

A Christmas Carol tells the story of Ebenezer Scrooge, a cold-hearted miser concerned exclusively with his own business, who regards the good fellowship of Christmas as 'humbug'. As he retires for the night on Christmas Eve he is visited by a succession of ghosts, starting with that of his late business partner, warning him of the consequences if he does not mend his ways. The Ghost of Christmas Past shows Scrooge how his selfishness drove away a former love and contrasts his indifference to Fred, his nephew, with the sympathy that Fred's mother once bestowed on Scrooge during his own unhappy childhood. The Ghost of Christmas Present takes Scrooge on a countrywide tour of the Christmas celebrations staged by even the poorest families, including that of his clerk, Bob Cratchit, whose invalid son, Tiny Tim, will die if Scrooge does not become more charitable. The Ghost of Christmas Yet to Come is a dark, hooded figure who does not speak but whose bony hand points to Scrooge's own depressing demise, robbed on his deathbed

1638 – THE SCOTTISH NATIONAL COVENANT

The declaration of resistance to King Charles I's efforts to enforce High Church Episcopalian practices upon the defiantly Presbyterian Church of Scotland was signed in multiple copies by much of the Scottish nobility and clergy as well as by other Scots. This copy was signed in 1639 by Lord George Gordon who died six years later at the Battle of Alford – fighting for the King.

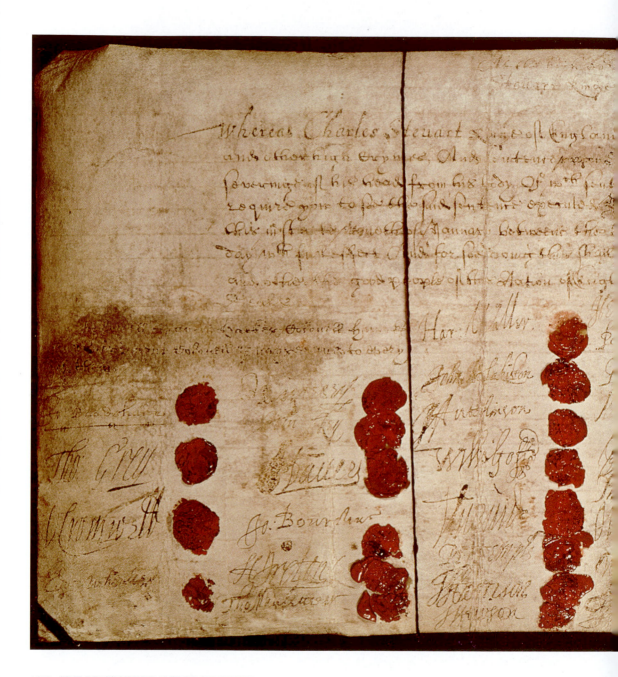

1649 – THE DEATH WARRANT OF CHARLES I

Charles I's death warrant, signed and with the seals of the fifty-nine regicides.
Oliver Cromwell signed third on the left-hand column.

The Plumb-pudding in danger: – or State Epicures taking un Petit Souper

"the great Globe itself, and all which it inherit," is too small to satisfy such insatiable appetites.

1707 – THE ACT OF UNION

When the Act of Union passed into law in the Westminster Parliament, Queen Anne had this illuminated 'Exemplification' of the Act presented as a gift to the Scottish Parliament that the legislation abolished. Queen Anne is depicted in the top left-hand corner of the title page. The three holes at the bottom of the parchment were made by the tags attaching the Great Seal.

1805 – JAMES GILLRAY'S *THE PLUM-PUDDING IN DANGER*

William Pitt the Younger and Napoleon Bonaparte fight for the mastery of sea and land.

and unmourned in his grave. Perturbed and frightened, Scrooge repents and on Christmas morning begins his path to rehabilitation. He joins his nephew Fred's lunch party, joyfully gives money to charity, sends a large turkey anonymously to the Cratchit family for their Christmas feast and decides he should henceforth be like a second father to poor Tiny Tim. Through living all year long in the Christmas spirit, Scrooge finds redemption.

Charles Dickens's original manuscript: the opening page of A Christmas Carol, *1843.*

Marley's Ghost. John Leech's etching for the first edition of A Christmas Carol.

A Christmas Carol was published at a time when few workers had more than one day's festive holiday and the habit of exchanging presents was not widespread. It reminded readers of the fate of disadvantaged children in the month of the commemoration of Christ's Nativity. Furthermore, it warned the well-off that giving was an obligation as well as a pleasure. They should not close their eyes to the fate of the poor and pretend that the dehumanizing workhouse was all that they deserved.

No other secular work did more to revive the notion of Christmas as the season of goodwill than Dickens's simple morality tale. Coincidentally, it was published at almost exactly the same moment that Henry Cole (subsequently the promoter of the Great Exhibition) commissioned for sale the first printed Christmas card – of a family united at the dinner table celebrating a festive meal. Dickens's offering was an immediate success, although he did not greatly benefit personally. Because of the high production costs that he had chosen to incur, having fallen out with his publisher Chapman and Hall, he made only £130 from the initial sale. When he sued the publishers of an unauthorized edition for piracy, he won the case but had to meet the £700 legal costs himself.

Nonetheless, the speed with which others rushed to make money from the book, not least in the theatrical adaptations that attracted eager audiences, testified to its wide appeal, on the far side of the Atlantic as well as at home. In the United States, Dickens is also celebrated as a founding father of the traditions of the modern Christmas. It was one of President Franklin D. Roosevelt's annual rituals to read Scrooge's story aloud from beginning to end. In Britain, too, the tale seems destined to remain relevant for many a Christmas yet to come.

1851

THE 'CRYSTAL PALACE' DESIGN
FOR THE GREAT EXHIBITION

JOSEPH PAXTON'S INNOVATION IN
ARCHITECTURAL DESIGN

O n 1 May 1851, Queen Victoria opened the 'Great Exhibition of Works of Industry of All Nations' in London's Hyde Park, describing the occasion as the greatest day in the country's history. It was the world's first major international exhibition and, over the next six months, 6 million visitors came to see what the industrial and commercial revolution was bequeathing mankind. The single greatest wonder, however, was the 'Crystal Palace' that housed it.

It was the satirical magazine *Punch* that christened the temporary exhibition hall with the name by which it would be forever celebrated. Surprisingly, the revolutionary structure was not the work of any of the great Victorian architects but rather of a garden expert.

Joseph Paxton (1803–65) started his professional life tending the flora of a park in Bedfordshire before becoming head gardener at Chatsworth, the magnificent Derbyshire estate of the dukes of Devonshire. There, he demonstrated his self-taught technical expertise by designing a deceptively delicate conservatory that was, at the time, the largest glass building in the world.

The principles upon which the glasshouses of Chatsworth soared informed Paxton's greatest project. He had observed the strength of a species of giant water lily, the *Victoria amazonica*, by sitting his daughter Annie upon one and floating her across a pond. It inspired Paxton to demonstrate how modern materials and natural forms could unite to produce vast buildings that were structurally strong, yet simple in form and relatively cheap to construct.

Having been drafted in to produce a design for the Great Exhibition's main hall at short notice, Paxton did so on blotting paper with a sketch doodled while attending a board meeting. In this approach, as in its method of execution,

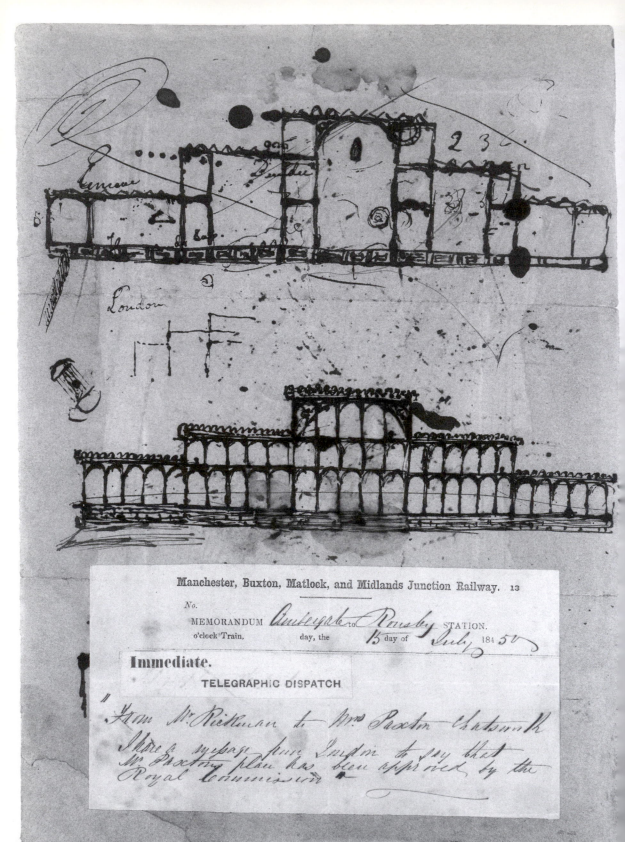

Manchester, Buxton, Matlock, and Midlands Junction Railway. 13

No.

MEMORANDUM *Ambergate* to *Rowsby* STATION.

o'clock Train, day, the *15* day of *July* 184 *5*

Immediate.

TELEGRAPHIC DISPATCH

"From Mr Rickman to Mrs Paxton Chatsworth

I have a message from London to say that

Mr Paxton's plan has been approved by the

Royal Commission"

Paxton's proposal could not have been more different from the mostly laboured and heavily ornamental schemes offered by the 245 architects who had originally submitted entries. Paxton's solution could be assembled quickly (in itself a major recommendation, given the fast-approaching deadline) by slotting together prefabricated sections. Indeed, the structure was completed within nine months of the submission of his plans. Wrought-iron ribs were raised into position to provide the frame and backbone, supplemented with wood casements and 293,000 panes of glass. Modern construction methods were used. Sliding along a trolley on rails, each glazier could fit over one hundred panes a day. A public outcry at the prospect of felling Hyde Park's ninety-foot-high elm trees meant that the building had to be tall enough to accommodate them inside. When it was finished, it was, at over a third of a mile long, the largest enclosed space in the world. With its nave and transept, it resembled a secular cathedral, one that proclaimed the birth of modern architecture.

The early impetus for the exhibition had been provided by Henry Cole, an Assistant Keeper of Public Records. In 1845, while campaigning for free trade and cheaper bread, the Anti-Corn Law League had successfully run bazaars showcasing British manufactures and raising money through company stalls. Cole proposed an altogether grander venture, which, being international in scope, would provide a forum for British and foreign leaders of industry and commerce to meet, learn and exchange ideas. His scheme attracted the influential support of Queen Victoria's husband, Prince Albert, who chaired the Royal Commission established to investigate its practicality.

THE AGE OF VICTORIA

1837 Queen Victoria succeeds her uncle, William IV. Charles Dickens publishes *Oliver Twist*.

1840 Victoria marries Prince Albert.

1841 Augustus Pugin's *True Principles* sets out the argument for the Gothic Revival in architecture.

1843 The 'Disruption' occurs between the Church of Scotland and the Free Church of Scotland.

1845–9 The Irish suffer the potato famine.

1846 The Corn Laws are repealed.

1847 The 'Ten-Hour' Factory Act is introduced.

1851 The Great Exhibition is mounted in Hyde Park.

1853–6 The Crimean War is fought by Britain, along with France and the Ottoman Empire, against Russia.

1857 The Indian Mutiny challenges British rule.

1858 The first transatlantic telegraph cable is laid: permanent connection is achieved in 1866.

1859 Charles Darwin's *Origin of Species* and J. S. Mill's *On Liberty* are published.

1861 Prince Albert dies, sending Victoria into years of mourning and public withdrawal.

1865 Lewis Carroll publishes *Alice's Adventures in Wonderland*.

1868 The last public execution takes place.

1876 Queen Victoria becomes Empress of India. Alexander Graham Bell patents the telephone.

1878 W. S. Gilbert and Arthur Sullivan's *HMS Pinafore* is performed.

1886 The first Irish Home Rule bill is defeated. The Liberal Party splits.

1895 The National Trust is founded.

1899–1902 The second Anglo-Boer War is fought.

OPPOSITE: Joseph Paxton's inspirational doodle on blotting paper for the 'Crystal Palace'.

Upon opening, the Great Exhibition featured displays from 17,000 exhibitors, which ranged from machinery to fine art. It also attracted visitors from all ranks of society, many of whom availed themselves of another novelty provided for their convenience – public lavatories. Arranging a deal with the Midland Railway, travel promoters like Thomas Cook helped organize the flood of tourists. By the time it closed in October 1851, the Exhibition's profitability was such that the proceeds were used to buy land in South Kensington upon which, in time, the Science, Natural History and Victoria and Albert museums were built: a considerable cultural, scientific and educational legacy.

Paxton was knighted, became MP for Coventry and designed Mentmore Towers in Buckinghamshire for the Rothschild family in a rich, neo-Jacobean style, which, while aesthetically magnificent, was far removed from the masterwork that made him one of the most influential fathers of modern architecture. Conceived at rapid speed as a temporary structure, the Crystal Palace endured for eighty-five years. It was disassembled and put back together again on Sydenham Hill, where it remained as a venue for exhibitions and concerts until destroyed by fire in 1936.

1863

THE RULES OF
ASSOCIATION FOOTBALL

THE 'BEAUTIFUL GAME' TAKES ITS MODERN FORM

Britain's most successful export was cobbled together in a London pub by a group of English public-school boys. Whilst those who gathered at the Freemason's Tavern in Great Queen's Street, Lincoln's Inn Fields, between 26 October and 8 December 1863 may not have actually invented the game of football, it was their codification of it that the rest of the world subsequently accepted as the genuine article.

Football's origins are disputed. By the Middle Ages, rival villages were kicking a ball – and each other – about in various forms, whose common feature may more closely have resembled modern off-pitch hooliganism than on-pitch ball skills. The authorities disapproved of its rowdiness, as well as its tendency to distract young men from militarily useful pursuits like archery, and it became one of the 'idle games' banned by King Edward III in 1363. Not to be outdone, King James I of Scotland also passed a law in 1424 commanding that 'Nae man shall play at fute-ball.'

It was not these ineffectual commands so much as the process of industrialization and urbanization that, by the early nineteenth century, had stifled football as a popular entertainment. That it survived in an organized form was largely thanks to the public schools, where it provided an outlet for adolescent energy and aggression while also offering an opportunity for team-building.

The problem was that each of the schools played it according to their own rules. At Rugby School – and elsewhere – this came to involve the ball-handling techniques that were later codified as rugby football. Other schools also had a variety of traditions in relation to the ethics and the efficacy of tackling, hacking, bundling and drop-kicking. However, when the former public-school boys became undergraduates at Oxford and Cambridge universities, their different experiences of how football was played led to constant argument.

To overcome the mutual incomprehension, in 1848 nine Cambridge under-graduates – old boys of the schools of Eton, Harrow, Marlborough, Rugby, Shrewsbury and Westminster – met to agree a common set of rules. The resulting 'Cambridge Rules' formed the basis for the code adopted in the first meetings of the Football Association (FA) in 1863.

The idea to form the FA as a body that would govern the sport came from a keen rower and footballer for the Barnes Club named Ebenezer Cobb Morley (1831–1924). The clubs that responded to his suggestion to agree the rules were Barnes, Blackheath, Blackheath School and another Blackheath team called Perceval House, together with Forest (the nucleus of the Wanderers, a club based in Battersea), the enigmatic 'N. N. (No Name) Club' of Kilburn, Crusaders, Crystal Palace (unrelated to the current Crystal Palace FC), Kensington School and Surbiton. Charterhouse school also sent a representative before deciding not to affiliate. Similarly, Blackheath opted out when its motion to allow handling and running with the ball was defeated.

The creation of the FA formalized the breach between the ball-handling and non-handling versions, or, in the Oxbridge-lingo of the time, 'rugger' and 'soccer' (that is, 'Association' Football). Those who preferred Blackheath's version formed their own Rugby Football Union in 1871. The rules that the FA agreed were essentially the Cambridge Rules but with minor modifications. It fell to Barnes and Richmond to play the first match under 'Association' auspices. Despite a goal-less draw, *The Field* pronounced it a success, observing: 'Very little difficulty was experienced on either side in playing the new rules, and the game was characterised by great good temper, the rules being so simple and easy of observance that it was difficult for disputes to arise.'

The rules were certainly simple. There were only thirteen of them and authority had not yet been ceded to a single referee. Additions and revisions quickly followed. In 1865, a tape crossbar was added to create a goal height of eight feet and the offside rule came into operation the following year. Football officially became 'a game of two halves' when changing ends after each goal was replaced by swapping at half-time.

The formative influences on the FA came primarily from Cambridge and the public schools rather than from the version of the game played during the 1850s and 1860s in Sheffield. Nevertheless, the FA's success was assured only when working-class clubs from the Midlands and the North sought to affiliate. In this way, the FA rules became the national rules and were also adopted by the

THE RISE OF SPORT IN BRITAIN

1780 'The Derby' is inaugurated at Epsom.

1787 Marylebone Cricket Club (MCC) is founded.

1823 The Rugby schoolboy William Webb Ellis allegedly picks up the ball and runs with it.

1829 The first Oxford v. Cambridge Boat Race takes place: 20,000 spectators watch Oxford win.

1839 The Grand National is inaugurated at Aintree (a similar race had been held there since 1836).

1848 The 'Cambridge Rules' establish a common code for playing football.

1859 George Parr's All-England XI tours Canada and the United States: the first foreign tour of an English cricket team.

1860 At Farnborough, the British champion Tom Sayers fights the American champion John Heenan in the last major bare-knuckle boxing match.

1863 The Football Association (FA) is established, and adopts a code of laws based on the earlier Cambridge rules.

1864 The first county cricket championship.

1867 The 'Queensberry Rules' are established for boxing.

1871 The Rugby Football Union is established, and Scotland beats England in the first rugby international.

1872 The Wanderers beat the Royal Engineers 1–0 in the first FA Cup final; the first football international ends goalless, played between Scotland and England.

1874 At the first Scottish Cup final, Queen's Park beat Clydesdale 2–0 in front of a crowd of 3,000.

1877 The first Wimbledon Lawn Tennis Championship is played. At the first Test match, Australia beats England in Melbourne by 45 runs.

1878 The Bicycle Union (from 1883 National Cyclists' Union) founded to represent exponents of the new cycling craze. Responding to police pressure, in 1890 the union bans racing on roads and restricts competitions to velodromes.

1880 The first cricket Test match in England takes place: England beats Australia by five wickets at the Oval.

1882 Australia defeats England at the Oval by seven runs. A mock obituary notice to English cricket in the *Sporting Times* creates the tradition of 'The Ashes'.

1885 The FA permits professionalism.

1888 The Football League is created on the initiative of a Scottish draper, William MacGregor. The first winner is Preston North End.

1891 The inaugural Scottish Football League is jointly won by Rangers and Dumbarton.

1895 Rugby league splits from rugby union.

1907 Local landowner Hugh Locke King constructs the world's first purpose-built motor racing circuit at Brooklands in Surrey.

1908 The Olympic Games are held at the White City Stadium, London.

Football Association, Laws of the Game, 1863

1. The maximum length of the ground shall be 200 yards, the maximum breadth shall be 100 yards, the length and breadth shall be marked off with flags; and the goal shall be defined by two upright posts, eight yards apart, without any tape or bar across them.

2. A toss for goals shall take place, and the game shall be commenced by a place kick from the centre of the ground by the side losing the toss for goals; the other side shall not approach within 10 yards of the ball until it is kicked off.

3. After a goal is won, the losing side shall be entitled to kick off, and the two sides shall change goals after each goal is won.

4. A goal shall be won when the ball passes between the goal-posts or over the space between the goal-posts (at whatever height), not being thrown, knocked on, or carried.

5. When the ball is in touch, the first player who touches it shall throw it from the point on the boundary line where it left the ground in a direction at right angles with the boundary line, and the ball shall not be in play until it has touched the ground.

6. When a player has kicked the ball, any one of the same side who is nearer to the opponent's goal line is out of play, and may not touch the ball himself, nor in any way whatever prevent any other player from doing so, until he is in play; but no player is out of play when the ball is kicked off from behind the goal line.

7. In case the ball goes behind the goal line, if a player on the side to whom the goal belongs first touches the ball, one of his side shall be entitled to a free kick from the goal line at the point opposite the place where the ball shall be touched. If a player of the opposite side first touches the ball, one of his side shall be entitled to a free kick at the goal only from a point 15 yards outside the goal line, opposite the place where the ball is touched, the opposing side standing within their goal line until he has had his kick.

8. If a player makes a fair catch, he shall be entitled to a free kick, providing he claims it by making a mark with his heel at once; and in order to take such kick he may go back as far as he pleases, and no player on the opposite side shall advance beyond his mark until he has kicked.

9. No player shall run with the ball.

10. Neither tripping nor hacking shall be allowed, and no player shall use his hands to hold or push his adversary.

11. A player shall not be allowed to throw the ball or pass it to another with his hands.

12. No player shall be allowed to take the ball from the ground with his hands under any pretence whatever while it is in play.

13. No player shall be allowed to wear projecting nails, iron plates, or gutta-percha on the soles or heels of his boots.

Scottish Football Association at its foundation in 1873.

Inevitably, this geographical and social spread of FA-affiliated clubs created a clash of cultures between the erstwhile public-school boys, who played for the South's amateur clubs, and the working-class players, who often received expenses and even modest incomes for playing in 'professional' clubs. Initially it was amateur clubs like Wanderers who won the FA Cup, but in the 1883 final Old Etonians were beaten 2–1 by the northern semi-professionals of Blackburn Olympic. After protests, professionalism was formally condoned two years later and the amateurs fell back upon the consolations of contesting their own competitions. The sport's regeneration as the people's game was evident when, in 1888, the Football League began with twelve clubs, all from the Midlands and the North. A second division was added in 1892 and the Scottish League began in 1890. By the beginning of the twentieth century attendances at the biggest matches surpassed 100,000.

By then, football had begun to take root on foreign turf, British expats having exported it to South America, Europe and Russia. When the Fédération Internationale de Football Association (FIFA) was founded as the embryonic international governing body in Paris in 1904, it enforced a single code as the only form of the game it would recognize worldwide. The form chosen was, of course, the rule book of the FA.

1882

THE MARRIED WOMEN'S PROPERTY ACT

WOMEN GAIN THE SAME RIGHTS AS MEN TO OWN PROPERTY AND RUN BUSINESSES

The marriage of Queen Victoria to Prince Albert in 1840 did not diminish the rights of Britain's female head of state. She remained a constitutional monarch, her powers intact, while Albert – for all his advice and influence – was merely her consort.

Other women were not so lucky. At the outset of Victoria's reign, a married woman had no legal identity. As the eighteenth-century jurist Sir William Blackstone put it, 'In law husband and wife are one person, and the husband is that person.' As a result, any property a wife inherited or any income she earned legally belonged to her husband. She could not make contracts or even a will. While there were many instances of a wealthy father employing a lawyer to draft a marriage settlement that safeguarded in trust his daughter's inheritance from a prospective son-in-law, even among the rich these were the exception rather than the rule.

The first changes to matrimonial law were prompted not by a feminist but by a successful poet and novelist who nevertheless wrote to *The Times* in 1838 to insist that 'The natural position of woman is inferiority to man...I never pretended to the wild and ridiculous doctrine of equality.' Yet the legal wrong done to the letter writer, Caroline Norton (1808–77), was so spectacular that it turned the non-rights of wives into a *cause célèbre*.

Her husband, George Norton, was an unfeeling and physically violent man who partly lived off his wife's literary earnings and the useful social connections she made for him. In 1836, he hoped to prepare the way for a divorce by taking her to court on a charge of criminal conversation (adultery) with the prime minister, Lord Melbourne. As a married woman, Caroline Norton was legally disbarred from giving evidence in her own defence. Nonetheless, the – probably groundless –

charge made against her and Melbourne was thrown out for want of evidence. Consequently unable to divorce her, George Norton retaliated by exercising his right as a husband to refuse her access to her children.

Caroline Norton was not so easily crushed and she launched a public campaign to reform the law. Parliament obliged in 1839 with the Infant Custody Act. The legislation provided that wives who had not been found guilty of adultery had the right to custody of their children until they reached the age of seven, with access rights granted to the non-custodial parent thereafter. In itself, it was a modest provision but it represented the first crack in the defence that the husband's rights over his family were absolute.

It did nothing to alter George Norton's right to help himself to his estranged wife's inheritance when her mother died in 1851, an issue that became the next of Caroline Norton's legal battles. She could not divorce him since the law permitted a wife to bring proceedings only on grounds of incest or bigamy (although adultery was sufficient grounds for a husband to divorce his wife). This imbalance, together with the huge cost of bringing proceedings and the necessity of an Act of Parliament to end each marriage, ensured that in England and Wales, between 1800 and 1857, only 186 men and four women obtained divorces.

In 1857 two former lord chancellors, the Tory Lord Lyndhurst and the Whig Lord Brougham, teamed up to steer through the Matrimonial Causes Act, despite the opposition of High Church Anglicans. Henceforth, divorce courts would deal with petitions that had previously lumbered through ecclesiastical courts, criminal courts and Parliament. Over the next thirty years the number of divorces averaged 239 annually (compared to an annual figure of 187,000 marriages being contacted annually). The act gave a wife the right to divorce her husband if his infidelity was compounded by other affronts, like desertion, bigamy or extreme cruelty. For men, however, a wife's adultery was still sufficient grounds alone. This inequality continued in England and Wales until 1923, although Scotland had long regarded adultery by either party to be sufficient grounds.

The campaign to give wives the entitlement to their own inheritance and income was led outside Parliament by a committee of women led by Barbara Leigh Smith and Ursula Mellor Bright. It was also prominently supported by the liberal philosopher and advocate of sexual equality, John Stuart Mill, and had a large measure of cross-party support in the House of Commons. When the Tory MP, Russell Gurney, introduced a bill in 1869, the Liberal government smoothed its passage. Despite qualifying amendments inserted by the House of Lords, the bill

From the Married Women's Property Act, 1882

The fact that any such deposit, annuity, sum forming part of the public stocks or funds, or of any other stocks or funds transferable in the books of the Bank of England or of any other bank, share, stock, debenture, debenture stock, or other interest as aforesaid, is standing in the sole name of a married woman shall be sufficient prima facie evidence that she is beneficially entitled thereto so as to authorise and empower her to receive or transfer the same, and to receive the dividends, interest, and profits thereof, without the concurrence of her husband.

permitted married women to keep their own earnings and investments, as well as to inherit property in their own right. It touched the poor as much as the rich, for, while working-class wives had seldom brought much in the way of property into their marriages, they at last gained the entitlement to keep their own earnings, rather than being legally obliged to surrender their weekly wages to their husband.

Nonetheless, various restrictions still remained and it took the Married Women's Property Act of 1882 to fully banish the notion that a woman's independent legal identity was submerged upon getting married. This removed the legal distinction in property rights between married and single women, while establishing the principle of husbands and wives having separate property rights. That was not all. More than any other legislative statute before or since, it was the 1882 Act that made possible the development of the businesswoman. Until 1882, married women could neither sue nor be sued, which made it hard for them to run a business. By removing sexual inequality with regard to litigation, the Married Women's Property Act opened the way for women to marry and run their own businesses without legal fetter.

1898–9
CHARLES BOOTH'S 'POVERTY MAP' OF LONDON

ANALYZING THE EXTENT AND NATURE
OF LONDON POVERTY

Charles Dickens had used his novels to draw attention to the poverty and distress that disfigured mid-Victorian London. Nearly half a century later, as the Victorian age drew to its close, it was the work of a sociologist, Charles Booth (1840–1916), that most starkly exposed the deprivation still enduring in the world's greatest metropolis.

Dickens and Booth came from dissimilar backgrounds, were temperamentally unalike and deployed wholly different methods. Whilst Dickens had known poverty in his childhood, Booth was born into a wealthy Liverpool merchant family and went into the lucrative shipping business with his elder brother. Brought up a Unitarian, he became disillusioned with religion as well as with sentimental attitudes, the effectiveness of traditional charitable giving and organized politics. Concluding that neither greater philanthropy nor better government were enough, he expressed his faith in an altogether less personal force, writing in 1870 that 'Science must lay down afresh the laws of life'.

He used some of the profits from his shipping company to finance a series of sociological surveys that would chart the nature of poverty, industry and religious adherence in late nineteenth-century London. He organized teams of investigators to move from street to street, compiling – through house enquiries, questionnaires and information gathered from school-board visits – the data he deemed essential to explain the reality of life in London. The project took fifteen years and was finally published in 1902, complete in seventeen volumes, as *Life and Labour of the People of London*. Many of his findings had already been released over the preceding years. By 1889, for example, he was able to calculate that 30.7 per cent of Londoners lived in poverty.

A part of Charles Booth's 'Poverty Map' of London is depicted in the fourth plate section.

289

Booth recognized that poverty came in different forms and with varying levels of intensity. His work classified the London population into eight categories, ranging at the bottom from Class A (the criminal underclass) and Class B (casual labour) through to Class H (the upper middle class). These divisions were most graphically illustrated in colour-coded street maps, showing which groups lived where in the capital. Other findings suggested that – with the exception of Catholic immigrants – the poorer the families, the less likely they were to attend church or chapel.

However, the primary intention was not just to categorize but to explain the causes of poverty and suggest remedies. While social reformers and the Poor Law had long struggled with the problem of how to differentiate between the 'deserving' and the 'undeserving' poor, Booth concluded that personal fecklessness and moral shortcomings, although evident, were not the major reasons for widespread poverty. Rather, he pinpointed not the criminal underclass but those who were a little higher up the scale as being the unintentional root of the problem. These were 'Class B' families, dependent on labour that was casual, seasonal, or at the mercy of regular 'boom and bust' trade cycles. The continued existence of this pool of cheap and disposable labour – sometimes immigrant – had the effect of dragging down the incomes of those in more regular employment, for whom poverty was also either a dismal prospect or a hard reality.

The social researcher and philanthropist Charles Booth (1840–1916).

Booth wanted the problem of the casual poor to be addressed both by a restructuring of the economy in addition to reform of welfare provision. Industry should be better organized so that it did not both create and rely on this group. To help the casual labourers improve their own chances, education and training should be focused on improving their skills. Those who failed to respond should be taken out of the market place and put to work in labour camps. As for the existing Poor Law, it had failed in its intentions. Workhouses were most commonly populated not with the work-shy destitute but with the elderly, whose working lives lay far behind them. Instead of confining them to such degrading institutions, he declared, they should receive old-age pensions.

There were problems with Booth's methodology. As a sociological snapshot of London at the nineteenth century's end, his work had no equal. What it could not do was provide a historical perspective, and it therefore failed to adequately address questions such as whether conditions were generally improving over time or how the patterns of poverty shifted with social mobility. Nor was it an infallible pointer to the future. No sooner was it completed than the creation of new suburbs changed London's demography and population density.

Nonetheless, while Booth's work may not have enjoyed Dickens' breadth of audience, it was extremely influential with policy-makers. The sociological researcher, social reformer and industrialist Benjamin Seebohm Rowntree adapted Booth's techniques and in 1901 produced a survey of York that suggested that a third of its citizens also lived in poverty. Booth's advocacy of old-age pensions was shared by the Liberal chancellor of the exchequer, David Lloyd George, who in 1908 introduced them for those over seventy. Indeed, during the first half of the twentieth century the remnants of the Victorian Poor Law were dismantled by successive Liberal, Conservative and Labour administrations. Through his cousin-in-law, the social reformer Beatrice Webb (who helped him with his research), Booth's work became a major influence on the 'Fabian' gradualist strand of socialist thinking, with its emphasis on planning and creating social 'efficiency'.

In economic policy, however, Booth rejected free trade, which both the Liberal Party and the early Labour Party supported. Ignoring the effect that cheaper foreign imports had in reducing the cost of living and in encouraging enterprise and diversification, Booth believed they harmed the security of working people's jobs. In 1903, in a supreme irony, he endorsed the protectionist tariff campaign of Joseph Chamberlain, the one-time Liberal radical who had in the end become a Tory imperialist.

VIII

FROM EMPIRE TO
THE WELFARE STATE

THE ANGLO-FRENCH ENTENTE CORDIALE

CROSS-CHANNEL RAPPROCHEMENT

Between the Norman Conquest and Napoleon's defeat at Waterloo in 1815, there had been almost 750 years of suspicion, enmity and conflict between England (and subsequently Britain) and France. However, after the Napoleonic Wars relations between the world's two greatest colonial powers became, by past standards, relatively untroubled. Indeed, during the Crimean War (1854–6) Britain and France even fought on the same side against tsarist Russia.

Nonetheless, their period as allies was a temporary expediency, not a settled policy. No British regiment stirred when the Prussian army invaded France and besieged Paris in 1870. Indeed, successive governments in London pursued a foreign policy of 'splendid isolation' – the avoidance of being drawn into continental entanglements.

Cross-Channel relations slipped back into rancour as the nineteenth century drew to a close. In 1898, during the so-called 'Scramble for Africa' by the European powers, it briefly looked as if shots would be exchanged at Fashoda on the Upper Nile. Instead, cooler heads prevailed and British dominance of Egypt and the Sudan was assured. Yet over the following three years, Britain's international reputation was tarnished by its conduct in South Africa during the Second Anglo-Boer War, notably its internment of Boer (Afrikaner) civilians in 'concentration camps'. At the same time, Joseph Chamberlain, the colonial secretary, investigated the possibilities of an Anglo-German alliance. His endeavours came to nothing, but it was a sign that Britain was preparing to depart from the principles of splendid isolation.

France and Russia had signed a mutual defence pact in 1892 in which each agreed to go to the military aid of the other if attacked by Germany. In contrast, Britain had long been suspicious of Russian intentions towards India and was increasingly perturbed by her encroachments into China, where Britain had major commercial interests. With this in mind, in 1902 Britain formed an alliance with Japan. This involved supportive neutrality if either country was attacked by a single opponent but guaranteed military assistance if attacked by multiple opponents. Therefore, Britain did not assist Japan during her war with Russia between 1904 and 1905, but Japan did fight on Britain's side in the First World War.

The alliance was a further signal that Britain was ready to pursue a more active diplomatic policy. The French, deciding that this presented an opening that they should not leave to rivals to explore, began a policy of actively courting Britain. It was particularly helpful that although the new king, Edward VII, was the cousin of Germany's Kaiser Wilhelm II, he was a Franco-phile in his sentiments. When he made a state visit to Paris in April 1903 he was rapturously received. The compliment was returned only two months later when France's President Loubet visited London. The symbolic and psychological adjustments involved in these public and private displays created the conditions for a more formal diplomatic agreement.

The terms of the new understanding were negotiated by the British foreign secretary, Lord Lansdowne (1845–1927), and his counterpart, Théophile Delcassé. The aim was not to agree a formal military pact – which was far beyond what London could be persuaded to commit to – but rather to remove existing sources of rancour: in particular regarding France's growing predominance in Morocco, over which it was trying to establish a protectorate, and British power in Egypt. Agreement was reached and, on

THE ROAD TO THE GREAT WAR

1882 The Triple Alliance, a military pact, is formed between Germany, Austria-Hungary and Italy.

1892 The Franco-Russian alliance agrees terms for mutual assistance in the event of either being attacked.

1902 The Triple Alliance is renewed. The Anglo-Japanese agreement is signed.

1904 The Anglo-French Entente Cordiale is agreed.

1904–5 The Russo-Japanese War is fought, in which Russia is humiliated.

1905 The Schlieffen Plan is devised for a German invasion of France via Belgium. Anglo-French military talks commence.

1906 The Algeciras conference discusses Morocco.

1907 Eyre Crowe's memorandum on Anglo-French alliance warns of German threat.

1908 The 'Young Turks' take power in the Ottoman Empire; Bulgaria declares independence.

1909 Louis Blériot flies across the English Channel, and the spectre of aerial attack is raised.

1911 Germany foments the Agadir crisis.

1912–13 In the First Balkan War Montenegro, Serbia, Greece and Bulgaria fight the Ottoman Empire.

1913 In the Second Balkan War Bulgaria attacks Greece and Serbia.

28 June 1914 A Serb terrorist assassinates the Austrian Archduke Franz Ferdinand and his wife in Sarajevo.

23 July Germany sends an ultimatum to Serbia.

28 July Austria-Hungary declares war on Serbia.

31 July Russia begins general military mobilization.

1 August Germany declares war on Russia and issues an ultimatum to France.

3 August Germany declares war on France.

4 August Germany invades Belgium, and Britain enters the war.

From the Entente Cordiale, 1904

Art. I. His Britannic Majesty's Government declare that they have no intention of altering the political status of Egypt.

The Government of the French Republic, for their part, declare that they will not obstruct the action of Great Britain in that country by asking that a limit of time be fixed for the British occupation . . .

II. The Government of the French Republic declare that they have no intention of altering the political status of Morocco.

His Britannic Majesty's Government, for their part, recognize that it appertains to France, more particularly as a Power whose dominions are conterminous for a great distance with those of Morocco, to preserve order in that country, and to provide assistance for the purpose of all administrative, economic, financial, and military reforms which it may require.

They declare that they will not obstruct the action taken by France for this purpose, provided that such action shall leave intact the rights which Great Britain, in virtue of Treaties, Conventions, and usage, enjoys in Morocco, including the right of coasting trade between the ports of Morocco, enjoyed by British vessels since 1901.

III. His Britannic Majesty's Government, for their part, will respect the right which France, in virtue of Treaties, Conventions, and usage, enjoys in Egypt, including the right of coasting trade between Egyptian ports accorded to French vessels.

IV. The two Governments, being equally attracted to the principle of commercial liberty both in Egypt and Morocco, declare that they will not, in those countries, countenance any inequality either in the imposition of customs duties or other taxes, or of railway transport charges.

8 April 1904 the 'Entente' was signed in London by Lansdowne and the French ambassador to London, Paul Cambon.

The excited talk about this new Entente Cordiale went far beyond the very limited terms of the agreement. Lansdowne did not see it as intrinsically inimical also to reaching a better understanding with Germany. Berlin, however, elected to test the Entente's fibre, hoping to show France how little it could rely on British

words. On 31 March 1905 Kaiser Wilhelm ostentatiously arrived in Tangier, where he delivered speeches that questioned France's intentions in Morocco and demanded that German coaling stations to be set up there, while also posing as the champion of the sultan's freedom of action. Britain, however, stood by France and the resulting conference at Algeciras effectively confirmed France's sphere of interest in Morocco. Germany pulled a second stunt in the region in 1911 (the 'Agadir Crisis'), but again failed to separate Britain and France.

Emboldened by the understanding with Paris, in 1907 the new Liberal foreign secretary, Sir Edward Grey, made an agreement with St Petersburg, clarifying Russian and British spheres of interest in Persia (modern Iran). As with the Anglo-French Entente, this did not commit Britain to a formal military pact. Indeed, there was uncertainty within Whitehall whether Britain had any potentially hazardous obligations even towards France. In 1911, the senior Foreign Office official, Eyre Crowe, advised that Germany *did* present an increasing threat to the security of Europe and to Britain, but went on to add: 'The fundamental fact of course is that the Entente is not an alliance. For purposes of ultimate emergencies it may be found to have no substance at all. For the Entente is nothing more than a

'The generosity of the English!' A contemporary French cartoonist's sceptical view of the Entente of April 1904. Edward VII tells the French foreign minister, Théophile Delcassé, 'You give me beautiful Egypt and I will allow you to run after Morocco.'

frame of mind, a view of general policy which is shared by the governments of two countries, but which may be, or become, so vague as to lose all content.'

What kept it at the forefront of Britain's consciousness was mounting alarm at Germany's intentions, in particular its accelerated naval-building programme, which appeared to be aimed at confronting the Royal Navy rather than patrolling distant waters. The British army was restructured to include an Expeditionary Force that could, at short notice, be deployed in Europe. Even so, the Cabinet – after deep discussion – declared war on Germany in August 1914 only because Germany had invaded neutral Belgium on its way to attacking France, a violation of the 1839 Treaty of London, which bound Britain to guarantee Belgian neutrality.

Germany tried to dismiss the latter agreement as a 'scrap of paper' in a fatal disregard for the power of old documents. Without the infringement of Belgium's neutrality, Britain might either have stayed out of the conflict altogether or limited its intervention on France's side to naval assistance, without committing troops to a European land war. What we cannot know is whether, if Britain had not got into the habit of thinking of France as an ally because of the 1904 Entente, the British government might have tried to wriggle out of meeting its own obligations in 1914 by claiming that the 1839 Treaty was indeed merely a 'scrap of paper'.

1910–11

THE LIBERAL GOVERNMENT'S LIST OF NOMINEES FOR THE PEERAGE

∼

THE DESTRUCTION OF THE HEREDITARY PEERS' ABILITY TO VETO LEGISLATION

U ntil 1911, no legislation became law unless it had been approved by the House of Lords. Parliament's upper chamber of hereditary peers did not give up its ancient right lightly. Only the knowledge that resistance would ensure the creation of 500 new pro-reform peers frightened their Lordships into acquiescence. The aristocratic safety valve on popular democracy was finally prised away by the 1911 Parliament Act.

This constitutional revolution was sparked by an extraordinary miscalculation from the upper house. In 1906, the Liberal Party had won a landslide election victory and began implementing a series of major spending commitments, including the creation of old-age pensions and the funding of a naval arms race with Germany. To pay for the rising expenditure, in 1909 the chancellor of the exchequer, David Lloyd George (1863–1945), introduced a budget that proposed a 'supertax' on top of the income tax and the land tax. Although these measures targeted high earners, they also caused particular outrage among country landowners whose wealth had already been eroded by a long agricultural recession. These representatives of 'old money' were the backbone of the Tory-dominated House of Lords and they duly vetoed the so-called 'People's Budget' by 360 votes to 75. In the process they did something far more revolutionary than anything proposed by Lloyd George. The House of Lords had not vetoed a budget for 250 years, during which time a precedent had taken root that the hereditary chamber would not reject finance bills.

The peers claimed they wanted to force a referendum on the sweeping tax changes. Instead the Liberal prime minister, Herbert Asquith, called a snap general election with the slogan 'Peers versus People'. It proved a hard-fought, eight-week campaign, during which rival politicians traded claims of unconstitutional behaviour. Lloyd George did his best to add insult to injury, telling crowds that the peerage consisted of 500 'ordinary men chosen accidentally from among the unemployed'. The electorate was galvanized: at a time when 70 per cent of men had the vote, the January 1910 general election recorded a turnout of 92 per cent, proportionately the largest in British history. Closing the gap from their humiliating drubbing four years previously, the Tories staged an extraordinary recovery, winning 273 seats, only two fewer than the Liberals.

The result was a hung parliament with Asquith retaining power only with the help of the Irish Nationalists and the infant Labour Party. On 28 April 1910, the House of Lords acknowledged the election result and passed the budget without even a division. Now however, the government was determined to force through legislation that would permanently clip the hereditary chamber's right to veto legislation proposed by the democratic chamber.

The problem was that any such legislation would have to be passed by the hereditary peers for it to become law and the prospect of Tory peers voting to do so was analogous to turkeys voting for Christmas. Looking for leverage, Asquith asked King Edward VII whether he would be prepared to create new peers who would vote for the reform. The problem was that to get a majority would require ennobling over 500 people. All peerages were hereditary and creating this number of them would produce a wholly unwieldy upper chamber, as well as looking like an act of gerrymandering that would drag the monarch into political controversy. A conference was convened between the government and the opposition in the hope of finding a compromise that would make this contingency unnecessary. When it failed to reach agreement, the second general election of the year was called for December 1910. It changed nothing, Tories and Liberals tying on 272 seats each. Asquith remained in power with the support of the minority parties.

The prime minister now introduced the Parliament Bill, which aimed to make illegal any future attempt by the Lords to veto, or even amend, a finance bill. Furthermore, the bill would remove the Lords' veto on all other legislation so long as it had been passed three times in the Commons (with the proviso that two years needed to have elapsed between the initial second reading and the last, third reading). To highlight the Commons' responsiveness to the popular will, the length of time separating general elections was to be cut from seven years to five.

From the list of 500 peerage nominees

Sir George Otto Trevelyan, *Liberal politician and historian.*

Sir Harold Harmsworth, *co-owner of the* Daily Mail *and* Daily Mirror.

Sir Walter Runciman, *Liberal politician.*

Sir Philip Burne-Jones, *painter.*

The Hon. Bertrand Russell, *philosopher.*

General Sir Robert Baden-Powell, *soldier and founder of the Scout Movement.*

Joseph Rowntree, *chocolate maker and social reformer.*

Sir John Gorst, *lawyer and Conservative politician.*

General Sir Ian Hamilton, *soldier who later commanded the ill-fated Dardanelles campaign.*

Gilbert Murray, *classical scholar and Liberal activist.*

J. R. Spender, *editor of the pro-Liberal evening newspaper, the Westminster Gazette.*

Thomas Hardy, *novelist and poet.*

As they prepared to vote on the Parliament Bill, the peers learned that the new king, George V, had agreed that if they rejected the neutering legislation, he would indeed create the requisite number of new peerages to push it through. A paper drawn up by the government's chief whip, Alexander Murray, the Master of Elibank, contained the list of nominees. They ranged from the relatively obscure to the famous, including the historian Sir George Otto Trevelyan, the philosopher Bertrand Russell, the soldier and Boy Scouts founder Robert Baden-Powell, the novelist Thomas Hardy and the creator of *Peter Pan*, J. M. Barrie. What they had in common was that they were expected to do the Liberal government's bidding on parliamentary reform.

Appalled at these prospects, on 10 August 1911 the House of Lords passed the Parliament Bill by the narrow margin of 131 votes to 114. Many 'diehard' Tory peers revolted against their own party's official policy of abstention and the measure was thus passed only because another group of Tory peers, led by Lord Curzon, voted with the government in order to avoid the dilution of aristocratic purity that would otherwise be foisted upon the peerage. Henceforth, the House of Lords' historic powers were humbled. Its delaying powers were cut from two years to one year in 1947, and life peerages were introduced in 1958. In 1999 the hereditary right to sit in the Lords was abolished, with only ninety-two self-electing hereditary peers remaining – it was stated, temporarily – pending a more comprehensive reform.

However, it was the 1911 Parliament Act – made possible by the threat of 'packing' the House with government nominees – that was the single greatest institutional revolution at Westminster in the twentieth century. It did away with the notion that the upper chamber had the same rights to determine legislation as the lower chamber. Ever after, the House of Lords was reduced to being a chamber that revised, but did not determine, legislation. The power of Britain's aristocracy would never be the same again.

FOURTEEN REASONS FOR SUPPORTING WOMEN'S SUFFRAGE

THE RIGHT OF WOMEN TO VOTE

'Deeds not words' was Mrs Emmeline Pankhurst's exhortation to her Women's Social and Political Union (WSPU). Suffragette militancy might therefore be better represented by a brick and shards of broken glass, or a padlock attached to iron railings, than by a document. Whether direct action helped or hindered the cause of women's enfranchisement is still actively disputed today. Such tactics were denounced at the time by the far more popular National Union of Women's Suffrage Societies (NUWSS), which campaigned tirelessly and, ultimately, successfully to win the moral and intellectual high ground of the debate.

When localized female suffrage groups came together to found the NUWSS in 1896, it seemed likely that at least some women were about to be granted the vote in national elections. The following year, a private members' bill reached as far as the second reading stage at Westminster, where it was approved by 230 votes to 159 before running out of parliamentary time. Rationally, it seemed a logical extension of what had already been enacted for local government, where women ratepayers had won the right to vote in 1869 and had been able to sit on parish and district councils since 1894. With increasing numbers of them paying their own taxes, the old cry of the American colonists was revived: 'No taxation without representation.'

Yet, despite the mildly supportive views of two successive Conservative prime ministers, Lord Salisbury and Arthur Balfour, not a single bill or even a resolution was brought before Parliament between 1897 and 1904. Hope for change was revived when the Liberal Party's landslide election victory of 1906 created a House

NATIONAL UNION OF WOMEN'S SUFFRAGE SOCIETIES,

25, VICTORIA STREET, WESTMINSTER, S.W.

President—Mrs. HENRY FAWCETT, LL.D.

14 REASONS

For Supporting Women's Suffrage.

++++++++++++++++++++++++++++++++

1.—Because it is the foundation of all political liberty that those who obey the Law should be able to have a voice in choosing those who make the Law.

2.—Because Parliament should be the reflection of the wishes of the people.

3.—Because Parliament cannot fully reflect the wishes of the people when the wishes of women are without any direct representation.

4.—Because most Laws affect women as much as men, and some Laws affect women especially.

5.—Because the Laws which affect women especially are now passed without consulting those persons whom they are intended to benefit.

6.—Because Laws affecting children should be regarded from the woman's point of view as well as the man's.

7.—Because every session questions affecting the home come up for consideration in Parliament.

8.—Because women have experience which should be helpfully brought to bear on domestic legislation.

9.—Because to deprive women of the vote is to lower their positions in common estimation.

10.—Because the possession of the vote would increase the sense of responsibility amongst women towards questions of public importance.

11.—Because public-spirited mothers make public-spirited sons.

12.—Because large numbers of intelligent, thoughtful, hard-working women desire the franchise.

13.—Because the objections raised against their having the franchise are based on sentiment, not on reason.

14.—**Because**—to sum all reasons up in one—**it is for the common good of all.**

of Commons with, at least notionally, a far stronger majority in favour of women's suffrage, although the new government failed to actively promote legislation. Neither the prime minister from 1908, Herbert Asquith (still less Mrs Asquith), nor successive home secretaries supported the cause.

The attitude of the Liberal government was disappointing to the NUWSS, whose president, Millicent Garrett Fawcett (1847–1929) was the widow of a noted Liberal MP. In Manchester, it was as much frustration with the half-hearted attitude of the national Independent Labour Party that stirred the widow of one of its activists, Emmeline Pankhurst (1858–1928), to found the WSPU in 1903.

Initially, Mrs Fawcett's NUWSS and Mrs Pankhurst's WSPU ran rival but essentially complementary campaigns. The former were known as Suffragists and the latter as Suffragettes (a term actually coined by the *Daily Mail*). To begin with, Suffragists neither joined in with nor greatly condemned the more headline-grabbing tactics of Suffragettes, whose efforts to keep the issue at the centre of attention included disrupting public meetings, heckling Liberal politicians and serving prison terms for breaching the peace.

OPPOSITE: The NUWSS's fourteen-point statement of 1912, arguing the case for women's suffrage.

Millicent Fawcett, who did not support fighting for constitutional liberties by unconstitutional means, came to deplore Emmeline Pankhurst's belief that 'the argument of the broken pane, is the most valuable argument in modern politics'. The two groups began to diverge sharply when the Suffragettes turned first to vandalism, smashing windows and slashing Velasquez's *Rokeby Venus* in the National Gallery, then to arson – including an attack on a station and a school – and ultimately to planting bombs, whose failure to kill anyone was as much chance as design.

Efforts in Parliament to pass suffrage legislation were hampered for several reasons. Some MPs no longer wished to be associated with a cause being advocated through intimidation (and it can probably be safely assumed that not many converts at Westminster were won over by the call for 'Votes for Women, Chastity for Men', the new slogan of Mrs Pankhurst's daughter and fellow activist, Christabel). The parliamentary arithmetic also became less promising after 1910 when the eighty-four Irish Nationalist MPs decided to oppose women's suffrage on the grounds that it would take up legislative time that was better spent passing Irish home rule. The prevalence of women activists in the campaign against the 'demon drink' led some politicians to fear that the practical consequence of giving them the vote would be the introduction of Prohibition, while those of an imperialist frame of mind questioned whether the empire could be defended by female voters.

For many MPs, of course, the real root of their objection was naked misogyny.

There was also the question of which women should get the vote. With a third of adult males still unenfranchised, the options were either for all women to gain the suffrage as part of a universal adult franchise bill or for prospective women voters to be subject to the existing property qualifications applicable to men. Whilst the NUWSS were prepared to settle, as an interim measure, for the latter, some Liberals saw it as an unattractive compromise calculating that it would merely add more Tory voters to the electoral register. The best chance of getting legislation onto the statute books came in 1913, when an amendment to include women was attached to legislation extending the male franchise. The opportunity was lost when the Speaker of the House of Commons ruled it out of order on the grounds that it fundamentally altered the nature of the bill.

How Punch *magazine depicted Suffragette militancy in the early 1900s.*

Where the Suffragette campaign did succeed was in inciting the brutality of the state. Imprisoned Suffragettes went on hunger strike and were force-fed through

THE SUFFRAGETTE THAT KNEW JIU-JITSU.
THE ARREST.

methods indistinguishable from torture. In 1913, the home secretary introduced a legal novelty with the 'Cat and Mouse' Act, which released women prisoners on hunger strike only to reimprison them once they had recovered. In that year the cause also gained its martyr when Emily Wilding Davison either threw herself or fell (she took her intentions to the grave) under the king's horse at the Derby. It was a time of desperation. The Pankhursts' Suffragette movement suffered splits and, with the number of new recruits dwindling, stopped publishing details of new members once they fell below 1,000 a year. In contrast, the membership of Millicent Fawcett's non-violent Suffragist NUWSS soared from 21,000 in 1910 to nearly 100,000 by 1914. In choosing to ally itself with the Labour Party, the NUWSS appeared likely to cause the Liberals significant damage, prompting David Lloyd George to open talks with the NUWSS to secure a measure of women's suffrage ahead of the next election. Before anything could be finalized, the First World War broke out.

Winding down their campaign, some Suffragists, including Mrs Fawcett, supported the war, many of them getting involved in nursing and relief work, although some ran pacifist campaigns. Both Emmeline and Christabel Pankhurst loudly backed the war. The common effort against Germany created a new situation in which former domestic foes could be reconciled. With the argument for granting adult male suffrage being enhanced by the patriotic endeavours of the armed forces in France, so the contribution that women were making to the war effort on the home front was cited as a reason for extending the vote to them too. Certainly, the assertion that the empire was not safe in women's hands was shot to pieces. When the conflict ended in 1918, the Representation of the People Act gave the vote to all men over twenty-one and all women over thirty.

Both the WSPU and the NUWSS disbanded, although the latter re-formed in a new guise to campaign for the removal of the remaining sexual discrimination in the age at which the vote was granted. Victory was won in 1928 when Stanley Baldwin's government finally introduced an equal franchise for all men and women over the age of twenty-one. Shortly afterwards, Mrs Pankhurst died, having been selected as the Conservative candidate for Whitechapel. By then, she, no less than British society, had undergone an extraordinary transformation.

1914
WAR RECRUITMENT POSTER

THE FIRST WORLD WAR AND THE PRINCIPLES
OF A VOLUNTEER ARMY

An iconic poster featuring Lord Kitchener is depicted in the fourth plate section.

Britain was the only major European country that went to war in 1914 with its armed forces made up entirely of volunteers. In contrast, the massed ranks fighting for the French republic, the tsar of Russia, the German Kaiser and the emperor of Austria-Hungary, were conscripts.

The differentiation was an important one for it went to the heart of British liberalism. Other states might force their citizens or subjects to serve in the armed forces – even in peacetime – but this was incompatible with British notions of a small state and the rights of the individual. Campaigns during the Edwardian period to introduce mandatory military service along continental lines were resisted by Herbert Asquith's Liberal government.

In the early stages of the war, long queues of volunteers lining the streets outside hastily opened recruitment offices, suggesting Britain had no need to turn to compulsion. The newly appointed secretary of state for war was the much decorated hero of the 1898 Sudanese campaign, Field Marshal Horatio Kitchener, Earl Kitchener of Khartoum (1850–1916), who now called for 100,000 volunteers. Within a month 300,000 had stepped forward. Although many needed no persuading, encouragement took the form of public exhortations to duty, peer pressure, propaganda about German atrocities (some true, some exaggerated, some made up) and poster campaigns.

No poster better caught the popular imagination than the famous Kitchener 'wants YOU'. The iconic image, dominated by the striking features of the field marshal with his finger outstretched towards the viewer, was the work of a professional illustrator, Alfred Leete (1882–1933). It was originally produced on the cover of *London Opinion*, a weekly magazine, before being reproduced across the nation's billboards. Thus was born one of the most familiar images in

BRITAIN IN ARMS 1914–18

1914

4 August Britain declares war on Germany.

23 April The British Expeditionary Force (BEF) engages the German advance at Mons.

8 October–22 November The First Battle of Ypres; the BEF holds its ground despite heavy losses.

29 October The Ottoman Empire enters the war on the German side.

1915

19 January The first Zeppelin raid hits Yarmouth and King's Lynn. By May 1916, 550 British civilians have been killed by Zeppelins.

22 April The Germans unleash chlorine gas on British troops in the Ypres salient.

25 April–20 December The Gallipoli landings fail to knock Turkey out of the war.

7 May A German U-boat torpedoes and sinks the British-registered cruise liner *Lusitania* off the Irish coast, killing 1,198 passengers, almost one hundred of them children.

17 May A cross-party coalition is formed; Herbert Asquith remains prime minister.

7 December Ottoman troops besiege British and Indian forces at Kut, south-east of Baghdad. After holding out for 147 days, the remaining 13,000-strong Anglo-Indian garrison surrender on 29 April 1916. The majority of them subsequently die in captivity.

1916

27 January Conscription is introduced.

24–30 April The Easter Rising by Irish nationalists in Dublin is suppressed.

31 May The naval battle of Jutland ends inconclusively.

1 July The Somme offensive starts, with 60,000 British casualties on the first day alone.

7 December David Lloyd George replaces Asquith as prime minister.

1917

1 February Germany launches unrestricted submarine warfare, intending to starve Britain into surrender within six months.

11 March Under the command of General Maude, the British Indian army takes Baghdad.

6 April The United States enters the war on the side of Britain and France.

7 June–12 November In the Third Battle of Ypres, British efforts to break out of the Ypres salient stall after 10,000 yards and 70,000 fatalities at Passchendaele.

20 November The first use of British tanks at the Battle of Cambrai briefly breaks through the Hindenburg Line.

9 December General Allenby takes Jerusalem.

1918

3 March Russia signs the Treaty of Brest-Litovsk and withdraws from the war.

21 March The German spring offensive drives the British army back.

11 April Field Marshal Haig issues his desperate 'backs to the wall' order.

8 August A massive British counter-attack takes place at Amiens, resulting in the 'black day of the German army'.

11 November The Armistice is signed.

the history of British advertising. It was also imitated across the Atlantic when the United States entered the war on 6 April 1917, albeit with the gesticulating Kitchener replaced by Uncle Sam.

Kitchener was among the few senior figures who had assumed from the start that the conflict would be a prolonged one. During 1915 it became clear to others that he was right and that, despite the early success of the recruitment campaign, Britain could run out of sufficient volunteers to plug the gaps. Now that the apparent risk of losing the war was rated as more serious than clinging to outmoded and complacent notions of individualism, the campaign became ever louder to match the other combatants' armies with conscription. In tandem came the belief that conscription was more equitable than a system in which public-spirited volunteers were slaughtered in the trenches while 'shirkers' prospered at home.

The Cabinet became increasingly divided on the issue while Asquith sought various compromise solutions. Lord Derby was put in charge of a scheme whereby civilian men of military age 'attested' – without compulsion – that they were willing to serve if called upon. This failed to placate those who argued that it was unfair for married men to make such a commitment when some unmarried men had still failed to do so. In January 1916, Asquith finally conceded that the age of volunteerism was over: the Military Service Act conscripted unmarried men between the ages of eighteen and forty-one. Thirty-four Liberal MPs forlornly voted against the bill and, although it made several Cabinet ministers uneasy, only Sir John Simon, the home secretary, carried his principles as far as to resign on the issue.

To pacify those who felt liberalism's soul had been sold, the status of the conscientious objector was recognized (unlike in most of Europe at the time). Few of those whom the tribunals excused from taking up arms found the alternatives to be soft options, for they included ambulance work or, for those unwilling to carry stretchers, labour camps. However, the greatest handicap to conscription was that many of those who had not volunteered were engaged in essential tasks at home, whether digging coal, in some area of factory activity still deemed unsuitable for the new influx of women workers, or in some other skilled and useful occupation. Hoping to tap the last remaining wells of manpower, in April 1916 the terms of military conscription were widened to make all men under forty-one eligible for call-up. No conscription was imposed upon Ireland, but the threat of its introduction in 1918 led to a huge increase in support for the hardline republicans of Sinn Féin.

By then, the individualist ideals behind the Kitchener poster had gone the way of the great field marshal himself. In June 1916 he was aboard HMS *Hampshire* when it hit a mine off the Orkney Islands, and he went down with the ship. His authority among his political and military colleagues was already waning although he had never lost his national popularity. As the prime minister's wife, Margot Asquith, observed, he remained 'a great poster'.

It is debatable whether the scrapping of volunteering played a role in winning the war. Auckland Geddes, who served as Director of National Service from 1917 to 1919, later concluded that 'the imposition of military conscription added little if anything to the effective sum of our war effort'. Nonetheless, it was reintroduced for the Second World War. The fact that conscription in 1939 was far less politically contentious than it had been in 1916 demonstrated not only how far the prospect of 'total war' had removed the old voluntary distinction between combatant and civilian but also the extent to which the balance between the state and the individual had shifted in the intervening period. More remarkable, conscription – as 'National Service' – was not disbanded until 1960, fifteen years after the Second World War had ended.

1918
CLAUSE IV OF THE LABOUR PARTY CONSTITUTION

THE PHILOSOPHY OF BRITISH SOCIALISM

The Labour Party was founded, as the Labour Representation Committee, in 1900 with the aim of securing parliamentary seats for working-class politicians. Drawn from various pre-existing groups and the trade unions, its members may have adhered to socialist tenets, but the promotion of socialist ideology was not the new organization's stated objective. Indeed, the failure to be explicitly doctrinal quickly ensured the disaffiliation of the Marxist Social Democratic Foundation.

In its first years, the Labour Party (as it became in 1906) drew strength from two developments. In 1903, it negotiated a secret deal with the Liberal Party to avoid running against each other in constituencies where the chances of splitting the progressive vote risked letting in a Conservative. Assisted in this way, Labour won twenty-nine seats in the 1906 general election and began to assume critical mass. The 'Lib-Lab' pact, however, did not survive the First World War. Of greater long-term significance, in terms of members, leverage and funding, was the Labour Party's role as the political wing of the trade union movement. Between 1910 and 1914, the number of trade unionists in Britain rose from 2.5 million to over 4 million. By 1920 it had doubled to more than 8 million.

The First World War provided Labour with both a test and an opportunity. Unable to support the conflict, the pacifist-minded Ramsay MacDonald (1866–1937) resigned as chairman of the Parliamentary Labour Party. However, his pro-war successor, Arthur Henderson (1863–1935), joined the Cabinet. Labour MPs were thus to be found sitting both on the government and on the opposition benches, yet the division in their ranks proved less strategically calamitous than those that tore the Liberal Party apart. The latter took the form of a highly personal fight between Herbert Asquith and David Lloyd George, with the result that in

Clause IV of the Labour Party Constitution, 1918

To secure for the workers by hand or by brain the full fruits of their industry and the most equitable distribution thereof that may be possible upon the basis of the common ownership of the means of production, **distribution and exchange**, and the best obtainable system of popular administration and control of each industry or service.

[words in **bold** added in 1929]

1916 the latter replaced Asquith as prime minister in the coalition government. To this clash of personalities was added the further fracturing of common Liberal purpose over differing notions of how the war should be prosecuted.

Although the war was still not won when Labour convened its party conference at Nottingham in January 1918, it found itself in a far stronger position than previously. The power of the state was being deployed to secure military victory, blowing away many former notions of *laissez-faire* non-interference. A collectivist spirit was allied to calls for ever greater redistribution of wealth. If soldiers were to be conscripted to win the war, so the argument ran, there should be a 'conscription of wealth' to follow. At the same time, the defection from liberalism of pacifist-minded, middle-class intellectuals, who were disgusted by the methods by which Lloyd George sought to win the war, ceased to make Labour merely a party of working-class men and trade unionists.

The consequence was the adoption at Nottingham of Clause IV of the Labour Party's constitution. The clause, which framed the aims and values of the party, was drafted by Sidney Webb (1859–1947), the Fabian Society thinker, a co-founder of the London School of Economics and an advocate of schemes for 'national efficiency'. It committed Labour for the first time to an explicitly socialist ideology – to secure for all workers 'the common ownership of the means of production and the best obtainable system of popular administration and control of each industry and service'.

The author of Clause IV, Sidney Webb.

THE RISE OF THE LABOUR MOVEMENT

1834 The Tolpuddle Martyrs, six agricultural workers in Dorset who covertly form a union, are convicted of making illegal secret oaths and transported to Australia for seven years. Following a public outcry, their sentence is cut to four years.

1868 The Trade Union Congress meets for the first time, in Manchester.

1892 Keir Hardie is elected an independent Labour MP for West Ham South; he loses his seat in 1895.

1893 Hardie co-founds the Independent Labour Party (ILP) in Bradford.

1900 The Labour Representation Committee (LRC) is founded at the Memorial Hall, Farringdon Street, by the ILP, the Fabians, the (Marxist) Social Democratic Federation and trade unions.

1903 One hundred and twenty-seven unions, with 847,000 members, are affiliated to the LRC.

1901 In the Taff Vale verdict the Law Lords rule that the unions may be financially liable for the cost of their strike action.

1906 The LRC wins twenty-nine seats in the general election and is renamed the Labour Party. The Trades Disputes Act reverses the Taff Vale decision and frees the unions from corporate liability for strike action.

1914 The Labour Party supports the war effort. Opposing it, Ramsay MacDonald resigns as chairman of the parliamentary Labour Party. The ILP also opposes the war.

1915 Labour's new leader, Arthur Henderson, enters the war coalition Cabinet.

1924 Ramsay MacDonald becomes the first Labour prime minister, but his minority administration loses power within ten months.

1926 The General Strike is called in defence of miners' demands: it is called off after ten days.

1927 The Trades Disputes Act makes 'sympathetic strikes' illegal.

1929 Labour is the largest party in the general election and forms a minority administration.

1931 The Labour government breaks up over whether to address the financial crisis with budget cuts. Expelled from Labour, MacDonald stays on as prime minister until 1935 in a coalition with the Conservatives.

1932 The ILP disaffiliates from the Labour Party.

1940 Labour joins Winston Churchill's wartime coalition, with Clement Attlee as deputy prime minister.

1945 Labour wins the July general election by a landslide.

1951 Labour loses the general election despite winning more votes: Churchill returns as Conservative prime minister.

1964 Labour wins the general election after thirteen years of Conservative rule: Labour leader Harold Wilson will serve three terms as premier (1964–66, 1966–70 and 1974–76).

1979 Margaret Thatcher defeats Labour prime minister Jim Callaghan in the general election; Labour suffers further election defeats in 1983, 1987 and 1992.

1995 Tony Blair, the architect of 'New Labour', repeals Clause IV.

1997 Labour returns to government after eighteen years in opposition, defeating John Major's Conservatives in a landslide, and remains in office until losing the 2010 general election.

What this phrase meant in practice was open to interpretation. It could involve the state's nationalization of private assets, or it could involve a 'syndicalist' approach in which various affiliations – whether trade unions, guilds or workers' co-operatives – effectively determined productivity, pay and conditions. All that was certain was that it intended to spell bad news for private enterprise. In the event, nationalization proved to be the favoured method, although the unions were appeased and consulted as part of a corporatist approach to economic planning.

Common ownership was not advanced during Labour's first two brief spells in government, in 1924 and 1929–31, under Ramsay MacDonald. There was neither the parliamentary majority nor the will to push forward the principles of Clause IV. This changed with the massive election victory won by Labour in 1945, after which Clement Attlee's government nationalized the 'commanding heights' of industry – including coal, iron and steel, gas, electricity, telecommunications, aviation, road haulage and the railways. This proved to be the apex of the movement for state control.

An attempt to amend Clause IV was defeated in 1959, but the Labour Left's efforts to nationalize Britain's top twenty-five companies in the 1970s were resisted by the party leadership. Thereafter, the most explicitly socialist commitments were made in the 1983 manifesto, and their overwhelming rejection by the electorate began a process of retreat from this form of state control. Its last rites were symbolically read in 1995 when Tony Blair secured the repeal of Clause IV and its substitution with a more anodyne form of words:

> The Labour Party is a democratic socialist party. It believes that by the strength of our common endeavour we achieve more than we achieve alone, so as to create for each of us the means to realise our true potential and for all of us a community in which power, wealth and opportunity are in the hands of the many, not the few, where the rights we enjoy reflect the duties we owe and where we live together freely, in a spirit of solidarity, tolerance and respect.

1921
THE ANGLO-IRISH TREATY

IRISH HOME RULE AND THE CREATION
OF NORTHERN IRELAND

The 'Irish Question' had been the most bitterly contested issue in British politics for nearly thirty years between 1886 and 1914. The decision of William Ewart Gladstone (1809–98) to advocate self-government for Ireland had split his Liberal Party, prompting a wave of defections. Augmented by leading ex-Liberals, the Conservative Party regarded the issue as so central to its purpose that for most of this period it was known as 'the Unionist Party'. This Unionist alliance defeated Gladstone's Irish home rule bills of 1886 and 1893. After 1910, Herbert Asquith's Liberal government became dependent for its parliamentary majority on the Irish Nationalist MPs and could not prevaricate on the matter indefinitely. With the House of Lords' powers of legislative veto removed by the 1911 Parliament Act, it was finally possible to bring Irish home rule onto the statute books despite the strong hostility of the opposition. The act received the royal assent in September 1914.

It was not, however, put into operation. The First World War had broken out the previous month and – with the support of the Irish Nationalist leader, John Redmond – the decision was taken to delay making the legislation effective until the hostilities were over. This was, of course, based on the assumption that the war would last nowhere near as long as its eventual four-year duration. London hoped that the pause would provide a breathing-space to finalize the details of a late amendment that appeared to give those northern Irish counties of Ulster that had Protestant majorities temporary exclusion from rule by the proposed Dublin Parliament.

Determined that the legislation should apply equally to all of Ireland, the Irish Nationalists opposed giving Ulster special treatment. However, any attempt to coerce the predominantly Protestant North into going in with the predominantly Catholic South seemed certain to result in civil war. In 1912, half a million Ulstermen

IRISH NATIONALISM 1886–1938

1886 The first Irish home rule bill is defeated in the Commons.

1890 Charles Stewart Parnell is cited in a divorce case and forced to resign as leader of the Irish Nationalist MPs.

1893 A second Irish home rule bill passes in the Commons but is defeated in the Lords.

1905 Arthur Griffith founds Sinn Féin ('We Ourselves').

1912 A third home rule bill is introduced. In Ulster, half a million sign the Solemn League and Covenant opposing home rule.

1913 Rival paramilitaries, the Ulster Volunteer Force and the Irish Volunteers (later the Irish Republican Army, or IRA), are formed.

1914 The Curragh 'Mutiny'. The Home Rule Act is passed but suspended for the duration of the First World War.

1916 The 'Easter Rising' in Dublin is suppressed and some of its ringleaders are executed.

1918 The threat of wartime conscription boosts Sinn Féin, which wins most Irish seats in the general election.

1919–21 The Anglo-Irish war pits the IRA against the 'Black and Tans'.

1920 The Government of Ireland Act proposes separate home rule assemblies for Northern Ireland in Belfast and Southern Ireland in Dublin.

1921 The Ulster Unionists win 67 per cent in Northern Ireland's first general election, and Sir James Craig becomes prime minister. The Anglo-Irish Treaty ends the conflict between the British government and Irish Nationalists, but Ireland is partitioned.

1922 The Irish Free State endorses the treaty in a general election. The insurrection by elements of the IRA opposed to the Anglo-Irish Treaty starts a civil war. Sectarian riots break out in Northern Ireland.

1923 Pro-treaty forces win the civil war in the Irish Free State.

1924 The anti-treaty leader, Eamon de Valera, founds Fianna Fáil ('Soldiers of Destiny').

1931 The IRA is declared an illegal organization in the Irish Free State.

1932 De Valera forms a Fianna Fáil government and institutes highly protectionist economic policies.

1937 A new constitution is approved in the Irish Free State, which formally lays claim to Northern Ireland.

1938 Britain hands over its naval bases at Berehaven, Queenstown and Lough Swilly to the Irish Free State.

1949 Ireland formally becomes a republic and leaves the British Commonwealth.

and women had signed a 'Solemn League and Covenant', affirming their loyalty to Britain and making clear they would refuse to recognize an Irish government. It was clear that they intended insurrection from the formation of the paramilitary Ulster Volunteer Force in early 1913 to resist forcible integration into a Dublin-based state. It was armed by well-wishers – many of them British Conservatives – and the trouble-stirring German government. After an officers' 'mutiny' at the Curragh

months from the date hereof.

18.   This instrument shall be submitted forthwith by His Majesty's Government for the approval of Parliament, and by the Irish signatories to a meeting summoned for the purpose of the members elected to sit in the House of Commons of Southern Ireland, and if approved shall be ratified by the necessary legislation.

Decr 6th 1921.

On behalf of the
British Delegation

D Lloyd George

Austen Chamberlain

Birkenhead.

Winston S. Churchill

L. Worthington-Evans

Hamar Greenwood

Gordon Hewart.

On behalf of the Irish
Delegation

Art Ó Gríobhtha (Arthur Griffith)

Mícheál Ó Coileáin

Riobárd Bartún

E. S. Ó Dúgáin

Seóirse Ghabháin Uí Dhubhthaigh.

camp in 1914, it seemed doubtful whether the British army would obey orders to forcibly put down an attempt by Ulster to stay loyal to Britain. To further inflame an already combustible situation, in late 1913 a rival southern paramilitary force, the Irish Volunteers, had been established with the goal of fighting – if it came to that – to ensure that an All-Ireland government was installed. In this state of affairs it was hard to see a way out of bloodshed, whatever course was pursued.

Rather than await a future round of negotiations when the First World War ended, republican militants took events into their own hands. In April 1916 they launched the Easter Rising in Dublin, which at first drew little popular support. However, the heavy-handed manner of its suppression (fifteen of the Rising's leaders were subsequently executed by firing-squad, while Sir Roger Casement, who had conspired with the Germans, was hanged) brought a wave of sympathy and vehement condemnation of British brutality. Belatedly, London tried to bring forward the date of introducing Irish home rule, only to find negotiations breaking down over whether Ulster would be temporarily or indefinitely excluded from it. Mistrust of British intentions, combined with a fear that conscription might be introduced in Ireland, undermined constitutional groups and, in the South, delivered an overwhelming victory in the 1918 general election for the uncompromising republicans of Sinn Féin.

Within weeks, Sinn Féin representatives met in Dublin where they issued a unilateral declaration of independence from the United Kingdom and convened themselves as the parliament of the Irish Republic – the Dáil Éireann. London treated this as a *coup d'état* and refused to recognize the new body. The Dáil claimed sovereignty over the North as well, despite the reality that – having already resolved to stay out of Irish self-government – Ulster's Protestant majority were even less keen to have anything to do with Sinn Féin-led Irish independence. The 1914 legislation was thus, from both sides of the divide, a dead letter.

Coming to terms with this reality, the prime minister, David Lloyd George, tried to wrest back the initiative with a new settlement, the 1920 Government of Ireland Act. Passed by Westminster, the act established two home-rule assemblies – one for Northern Ireland, meeting in Belfast; and one for southern Ireland, meeting in Dublin. The Northern Irish Parliament was successfully instituted at Stormont in the outskirts of Belfast the following year, but few in the South acknowledged the legitimacy of Lloyd George's Dublin Parliament. The Sinn Féin-controlled assembly, the Dáil Éireann, and its president, Eamon de Valera, continued to act as the *de facto* power in the south.

OPPOSITE: *The signatories of the Anglo-Irish Treaty. For the British delegation: David Lloyd George (prime minister), Austen Chamberlain (Lord Privy Seal and Conservative Party leader), Lord Birkenhead (lord chancellor), Winston Churchill (colonial secretary), Laming Worthington-Evans (war secretary), Hamar Greenwood (chief secretary for Ireland), Gordon Hewart (attorney general). For the Irish delegation (who signed in Irish): Arthur Griffith (foreign secretary), Michael Collins (finance secretary), Robert Barton (economic affairs secretary), Eamonn Duggan (chief liaison officer) and George Gavan Duffy (Sinn Féin MP).*

Rather than concede that the Dáil was an established fact, London continued to treat it as a revolutionary tribunal. Under the charismatic leadership of a former post-office clerk and veteran of the 1916 Rising, Michael Collins (1890–1922), the Irish Volunteers were turned into an effective guerrilla force, the Irish Republican Army (IRA), which, in 1919, began hit-and-run terror attacks on individuals and institutions that remained loyal to the British Crown. The latter responded by meeting terror with terror, its instruments of restoring order – the paramilitary 'Black and Tans' and the Auxiliary Division of the Royal Irish Constabulary – being as indiscriminately violent as the IRA. By 1921, the IRA had killed about 500 police and 200 soldiers, while around 750 real or suspected republicans had died. Ireland was, to all intents and purposes, in a state of war.

When a truce was signed on 8 July 1921, it suited both sides. Michael Collins later told Hamar Greenwood, the chief secretary for Ireland, 'You had us dead beat. We could not have lasted another three weeks.' On the other hand, the British forces were effectively fighting for an unsustainable cause. Formal negotiations began in London in October. The Irish delegation was led by Collins and Arthur Griffith, Sinn Féin's founder, and the British team included Lloyd George, Winston Churchill, Lord Birkenhead and the Conservative Party leader Austen Chamberlain. A deal was struck early on 6 December. Southern Ireland would gain virtual independence as the Irish Free State (this represented far more autonomy than the 1914 Home Rule Act had offered). Nonetheless, it would remain in the British Commonwealth with dominion status similar to that enjoyed by Canada.

This created a debate about whether members of the Dáil should therefore swear an oath of allegiance to the king. In the end it was agreed that they would do so, but only subordinately within the context of the common citizenship that dominion status entailed. Their primary oath would be to uphold the Irish Constitution. The treaty also guaranteed to the Royal Navy the continued use of three deep-water Irish ports. Crucially, the new Irish Free State would not have sovereignty over six counties of Ulster, which retained the right to remain within the United Kingdom.

The Irish delegates may have accepted partition because Lloyd George hinted to them that a future boundary commission might make the northern province effectively unsustainable, forcing it to join the South. In the event, no such alteration took place. The best reason for signing though, was the grimness of the alternative: a resumption of hostilities.

As the delegates' names were added to the treaty, Lord Birkenhead quipped that he might be signing his political death warrant. Michael Collins's riposte

was, 'I may have signed my actual death warrant.' This proved prophetic. The Dáil narrowly approved the treaty by 64 votes to 57 and a general election in the South voted 72 per cent in favour of pro-treaty parties. Having stayed away from the negotiations, de Valera declared them a betrayal and denounced the partition of the island. His wing of the IRA, the 'Irregulars', went to war with the new Irish Free State forces. Collins was ambushed and shot dead by anti-treaty IRA gunmen in his home county of Cork in August 1922.

Eventually, in May 1923, Irish government forces succeeded in suppressing de Valera's insurrection. However, as leader of a new republican party, Fianna Fáil, de Valera would be elected to power in 1932, proceeding to guide his nation's fortunes until 1959, and thereafter, in the more honorific role as president until 1973. Britain returned the 'treaty ports' in 1938, and the Irish Free State, Gaelicized as Éire, was effectively a republic from 1937. It was formally declared as such in 1949 when it left the British Commonwealth. Its constitution continued to lay claim to the 'six counties' of Northern Ireland until 1999.

Michael Collins leaving 10 Downing Street during the peace talks, October 1921.

c.1925
SCHOOL MAP OF
THE BRITISH EMPIRE

IMPERIAL PRIDE, TRADE AND KINSHIP

A map of the British Empire is depicted in the fourth plate section.

Although later generations came to associate the zenith of the British Empire with the reign of Queen Victoria, it actually reached its greatest extent in the 1920s, twenty years before its rapid dissolution began.

During that period, the Union Jack fluttered over a quarter of the world's population and landmass. The First World War had brought about the collapse of the Russian, German, Austro-Hungarian and Ottoman empires, but Britain's had endured. Indeed, Britain found herself taking responsibility for additional colonies that had formerly been ruled by the vanquished. The League of Nations (the predecessor to the United Nations) approved Britain's mandate to run ex-German colonies in Africa, while in the Middle East Britain took over large parts of the disintegrated Ottoman Empire, gaining mandates for Palestine, Transjordan and Iraq.

It would have been impossible for a country the size of the United Kingdom, especially after the financial and material strain of the First World War, to have run all of this vast empire directly. While Britain was the administrative authority in many colonies, by the early decades of the twentieth century the term 'empire' was innappropriate for the majority of the most important countries.

Dominion status conferred home rule to Canada, Newfoundland, South Africa, Australia, New Zealand and the Irish Free State. In most areas of domestic policy these countries ran their own affairs. In foreign policy the relationship was more complicated, not least because it was entwined with the notion of a co-ordinated 'imperial defence'. However, each of the dominions was represented as a separate entity in the League of Nations and could not be forced to declare war on Britain's enemies without the approval of its own government.

India remained, in the well-worn phrase, the 'jewel in the crown'. Nonetheless, even there, British rule was not quite as absolute as the pink colouring on the map of the world implied. The fact that a mere 500 Britons staffed a civil service responsible for 320 million inhabitants might be considered a testament to bureaucratic efficiency, even if it was as much a sign of light administration. Far from intervening in every aspect of Indian life, no social legislation was imposed on the subcontinent between the revision of the penal code in 1861 and the Age of Consent Act in 1921. Although ultimately what underpinned the Raj was force, this still comprised only 60,000 British soldiers. Indeed, almost half the land area of India was not even run by the British but rather by the maharajahs, nizams and nawabs of its more than 500 princely states. They pledged loyalty to the British Crown as the paramount power and, in return for not making trouble, were mostly left to their own devices.

There was a contradiction at the heart of Britain's relations with her dominions and colonies, in that a country that, until 1932, pursued policies of free trade with foreign countries continued to permit its imperial possessions to slap tariffs on British trade. For instance, by 1931 'British' India's general tariff on importing British goods reached 25 per cent. Dominion governments also protected their home market against the 'mother country' and although negotiated reductions were made in 1932, the Imperialists' goal of Empire Free Trade still remained elusive when the Second World War broke out seven years later.

Yet the worth of the empire – at any rate to Britain – was never more apparent than in 1939 when (apart from the Irish Free State) even those of its members best able to exercise

THE HIGH NOON OF EMPIRE

1899–1902 Britain prevails in the Second Boer War in South Africa.

1901 The Commonwealth of Australia is formed. The protectorate of Nigeria is established.

1904 Empire Day (24 May: Queen Victoria's birthday) is first celebrated.

1906 The Muslim League is founded in Bengal.

1907 New Zealand is granted dominion status.

1910 The Union of South Africa is created, with dominion status.

1911 The 'Coronation Durbar' in New Delhi celebrates the coronation of George V as India's emperor.

1912 The African National Congress (initially the South African Native National Congress) is founded in Bloemfontein to campaign for black rights.

1914 Egypt is formally made a British protectorate. Volunteers from across the empire rally to Britain's war effort.

1919 In India's Amritsar Massacre, troops fire on unarmed protestors killing 379.

1920 Britain is awarded the mandate to administer Palestine. British East Africa becomes the colony of Kenya.

1922 Egypt is given independence. The Palestine Mandate incorporates Transjordan.

1925 Cyprus becomes a British colony.

1930 Mohandas K. Gandhi steps up his civil disobedience campaign in India.

1931 The Statute of Westminster establishes the legislative equality and independence of all six dominions (Australia, Canada, the Irish Free State, New Zealand, South Africa and Newfoundland).

1939–45 The dominions volunteer to fight alongside Britain during the Second World War.

1947 Indian independence from Britain marks the start of Britain's withdrawal from empire.

free will chose to rally to Britain's side. In 1940, with the British Expeditionary Force trapped and awaiting rescue at Dunkirk, the defence of a large sector of southern England was in the hands of Canadian soldiers. By the time the conflict was won, the Canadian government had effectively donated to Britain $4 billion in money and supplies. India supplied the largest volunteer army in history. Even in the darkest days of 1940–1, Britain was never quite 'alone' when she had a vast empire of countries transporting men and resources.

It was the so-called 'white dominions' that were the most popular empire destination for generations of British emigrants. Funds were on offer between the 1920s and 1970s to help populate them (and keep them white). Well-intentioned – if sometimes misguided – philanthropy also dispatched orphans and the underprivileged to what was hoped would be a better life in the sun than in the slums of industrial Britain. Nonetheless, it is telling how little this huge migration was directed by officialdom.

That fact itself is one indicator of the considerable pull that the empire exerted on the imagination despite the criticisms made by some, particularly on the Left, of both its principles and the reality. Popular books and films helped keep alive faith in its moral purpose, whether as a bulwark of democracy (in places where it *was* democratic), as a force for extending law and order, as an environment for promoting missionary work and social improvements, or merely as a means of preventing other countries seizing the same territories and claiming the glory for themselves.

Rudyard Kipling's stories of India enjoyed a wide audience, particularly among children with a sense of adventure. Special events also reinforced the message. Empire Day was launched in 1904 by the Anglo-Irishman Lord Meath, and it continued to be observed, principally by schoolchildren (who got the afternoon off), throughout the inter-war period. With its pavilions and purpose-built Wembley Stadium, the Empire Exhibition of 1924–5 proved even more popular than the Great Exhibition of 1851, drawing a record 27 million visitors. A Canadian track and field manager, Melville Marks 'Bobby' Robinson, organized the first Empire (subsequently Commonwealth) Games in Hamilton, Canada, in 1930.

The most formative influence on young minds, however, must surely have been the map of the world with the imperial possessions coloured in pink. Vast numbers were produced during the period, whether by educational publishers or distributed as special offers to newspaper readers. They were more than an indispensable teaching aid. Almost standard classroom decoration, they were the ever-present focal point on which generations of wandering thoughts must daily have fixed.

1927
THE ROYAL CHARTER
OF THE BBC

❧

BRITAIN'S NATIONAL BROADCASTING CORPORATION

The BBC was the world's first regular television broadcaster and is still the world's largest broadcasting corporation. Even aside from its international reach and reputation, its influence on the knowledge, culture and shared experiences of the British people is beyond calculation.

It started in 1922 as a private enterprise, the British Broadcasting Company Ltd. Its major shareholders were six wireless-set manufacturers, including the business of the pioneer of the technology, Guglielmo Marconi, and British subsidiaries of the American-owned General Electric Company. They hoped to sell more sets, a prospect likely to be achieved only if radio broadcasting was allowed to reach a substantial audience.

Regulating wireless telephony was the responsibility of the Post Office. It wanted to avoid the chaotic race to start up radio stations that had just occurred in the United States, where the result was congestion and interference on the airwaves, low-quality programme-making and bankrupt companies. As favouring the BBC seemed the perfect means of avoiding this outcome, the Post Office granted it the exclusive right to construct transmitters across the country from which to broadcast. It would receive half of the 10-shilling (50p) fee that the Post Office charged listeners for their annual receiving licences.

The BBC's general manager, John Reith (1889–1971), had no background in broadcasting but demonstrated an unremitting determination to use what he described as 'the brute force of monopoly' as a power for moral and cultural enlightenment. He envisaged the BBC as bringing to homes across the country 'all that was best in every department of human knowledge, endeavour and achievement' in its mission to inform, educate and entertain. His first great test came in 1926 when the General Strike brought much of the country to a standstill

From the BBC's Royal Charter, 1927

Whereas it has been made to appear to Us that more than two million persons in Our Kingdom of Great Britain and Northern Ireland have applied for and taken out Licences to instal and work apparatus for . . . the purpose of receiving Broadcast programmes and whereas in view of the widespread interest which is thereby shown to be taken by Our People in the Broadcasting Service and of the great value of the Service as a means of education and entertainment, We deem it desirable that the Service should be developed and exploited to the best advantage and in the national interest . . . [by] a Corporation charged with these duties . . . [and] created by the exercise of Our Royal Prerogative.

and shut down the traditional Fleet Street newspapers. Reith resisted the efforts of some Cabinet ministers to commandeer the BBC for government propaganda, in the process enhancing the company's reputation for independence.

At the same time, Parliament was considering the future of the medium. The Crawford Committee recommended revoking the BBC's licence and transforming the company into a public corporation, guided by the responsibility to be a 'Trustee for the national interest'. Stanley Baldwin's Conservative government endorsed the Crawford Committee's proposals, and on New Year's Day 1927 the BBC was re-established by royal charter as the British Broadcasting Corporation. To avoid commercial advertising, the licence-fee model of funding was retained. There were already over 2 million receiving licences and it was clear millions more were on the way.

The new corporation was the state broadcaster, enjoying a monopoly of all output, with a board of governors nominated by the government. Nevertheless, it had operational and editorial independence. To minimize the risk that it would destroy competition from other forms of media or even peddle an agenda of its own, its news output was at first strictly limited. It was not permitted to broadcast news bulletins until 7 p.m. in order to avoid detracting from the newspaper market, the bulletins being strict summaries of news compiled from the press agencies. The emphasis was on avoiding contentious discussion and any analysis of current affairs.

Gradually, these restrictions were pruned down and lifted, although they shaped an approach that, during the 1930s, tended to shy away from the articulation of unorthodox views. Winston Churchill was among those who complained that he was not given airtime to voice his opposition to the government's appeasement policy. Critics detected a longer legacy from this period that was evident in the corporation's deferential tone and failure to take risks. It was not until the 1960s that this broke down when the BBC was given a new direction by a modernizing director-general, Hugh Carleton Greene (the brother of the writer Graham Greene). The broadening appeal was not to everyone's taste – the 'Clean-Up TV' campaigner, Mary Whitehouse, concluded that Greene was 'more than anybody else . . . responsible for the moral collapse in this country'.

By then, the BBC was as much a television as a radio broadcaster. The prospect of television was loathed by Reith, a dour Presbyterian Scot who made even his radio announcers read the news in black tie. Nonetheless, it was during his tenure as director-general between 1927 and 1938 that the corporation adopted the medium. At 3 p.m. on 2 November 1936, Leslie Mitchell announced live to camera, 'This is the BBC Television Station at Alexandra Palace,' and Britain's fascination with 'telly' began.

Sir John Reith, who took the BBC from a company to a corporation and served as its first director general from 1927 to 1938.

The first TV programmes were broadcast using two different formats one after the other, John Logie Baird's mechanical electronic system, followed by the wholly electronic Marconi–EMI technology. The latter's better picture quality and scope for future improvement quickly won the day. Because of the cost and limitations of early television sets the audience was small and based in the South-East, where 20,000 sets could receive the BBC's twenty hours a week of programmes in 1939 until the service was shut down for the war. Broadcasting resumed in 1946, and its popularity was hugely boosted by its coverage of Queen Elizabeth II's coronation in 1953.

Since then, the BBC's charter has been renewed and it has remained a public service broadcaster, funded by the licence fee. Despite the best efforts of the welfare state advocate, William Beveridge, its monopoly proved indefensible. In 1954, Winston Churchill's government secured the passage of the Television Act.

SIX DECADES OF HIT TV: THE MOST WATCHED PROGRAMMES

		Channel	Date	Audience (in millions)
1950s				
1	*Wagon Train*	ITV	30/11/1959	13.63
2	*Take Your Pick*	ITV	11/12/1959	13.16
3	*Sunday Night at the London Palladium*	ITV	6/12/1959	13.08
4	*Armchair Theatre: Suspicious Mind*	ITV	22/11/1959	12.74
5	*The Army Game*	ITV	11/12/1959	12.60
1960s				
1	The World Cup Final, 1966	BBC1	30/7/1966	32.30
2	*The Royal Family*	BBC1 & ITV	21/6/1969 (BBC1)/ 28/6/1969 (ITV)	30.69
3	*Royal Variety Performance*, 1965	ITV	14/11/1965	24.20
4	News [John F. Kennedy Assassination]	BBC & ITV	22/11/1963	24.15
5	*Miss World*	BBC1	19/11/1967	23.76
1970s				
1	Apollo 13 splashdown	BBC1 & ITV	17/4/1970	28.60
2	FA Cup final replay: Chelsea v. Leeds United	BBC1 & ITV	29/4/1970	28.49
3	Princess Anne's wedding	BBC1 & ITV	14/11/1973	27.60
4	*To the Manor Born*	BBC1	11/11/1979	23.95
5	*Miss World*	BBC1	20/11/1970	23.76
1980s				
1	*EastEnders*	BBC1	25/12/1986	30.15
2	Royal wedding ceremony	BBC1 & ITV	29/7/1981	28.40
3	*Coronation Street*	ITV	19/3/1989	26.93
4	*Dallas*	BBC1	22/11/1980	21.60
5	*To the Manor Born*	BBC1	9/11/1980	21.55
1990s				
1	Funeral of Princess Diana	BBC1 & ITV	6/9/1997	32.10
2	*Only Fools and Horses*	BBC1	29/12/1996	24.35
3	*EastEnders*	BBC1	2/1/1992	24.30
4	Torvill and Dean: Winter Olympics, 1994	BBC1	21/2/1994	23.95
5	World Cup, 1998: England v. Argentina	ITV	30/6/1998	23.78
2000s				
1	*Only Fools and Horses*	BBC1	25/12/2001	21.34
2	Euro 2004: England v. Portugal	BBC1	24/6/2004	20.66
3	*EastEnders*	BBC1	5/4/2001	20.05
4	*Coronation Street*	ITV	24/2/2003	19.40
5	World Cup, 2006: England v. Sweden	BBC1	20/6/2006	18.50

(Source: BFI)

It permitted commercial television, with various regional companies – operating under fixed-term franchises – producing their own material under the umbrella of Independent Television (ITV) and its regulator, the Independent Television Authority. The development was initially opposed by the Labour Party, which believed greater choice would diminish quality. The viewing preferences of Labour's core voters forced an urgent rethink.

The BBC responded with more channels, launching BBC2 in 1964 (which was the first to broadcast in colour, in 1967) and rearranging its radio output into four (later five) national stations plus various regional stations. Further independent competition came from Channel 4 in 1982 and Sky satellite television in 1989. With the advent of the internet, the 1990s brought a new threat that the corporation decided to embrace, first with its own news website and, in 2007, by streaming its programmes online. Whether its unique funding formula will survive indefinitely remains a matter for debate, although remarkably the BBC's listening and viewing figures have held up surprisingly well, despite the swelling number of competing channels and alternative entertainments on offer. Its modern embrace of popular tastes and periodic vulgarity would have horrified Reith, yet it has still broadly tried to honour his guiding principles – if not his style – to inform, educate and entertain.

1936

EDWARD VIII'S INSTRUMENT OF ABDICATION

THE ABDICATION CRISIS

There was a widespread fear that the monarchy might not survive the abdication of King Edward VIII. Despite all the dramas of peace and war over the centuries, the prime minister, Stanley Baldwin, thought it appropriate to tell the House of Commons: 'No more grave message has ever been received in Parliament.'

In the seventeenth century Charles I had been executed and his son, James II, had fled into exile. Thereafter, Britain had experienced almost 250 years of constitutional monarchy, its kings and queens having died while still in office. The very idea that Edward VIII (1894–1972) should throw his throne away – within a year of ascending to it – for the love of Mrs Wallis Simpson (1896–1986), a woman who was an acquired taste, dumbfounded many. As Edward's mother, Queen Mary, later told him, it remained 'inconceivable to those who had made such sacrifices during the war that you, as their King, refused a lesser sacrifice'.

Having succeeded his widely respected father, George V, in January 1936, Edward appeared to be an affable, handsome, modern-minded monarch. Yet behind the scenes, his flippant attitude to his duties and his growing attachment to Wallis Simpson caused consternation among those more closely acquainted with him. The general public knew nothing of this until 1 December, when the bishop of Bradford chose the occasion of a diocesan conference to lament the king's failure to recognize that he was in need of God's grace. Reluctant to engage in self-imposed censorship any longer, the press regarded this as the moment to break a story in Britain that was already filling the column inches of the foreign press.

Edward hoped he could marry his twice-married American lover and retain his throne. The Church of England, of which he was supreme governor, forbade

INSTRUMENT OF ABDICATION

I, Edward the Eighth, of Great Britain, Ireland, and the British Dominions beyond the Seas, King, Emperor of India, do hereby declare My irrevocable determination to renounce the Throne for Myself and for My descendants, and My desire that effect should be given to this Instrument of Abdication immediately.

In token whereof I have hereunto set My hand this tenth day of December, nineteen hundred and thirty six, in the presence of the witnesses whose signatures are subscribed.

SIGNED AT
FORT BELVEDERE
IN THE PRESENCE
OF

The Instrument of Abdication signed by Edward VIII and his three brothers – Albert, duke of York (thereafter George VI), Henry, duke of Gloucester and George, duke of Kent.

THE LIFE OF EDWARD VIII

1894 Edward Albert Christian George Andrew Patrick David is born in Richmond, Surrey.

1907 Aged thirteen, Edward is sent to naval college.

1910 Death of Edward VII and accession of George V.

1911 Edward is invested as Prince of Wales.

1912 Edward studies – briefly – at Magdalen College, Oxford.

1919–35 Edward undertakes sixteen tours to various parts of the British Empire.

1933 Edward begins his affair with Wallis Simpson, an American divorcee.

1936 Edward ascends the throne only to abdicate it when the government effectively prevents him from marrying Wallis and remaining king.

1937 Accorded the titles duke and duchess of Windsor, Edward and Wallis marry at the Château de Candé in France. They go on to tour Germany as guests of Hitler.

1940 After undistinguished and potentially compromising war service, the duke (with the duchess) flees France for Lisbon. The duke is made Governor of the Bahamas for the duration of the war, largely to get him out of the way of trouble.

1945 The duke and duchess settle in Paris, supported by a government allowance and an exemption from French income tax.

1951 The duke's largely ghost-written autobiography, *A King's Story*, is published.

1972 The duke of Windsor dies of cancer and is buried with other members of the royal family at Frogmore, Windsor. The duchess becomes increasingly reclusive and bed-ridden.

1986 The duchess of Windsor dies at her home in the Bois de Boulogne, Paris.

a church wedding to divorced persons whose former spouses were still alive. Inconveniently in Mrs Simpson's case, she had *two* living ex-husbands. It was a difficult situation, which, whatever the state of popular opinion, might have been smoothed if only the Church and the political Establishment had wished to do their monarch's bidding. Instead, they saw little in his private demeanour or public posturing to justify conniving in so controversial an action. The possibility that he might contract a morganatic marriage – whereby Wallis Simpson would become his wife but not queen and any children would not succeed to the throne – was effectively ruled out by Baldwin, who assured his king that Parliament would not agree to it.

As prime minister, Baldwin was the decisive figure throughout the crisis. He tightened the screw by insisting that the government would resign if the king persisted with his marriage plans. Baldwin had even taken the precaution of securing the Labour opposition's word that it would refuse to form a government in this eventuality. Alternative politicians lacked either the credibility or a parliamentary majority to carry out the king's wishes. If Edward did not back down, his realm would have no functioning government.

He pleaded for time, but Baldwin insisted on a speedy decision in order to prevent the country becoming divided. His Majesty's own government refused him permission to broadcast directly to his people. Outmanoeuvred, he realized that further prevarication was useless and chose love over duty.

Edward signed the Instrument of Abdication on 10 December. His brothers also appended their signatures to it, including his successor, Prince Albert, duke of York, who signed under his first name, but who reigned as George VI. An Act of Parliament was rushed through Westminster the following day, giving the abdication document legal effect. Only with the deed done was Edward permitted to broadcast a farewell to his former subjects and to pledge allegiance to his brother, who, as Edward rather pointedly observed, enjoyed the 'matchless blessing enjoyed by so many of you and not bestowed on me – a happy home with his wife and children'.

Indeed, the new king's family, in particular his wife, Queen Elizabeth, and elder daughter, the Princess Elizabeth, were to prove a great support to George VI, a shy, stuttering man who had never wanted his brother's throne but was determined to overcome his limitations in order to do the duty Edward shirked. Created duke of Windsor, Edward married Wallis in June 1937 in a private ceremony, attended by only a few friends, in France, where they were to spend much of the rest of their lives. A perspective on their subsequent level of contentment was eventually offered by Wallis when she confided: 'You have no idea how hard it is to live out a great romance.'

Nothing in Edward's subsequent conduct contradicted the suggestion that the Instrument of Abdication was anything other than a godsend for the monarchy and the British realm.

R. J. MITCHELL'S DESIGN FOR THE SUPERMARINE SPITFIRE, MARK I

A CLASSIC DESIGN THAT HELPED SAVE BRITAIN FROM INVASION IN 1940

No other British airplane, whether civil or military, has remained as deeply in the nation's affection – or gratitude – as the Spitfire. In 1940, it played a crucial role in thwarting the Luftwaffe during the Battle of Britain. Of course, it did not perform this task alone. Aside from the extraordinary bravery of the pilots and the dedication of their ground crews, the honour for winning the Battle of Britain must also be shared with radar and another fighter plane, the Hawker Hurricane. Nonetheless, there was something about the Spitfire that captivated those who flew it as well as catching the imagination of the wider population. It was a delight to fly and a joy to behold.

Even from far off, it was distinctive from the other aircraft circling the skies of southern England during the summer of 1940, particularly in the unusual elliptical shape of its wings. Almost everything about the Spitfire, from its slim nose to its tail, exemplified an aerodynamic appearance. Nor did it merely look good: it had incredible manoeuvrability, with an ability to soar, plunge and make tight turns that often gave it the upper hand in dogfights.

The fact that it ever went into mass production was no small miracle in itself. It had been widely assumed by both the RAF and the Air Ministry in the interwar period that fighters could do little to deter mass attacks by bombers. This attitude, summed up in the oft-repeated statement of ultimate fatalism, 'The bomber will always get through', reinforced the thinking of those who believed that the only means to counter the saturation bombing of Britain was to have the power to threaten comparable retaliation on the enemy. Consequently, priority was given to the construction of bombers. It was against this orthodoxy that the Supermarine Aviation Works, based in Southampton, persevered with designs for fighter aircraft.

The government had pulled out of funding Supermarine's S 6B flying boat in 1931. It was only because Lady Houston wrote a £100,000 cheque to overcome what she condemned as the parsimony of the prime minister, Ramsay MacDonald, that the S 6B proceeded to win the much-coveted Schneider Trophy later that year and break the world air-speed record. A remarkable monoplane at a time when aircraft were still mostly canvas-covered biplanes, it demonstrated the visionary talent of its designer, R. J. Mitchell. Impressed by Mitchell, in December 1934 the Air Ministry awarded Supermarine £10,000 (almost half the initial cost) towards funding the prototype of a high-powered fighter that retained many of the S 6B's features. The resulting K5054, of which only one was constructed, made its maiden flight in 1936. The Air Ministry promptly ordered 310 of what became the Spitfire Mark I for the RAF.

The Spitfire got its chance because of the fundamental shift in RAF policy. The advocates of change were chief of the air staff, Sir Edward Ellington, and Air Chief Marshal Sir Hugh Dowding. They wanted to see resources switched from bombers to fighters and, crucially, Dowding persuaded the air secretary, Viscount Swinton. Becoming prime minister in 1937, Neville Chamberlain also favoured prioritizing

THE MARKS OF A LEGEND

The dates refer to the first and final placing of orders for production of a particular mark. (PR stands for photo reconnaissance.)

1934	Prototype K5054
June 1936–August 1940	Mk I
April 1939	Mk II; Mk III (order cancelled before production); Mk IV (prototype)
August 1939–October 1941	Mk V
August 1939	Mk VI
August 1940	PR IV
October 1940	Mk VII
January 1942	Mk VIII
April 1942	PR VIII
October 1941–April 1944	Mk IX
August 1941	Mk XI
August 1941	Mk XII
March 1942	F 21
April 1942	F 20 (test flight)
May 1942	Mk X
May 1942	Mk XVI
June 1942	F 22
July 1942–February 1945	Mk XIV
August 1942	Mk XIII
December 1942	Mk XVIII
June 1943	Mk XIX
June 1942–November 1945	F 24
October 1943	F 23

an essentially defensive rather than offensive strategy. With these three influential backers, the newly formed Fighter Command began to take shape, helped by vastly improved financing. In 1935, the air force's £17 million budget had been just half

R. J. Mitchell's original chalk drawing for the Spitfire. Even at the prototype stage, the key aspects of the aircraft's aerodynamic elegance and elliptical wing design were well developed.

that spent on the army and a quarter that of the navy. By 1939, prompted largely by the threat of the expanding Luftwaffe, its budget had risen to £133 million, more than either of the other two armed services.

The Spitfire's designer, Reginald Joseph Mitchell, had been born near Stoke-on-Trent in 1895, eight years before the Wright brothers made the world's first powered flight. While working as an apprentice at a local locomotive-building firm, he spent his evenings at night school learning engineering, mechanics and advanced mathematics. In 1917 he joined the Supermarine company, quickly becoming its chief engineer, and he continued in this position after the company was bought by Vickers. Unlike many aircraft designers, in 1934 he even learned to fly.

Mitchell wanted to call the plane that would become a legend the 'Shrew'. When told that the Air Ministry had instead decided upon 'Spitfire', he grumbled, 'It's the sort of bloody silly name they would give it.' In fact, the brilliantly conceived moniker was the suggestion of Sir Robert McClean, the chairman of Vickers – 'Spitfire' being the affectionate nickname he gave his hot-tempered daughter, Anna. It had an Elizabethan/Jacobean provenance: Shakespeare had used the phrase in *King Lear*, 'Rumble thy bellyful! Spit, fire! spout, rain!' (However, Katharine Hepburn may have helped give the word more contemporary resonance by starring in a Hollywood film entitled *Spitfire* in 1934; it had also been the name of several Royal Navy ships.)

The first of the Mark I Spitfires entered the RAF's service in August 1938. Alas, its creator was not there to see his vision take flight. Mitchell had been fighting his own personal battle since being diagnosed with bowel cancer in 1933 and died on 11 June 1937, aged just forty-two. Despite the pain of his illness, he had stuck to his task until the end and, after his death, his chief draughtsman, Joseph Smith, carried through his design, making a series of small but successful modifications. The major drawback was that the Spitfire, with its hand-fabricated aluminium fuselage, was slower to produce than other contemporary fighters, including the wooden-framed Hawker Hurricane. Supermarine and its subcontractors struggled to make it in sufficient numbers. By the outbreak of war in September 1939, only 187 were in full service with their squadrons.

Fortunately, the feared strike by the Luftwaffe did not come until the summer of 1940, by which time Fighter Command was able to defend the country with nineteen Spitfire and twenty-five Hurricane squadrons. Both aircraft drew their strength from a 12-cylinder piston-powered Rolls-Royce Merlin engine. The Spitfire's armament consisted of eight rapid-firing 0.303 inch Browning machine-guns in its wings. (During the Battle of Britain, the most experienced Spitfire squadron, No. 19, was temporarily fitted with cannon, but they tended to jam.) The Mark I was twenty-nine feet twelve inches long, with a wingspan of thirty-six feet ten inches and could fly at a maximum speed of 362 mph (at 18,500 feet). As one Battle of Britain fighter ace, Adolph 'Sailor' Malan, put it, 'She was a perfect lady. She had no vices. She was beautifully positive. You could dive till your eyes were popping out of your head … she would still answer to a touch.' Pilots of the

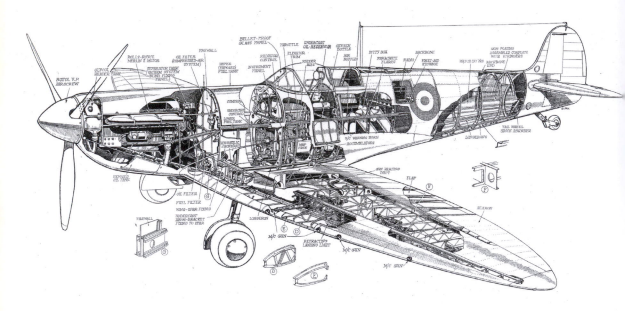

A cutaway drawing of the Spitfire Mk I published in The Aeroplane *on 12 April 1940.*

Luftwaffe's premier fighter, the Messerschmitt Me (or Bf) 109, developed a healthy respect for Mitchell's aircraft.

Of the forty-six different marks and designations produced, the Mark V and Mark IX were the most widely flown. Successive modifications made the Spitfire progressively heavier, faster, and more potently armed, with two 20mm cannons (teething problems now solved) replacing four of the machine guns. By 1943, the Merlin engine had been replaced by the even more powerful Rolls-Royce Griffon, which took the plane to speeds of 454 mph at 26,000 feet. During the course of the conflict, the fighter was deployed in almost every theatre of war. By the time the last Spitfire was completed in 1947, over 20,000 had been built, more than any other RAF fighter plane. Over forty still survive in flying condition.

The last of the Spitfires ceased regular service with the RAF following operational missions in Malaya, in 1954. By that year the Lightning, a supersonic jet fighter, was in development. Yet the passing of the propeller age saw no diminution in the Spitfire's place in the collective consciousness. Even those with no interest in aeronautics recalled her role flown by 'the Few' in her country's 'Finest Hour'. All these years on, who does not still associate the very words 'British freedom' with the soaring image of a lone Spitfire tilting its beautifully crafted wings in acknowledgement?

HITLER AND CHAMBERLAIN'S NOTE: THE MUNICH PACT

THE APPEASEMENT OF NAZI GERMANY

By the early 1930s, Britain's sense of relief at having been on the winning side in the Great War had been swamped by a solemn recognition of the scale of sacrifice involved. Economic depression and the rise of fascism in Europe reinforced the feeling of futility. Amid a growing mood of anti-militarism, many Britons, especially on the Left, looked to the League of Nations (the forerunner to the United Nations) to replace old balance-of-power politics with a 'collective security' approach to problems.

The revulsion at the prospect of rearmament and a dislike of traditional 'sabre-rattling' made the British government's appeasement of Adolf Hitler's regime both possible and, until late in the day, popular. Diplomatic measures to restrict German aggression had been framed by the 1919 Treaty of Versailles, but by the mid-1930s the agreement was widely criticized as one of the causes of Germany's lurch into fascism. Neither Britain nor France chose to uphold the treaty's clauses – not when Hitler remilitarized the Rhineland in March 1936, nor when he annexed Austria two years later. The newsreels showing jubilant crowds welcoming the German army into these areas effectively blunted claims that Hitler's actions lacked the popular support of the very groups they affected.

Hitler's efforts to annex the Sudetenland – the German-speaking region of Czechoslovakia – was far more contentious. Unlike London, Paris had an agreement with Prague to defend the territorial integrity of Czechoslovakia. Although the Sudetenland's German-speaking majority appeared to welcome German annexation, permitting the redrawing of the boundary would effectively make the remaining Czechoslovak state strategically vulnerable should Hitler threaten it at a later date.

Neville Chamberlain (1869–1940), who had been prime minister since May 1937, was determined to take the diplomatic lead in order to permit the transferral

We, the German Führer and Chancellor and the
British Prime Minister, have had a further
meeting today and are agreed in recognising that
the question of Anglo-German relations is of the
first importance for the two countries and for
Europe.

We regard the agreement signed last night
and the Anglo-German Naval Agreement as symbolic
of the desire of our two peoples never to go to
war with one another again.

We are resolved that the method of
consultation shall be the method adopted to deal
with any other questions that may concern our two
countries, and we are determined to continue our
efforts to remove possible sources of difference
and thus to contribute to assure the peace of
Europe.

Neville Chamberlain

September 30. 1938.

of the Sudetenland to Germany in an orderly and peaceful manner that did not provoke Franco-German, and possibly European-wide, war. He flew to Germany to negotiate directly with Hitler, whose stated intention was to invade the Sudetenland regardless of the consequences. Chamberlain thought his efforts had failed, until, on 28 September 1938 – with Hitler's troops poised to cross the Czech border – he was summoned to a conference the following day at Munich. There, he met Hitler, the French prime minister Edouard Daladier, and the Italian fascist leader Benito Mussolini. Together, they agreed that Germany could annex the Sudetenland without fear of retaliation. Deserted by her allies (and not even invited to the conference), the Czechs were forced to acquiesce in the carve-up of their country.

Believing world war had been averted, Chamberlain returned to Britain on 30 September and received a hero's welcome. He believed his great personal achievement during the negotiations had been to come back with a piece of paper (which he held up to the cheering crowds at Heston aerodrome) that he had persuaded Hitler to sign. In this note, the German Führer and the British prime minister renounced war and determined to resolve their future differences purely through diplomacy.

OPPOSITE: The Munich 'piece of paper,' signed by Adolf Hitler and Neville Chamberlain, pledging the peaceful resolution of Anglo-German disputes.

This proved to be the zenith of Britain's appeasement policy. Six months later, and without warning, Hitler invaded the rump Czechoslovakian state that Chamberlain's diplomacy had helped render virtually defenceless. Scrambling to limit further Nazi expansion in Central and Eastern Europe, Britain rushed to offer Poland a guarantee of military support in the event of German invasion. On 3 September 1939, this

'Here is the paper which bears his name upon it as well as mine' – Neville Chamberlain tells the crowds greeting him at Heston aerodrome that Hitler has given him his word at Munich. On the far left of the picture, a tall man is observing intensely. He is the foreign secretary, Lord Halifax.

COUNTDOWN TO WAR: 1939

14 March At Hitler's prompting, Slovakia's provincial assembly declares independence from Czechoslovakia.

15 March Germany invades the remaining rump of the Czech state.

22 March Germany annexes Memel from Lithuania.

28 March–1 April The Spanish Civil War ends in victory for Franco's German- and Italian-backed Nationalists.

31 March Britain announces it will guarantee Poland's sovereignty against attack.

7 April Italy invades Albania.

22 May Germany and Italy agree a 'Pact of Steel'.

24 May The Cabinet agrees to explore terms for a military pact with the Soviet Union.

23 August The Molotov–Ribbentrop non-aggression pact is signed between Germany and the Soviet Union.

24 August Parliament is recalled. The Emergency Powers Act is rushed through.

25 August The British guarantee regarding Poland's security is given legal status.

31 August The Royal Navy is mobilized. The evacuation of children from London begins.

1 September Germany invades Poland.

3 September At 9 a.m. Britain sends Germany a two-hour ultimatum to begin withdrawing from Poland. When no undertaking is received, at 11 a.m. Britain declares war on Germany. At 11.15 a.m. Neville Chamberlain broadcasts to the nation, announcing that it is at war. At 5 p.m. France declares war on Germany.

agreement brought Britain (joined by France) into all-out war with Germany for the second time in twenty-one years.

Chamberlain's agreement at Munich came to be seen as a betrayal of the democratic Czechoslovakian state in a desperate – and ultimately futile – effort by Britain to save herself from war. Indeed, appeasing Hitler at Munich only appeared to give the Führer the wrong impression that he could continue with the forcible annexation of his neighbours with impunity. These 'lessons of Munich' influenced post-war British and American foreign policy, encouraging a more bellicose attitude towards dictatorial regimes, with varying levels of success, including against the Soviet Union in the Cold War, Egypt's President Nasser in the 1956 Suez Crisis and Iraq's Saddam Hussein over his invasion of Kuwait in 1990.

A rival interpretation of Chamberlain's actions at Munich eventually developed in which some historians argued that appeasement saved Britain from fighting a war in 1938 for which she was militarily ill-prepared. This was true, although it also bought Germany eleven months in which to further her own rearmament programme as well. For instance, the Munich agreement delivered into the hands of Hitler's Reich the Skoda armaments factory in the Sudetenland, whose output between October 1938 and September 1939 was almost equal to all British armaments factories put together.

Nevertheless, Chamberlain's aim at Munich was to prevent, rather than defer, war. As his adviser Horace Wilson admitted in 1962: 'Our policy was never designed just to postpone war, or enable us to enter war more united. The aim of appeasement was to avoid war altogether, for all time.' Chamberlain had said as much when he greeted the crowds on his return from Munich with his famously ill-fated comment that he hoped he had brought home 'peace for our time'.

1942
THE BEVERIDGE REPORT

BLUEPRINT FOR THE WELFARE STATE

In December 1942, in the midst of the Second World War, a government white paper became a best-seller. This was Sir William Beveridge's official report, *Social Insurance and Allied Services*, and 635,000 copies of it were snapped up by a British public intrigued and excited by its promise to provide 'freedom from want by securing to each a minimum income sufficient for subsistence.'

It was not just socialists and romantic William Blake-quoting idealists who saw Beveridge as the architect for the New Jerusalem that would rise from the rubble and sub-standard housing of capitalist war-torn Britain. For all sorts of people, his report's proposals became an additional reason for Britain to be fighting, along with self-survival and the defeat of Nazism. Soon after its release, an opinion poll conducted by the British Institute of Public Opinion (BIPO) suggested 86 per cent of respondents supported the report, while only 6 per cent opposed its findings. After the mass unemployment and means tests of the inter-war years, it offered a better tomorrow.

The report identified 'five giants' that needed taming – want, disease, ignorance, squalor and idleness. In the assault on these social ills, the central strategy was to replace the existing varying and non-comprehensive insurance schemes with a standard level of benefit. Beveridge based that level on the assumption of an average household, in which a husband was the breadwinner for a wife and a child. He wanted national insurance to be universal, unlike the scheme established in 1911, which covered only manual workers and those on low incomes. He felt, too, that the scope of old-age pensions should be widened. In place of the remnants of the old Poor Law, taxpayers' money was to be funnelled to the needy and destitute through National Assistance. The taxpayer should also provide a supplementary benefit to families with two or more infants in the form of Child Allowances.

From *Social Insurance and Allied Services,* 1942

In proceeding from this first comprehensive survey of social insurance to the next task – of making recommendations – three guiding principles may be laid down at the outset.

The first principle is that any proposals for the future, while they should use to the full the experience gathered in the past, should not be restricted by consideration of sectional interests established in the obtaining of that experience. Now, when the war is abolishing landmarks of every kind, is the opportunity for using experience in a clear field. A revolutionary moment in the world's history is a time for revolutions, not for patching.

The second principle is that organisation of social insurance should be treated as one part only of a comprehensive policy of social progress. Social insurance fully developed may provide income security; it is an attack upon Want. But Want is one only of five giants on the road of reconstruction and in some ways the easiest to attack. The others are Disease, Ignorance, Squalor and Idleness.

The third principle is that social security must be achieved by co-operation between the State and the individual. The State should offer security for service and contribution. The State in organising security should not stifle incentive, opportunity, responsibility; in establishing a national minimum, it should leave room and encouragement for voluntary action by each individual to provide more than that minimum for himself and his family.

The Plan for Social Security set out in this Report is built upon these principles. It uses experience but is not tied by experience. It is put forward as a limited contribution to a wider social policy, though as something that could be achieved now without waiting for the whole of that policy. It is, first and foremost, a plan of insurance – of giving in return for contributions benefits up to subsistence level, as of right and without means test, so that individuals may build freely upon it.

Some saw the Beveridge Report as merely the completion of a legislative process that had its foundations laid by David Lloyd George, the chancellor of the exchequer in the Liberal government before the First World War, and extended by Winston Churchill and Neville Chamberlain as chancellor and minister of health respectively in the 1924–9 Conservative government. This was not how the report's author saw it. Beveridge made clear that 'My plan is not to develop social insurance:

it is a plan to give freedom from Want by securing to each citizen at all times . . . a minimum income sufficient for his subsistence needs and his responsibilities.' Moreover, his proposals went hand in hand with two important assumptions. The first was that future governments would be able to sustain full, or nearly full, employment in contrast to the high levels of unemployment of the Depression years. The second was that a National Health Service would be established. The report advocated the adoption of both these measures without providing a detailed plan for how they might be made to work.

Ironically, despite a life in social inquiry, it was with reluctance that Sir William Beveridge (1879–1963) accepted the Ministry of Health's request to chair the committee looking into social insurance. As a youthful civil servant in 1908 he had assisted Churchill at the Board of Trade in setting up labour exchanges before becoming director of the London School of Economics from 1919 to 1937 and thereafter Master of University College, Oxford. He wanted to spend the war assisting Ernest Bevin in planning manpower resources at the Ministry of Labour. However, Bevin could not abide Beveridge's conceited attitude and helped ensure his move to social insurance.

Churchill's coalition government accepted the Beveridge Report in principle, while making clear its implementation was a matter for a future, post-war administration. Had the Conservatives won the 1945 general election, much of it would have still been implemented. It was Churchill's Tory 'caretaker' Cabinet in 1945 that introduced the Child Allowance scheme and Beveridge had put on record his opinion that a future Conservative government provided the best chance of his proposals being properly adopted. On the whole, the electorate declined to agree, interpreting some Tories' qualifying statements as a portent that grim post-war economic reality would be cited as the reason for watering down the promised welfare state. After all, something similar had befallen Lloyd George's domestic pledges at the end of the First World War.

The Labour Party, by contrast, was clearly wholeheartedly behind the report and could be trusted not to flinch in the face of financial hardship. This commitment was certainly a factor in Labour's 1945 election triumph, even though creating full employment and nationalizing industries had pride of place in the party's manifesto. Among the casualties of the landslide victory was Beveridge himself, whose fleeting career as a Liberal MP ended in rejection by the voters of Berwick-upon-Tweed. Nonetheless, the influence of this father of the post-war welfare state would outstrip that of all but a few of the politicians elected then, or in subsequent parliaments.

1945
LONDON COUNTY COUNCIL MAP OF LONDON WAR DAMAGE

THE WAR AT HOME AND THE DESTRUCTION AND REBUILDING OF LONDON

One of London County Council's bomb damage maps is depicted in the fourth plate section.

The Second World War was a 'People's War', in which millions of civilians undertook war work. Britain's survival as a free nation was sustained on the farms and down the mines as well as in the munitions factories and on the front line. Merchant ships, bringing in essential resources, ran the same risks of being torpedoed as the Royal Navy. This was 'total war' and nothing better demonstrated the blurring of its distinction between combatants and non-combatants than the bombing of towns and cities.

During the war more than 60,000 British civilians were killed by aerial bombardment while over 2 million homes were destroyed or seriously damaged. In order to cripple the British war effort, the German Luftwaffe targeted cities like Coventry and Birmingham, where military material was rolling off the production lines, as well as ports and shipbuilding centres like Belfast, Clydeside, Portsmouth and Plymouth. The RAF retaliated, beginning what became the ultimately devastating 'strategic' bombing of Germany. Following an RAF attack on the ancient Baltic port city of Lübeck, the Luftwaffe launched attacks on historic British cities such as Bath, Exeter and Canterbury – whose importance was not military but cultural – in what became known as the 'Baedeker Raids' after the famous travel guides. In June 1944, with its diminished air force pulled back to defend its threatened European empire, Germany began launching what it described as its 'vengeance' weapons: V-1 and V-2 missiles targeted at the civilian population where it was most densely concentrated.

The missiles' main target was London, the city that had also borne the brunt of the German assault on Britain in the 'Blitz' of 1940 and 1941. The battering that the capital received, as well as its citizens' determination to carry on, revealed a defining aspect of the British character, which was summed up as the 'Spirit of the Blitz'. Military planners had incorrectly assumed that the war would start with the saturation bombing of London and other major cities, promoting the mass evacuation of children during September 1939. In reality the attacks over the capital did not begin until the following September, in the closing weeks of the Battle of Britain. They intensified at the end of October 1940 when the Luftwaffe concentrated night-time bombing, pummelling London for seventy-six consecutive nights. Through 1941, the raids became more intermittent but no less severe.

The London Blitz (from the German word *Blitzkrieg*, or 'lightning war') represented a switch in strategy by the Luftwaffe whose original aim had been to knock out the airfields and aircraft of the RAF to ensure German air superiority for a full-scale invasion. It was the RAF's victory in the Battle of Britain, together with the ongoing threat posed by the Royal Navy to a Channel crossing, that forced Hitler to postpone his invasion plans indefinitely. Germany now concentrated instead on trying to obliterate London's docks and intimidate its citizens and politicians into suing for peace. The Luftwaffe dropped high-explosive bombs, which were intended to blast out buildings, as well as incendiary bombs, which were designed to spread fires. The worst attacks were the massive incendiary raids of 29/30 December 1940 and 10/11 May 1941, which, besides causing widespread damage, destroyed many of London's architectural jewels, including Baroque churches in the City and the chamber of the House of Commons. The attacks thereafter subsided while Hitler's attention switched to the invasion of the Soviet Union, on 22 June 1941, until recommencing shortly after D-Day in 1944, with the advent of the missile strikes.

It was in January 1941, while London was still burning, that plans were first devised for post-war reconstruction. To prepare for this, staff of the London County Council's Architect's Department were engaged to plot the damaged areas on 110 ordnance survey maps covering the 117 square miles under the LCC's authority. They continued their work until the last V-2 ballistic missile fell on 27 March 1945, a mere six weeks before Germany's unconditional surrender.

During the course of the war, over 1 million London houses were hit. The highest density of bombs fell in Stepney, the City of London and Holborn, all of which

THE WAR AT HOME

Civilians killed in Britain	
1939–1940	23,767
1941	19,918
1942	3,236
1943	2,372
1944	8,475
1945	1,860
Total civilian deaths in Northern Ireland	967
United Kingdom total	60,595

were struck by more than 600 bombs per 1,000 acres. The LCC maps provide an extraordinarily detailed picture of the extent and concentration of war damage on the capital. The only omissions were a few especially prominent buildings, including railway stations and the Palace of Westminster. Otherwise, the fate of virtually every property – from the giant warehouse to the fine townhouse to the meanest rented apartment – was recorded. Circles marked where the V-1 and V-2 missiles landed. Buildings painted black represented those totally destroyed, and the colour code ranged through the other varying degrees of damage inflicted. Light-blue colouring (which the passage of time has turned greenish-blue) designated areas where the whole area was marked for total clearance and redevelopment.

Although the human cost appalled all, modern architects viewed with excitement the opportunities for redevelopment on so vast a scale, giving them their chance to put right what they saw as London's generations of ill-planned growth. In July 1943, the LCC's architect and chief planner, J. H. Forshaw, and Professor Patrick Abercrombie published the County of London Plan, which went through various changes. There was ambitious talk of creating a modern, integrated city. Comparisons were drawn with Sir Christopher Wren's (unexecuted) plan for rebuilding London after its last great devastating fire, in 1666.

The Wren analogy flattered the talents of those who recast post-war London. While the loss of many pre-war slums was hardly to be regretted on either aesthetic or sanitary grounds, the quality of what replaced them only rarely set spirits soaring. The crude office blocks that rose around St Paul's Cathedral were a particularly offensive insult to their setting. Indeed, it was perhaps fortunate that the more sweeping aspects of the London Plan were never put into practice. Aside from the Royal Festival Hall and a few other modern masterpieces, it was a sorry indictment that, over half a century later, most Britons were thankful not for the new buildings that replaced old favourites, but rather for the instances in which badly damaged buildings were repaired and, in many places, successfully restored.

St Paul's Cathedral survived the destruction of the Blitz and also outlived the post-war modernist blocks that were built on the bomb sites around it.

349

1945
BRIEF ENCOUNTER,
FILM SCRIPT

NOËL COWARD, DAVID LEAN
AND BRITAIN'S STIFF UPPER LIP

*OPPOSITE: A page
from the original* Brief
Encounter *film script:
Laura fears love's
consequences.*

ew dramatists better expressed aspects of the British character than Noël
Coward. His many artistic gifts embraced playwriting, acting, theatre
direction, and the composition of songs that are now synonymous with
their period.

Coward's louche persona – redolent of cocktails, cigarette holders and the
wearing of silk dressing-gowns – was among his most successful creations. He
had actually been born, in 1899, in suburban Teddington into the struggling
lower middle class. His father, a failed piano salesman, was driven to drink, but
his mother harboured social ambitions for something better. Her son's formal
schooling ended when he was nine, at which point his career as a child actor
began. From then on, his extraordinary ascent was driven by hard work and
voracious reading.

He was only twenty-four when he made his name with his first stage hit, *The
Vortex*. The drama, involving a drug-taking son and his nymphomaniac mother,
was considered by some to be unseemly. Only slightly less bohemian was the plot
of *Private Lives* (1930), which revolves around Amanda and Elyot, a once-married
couple, who find themselves in neighbouring honeymoon suites with their new
partners.

Coward, however, was at root no political revolutionary. His ambitious
1931 play, *Cavalcade*, celebrated Britain's recent imperial history. In 1933 his
review *Words and Music* included his composition 'Mad Dogs and Englishmen',
which simultaneously sent up and exalted the colonialists who shouldered
Rudyard Kipling's 'white man's burden'. This combination of gentle mockery
and affection towards its target was evident in Coward's comic lines and lyrics,

53.

                    DISSOLVE to a shot of the car pulling
                    up near a small bridge over a stream.

LAURA'S VOICE:
          When we were out in the real country - I think it
          was a few miles beyond Brayfield - we stopped the
          car just outside a village and got out. There was
          a little bridge and a stream and the sun was making
          an effort to come out but really not succeeding
          very well. We leaned on the parapet of the bridge
          and looked down into the water. I shivered and
          Alec put his arm around me.

ALEC: Cold ?

LAURA: No - not really.

ALEC: Happy?

LAURA: No - not really.

ALEC: I know what you're going to say - that it isn't
          worth it - that the furtiveness and the necessary
          lying outweigh the happiness we might have together
          - wasn't that it ?

LAURA: Yes, something like that.

ALEC: I want to ask you something - just to reassure
          myself.

LAURA: (her eyes filling with tears) What is it ?

ALEC: It is true for you isn't it? This overwhelming
          feeling that we have for each other - it is as true
          for you as it is for me - isn't it ?

LAURA: Yes - it's true.

                    She bursts into tears and Alec puts his
                    arms closer around her. They stand in
                    silence for a moment and then kiss each
                    other passionately.

                    DISSOLVE to a long shot of Alec and Laura
                    still standing on the bridge.

LAURA'S VOICE:
          I don't remember how long we stayed on that bridge
          or what we said. I only remember feeling that I
          was on the edge of a precipice, terrified yet want-
          ing desperately to throw myself over.

a distinctively British form of satire that would later be exemplified by the 1960s double act of Michael Flanders and Donald Swann.

With the outbreak of war, Coward was keen to play his part in stiffening morale, entertaining troops in Burma and the Middle East, and writing the great patriotic song of the Blitz, 'London Pride'. He also starred in a film celebrating the heroism of the Royal Navy, *In Which We Serve*, his first collaboration with the film director David Lean (1908–91). Lean, who went on to direct some of the greatest epics of British cinema, including *Lawrence of Arabia* and *The Bridge On the River Kwai*, also directed film versions of Coward's plays *This Happy Breed*, *Blithe Spirit* and, most memorably of all, *Brief Encounter*.

Brief Encounter's first incarnation was as *Still Life*, one of ten, single-act plays performed in Coward's 1936 dramatic cycle *To-Night at 8.30*. The film version starred Trevor Howard as Alec, a GP, and Celia Johnson as Laura, a conventional, middle-class housewife and mother of twins who is married to a well-meaning but passionless husband. After a chance meeting on a railway platform, they find themselves edging towards an affair. It is a tale of the conflict between surrendering to personal desire and staying true to an ethos of self-denial, honouring social mores and family responsibilities. Ultimately, the latter triumphs and the doomed lovers part. The fact that it was originally staged shortly before Edward VIII did the opposite, abdicating his royal duties for 'the woman I love', gave it an unintended topical piquancy. The film version was released in 1945, at a time when the disruptions of the Second World War had provided plenty of opportunity for extramarital affairs.

Coward juxtaposed the tragic dilemma of his repressed, provincial leads with the uncomplicated, guiltless fun enjoyed by the working-class characters played by Stanley Holloway and Joyce Carey. In this, there were echoes of E. M. Forster's critique of emotionally stultifying suburban values in his Edwardian novels *A Room with a View* and *Howard's End*. Unlike Forster, with his liberal message of emancipation, Coward – whose politics were Conservative despite his off-screen homosexuality – was more sympathetic to bourgeois ethics, appreciating the nobility involved in renunciation.

Brief Encounter was an immediate hit, critically and commercially, at a time when British cinema was at the summit of its popularity. It proved to be the last of Coward's successes for some time. Although they enjoyed frequent revivals from the later 1960s onwards, his carefully crafted dramas were deemed stylized and old-fashioned by the new generation of 'kitchen sink' playwrights of the 1950s and

early 1960s, many of whom saw the theatre as a place for revealing social reality and a platform for agitating for change. On a different plane, his sophisticated comedies were far removed from the saucy innuendos of the *Carry On* films. Similarly, *Brief Encounter*'s tragic lovers, turning away from personal gratification, seemed hopelessly dated to the 1960s generation of social and sexual liberation. That, however, did not make the national characteristics that Coward depicted any less meaningful, potent or real.

Celia Johnson and Trevor Howard wrestle with their emotions in Brief Encounter.

1948

THE BRITISH NATIONALITY ACT

OPENING THE DOOR TO MASS IMMIGRATION
FROM THE COMMONWEALTH

The 1948 British Nationality Act transformed the racial make-up of Britain. At the time that the legislation passed into law, non-white faces were a rare sight in all but a few parts of the country. Even the immigrant communities, new or old, were overwhelmingly European. By holding wide open Britain's door of entry to anyone born anywhere within the borders of her empire and Commonwealth, the 1948 Act forever changed the national composition and set the United Kingdom on a path towards a multiracial, multicultural future.

It may have seemed counter-intuitive for Clement Attlee's government to make so affirmative an expression of faith in the unity of empire only months after India and Pakistan had been granted independence from it. The loss of the 'jewel in the crown' was indeed the beginning of a process of decolonization that would be completed in 1997 with the handover of Hong Kong to China. Nonetheless, in the post-war years there was widespread faith in the future of the British Commonwealth (of which India and Pakistan became members). This was not just a reflexive scramble for a face-saving idea to conceal the reality of a world power in decline. The many peoples of the empire, of all faiths and colours, who had volunteered to fight in the common cause between 1939 and 1945 demanded a retrospective expression of gratitude from – depending on their political viewpoint – their mother country or colonial master.

POST-WAR IMMIGRATION

Year	Total foreign-born population of the UK (in millions)	% of total UK population
1951	2.1	4.2
1961	2.5	4.9
1971	3.2	5.8
1981	3.4	6.2
1991	3.8	6.7
2001	4.9	8.3
2008	6.5	10.7

From the British Nationality Act, 1948

1.—(1) Every person who under this Act is a citizen of the United Kingdom and Colonies or who under any enactment for the time being in force in any country mentioned in subsection (3) of this section is a citizen of that country shall by virtue of that citizenship have the status of a British subject.

(2) Any person having the status aforesaid may be known either as a British subject or as a Commonwealth citizen; and accordingly in this Act and in any other enactment or instrument whatever, whether passed or made before or after the commencement of this Act, the expression "British subject" and the expression "Commonwealth citizen" shall have the same meaning.

(3) The following are the countries hereinbefore referred to, that is to say, Canada, Australia, New Zealand, the Union of South Africa, Newfoundland, India, Pakistan, Southern Rhodesia and Ceylon.

Directly prompted by changes in Canada's citizenship laws, the 1948 Act primarily had in mind the right of entry of those of British descent from the 'white dominions' of Canada, South Africa, Australia and New Zealand. Strictly speaking, it reaffirmed an old policy dating from the start of a previous call to imperial arms. The 1914 British Nationality and Status of Aliens Act gave British citizenship to 'any person born within His Majesty's dominions and allegiances'. As a result, 400 million subjects of the British Empire had effectively been granted the right to settle on a small island off the European continent, but very few of them had done so. Opportunities for migrants usually appeared better for those going to the 'white dominions' than to Britain and the cost of long-distance travel was beyond the means of most Indians, Africans or inhabitants of the Caribbean. Although the history of black settlers in Britain went back at least to the sixteenth century (when Queen Elizabeth I complained there were too many of them) and they had long formed strong communities in port cities like Liverpool and Cardiff by the 1930s, the non-white population of Britain numbered only a few thousand.

The 1948 British Nationality Act came at a time when the cost of travel was falling. The result was immigration from the 'New Commonwealth' (essentially,

The Empire Windrush's passenger list, 21 June 1948.

the Indian subcontinent, Africa and the West Indies) on a scale that the framers of the legislation had never imagined. The influx began when an old troopship, the *Empire Windrush*, docked at Tilbury on 22 June 1948 with 492 migrants travelling from Jamaica. Immigrants from the Caribbean had traditionally gone to the United States, but in 1952 the US government restricted their entry. Britain became their destination instead. Census returns pointed to a rise in Britain's 'coloured' population from 74,500 in 1951 to 336,000 in 1961. Of these, by far the largest proportion (171,800) had come from the West Indies, while 81,400 were from India, 24,900 from Pakistan and 19,800 from West Africa.

The immigrants' contribution became particularly evident in the transport sector and the health service. Subsequent generations, particularly of Asian descent, brought an entrepreneurial spirit and entered the professions. Yet the argument raged over whether many of them were doing important, otherwise unfillable, jobs or were changing the nature of the country in a way that left many native-born Britons uncomfortable. During the 1950s, successive Conservative administrations considered plans to reduce the inflow but did not implement them, in part because of a reluctance to be seen to discriminate between black migrants from the New Commonwealth and those of British descent from the 'white dominions', whom they still regarded as 'kith and kin'.

The first restrictions came with the 1962 Commonwealth Immigrants Act, which stemmed the flow by insisting on the possession of employment vouchers. Having opposed restrictions while in opposition, Harold Wilson's Labour government after 1964 tightly controlled the number of vouchers available. However, the government tried to make life more tolerable for those who had already arrived by passing the 1965 Race Relations Act, which made racial discrimination illegal.

The first wave of arrivals were overwhelmingly young males, mostly unskilled or semi-skilled, coming in search of work. Many repatriated some of their earnings back home. Over time, their families came out to join them in Britain, a major factor in the rate of entry remaining above 50,000 a year after the 1962 Act. Faced with an influx from East Africa, in 1968 legislation finally discriminated against those who had not been born in Britain or, failing that, had a parent or grandparent born there.

The heated debate focused on only one aspect of migration policy. In fact, net emigration from Britain exceeded net immigration every year from 1946 to 1979. This was overwhelmingly the result of Britons starting new lives in the sun rather than recent arrivals returning back to the warmer climes they had left behind. Southern Rhodesia (modern Zimbabwe) was a popular destination in the 1950s; during the 1960s, British emigration to Australia and New Zealand ran at between 80,000 and 100,000 a year.

Another aspect of policy that caused a significant migration shift within the British Isles concerned the favourable status accorded the Southern Irish. In 1947, Ireland announced that it was formally becoming a republic and leaving the Commonwealth. Rather than draw the perhaps natural conclusion that the link with Dublin was severed, the 1948 British Nationality Act guaranteed Irish citizens the rights to reside and to vote in Britain. Many took up the offer. In this way, non-members of the Commonwealth ended up enjoying easier entry than Commonwealth members. This process was completed when Britain became part of the free movement of peoples within the European Community.

357

1949
THE NORTH ATLANTIC TREATY

BRITAIN'S ROLE IN THE COLD WAR

The North Atlantic Treaty was one of the most significant achievements of the post-war Labour government. Through it, the North Atlantic Treaty Organization (NATO) became the cornerstone of British foreign policy for the rest of the century, perpetuating the wartime 'special relationship' between Washington and London, and securing Britain's role as deputy leader of the 'Free World'.

It nonetheless involved the sort of commitment that, after the defeat of Germany in 1945, both Britain and America had hoped to avoid. A year after VE-Day, the number of American troops stationed in Europe had fallen from over 3 million to under 400,000, British troops from 1.3 million to 488,000, and the Canadians from 300,000 to none. In contrast, the Soviet forces remained close to full strength and on a war footing. Despite signing the 1947 Treaty of Dunkirk, an Anglo-French defence pact, Britain's main plan in the event of a Soviet attack on Western Europe was to re-enact the 1940 Dunkirk evacuation and scurry her continental forces back across the English Channel for home defence. In May 1948 the order changed to command them to stand and fight on European soil. It was not until 1950 that the minor comfort of reinforcements was promised in the event of British troops being forced to make a suicidal last stand against the massed divisions of Comrade Stalin. Only the threat of launching an American nuclear strike told in the Western allies' favour.

Even before the Second World War was over, Winston Churchill had begun to fear future Soviet intentions. American public and political opinion was slower to reach the same conclusion but, when it did, it manifested itself forcibly. In March 1947, President Harry Truman addressed Congress on the need to contain the further spread of communism. This 'Truman doctrine' was echoed the following January by Clement Attlee, who warned the British people in a broadcast that 'Soviet Communism pursues a policy of imperialism in a new form – ideological,

The British foreign secretary, Ernest Bevin, signs the North Atlantic Treaty in Washington, DC on 4 April 1949.

economic, and strategic – which threatens the welfare and way of life of the other nations of Europe.'

During 1948, 'Marshall Aid' began, pouring American development money into the shattered economies of Britain and Western Europe in the hope of getting them back on their feet and bolstering resistance to the lure of communism. The Soviet Union refused to allow the Eastern European countries that it occupied to join the scheme. Two Moscow-backed moves further confirmed Western suspicions. In February 1948, communists seized power in Czechoslovakia. Four months later, Soviet forces blockaded the Allied sectors of Berlin. Rather than capitulate, the British and Americans responded by a daring airlift of vital supplies into the city and, after eleven months, the siege was lifted. Impressed, German citizens noted that British and American airmen who had previously helped destroy their city now risked their lives to save it. Ignoring Soviet objections, the Western powers began the process of creating West Germany as a free and independent state.

Britain's foreign secretary was Ernest Bevin (1881–1951), a former general secretary of the Transport and General Workers Union, wartime minister of labour and passionate anti-communist. With Germany disarmed and France's martial traditions needing refounding, Bevin recognized both that Britain was the only European military power of consequence and that she could not hold the continent alone. While he negotiated the Brussels Treaty, a defence pact between Britain, France and the Low Countries in March 1948, his greater aim was to draw this grouping into a wider transtlantic alliance. The result was a ceremony in Washington, DC, in April 1949 in which Bevin joined the representatives of the United States, Canada, France, Italy, Belgium, the Netherlands, Luxembourg, Denmark, Iceland, Norway and Portugal in signing the North Atlantic Treaty. Its core principle was that each signatory state considered a military attack on any one of them to be an attack on all of them. This was the ultimate embodiment of collective security.

During the negotiations, Bevin successfully quashed an American proposal of a presidential guarantee to defend Western Europe rather than a formal alliance. As Bevin well understood, a guarantee was much easier for future presidents, perhaps with hostile Congresses, to water down. Furthermore, in the coming age of nuclear strikes, Britain could hardly hold the line long enough to allow the United States to begin mobilizing troops to send across the Atlantic. What was needed was the forces of a permanent, continent-based alliance and this is what Bevin got.

Even so, the wording of Article 5 still left latitude over whether the response to an attack on one member had to be military rather than merely diplomatic or economic. It was only in 1950, with the Western allies fighting together under UN auspices to repel the communist invasion of South Korea, that the North Atlantic Treaty was transformed from essentially a mutual defence pact into a military organization with an integrated command structure. Its standing body was led by the United States, with General Eisenhower as supreme commander and Britain's Lord Ismay as secretary-general. This replicated the relative importance of the two countries. Britain, as co-instigator and (from 1952) with its own nuclear deterrent, remained the second most important power within NATO even after it had expanded to include Greece and Turkey in 1951, West Germany in 1955, Spain in 1985 and then, with the end of the Cold War, Eastern Europe as well. Beyond its nuclear capacity, the heart of Britain's

From the North Atlantic Treaty, 1949

Article 5: The Parties agree that an armed attack against one or more of them in Europe or North America shall be considered an attack against them all and consequently they agree that, if such an armed attack occurs, each of them, in exercise of the right of individual or collective self-defence recognised by Article 51 of the Charter of the United Nations, will assist the Party or Parties so attacked by taking forthwith, individually and in concert with the other Parties, such action as it deems necessary, including the use of armed force, to restore and maintain the security of the North Atlantic area.

> Any such armed attack and all measures taken as a result thereof shall immediately be reported to the Security Council. Such measures shall be terminated when the Security Council has taken the measures necessary to restore and maintain international peace and security.

Article 6 (1): For the purpose of Article 5, an armed attack on one or more of the Parties is deemed to include an armed attack:

> on the territory of any of the Parties in Europe or North America, on the Algerian Departments of France,[*] on the territory of or on the Islands under the jurisdiction of any of the Parties in the North Atlantic area north of the Tropic of Cancer;

> on the forces, vessels, or aircraft of any of the Parties, when in or over these territories or any other area in Europe in which occupation forces of any of the Parties were stationed on the date when the Treaty entered into force or the Mediterranean Sea or the North Atlantic area north of the Tropic of Cancer.

[* this clause ceased to be applicable after Algeria's independence in 1962.]

NATO contribution was the British Army of the Rhine (BAOR), stationed on the German front line, and the Royal Navy patrolling the North Sea, which from the 1960s could deploy Polaris submarine-launched nuclear missiles. Like France, Britain's position in NATO was supplemented by its permanent seat on the UN Security Council; unlike France, it did not opt out of NATO's integrated command structure (which President Charles de Gaulle regarded as incompatible with French sovereignty).

BRITISH SPENDING ON DEFENCE

Year	Defence budget (£bn)	Budget as % of GDP
1955/56	£1.4	7.1 %
1960/61	£1.6	6.1 %
1965/66	£2.1	5.6 %
1970/71	£2.5	4.7 %
1975/76	£5.3	4.8 %
1980/81	£11.2	4.7 %
1985/86	£17.9	4.9 %
1990/91	£22.3	3.9 %
1995/96	£21.5	2.9 %
2000/01	£23.6	2.4 %
2005/06	£30.6	2.4 %
2008/09	£36.4	2.5 %

The alliance's united stance appeared vindicated by communism's collapse and the disintegration of the Soviet Union between 1989 and 1991. In an extraordinary transformation from putative enmity to fraternity, Eastern European former members of the Warsaw Pact, when freed to pursue their own destiny, rushed to join NATO as a security against any future reassertion of Russian might. In the meantime, NATO sought new purpose as a policeman of what was optimistically termed the 'new world order' – involving itself, for instance, in trying to resolve the conflicts of the former Yugoslavia where a 60,000-strong NATO Implementation Force (IFOR) was dispatched in 1995.

When, three years later, NATO launched air strikes against Serbia in order to persuade President Slobodan Milošević to withdraw his forces from the disputed Serbian territory of Kosovo, where mounting ethnic violence threatened to create a humanitarian catastrophe, it demonstrated how much it had changed its purpose. The Kosovo campaign was the first time in NATO's history that it had attacked a sovereign country whose boundaries were recognized in international law. Despite the humanitarian intentions, the air strikes did not have direct UN sanction and exposed tensions within the alliance.

These tensions grew more significant after 2001 when the United States responded to the al-Qaeda outrages in New York and Washington, DC, by declaring a broad-ranging 'war on terror' and sought partners to assist with operations in Afghanistan and later Iraq. The British government responded fully, but other NATO countries displayed varying degrees of enthusiasm. Some commentators questioned whether the alliance's unity of purpose still existed in the absence of the Soviet threat to mainland Europe. Indeed, many felt that international terrorism and the consequences of 'failed states' around the world called for a thorough debate about NATO's future role. The more it adapted to the new challenges, the more manifest became the uncertainty over where the parameters for action were – or should be – set.

1950

THE EUROPEAN CONVENTION ON HUMAN RIGHTS

∽

HUMAN RIGHTS, FROM EUROPEAN CONVENTION TO BRITISH LAW

Jack Straw, the home secretary in Tony Blair's first administration, described the passage of the Human Rights Act in 1998 as the greatest constitutional change since Magna Carta. It incorporated the European Convention on Human Rights into British law. Even in the half-century between the Convention's adoption in 1950 and the Human Rights Act, the former had an effect on British legal developments. In the twenty-first century, it seemed destined to be ever more central to judicial deliberations.

The drafting of the European Convention on Human Rights was undertaken by a committee guided by a leading British politician and lawyer, Sir David Maxwell-Fyfe (1900–67). The son of an impecunious Scottish schoolmaster, Maxwell-Fyfe showed early ambition at George Watson's College in Edinburgh and at Oxford University. At the age of thirty-four he became the youngest King's Counsel (KC) for 250 years and the following year was elected as a Conservative MP in Liverpool. In Churchill's wartime coalition government he was solicitor-general and, in part owing to the work he had undertaken while in that office, he was appointed deputy chief prosecutor in the Nuremberg trial of Nazi leaders. There he succeeded – where others had failed – in cracking the courtroom self-confidence of the most important defendant, Hermann Goering.

The fact that Germany, one of the world's most cultured nations, could have succumbed to the moral degradation of the Third Reich provided a shocking example of what could happen when the rights of the individual were disregarded by an all-powerful totalitarian state answerable only to itself. To Maxwell-Fyfe and his fellow enthusiasts for European integration, it seemed essential that the post-war continent should be rebuilt with stronger legal protection for its citizens. In 1949,

From the European Convention on Human Rights, 1950

ARTICLE 1

The High Contracting Parties shall secure to everyone within their jurisdiction the rights and freedoms defined in Section I of this Convention.

SECTION I

ARTICLE 2

Everyone's right to life shall be protected by law. No one shall be deprived of his life intentionally save in the execution of a sentence of a court following his conviction of a crime for which this penalty is provided by law.

Deprivation of life shall not be regarded as inflicted in contravention of this article when it results from the use of force which is no more than absolutely necessary:

(a) in defence of any person from unlawful violence;

(b) in order to effect a lawful arrest or to prevent escape of a person lawfully detained;

(c) in action lawfully taken for the purpose of quelling a riot or insurrection. . . .

ARTICLE 3

No one shall be subjected to torture or to inhuman or degrading treatment or punishment.

ARTICLE 6

In the determination of his civil rights and obligations or of any criminal charge against him, everyone is entitled to a fair and public hearing within a reasonable time by an independent and impartial tribunal established by law. . . .

Everyone charged with a criminal offence shall be presumed innocent until proved guilty according to law. . . .

ARTICLE 7

No one shall be held guilty of any criminal offence on account of any act or omission which did not constitute a criminal offence under national or international law at the time when it was committed. Nor shall a heavier penalty be imposed than the one that was applicable at the time the criminal offence was committed.

This article shall not prejudice the trial and punishment of any person for any act or omission which, at the time when it was committed, was criminal according the general principles of law recognized by civilized nations.

ARTICLE 8

Everyone has the right to respect for his private and family life, his home and his correspondence.

There shall be no interference by a public authority with the exercise of this right except such as is in accordance with the law and is necessary in a democratic society in the interests of national security, public safety or the economic well-being of the country, for the prevention of disorder or crime, for the protection of health or morals, or for the protection of the rights and freedoms of others.

ARTICLE 9

Everyone has the right to freedom of thought, conscience and religion; this right includes freedom to change his religion or belief, and freedom, either alone or in community with others and in public or private, to manifest his religion or belief, in worship, teaching, practice and observance.

Freedom to manifest one's religion or beliefs shall be subject only to such limitations as are prescribed by law and are necessary in a democratic society in the interests of public safety, for the protection of public order, health or morals, or the protection of the rights and freedoms of others.

ARTICLE 10

Everyone has the right to freedom of expression. This right shall include freedom to hold opinions and to receive and impart information and ideas without interference by public authority and regardless of frontiers. This article shall not prevent States from requiring the licensing of broadcasting, television or cinema enterprises.

The exercise of these freedoms, since it carries with it duties and responsibilities, may be subject to such formalities, conditions, restrictions or penalties as are prescribed by law and are necessary in a democratic society, in the interests of national security, territorial integrity or public safety, for the prevention of disorder or crime, for the protection of health or morals, for the protection of the reputation or the rights of others, for preventing the disclosure of information received in confidence, or for maintaining the authority and impartiality of the judiciary.

ARTICLE 11

Everyone has the right to freedom of peaceful assembly and to freedom of association with others, including the right to form and to join trade unions for the protection of his interests.

No restrictions shall be placed on the exercise of these rights other than such as are prescribed by law and are necessary in a democratic society in the interests of national security or public safety, for the prevention of disorder or crime, for the protection of health or morals or for the protection of the rights and freedoms of others. This article shall not prevent the imposition of lawful restrictions on the exercise of these rights by members of the armed forces, of the police or of the administration of the State.

ARTICLE 12

Men and women of marriageable age have the right to marry and to found a family, according to the national laws governing the exercise of this right.

Britain joined France, Italy, Denmark, Sweden, Norway, Belgium, the Netherlands, Luxembourg and Ireland in signing the Treaty of London, which established the Council of Europe. While political and economic integration became the task of a separate entity, the EEC (later the EU) from 1957, the Council of Europe's main preoccupation was with upholding human rights upon principles laid out by a convention.

As Maxwell-Fyfe was chairman of the Council of Europe's legal and adminis-trative council and *rapporteur* on the drafting committee of the Convention on Human Rights, his considerable energies were brought to the fore. The convention was completed in 1950. However, signatories, including Britain, agreed to abide by it only as part of international treaty law, a legal framework of obligation between nations, rather than between state and citizen. There was initially no European court to hear cases individuals might bring. This changed in 1959 with the establishment of the European Court of Human Rights, with its own judges sitting in Strasbourg and adjudicating on cases brought to them by the citizens of member states. However, Harold Macmillan's government (in which Maxwell-Fyfe, as Lord Kilmuir, was lord chancellor) kept Britain out of this jurisdiction. It was Harold Wilson's Labour government of 1964–70 that gave Britons the belated right to challenge national judgments at Strasbourg. And following the 1998 Human Rights Act, the trek to Strasbourg became less necessary. Fully operational in 2000, the legislation forced all British courts to act in accordance with the Convention on Human Rights.

These changes were heralded as an advance for equal rights and personal liberty. However, critics of the Human Rights Act have argued that the European convention has ceased to be a basic bulwark against arbitrary rule and has instead become a tool of judicial activism. Certainly, it has led to judges interpreting the broadly phrased wording of the convention in ways that would have horrified Maxwell-Fyfe. For instance, as home secretary between 1951 and 1954, Maxwell-Fyfe supported the death penalty (notoriously refusing clemency in 1953 for Derek Bentley, an illiterate epileptic eighteen-year-old who was hanged for being party to the murder of a policeman) and vigorously opposed the decriminalizing of homosexuality. Yet in 2000 the European Court interpreted the convention's Article 8 ('Everyone has the right to respect for his private and family life') to include group participation in sadomasochist gay sex, effectively overruling the existing British law that had found those who did so guilty of 'gross indecency'.

Following the full implementation of the Human Rights Act, the convention's effects began to be ever more apparent in domestic legal judgments. There were, in particular, profound implications for where the balance was henceforth to be struck between press freedom and the privacy of the individual, and for how terrorist suspects should be treated. A small number of highly controversial judgments threatened to undermine popular support for the supremacy of the convention in British law. At the core was a debate over whether civil society remained workable if the ultimate legal document stressed human rights but not mutual responsibilities. Totalitarian regimes had shown the pitfalls of disregarding the rights of the individual. Maxwell-Fyfe's intentions were not only to prevent a return to Nazism but also to establish the convention as the first trip-wire against the future spread of communism. In 1950, this danger had seemed a real possibility. Yet after sixty years of peace and democracy, judicial interpretation has developed the convention from being an ennobling, if limited, declaration against serious abuses of power into becoming a forum in which even minor day-to-day decision-making by any public body can be legally challenged. The potential costs and restrictions that this imposes upon public bodies are considerable, the consequences for the principles upon which society has long organized itself, transformative.

IX

ELIZABETH II'S BRITAIN

IAN FLEMING'S MANUSCRIPT FOR *CASINO ROYALE*

CREATING THE BRITON WHO COULD SAVE THE WORLD

Ian Fleming was forty-three years old when he departed from Goldeneye, his Jamaican retreat, bound on his honeymoon. Accompanying him was Anne, his wife, and an attaché case containing the manuscript for his first James Bond novel, *Casino Royale*. Thirteen years later Fleming would be dead, but in that short span he published fourteen Bond adventures and bequeathed to the world the ultimate fictional British hero.

Over 100,000,000 Bond books have been sold. Less verifiably, it has been calculated that more than half the world's population has seen at least one Bond film. As for the character at the centre of it, he has sprung from the written page to evolve into a global cinema phenomenon, outgrowing the original canon of novels but continuing to visit glamorous locations and grapple with international villains and *femmes fatales*. Even today, 007 (Licence to Kill) remains the most famous embodiment of Her Majesty's secret service.

'Everything I write has a precedent in truth,' claimed James Bond's creator. Ian Fleming had been born in 1908 into a privileged background. His Scottish grandfather had founded Fleming's, a merchant bank. His father, an MP, was killed in the First World War when his son was aged only eight. Sent to Eton, Ian Fleming excelled at sport, but his progression to Sandhurst was cut short by illness and his realization that he did not wish to conform. Rejected by the Foreign Office, he worked first for the Reuters news agency (where he honed his ability to write the short, punchy sentences that were to mark his subsequent literary style) and then in stockbroking. It was the outbreak of war in 1939 that generated the experiences that would later inform his novels.

His mother wrote to Winston Churchill to advertise her son's untapped talent and following this and other approaches, Fleming was appointed assistant to

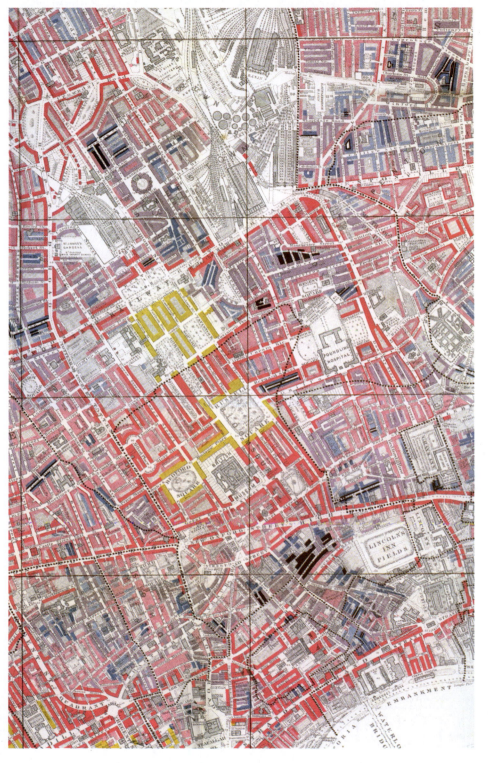

1898–9 – CHARLES
BOOTH'S
'POVERTY MAP'
OF LONDON

*Charles Booth's poverty
maps of central London
provided a colour-coded
guide to the varying
prosperity of late-
Victorian London. The
affluence of Bloomsbury
contrasted with the
abject poverty endured
only a few streets away
between Covent Garden
and Lincoln's Inn Fields.*

- *Lowest class. Vicious,
  semi-criminal.*

- *Very poor, casual.
  Chronic want.*

- *Poor. 18 to 21
  shillings a week for a
  moderate family.*

- *Mixed. Some
  comfortable, others
  poor.*

- *Fairly comfortable.
  Good ordinary
  earnings.*

- *Well-to-do. Middle
  class.*

- *Upper-middle
  and upper classes.
  Wealthy.*

OPPOSITE: 1945 – LONDON COUNTY COUNCIL MAP OF LONDON WAR DAMAGE

The London County Council's bomb damage maps graphically displayed the extent of both the Blitz and of subsequent rocket attacks on the capital, where one million houses were hit. While much of west London escaped with only sporadic damage, whole swathes of the City of London and the East End were erased – either during the war or in the redevelopment that followed it.

1914 – WAR RECRUITMENT POSTER

Alfred Leete's iconic poster of 1914, featuring Lord Kitchener and his appeal for 100,000 volunteers.

1927 – MAP OF THE BRITISH EMPIRE

Maps showing the extent of the British Empire were often to be found in school rooms and other public places as well as in private homes. This design was produced in 1927 by the Empire Marketing Board, a government-funded body founded the previous year to promote the purchase of goods from the Dominions and Colonies. The Board was wound up in 1933 following the introduction of tariffs against many non-Empire imports.

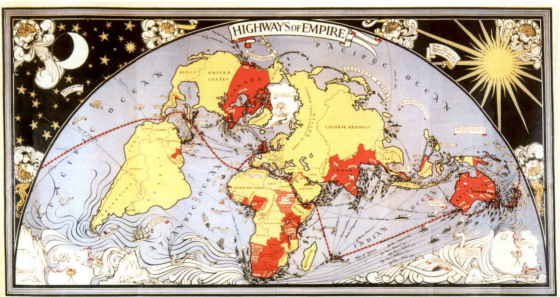

1967 – THE BEATLES' *SGT. PEPPER* ALBUM COVER

Peter Blake's album cover for The Beatles' Sgt. Pepper's Lonely Hearts Club Band is recognized as a defining image of Pop Art and an intriguing expression of the emerging cult of celebrity. EMI, the record company, worried about the cost of constructing the collage, though – with the copyright signed away – Blake made only about £200.

1997 AND AFTER – CONDOLENCE BOOKS AND POPULAR INSCRIPTIONS TO DIANA, PRINCESS OF WALES

Upon the death of Diana, Princess of Wales, condolence books were opened across the world to cater for an extraordinary outpouring of mass emotion. In Harrod's department store, in Knightsbridge, condolence books were still being signed on a daily basis in 2010, more than a decade after Diana's death. Dodi Fayed, the son of Mohamed Al-Fayed, who owned Harrod's until 2010, died alongside the princess.

Admiral John Godfrey, the director of naval intelligence. Commander Fleming found himself privy to vital secret operations. He was called upon to devise plans to capture enemy Enigma codebooks and helped organize 30 Assault Unit, a Commando unit charged with seizing important enemy materials before they could be destroyed. He lived life to the full, his work bringing him into contact with extraordinary men. Patrick Dalzel-Job and Wilfred 'Biffy' Dunderdale were among those who provided inspiration for the character of James Bond.

After the war, Fleming was employed as foreign manager of the *Sunday Times* and also wrote travel articles for the paper. In these roles, he dispatched correspondents to report on the emerging Cold War whilst enjoying lavish expenses travelling to exotic places, all of which he drew upon in creating James Bond (whose name he appropriated from the author of a noted book on West Indies ornithology because it sounded 'brief, unromantic, Anglo-Saxon and yet very masculine').

Bond's creator, Ian Fleming (1908–64).

Published by Jonathan Cape in 1953, *Casino Royale* was an instant success. A three-book deal followed. The world in which Bond and his creator moved with its martinis (shaken, not stirred) and fine wines, casinos, fast cars and seductive women appeared extraordinarily glamorous compared to the stark reality of post-war Britain. While Bond sampled beluga caviar, his homeland still endured meat rationing until 1954. This level of escapism was matched by another need that Bond filled. Britain had lost her empire and was humiliated by the Suez Crisis in 1956 (after which disaster Anthony Eden opted to recuperate at Goldeneye). Reassuringly, Bond represented the central role Britain still played in the security of the West in the Cold War. Appropriately, he was periodically extracted from a tight spot by an American CIA operative, Felix Leiter. In 1962, the release of *Dr No*, the first – American-produced – film adaptation, brought Bond's mixture of British cunning and bravery to an ever widening audience. Alongside The Beatles, 007 was quickly established as an internationally recognizable British brand after a long period in which most manifestations of popular culture were either American or Americanized.

Bond's appeal was less agreeable to those who found the character personally and politically repugnant. The left-wing *New Statesman* dismissed the novels as nothing more than 'sex, snobbery and sadism'. Others were no less snooty. Fleming

23

```
half a measure of Kina Lillet. Shake it very well until its ice-cold
then add a large thin slice of lemon-peel. Got it ? [ Certainly, Monsieur.
                  Seemed
The barman was clearly pleased with the idea, of the mixture.
           Gosh, that's certainly a man's drink, said Leiter.
Bond laughed. - When hm - er - concentrating, he explained,
           I never have more than one drink before dinner, apologised Bond.
         do    one
But I like that, to be large and very strong and very cold and very
                                                        when they
well-made. I hate small portions of anything, particularly if its tastes
bad. This drink's my own invention and I'm going to patent it when I can
                                                       became
think of a good name. [ He watched carefully as the deep glass frosted
                                                            ^
with the pale golden drink, slightly aerated by the bruising of the
             reached for it a
shaker. He lifted his glass to Leiter and took a long sip. [ Excellent,
he said to the barman, but if you can get a vodka made with grain
                                               "mais n'en culons
instead of potatoes, you will find it still better." he added   an aside to the barman. The barman
pas des mouches"                                                 He laughed &
         You certainly think things out, said Leiter with amused respect
grinned.
         as they carried their glasses to a corner of the room, and in an
lowered his voice                                 Escape
undertone, ' you'd better call it the Blue Case Special after that
                       someone else
                    someone
something similar they threw at you this afternoon.
                    ^ (in an isolated corner
         somxmxlaughed They sat down, Bond laughed. [ I see the spot marked
X has been roped off from the public and they're making cars take a
detour over the pavement. I hope it has'nt frightened away any of the
```

Fleming's original manuscript for Casino Royale: *Bond orders his favourite martini. He subsequently decides to call it a 'Vesper' after the book's femme fatale, Vesper Lynd.*

once returned home unexpectedly to find his wife's literary friends in his drawing room reading out passages and laughing derisively. Even his publisher suggested he tone down the sexual content.

Defending his novels against those who yearned for a return to the clean-living Edwardian heroism of 'Bulldog' Drummond or Richard Hannay, Fleming retorted that 'All history is sex and violence.' Nonetheless, the works of Fleming shared some common factors with those of 'Sapper' (H. C. McNeile) and John Buchan in the streak of chauvinism and the propensity of villains to be foreigners, often with physical deformities. Envisaging how scientific and technological advances made it increasingly possible to hold the world to ransom, Fleming wrote, 'These politicians can't see that the Atomic Age has created the most deadly saboteur in the history of the world, the little man with the heavy suitcase.' Yet while such a villain might spring schemes of dastardly depravity, Bond, like Buchan's heroes before him, exemplified an idea more uplifting: that a sufficiently brave individual could bring about change and even save the world from deadly peril.

1956
THE SÈVRES PROTOCOL

THE SECRET DOCUMENT BEHIND THE SUEZ CRISIS

The Sèvres Protocol was top secret. It engineered the Suez Crisis, one of the most calamitous – and shameful – episodes in British foreign policy. Having destroyed his copy of the incriminating document, Anthony Eden, the prime minister, always denied it had ever existed. Unfortunately for his reputation, the Israeli government kept its copy.

In post-war strategy, successive Labour and Conservative administrations regarded the Middle East as being of vital national importance. The region was host to major British economic investments (especially oil) as well as to British naval and air bases from which to counter the Soviet threat. Clement Attlee's Cabinet considered, before deciding not to use, military action against Iran when it nationalized the Anglo-Iranian Oil (subsequently BP) refinery at Abadan in 1951. However, two years later, the British and United States governments ensured the restoration of their oil concessions by providing backing for a coup in Tehran that overthrew the Iranian leader, Mohammad Mosaddeq.

Meanwhile, in 1952 a military coup in Cairo had removed Britain's client rulers in Egypt and set the path for Gamal Abdel Nasser, an Arab nationalist, to come to power. Although Britain negotiated an orderly withdrawal from its Egyptian bases, it considered as sacrosanct the maintenance of the Suez Canal as an international shipping lane and conduit for Europe's oil supplies. When, on 26 July 1956, Nasser nationalized the Suez Canal, the new British prime minister, Anthony Eden, feared the worst.

Eden's foreign secretary, Selwyn Lloyd, was dispatched to the United Nations in New York to try to broker a settlement. On 14 October, Eden was visited at Chequers, the prime ministerial weekend home, by General Maurice Challe, the deputy chief of staff of the French armed forces, and the French minister for social affairs (deputizing for the foreign minister), Albert Gazier, who put to him an

THE RETREAT FROM EMPIRE: BRITAIN'S FORMER COLONIES GAIN THEIR INDEPENDENCE

1947 India gains independence (and is partitioned, creating also West and East Pakistan).

1948 Ceylon (Sri Lanka) and Burma gain independence.

1949 The Republic of Ireland leaves the Commonwealth.

1954 British troops vacate Egypt and Sudan gains independence.

1957 The Gold Coast (Ghana) gains independence, as does the Federation of Malaya (Malaysia).

1960 Cyprus, British Somaliland and Nigeria gain independence.

1961 Sierra Leone, British Cameroon and Tanganyika gain independence. South Africa, under National Party rule, leaves the Commonwealth.

1962 Jamaica, Trinidad and Tobago, Western Samoa and Uganda gain independence.

1963 Kenya and Zanzibar gain independence, the latter to merge with Tanganyika to form Tanzania.

1964 Northern Rhodesia (Zambia), Nyasaland (Malawi) and Malta gain independence.

1965 Southern Rhodesia makes its unilateral declaration of independence (UDI) from British rule, to avoid black-majority rule. The Gambia gains independence.

1966 Barbados, Lesotho and Botswana gain independence.

1967 Aden (South Yemen) gains independence.

1968 Mauritius and Swaziland gain independence.

1970 Fiji and Tonga gain independence.

1971 Bahrain and Qatar gain independence.

1973 The Bahamas gain independence.

1974 Grenada gains independence.

1976 The Seychelles gain independence.

1978 Dominica gains independence.

1979 The Gilbert Islands (Kiribati) gain independence.

1980 Zimbabwe (formerly Southern Rhodesia) gains independence after a prolonged liberation struggle.

1981 Belize gains independence.

1984 Brunei gains independence.

1996 South Africa under Nelson Mandela rejoins the Commonwealth.

1997 Hong Kong is reunited with China following the expiration of its lease to Britain.

extraordinary proposal. They suggested that if Israel could be persuaded to attack Egypt across the Sinai peninsula this would provide a convenient pretext for the British and French to land peacekeeping forces along the Suez Canal zone. Having secured it, they could from there help bring down Nasser's regime.

Regrettably, Eden thought this was a sound idea. Two days later he travelled with Lloyd to France for talks at the Palais Matignon with Guy Mollet, the French prime minister and his foreign minister, Christian Pineau. Lloyd did not like the plan but lacked the courage to stand up to Eden, whose reputation in foreign policy was high (he had three times been foreign secretary, in 1935–8, 1940–45 and 1951–5). Eden became obsessed with the notion that Nasser was another Hitler whose ambitions it would be calamitous to appease. Fearful of Nasser's support for Algerian nationalists, the French had as much – indeed more – reason than the British to want to see the regional troublemaker toppled. Crucially, Israel had to be brought into the conspiracy too.

The vital negotiations were conducted, in tight secrecy, between 22 and 24 October, at a suitable location – on the Rue Emanuel Girot in the Paris suburb of Sèvres in an elegant villa that had been a hideout for the French Resistance during the war. The talks began with the French delegation, led by Mollet and Pineau, trying to persuade the reluctant Israelis to do their bidding. The Israeli team, led by their prime minister and defence minister, David Ben-Gurion, included Moshe Dayan and Shimon Peres. They were then joined by the British, looking distinctly uncomfortable, in the guise of Selwyn Lloyd and his private secretary, Donald Logan.

Eden preferred not to attend in person and his aloofness was understandable. After all, it was a covert meeting of those conceiving an international conspiracy. Lloyd was ill at ease and it was only after his departure that relations between the French and Israelis improved on the second day. That night, back in London, Lloyd and Eden discussed progress with Pineau. Brushing aside moral and practical complaints, Eden remained enthusiastic. All was set for the third and final day's negotiations at Sèvres. With Lloyd unable to attend, Britain was represented there by Donald Logan and Patrick Dean, an assistant under-secretary of state at the Foreign Office.

The Israelis were finally persuaded, seeing the scheme as a chance to be rid of Nasser, a potentially implacable enemy, whilst cementing better relations with the French and British. It was agreed that Israel would initiate the crisis by invading the Sinai peninsula on 29 October. Feigning shock, the British and French would

3. -

3° - Dans le cas où le Gouvernement EGYPTIEN n'aurait pas dans les délais fixés donné son accord aux clauses de l'appel qui lui a été adressé, les Forces Anglo-Françaises déclancheront le 31 octobre dans les premières heures de la matinée les opérations militaires contre les Forces Egyptiennes.

4° - Le Gouvernement Israélien enverra des Forces afin d'occuper la côte OUEST du Golfe d'AKABA et le groupe des Iles TIRAN et SANAFIR pour assurer la liberté de navigation dans le golfe d'AKABA.

5° - Israël s'engage à ne pas attaquer LA JORDANIE pendant la période des opérations contre l'EGYPTE.

Mais, au cas où dans la même période la JORDANIE attaquerait Israël, le Gouvernement Britannique s'engage à ne pas venir en aide à la JORDANIE.

6° - Les dispositions du présent PROTOCOLE doivent demeurer rigoureusement secrètes.

7° - Elles entreront en vigueur après l'accord des Trois Gouvernements.

A surviving copy of the incriminating document that Anthony Eden denied existed. The Sèvres Protocol was hurriedly typed up in French and signed by the French foreign minister, Christian Pineau, the British under-secretary of state, Patrick Dean, and the Israeli prime minister, David Ben-Gurion.

The Sèvres Protocol, 1956

The results of the conversations which took place at Sèvres from 22–24 October 1956 between the representatives of the Governments of the United Kingdom, the State of Israel and of France are the following:

1. The Israeli forces launch in the evening of 29 October 1956 a large scale attack on the Egyptian forces with the aim of reaching the Canal Zone the following day.

2. On being apprised of these events, the British and French Governments during the day of 30 October 1956 respectively and simultaneously make two appeals to the Egyptian Government and the Israeli Government on the following lines:

   A. To the Egyptian Government
      a) halt all acts of war.
      b) withdraw all its troops ten miles from the Canal.
      c) accept temporary occupation of key positions on the Canal by the Anglo-French forces to guarantee freedom of passage through the Canal by vessels of all nations until a final settlement.

   B. To the Israeli Government
      a) halt all acts of war.
      b) withdraw all its troops ten miles to the east of the Canal.

   In addition, the Israeli Government will be notified that the French and British Governments have demanded of the Egyptian Government to accept temporary occupation of key positions along the Canal by Anglo-French forces. It is agreed that if one of the Governments refused, or did not give its consent, within twelve hours the Anglo-French forces would intervene with the means necessary to ensure that their demands are accepted.

   C. The representatives of the three Governments agree that the Israeli Government will not be required to meet the conditions in the appeal addressed to it, in the event that the Egyptian Government does not accept those in the appeal addressed to it for their part.

3. In the event that the Egyptian Government should fail to agree within the stipulated time to the conditions of the appeal addressed to it, the Anglo-French forces will launch military operations against the Egyptian forces in the early hours of the morning of 31 October.

4. The Israeli Government will send forces to occupy the western shore of the Gulf of Aqaba and the group of islands Tirane and Sanafir to ensure freedom of navigation in the Gulf of Aqaba.

5. Israel undertakes not to attack Jordan during the period of operations against Egypt. But in the event that during the same period Jordan should attack Israel, the British Government undertakes not to come to the aid of Jordan.

6. The arrangements of the present protocol must remain strictly secret.

7. They will enter into force after the agreement of the three Governments.

(signed)

CHRISTIAN PINEAU   PATRICK DEAN   DAVID BEN-GURION

issue separate appeals for both sides to disengage and then land their own forces in the canal zone as a buffer between the rivals, supposedly destabilizing Egypt and thereby threatening Nasser's position. Much as the British would have preferred to keep the details off the record, they felt it might look suspicious if they refused Ben-Gurion's request that a summary of what had been agreed should be drawn up and signed.

The resulting protocol was hurriedly typed up in French on a portable typewriter – seemingly without sufficient time to correct minor typing errors and its irregular layout. Three copies were made, one for each of the participating delegations. Pineau signed for the French and Ben-Gurion for the Israelis. Dean initialled each page on behalf of Britain and signed at the end. Stilted congratulations were exchanged over a glass of champagne. The party became more amicable after the British left, when the French and Israelis felt able to toast another consequence – separate and unknown to the British – of their collaboration: namely, French assistance in turning Israel into a nuclear power.

Back in Britain, Eden endorsed Dean's actions whilst being furious that a formal record had been kept. He had the British copy destroyed and tried – in vain – to get the French and Israelis to do likewise (although the French copy was subsequently mislaid).

The Israeli attack went according to plan; British and French troops landed without serious losses, but the plotters had failed to take sufficient account of a crucial factor: the hostility of the United States. Transatlantic relations turned sour. Oil sanctions were threatened. Critically, there was a run on the pound. Lacking the reserves to support the plummeting value of the currency, Harold Macmillan, the chancellor of the exchequer, performed a dramatic

U-turn, arguing in Cabinet for the suspension of the military operation as the only means of securing the vital American financial support that was currently being withheld. Reluctantly, Eden felt compelled to bow to the pressure of the money markets. A ceasefire was arranged for 5 p.m. on 6 November and on 2 December the government formally announced that all British forces were being immediately withdrawn from Egypt.

For Britain it was an unqualified humiliation. The episode appeared to show that this once great power was so economically weak that it could no longer operate a foreign policy independent of American support. The domestic political repercussions were also enormous. The Labour Party found a strong and united voice in opposing the adventure. Middle-class liberals felt alienated by the actions of a Conservative leader they had previously admired. Still suffering from the severe stress that undermined his judgment during the crisis, Eden fell genuinely ill from a bungled gall-bladder operation and resigned in January 1957.

The humbling of Britain's global pretensions was not the least of it. Moscow had previously decided not to intervene against the reformist government in Hungary, but changed its mind when the Suez Crisis provided the necessary distraction. While the world was watching events on the Sinai peninsula, Soviet soldiers and tanks were sent in to crush Budapest's assertion of independence, killing 20,000 Hungarians in the process. The cracks in the Iron Curtain were filled up again with devastating consequences for the world.

Both in Britain and abroad there was widespread suspicion from the first that the Suez Crisis was the consequence of collusion between the British, French and Israelis. Eden had mentioned in a Cabinet meeting of 23 October 'secret conversations which had been held in Paris with representatives of the Israeli Government' about which none of his colleagues chose to challenge him. Only the minister of state at the Foreign Office, Anthony Nutting, resigned. Eden then lied to the House of Commons on 20 December when he stated: 'to say it quite bluntly to the House there was not foreknowledge that Israel would attack Egypt – there was not', a pretence he maintained subsequently.

Nutting was the first official to publicly admit – in his autobiography of 1967 – that there had been collusion at Sèvres. The French and Israeli participants followed suit. It is only because the Israelis refused Eden's request that they burn the secret protocol that we have unanswerable proof of the full extent of the Franco-British conspiracy.

1965

ANTHONY CROSLAND'S DEPARTMENT OF EDUCATION CIRCULAR 10/65

THE ABOLITION OF GRAMMAR SCHOOLS AND THE CREATION OF COMPREHENSIVE SCHOOLS

Before the Second World War, four out of five children never formally acquired a secondary education. They remained at elementary school until the age of fourteen, after which they went into employment. This system was ended by the 1944 Education Act, introduced by the Conservative secretary of state for education in the wartime coalition government, R. A. ('Rab') Butler. Henceforth, all children would leave elementary school at eleven and then have a minimum of four years' secondary schooling. How they performed academically at the age of eleven determined what sort of secondary school they would attend. The majority would be given places in secondary modern schools and from there go straight on to the workplace, while a few went to the small number of technical schools. Around a quarter of the most intelligent, as measured by the 'eleven plus' exam, would proceed to grammar schools, where they could expect a rigorous and challenging curriculum that was intended to prepare them for the prospect of university and a professional career.

The twenty years following the Butler Act witnessed a great breaking down of class barriers and the rise of social mobility, fuelled, in part, by a grammar-school system that provided a free but academically exacting education to those deemed best able to benefit from it regardless of their family's finances or circumstances. It was a motor of the new 'meritocracy', a term first coined in 1958. However, the undoubted excellence of the schooling provided for the gifted contrasted with the quality of what was offered to the majority in secondary moderns, where the bar of aspiration was set lower. To critics, it was inherently unfair to perpetuate a system that divided children at the age of eleven into two different forms of schooling that usually shaped their subsequent attainments.

In 1965, Anthony Crosland (1918–77) became education secretary in Harold Wilson's Labour government. Educated at Highgate, a highly academic private school, and at Oxford, where he was both a student and a don, Crosland was a convinced modernizer and author of a highly influential book, *The Future of Socialism*. Despite the advantages he had himself derived from it, he detested selective education and declared that he intended 'to destroy every f---ing grammar school' in the country. He wanted them replaced by comprehensive schools, the egalitarian, non-selective model that was already being tested by a number of local education authorities, most notably in Labour-controlled London.

To this effect, he issued Circular 10/65. Although it lacked the statutory power to enforce the comprehensive model, it made clear that this was nonetheless the will of Parliament and that local education authorities were accordingly expected to submit their plans 'for reorganising secondary education in their area on comprehensive lines' to the secretary of state. The circular was actively seized upon by those determined to smash the grammar schools. They argued that the two different models could not continue side by side, for the whole point of comprehensives was that they were mixed-ability institutions. Disingenuously, the claim was made that comprehensives were 'grammar schools for all'. Sceptics countered that better-resourced secondary moderns for all would be the reality.

Whilst comprehensives would have spread even without endorsement by central government, the impetus given to them by Circular 10/65 was palpable. When it was published, there were only 200 comprehensive schools in the country. Five years later, the number had risen to 1,000. In 1975, the returning Labour government carried on the assault on selective institutions by abolishing direct-grant schools, among which were some of the most venerable and high-performing schools in the country. Those that survived did so by becoming private schools – which was hardly what Labour had intended. Overall, the speed at which successful educational establishments, some of which had survived for three or four hundred years, were either closed or transformed beyond all recognition represented nothing short of a cultural revolution. By 1980, 90 per cent of Britain's schools had become comprehensives.

The results were open to interpretation. Social mobility went into decline, although the extent to which this was due to other government policies is debatable. The reputation of comprehensives has suffered because of a tendency

From Department of Education Circular 10/65

It is the Government's declared objective to end selection at eleven plus and to eliminate separatism in secondary education, The Government's policy has been endorsed by the House of Commons in a motion passed on 21st January 1965:

'That this House, conscious of the need to raise educational standards at all levels, and regretting that the realisation of this objective is impeded by the separation of children into different types of secondary schools, notes with approval the efforts of local authorities to reorganise secondary education on comprehensive lines which will preserve all that is valuable in grammar school education for those children who now receive it and make it available to more children; recognises that the method and timing of such reorganisation should vary to meet local needs; and believes that the time is now ripe for a declaration of national policy.'

The Secretary of State accordingly requests local education authorities, if they have not already done so, to prepare and submit to him plans for reorganising secondary education in their areas on comprehensive lines. The purpose of this Circular is to provide some central guidance on the methods by which this can be achieved.

to compare them with the academic grammar schools they replaced rather than the secondary moderns for which comprehensives were often an improvement. Nonetheless, the introduction of comprehensives coincided with new 'child-centred' approaches to teaching, which traditionalists thought lacked rigour. Those wishing to escape this style of teaching either moved to counties like Kent or Buckinghamshire, where many of the 164 residual grammar schools in England survived (as they did in Northern Ireland), or turned to private schools. The fact that the best comprehensives – judged by exam results – tended to be within the catchment areas of some of Britain's most expensive neighbourhoods suggested that Crosland's social experiment unintentionally acted to reinforce social barriers, rather than break them down. In most cases, the best education was still only available to those who could either pay school fees or afford an expensive mortgage.

More than forty years later, Circular 10/65 remained controversial, though the debate had shifted. The Conservative Party gave up attempting to bring back grammar schools, while Labour lost interest in eliminating the few that had survived. Instead, the argument focused on reforming the comprehensives.

1967

THE BEATLES' *SGT. PEPPER* ALBUM COVER

AN ICON OF BRITAIN'S 'SWINGING SIXTIES'

In the 1950s, Britain's youth imported pop music largely from the United States. Home-grown talent either performed cover versions of American hits or adopted an imitative transatlantic style.

By the beginning of the 1960s, rock 'n' roll appeared to be running out of ideas. Without an obvious successor, a variety of rival styles briefly vied for supremacy. It was during this period, in May 1962, that the trad-jazz clarinettist Acker Bilk became the first Briton to reach number one in the American billboard charts with his instrumental number 'Stranger on the Shore'.

Coincidentally, just days later The Beatles signed a contract with Parlophone, a record label owned by EMI, and promptly changed the face of pop music across the world. Within months 'Beatlemania' had conquered Britain and by 1964 had successfully crossed the Atlantic. So began a 'revolution in the head' that placed post-imperial Britain at the heart of a new, vibrant youth culture.

The Beatles were four Liverpudlians: the singer-songwriting duo of John Lennon and Paul McCartney – respectively guitar and bass guitar – with George Harrison also playing guitar and Ringo Starr on drums. They gained valuable professional assistance from their manager, Brian Epstein, and their producer at Parlophone, George Martin. None of this commercial expertise, however, masked the reality that these four working-class lads were the masters of their own destiny. The fact that they wrote their own music was a decisive mark of independence, far removed from the previous notion that pop singers merely performed the work of unseen professional songwriters. Together, Lennon and McCartney proved to be the most successful composers in British history. Despite the break-up of The Beatles in 1970, their popularity endured, as did their critical reputation. By the twenty-first century, they had sold over 1 billion albums worldwide.

The album cover of Sgt. Pepper's Lonely Hearts Club Band is depicted in the fourth plate section.

Over successive albums, The Beatles' style developed, as did its complexity. *Please Please Me*, their first album, was recorded in under 600 minutes. More albums followed. In particular, *Revolver* (1966) provided a major staging-post in their progress towards greater musical complexity and the broadening of their audience far beyond the original, if fickle, tastes of teenagers. In 1966 they stopped playing live concerts, choosing to devote more time to exploring new influences and technical advances. Released the following year, *Sgt. Pepper's Lonely Hearts Club Band* took 129 days to complete, devouring 700 hours in London's Abbey Road recording studios. The resulting sound transformed the genre, pointing the way towards the dreamlike 'psychedelic' scene of the late 1960s, with its drugs, freedom from inhibition and student revolt. Indeed, from the singalong – almost Edwardian music-hall – simplicity of 'When I'm Sixty-Four', to the near-heavy-metal instrumental opening of the title track, to the psychedelia of 'Lucy in the Sky with Diamonds', it was a work of extraordinary eclecticism. More than forty years later, it is still regularly cited as the most influential album in the history of popular music.

The *Sgt. Pepper* album cover was the outward sign of the group's ambitions. Breaking away from traditional reliance on the work of commercial designers (who provided a rejected design), a leading British artist was approached. This was Peter Blake, whose work often mixed images from advertising and other popular media. At the time of their first full-length film, *A Hard Day's Night* in 1964, The Beatles were promoted through images of being joyfully pursued across London by screaming and adoring fans. Two years later, the 'Fab Four' were tiring of the mass adulation that had accompanied their rise. For the *Sgt. Pepper* album cover they appeared thinly disguised in fancy dress as bandsmen, surrounded not by their fans, but by a background montage of the people of their choice.

'People We Like' was the artwork's title. The photo shoot took place at Chelsea Manor Studios, Flood Street, London on 20 March 1967, with the characters represented by life-size cut-outs pasted on to hardboard. George Harrison, who was increasingly influenced by Eastern spiritualism, opted for Indian gurus. Ever the controversialist, John Lennon chose Gandhi, Jesus and Hitler, none of whom made the final line-up. Ringo Starr, in contrast, was happy with whatever the rest of the band wanted. In its final form, the background crowd included such eclectic characters as Sir Robert Peel, Karl Marx, Diana Dors and Stuart Sutcliffe, the band's former member, and Lennon's close friend, who had died just before their rise to success. Permission had to be sought to represent people still living.

THE SWINGING SIXTIES

1960 The British paperback publication of D. H. Lawrence's *Lady Chatterley's Lover* is cleared in an obscenity trial. The year's best-selling single is Elvis Presley's 'It's Now or Never'.

1961 The contraceptive pill goes on sale (for married women only until 1970, but the Brook clinic prescribes it to unmarried girls from 1964). Elvis Presley's 'Are You Lonesome Tonight?' is the best-selling single.

1962 The Telstar 1 satellite provides the first live transatlantic television feed. The innovative BBC satire programme *That Was the Week That Was* is broadcast (despite massive popularity, it is scrapped after its second series in 1963). The film version of *Dr No* launches the James Bond films. Frank Ifield's 'I Remember You' is the best-selling single.

1963 The Profumo sex scandal rocks the government. Harold Macmillan resigns as prime minister due to ill-health. 'She Loves You' by The Beatles is the best-selling single.

1964 Labour narrowly wins the general election, ending thirteen years of Conservative government. Barbara Hulanicki opens her first Biba shop and Terence Conran his first Habitat store. Mods and Rockers clash at seaside resorts. Mary Whitehouse holds her first 'Clean Up TV' public meeting. 'Can't Buy Me Love' by The Beatles is the best-selling single.

1965 Sir Winston Churchill dies. Mary Quant's 'miniskirt' design is launched. The death penalty is abolished. 'Tears' by Ken Dodd is the best-selling single.

1966 England wins the football World Cup. Oil is discovered in the North Sea. A slag-heap disaster engulfs a school in Aberfan, killing 144 children. 'Green, Green Grass of Home' by Tom Jones is the best-selling single.

1967 Abortion is legalized in England, Wales and Scotland. The Sexual Offences Act permits homosexual acts for those over twenty-one in private in England and Wales (effective in Scotland in 1980 and Northern Ireland in 1982). 'The Summer of Love' marks the apex of the 'hippie' movement. Engelbert Humperdinck's 'Release Me' is the best-selling single.

1968 The 'I'm Backing Britain' campaign, launched to work an extra half-hour every day without pay to help the economy, is fleetingly popular. *Carry On Up the Khyber* hits the cinemas. 'Hey Jude' by The Beatles is the best-selling single.

1969 The first flight of supersonic airliner Concorde. The first broadcast of colour TV in the UK. The Divorce Reform Act (effective from 1971 in England and Wales) creates 'irretrievable breakdown' as grounds for divorce. *The Italian Job* hits the cinemas. 'Sugar, Sugar' by The Archies is the best-selling single.

Before a personal letter from the band persuaded her, Mae West initially refused, complaining, 'What would I be doing in a lonely hearts club?'

Returning from the Abbey Road studios at dawn to a flat off the King's Road (then a centre of London's 'swinging' fashion scene), the band placed speakers on the window ledge and serenaded the neighbourhood. Their press officer later recollected, 'All the windows around us opened up and people leaned out, wondering. It was obvious who it was on the record. Nobody complained. A lovely spring morning. People were smiling and giving us the thumbs-up.'

1972

THE ACCESSION TREATY TO THE EUROPEAN ECONOMIC COMMUNITY

BRITAIN AND EUROPEAN INTEGRATION

The United Kingdom's decision to sign up to the Treaty of Rome and its successor treaties led – over a thirty-year period – to the biggest transfer of sovereignty in the history of the British state. As far as England was concerned, it was potentially the greatest transferral of authority since 1211, when a temporarily humiliated King John offered his kingdom to the pope.

The rationale for doing so was partly idealistic. The European Economic Community (the European Union after 1993) represented the coming together of countries whose long histories of periodic hostility had been the precursor to two devastating world wars. It was also practical. The period after 1945 witnessed a steady deterioration in Britain's status as a global power. Hopes were raised that becoming a leading member of a new, greater entity could actually increase London's international influence. There was also the reality that in the fifteen years since the EEC's birth, its members' economies and standards of living had improved far more rapidly than had Britain's. In addition, some Conservatives who feared the anti-free-market policies of the left wing of the Labour Party believed that joining the tariff-free 'Common Market' would permanently clip the wings of native socialism, safeguarding the future of capitalism in Britain.

The government's attitude towards European political integration shifted over time. Although Winston Churchill had initially welcomed it, he also summed up Britain's relationship towards it as: 'We are with Europe but not of it. We are linked, but not combined. We are interested and associated, but not absorbed.' In essence, European integration was necessarily a Franco-German project, devised by two Frenchmen, Jean Monnet and Robert Schuman. Britain was not consulted when the Schuman Plan was devised for what became the European Coal and

Steel Community in 1952 and chose not to participate in the talks that led to the signing of the EEC's founding charter, the Treaty of Rome, by France, West Germany, Italy, Belgium, Luxembourg and the Netherlands in 1957. Harold Macmillan's belated attempt to secure British membership was vetoed in 1963 by France's president, Charles de Gaulle, who did so using arguments similar to Churchill's assessment of Britain's continental commitment.

The situation was radically altered by the election of the Conservative leader Edward Heath as prime minister in 1970. He not only saw EEC membership as a means to reverse Britain's relative economic decline but approached the prospect with the zeal of the committed idealist. Whilst the Tory election manifesto had weighed the pros and cons of membership before promising merely 'Our sole commitment is to negotiate; no more, no less', few who knew Heath could have doubted he was determined to get a deal at almost any payable price. It was in this spirit that terms were agreed by June 1971. Divisions on the issue of joining the EEC crossed party boundaries, with opinion polls suggesting widespread scepticism among the electorate. Nevertheless, in October the House of Commons endorsed entry by 356 votes to 244. Upon this mandate, Heath signed the Treaty of Accession in Brussels on 22 January 1972. The treaty was made law by the European Communities Act in October. Membership took effect from 1 January 1973.

The debate was not so easily concluded. At issue was not just what Britain had signed up to, but what she might subsequently find herself committed to in an organization dedicated to 'ever closer union'. Following the Heath government's fall in February 1974, the incoming Labour administration of Harold Wilson tried to paper over its own divisions in 1975 by offering the British electorate a referendum on whether – after a cosmetic renegotiation of the terms – to remain within the EEC. In the midst of an economic crisis, Britain's voters preferred by a ratio of two to one to stay in. The official 'yes' campaign pamphlet sent to every home stated that important decisions in Brussels 'can be taken only if all the members of the Council agree. The minister representing Britain can veto any proposal for a new law or a new tax if he considers it to be against British interests.' In reality, there were already plans to curtail the right to veto. By 1990, European judges were successfully striking down British Acts of Parliament.

European competence over British law received its greatest boost in 1987 when the Single European Act – passed after only a desultory Commons debate – established the Single Market. This process, which was completed by 1992,

Commemorative postage stamps marked Britain's entry into the European Communities in 1973.

1957 The Treaty of Rome creates the European Economic Community (EEC), comprising France, West Germany, Italy, Belgium, Netherlands and Luxembourg. The 'six' also set up Euratom with the aspiration of framing a common nuclear energy policy.

1958 The European Court of Justice is established to interpret the Treaty of Rome's provisions.

1960 The European Free Trade Association (EFTA) is launched to cut tariffs between the UK, Austria, Switzerland, Denmark, Norway, Sweden and Portugal while avoiding creating supranational institutions.

1961 The UK applies to join the EEC (the application is vetoed by France in 1963).

1967 The EEC, Euratom and the European Coal and Steel Community are brought together as the European Community (EC).

1968 The Common Market is completed, removing internal tariffs.

1973 Britain, Denmark and Ireland join the EC.

1975 British membership of the EC is upheld in a national referendum.

1979 The European Monetary System is established. Britain joins but does not commit sterling to the EMS's Exchange Rate Mechanism (ERM). The first direct elections to the European Parliament are held.

1981 Greece joins the EC.

1984 Margaret Thatcher secures a partial budget rebate of UK contributions to the EC.

1986 Spain and Portugal join the EC. The new European flag is unveiled (a circle of twelve gold stars on a blue background).

1987 The Single European Act enters into law, removing national vetoes across the market and instituting regulatory policies in order to create a 'single market'.

1990 Britain pegs sterling within the ERM.

1992 The Maastricht Treaty is signed (it comes into effect in 1993), creating the European Union (EU) and committing members to establishing the single currency, the Euro. Britain retains the right to opt out of the Euro and Social Chapter policies. European citizenship is created.

1992 Sterling is withdrawn from the ERM.

1995 Austria, Sweden and Finland join the EU. A Norwegian referendum rejects membership. The Schengen Pact begins removing border controls between members (though the UK and Ireland do not join).

1997 Britain opts into Maastricht's Social Chapter. The Amsterdam Treaty increases EU legal competence over asylum, immigration, and social and employment policies.

2002 The Euro replaces national currencies. The UK, Sweden and Denmark opt out.

2005 The EU expands to twenty-five members – bringing in Malta, Cyprus, Estonia, Latvia, Lithuania, Poland, Hungary, Slovenia, Slovakia and the Czech Republic. Referenda votes in France and the Netherlands reject an EU constitution.

2007 Romania and Bulgaria join the EU.

2009 The 2007 Lisbon Treaty becomes law, enforcing much of the (supposedly) defeated constitution proposals, further reducing national veto powers, strengthening the EU's common foreign and diplomatic policies, giving legal force to the Charter of Fundamental Rights, and establishing permanent positions for the European president of the Council and the high representative for foreign affairs.

secured the free movement of goods, services, money and people within the European Community (which had by then increased to twelve members) as well as introducing qualified majority voting procedures in related policy areas, thereby ending national vetoes. Generally welcomed by Britain's major exporters, it also brought in its wake a vast extension of new regulation. For its promoter, Margaret Thatcher, it came to represent the high-water mark after which her faith in the European 'project' subsided. Conversely, Labour Party and trade union leaders warmed to its decisive legal influence over working practices and other social issues.

Mrs Thatcher's successor as prime minister, John Major, signed the Maastricht Treaty in 1992, which transferred further areas of law-making to Brussels. In particular, it established monetary union and a single currency, the Euro, for its members – a vast transferral of monetary and economic authority from which Britain and Denmark opted out. In 2007 the Lisbon Treaty was signed with the aim of creating what was effectively a constitution for a European Union that – with the collapse of communism – had spread to twenty-seven members and embraced nearly 500 million people. Measures to coordinate foreign policy were also devised, with an eventual goal that Europe might speak to the world with one voice. The structure of a federal superstate was clearly discernible, if not fully operational.

Supporters of deeper integration maintained that sovereignty was distinct from power and that membership of the European Union enhanced British power. Nevertheless, there remained a democratic deficit at the heart of the project which reduced voters to electing MPs who, over large areas of legislation, were no longer responsible for making the law.

EEC Accession Treaty, 1972

HIS MAJESTY THE KING OF THE BELGIANS,
HER MAJESTY THE QUEEN OF DENMARK,
THE PRESIDENT OF THE FEDERAL REPUBLIC OF GERMANY,
THE PRESIDENT OF THE FRENCH REPUBLIC,
THE PRESIDENT OF IRELAND,
THE PRESIDENT OF THE ITALIAN REPUBLIC,
HIS ROYAL HIGHNESS THE GRAND DUKE OF LUXEMBOURG,
HER MAJESTY THE QUEEN OF THE NETHERLANDS,

THE PRESIDENT OF THE PORTUGUESE REPUBLIC,
HER MAJESTY THE QUEEN OF THE UNITED KINGDOM OF GREAT BRITAIN AND
NORTHERN IRELAND,

UNITED in their desire to pursue the attainment of the objectives of the Treaty
establishing the European Economic Community and the Treaty establishing the
European Atomic Energy Community,

DETERMINED in the spirit of those Treaties to construct an ever closer union among
the peoples of Europe on the foundations already laid,

CONSIDERING that Article 237 of the Treaty establishing the European Economic
Community and Article 205 of the Treaty establishing the European Atomic Energy
Community afford European States the opportunity of becoming members of these
Communities,

CONSIDERING that the Kingdom of Denmark, Ireland and the United Kingdom of
Great Britain and Northern Ireland have applied to become members of these
Communities,

CONSIDERING that the Council of the European Communities, after having
obtained the Opinion of the Commission, has declared itself in favour of the
admission of these States,

HAVE DECIDED to establish by common agreement the conditions of admission and
the adjustments to be made to the Treaties establishing the European Economic
Community and the European Atomic Energy Community and to this end have
designated as their Plenipotentiaries:

> The Right Honourable Edward Heath MBE MP,
> Prime Minister, First Lord of the Treasury, Minister for the Civil Service;

> The Right Honourable Sir Alec Douglas-Home KT MP,
> Her Majesty's Principal Secretary of State for Foreign and Commonwealth
> Affairs;

> The Right Honourable Geoffrey Rippon QC MP,
> Chancellor of the Duchy of Lancaster;

Who, having exchanged their Full Powers found in good and due form,
HAVE AGREED as follows:

ARTICLE 1

1. The Kingdom of Denmark, Ireland and the United Kingdom of Great Britain and Northern Ireland hereby become members of the European Economic Community and of the European Atomic Energy Community and parties to the Treaties establishing these Communities as amended or supplemented. . . .

ARTICLE 2

This Treaty will be ratified by the High Contracting Parties in accordance with their respective constitutional requirements. The instruments of ratification will be deposited with the Government of the Italian Republic by 31 December 1972 at the latest.

This Treaty will enter into force on 1 January 1973, provided that all the instruments of ratification have been deposited before that date and that all the instruments of accession to the European Coal and Steel Community are deposited on that date....

ARTICLE 3

This Treaty, drawn up in a single original in the Danish, Dutch, English, French, German, Irish and Italian languages, the Danish, Dutch, English, French, German, Irish and Italian texts all being equally authentic, will be deposited in the archive of the Government of the Italian Republic, which will transmit a certified copy to each of the Governments of the other signatory States.

In witness whereof, the undersigned Plenipotentiaries have affixed their signatures below this Treaty.

Done at Brussels on this twenty-second day of January in the year one thousand nine hundred and seventy-two.

1973

THE COMMUNIQUÉ OF THE SUNNINGDALE AGREEMENT

EFFORTS TO SOLVE NORTHERN IRELAND'S 'TROUBLES'

S ince 1921, the six counties of Northern Ireland had enjoyed a large measure of legislative autonomy. The province had its own Parliament, elected by universal adult suffrage, which met at Stormont, on the outskirts of Belfast. While retaining ultimate executive authority and providing subsidies, London's politicians largely left their Belfast counterparts to run their own affairs.

Irish Nationalist hopes at the signing of the 1921 Anglo-Irish Treaty – that partition would prove only a temporary expedient – were quickly confounded. As time passed, the prospect of a united Ireland receded. The promotion of overtly Catholic, culturally Gaelic and anti-British sentiments in the Irish Free State, particularly after Eamon de Valera came to power in 1932, was met in Ulster by a corresponding assertion of British defining characteristics. Despite the presence of a sizeable Catholic minority, Northern Ireland effectively had what its first prime minister, Lord Craigavon, termed 'a Protestant government for a Protestant people'.

Periodic acts of terror by the IRA between 1956 and 1962 entrenched rather than shifted this governing assumption. By 1968, however, a civil rights movement had successfully galvanized the province's Catholic/Nationalist minority in its demands for better housing and an end to the property qualification in local-government elections that had disproportionately reduced their voice in municipal affairs. Rival marches descended into violence. Responding to an appeal by the inspector general of the Royal Ulster Constabulary, and concluding that the Northern Irish authorities were incapable of restoring order in a non-sectarian fashion, Harold Wilson's government sent in British troops in 1969.

The euphemistically named 'Troubles' only escalated and by 1972 British troop deployment had reached 21,000. The Provisional IRA brought terror throughout the province and also to the mainland. Loyalist paramilitaries retaliated with no

392

greater concern for human life. Support for the IRA swelled on both sides of the border, as well as in the United States, when British paratroopers – in confused and disputed circumstances – shot dead thirteen protesters during a march on 'Bloody Sunday' on 30 January 1972. During the course of that year, almost 500 people were killed in the violence and the IRA detonated 1,300 bombs. When Stormont refused Westminster's request to take over responsibility for law and order, Edward Heath's government responded by suspending Stormont and imposing direct rule from London. Heath's intention was to respect the will of Ulster's majority to remain within the United Kingdom while addressing the underlying problem that the province's Catholics, electorally a permanent minority at Stormont, felt marginalized by existing Northern Irish institutions.

The result was a power-sharing arrangement. In place of direct rule, the province would be governed by an executive, which neither community could dominate, and a legislature, the Assembly (which replaced the suspended Stormont parliament). Using proportional representation, elections to the Assembly in June 1973 returned a majority for the agreement and a power-sharing administration was formed of Unionists, the moderate-nationalist SDLP and the small, non-aligned Alliance Party.

Ominously, the new power-sharing arrangement was opposed by both Sinn Féin (the Provisional IRA's political wing) and the more militant Ulster Unionists, but what tipped the scales against its survival was the next strand of the process. Cross-border rather than cross-community in nature, it was agreed by the British and Irish governments, along with leaders of the Stormont Executive, when they met at Sunningdale, Berkshire, in December 1973. The resulting communiqué announced the establishment of a Council of Ireland, composed of politicians from both Belfast and Dublin, with responsibility for issues of common interest to both the North and the South. The Irish Republic – which still laid constitutional claim to the North – would concede Ulster's right to self-determination and London made clear it would not oppose unification if the North voted for it.

Although the areas of common policy envisaged at Sunningdale were limited, Unionists perceived them as a Trojan horse by which Dublin would increasingly interfere in Ulster politics. The Ulster Unionist Party's governing council voted to withdraw from the agreement and, in the United Kingdom's general election of February 1974, pro-Sunningdale Unionist MPs lost their seats to their opponents. The likelihood, already fatally undermined, that power-sharing could be sustained without the commitment of the Unionist majority was put beyond question in

NORTHERN IRELAND'S TROUBLES

1968 A Civil Rights Association campaign is launched against discriminatory policies.

1969 Rioting in Londonderry and Belfast leads to British army troop deployment. The Provisional IRA is formed.

1970 Severe rioting in Londonderry and Belfast. The Nationalist SDLP is formed.

1971 Internment without trial is introduced for those suspected of paramilitary involvement. The Ulster Defence Association (UDA) and its terrorist unit, the Ulster Freedom Fighters, are formed.

1972 On 'Bloody Sunday', in Londonderry, thirteen civilians die from army gunshot wounds during a march. In retaliation, a mob burns down the British Embassy in Dublin. London imposes direct rule upon Northern Ireland. On 'Bloody Friday' the IRA explode twenty-two bombs in Belfast. The British army's 'Operation Motorman' retakes the 'no-go areas' established by republicans.

1973 Elections are held for a Northern Ireland Assembly. The Sunningdale Agreement is signed.

1974 Unionist strikes help bring down the Sunningdale Agreement. Direct rule is reimposed. The IRA bomb the House of Commons and pubs in Guildford and Birmingham.

1975 Internment is ended.

1976 Christopher Ewart-Biggs, the British ambassador to Ireland, is killed. 'Blanket protests' in the Maze prison.

1979 The Irish National Liberation Army (INLA) Republican splinter group murders the Tory politician Airey Neave. Eighteen British soldiers are killed by an IRA bomb at Warrenpoint. The Queen's cousin, Lord Louis Mountbatten, is murdered by the IRA.

1981 Ten republican prisoners die in hunger strikes at the Maze prison. Before his death, the IRA hunger striker Bobby Sands is elected an MP from prison.

1984 The IRA bomb Brighton's Grand Hotel, killing five in an attempt to murder Margaret Thatcher.

1985 The Anglo-Irish Agreement is concluded.

1987 The IRA bomb a Remembrance Sunday service at Enniskillen.

1991 The IRA launch a mortar attack on 10 Downing Street.

1993 The IRA explodes bombs at Warrington and the City of London.

1994 The IRA issues a seventeen-month ceasefire.

1996 The IRA bomb Manchester and London's new financial district at Canary Wharf.

1998 The Belfast Agreement is signed on Good Friday and approved in referenda in both Northern Ireland and the Irish Republic. The 'Real IRA', a dissident Republican group opposed to the peace process, bombs Omagh, murdering twenty-nine civilians.

1999 The Northern Ireland Assembly is re-established.

2001 The RUC is disbanded and replaced by the Police Service of Northern Ireland.

2005 The IRA puts its weapons 'beyond use'.

2007 British army operations in Northern Ireland are wound down. The Northern Ireland Executive is formed.

2010 Despite sporadic violence from splinter republican terror groups, the INLA and the UDA join the list of paramilitary organizations that put their weapons beyond use and the Independent International Commission of Decommissioning is disbanded.

May, when the province was paralyzed by a general strike that led to power cuts and barricades being erected across streets.

The strike was organized by the Ulster Workers' Council, an umbrella movement that included Protestant trade unionists and the loyalist paramilitary group, the Ulster Defence Association (UDA). Within fourteen days it had achieved its objective and brought down Sunningdale's four-month experiment in power-sharing. Rather than risk all-out insurrection by turning the troops on the strikers in order to restore a system of government that the majority party had rejected, Harold Wilson's administration mothballed Stormont. Direct rule was reimposed from London.

The result was a further twenty-four years of deadlock and violence. Wilson had ordered a study into an alternative strategy, which on 31 May outlined the argument for Northern Ireland's expulsion from the United Kingdom. In this scenario, it would become a self-governing dominion (although, peculiarly, excluded from the Commonwealth), its people still the Queen's subjects but constitutionally severed from Britain in almost every other respect.

Far from being a solution, such a British withdrawal threatened to plunge Ulster into all-out civil war, possibly prompting military intervention by the Republic of Ireland. It was extremely doubtful whether the republic's army, only 12,000 strong, was capable of securing the province, given the likelihood that the attempt would spark an armed uprising by the Unionist majority – as a separate study by the Irish government also concluded.

So Ulster's direct rule from Westminster continued. It was not until the Belfast Agreement of Good Friday 1998 that the process recommenced of restoring devolved government. The Irish government finally renounced its territorial claim to the North, while power-sharing initiatives (cross-community and cross-border) similar to those of 1973, were revived in Ulster. These arrangements had to be halted until the IRA finally declared its terror campaign over in 2005 and put its weapons beyond use. Thereafter, power-sharing began to look as if it might enjoy greater permanence only in 2007 when, improbably, the Democratic Unionist Ian Paisley and Sinn Féin's Martin McGuinness became, respectively, first and deputy first minister. By then, the violence had claimed over 3,500 lives, including more than 1,000 British soldiers and Royal Ulster Constabulary police personnel, and over 1,800 civilians. The 1998 agreement that had laid the ground for ending the Troubles was summed up by the SDLP's Seamus Mallon as 'Sunningdale for slow learners'.

The Ulster Unionist leader, Brian Faulkner (above) with the Irish Taoiseach, Lian Cosgrove (below), during the Sunningdale negotiations, December 1973.

From the Sunningdale Agreement, 1973

5. The Irish Government fully accepted and solemnly declared that there could be no change in the status of Northern Ireland until a majority of the people of Northern Ireland desired a change in that status. The British Government solemnly declared that it was, and would remain, their policy to support the wishes of the majority of the people of Northern Ireland. The present status of Northern Ireland is that it is part of the United Kingdom. If in the future the majority of the people of Northern Ireland should indicate a wish to become part of a united Ireland, the British Government would support that wish. . . .

7. The Conference agreed that a Council of Ireland would be set up. It would be confined to representatives of the two parts of Ireland, with appropriate safeguards for the British Government's financial and other interests. It would comprise a Council of Ministers with executive and harmonising functions and a consultative role, and a Consultative Assembly with advisory and review functions. The Council of Ministers would act by unanimity, and would comprise a core of seven members of the Irish Government and an equal number of members of the Northern Ireland Executive with provision for the participation of other non-voting members of the Irish Government and the Northern Ireland Executive or Administration when matters within their departmental competence were discussed. The Council of Ministers would control the functions of the Council. The Chairmanship would rotate on an agreed basis between representatives of the Irish Government and of the Northern Ireland Executive. Arrangements would be made for the location of the first meeting, and the location of subsequent meetings would be determined by the Council of Ministers. The Consultative Assembly would consist of 60 members, 30 members from Dail Eireann chosen by the Dail on the basis of proportional representation by the single transferable vote, and 30 members from the Northern Ireland Assembly chosen by that Assembly and also on that basis. . . .

8. In the context of its harmonising functions and consultative role, the Council of Ireland would undertake important work relating, for instance, to the impact of EEC membership. As for executive functions, the first step would be to define and agree these in detail. . . . Studies would be directed to identifying, for the purposes of executive action by the Council of Ireland, suitable aspects of activities in the following broad fields:

(a) exploitation, conservation and development of natural resources and the environment;

(b) agricultural matters (including agricultural research, animal health and operational aspects of the Common Agriculture Policy), forestry and fisheries;

(c) co-operative ventures in the fields of trade and industry;

(d) electricity generation;

(e) tourism;

(f) roads and transport;

(g) advisory services in the field of public health;

(h) sport, culture and the arts.

It would be for the Oireachtas and the Northern Ireland Assembly to legislate from time to time as to the extent of functions to be devolved to the Council of Ireland. Where necessary, the British Government will cooperate in this devolution of functions. Initially, the functions to be vested would be those identified in accordance with the procedures set out above and decided, at the formal stage of the conference, to be transferred. . . .

10. It was agreed by all parties that persons committing crimes of violence, however motivated, in any part of Ireland should be brought to trial irrespective of the part of Ireland in which they are located. The concern which large sections of the people of Northern Ireland felt about this problem was in particular forcefully expressed by the representatives of the Unionist and Alliance parties. The representatives of the Irish Government stated that they understood and fully shared this concern. Different ways of solving this problem were discussed; among them were the amendment of legislation operating in the two jurisdictions on extradition, the creation of a common law enforcement area in which an all-Ireland court would have jurisdiction, and the extension of the jurisdiction of domestic courts so as to enable them to try offences committed outside the jurisdiction. It was agreed that problems of considerable legal complexity were involved, and that the British and Irish Governments would jointly set up a commission to consider all the proposals put forward at the Conference and to recommend as a matter of extreme urgency the most effective means of dealing with those who commit these crimes. The Irish Government undertook to take immediate and effective legal steps so that persons coming within their jurisdiction and accused of murder, however motivated, committed in Northern Ireland will be brought to trial, and it was agreed that any similar reciprocal action that may be needed in Northern Ireland be taken by the appropriate authorities. . . .

1983

THE NEW HOPE FOR BRITAIN, THE LABOUR PARTY ELECTION MANIFESTO

THE NADIR OF BRITISH SOCIALISM

I n the general election campaigns of 1931, 1945 and 1983, the Labour Party promised sweeping nationalization and central planning. The results were decisive: a landslide triumph in 1945 and two landslide humiliations in 1931 and 1983. It was, however, the 1983 defeat that dealt a shattering blow to traditional socialist politics in Britain, leading the Labour politician Gerald Kaufman to dub the party's manifesto of that year 'the longest suicide note in history'.

Labour's defeat was all the more extraordinary given how low the fortunes of Margaret Thatcher's embattled Conservative administration had sunk by 1981. Her strategy to combat the runaway inflation that had bedevilled the British economy over the previous ten years coincided with a worldwide recession. This meant that traditional industries were decimated by a tight monetary squeeze, high interest rates and a strong currency that handicapped exports. Unemployment, which had stood at 1.25 million in May 1979 when Mrs Thatcher was elected, passed the 3 million mark by the beginning of 1983.

At the same time, the Labour Party was engulfed in a bitter internecine fight. Convinced that the parliamentary party and the leadership had failed to deliver effective socialist policies, constituency activists demanded an increased say in determining policy. At the 1980 party conference, they passed motions calling for the transformation of Britain into an isolationist, socialist state. A fortnight later, James Callaghan stood down as leader. In his place was elected Michael Foot, a left-wing intellectual and brilliant orator, whose misfortune it was to look even older and considerably more infirm than his sixty-seven years. In January 1981, Labour lurched further to the Left with the adoption of new rules that handed more power to the party's 'grass roots'. Henceforth, choosing the leader would be assigned to an electoral college system in which the unions had 40 per cent of the vote, activists 30 per cent and MPs 30 per cent.

The immediate consequence was that some of Labour's most popular moderate politicians – in particular the so-called 'gang of four' of Roy Jenkins, David Owen, Shirley Williams and Bill Rodgers – resigned from the party and formed a new force, the Social Democratic Party (SDP). Sensational by-election victories followed, suggesting that the SDP might, as it claimed, 'break the mould' of British politics, even though its politics – a 'mixed economy' of state-run and private companies, with incomes policies to cap salaries – were essentially those of the 1970s Labour leadership, merely shorn of its trade union ties. In order not to split the middle ground, the SDP formed 'the Alliance' with the Liberal Party.

The Alliance's rapid progress came to a sudden halt in April 1982 when Argentina's right-wing dictatorship seized the British dependency of the Falkland Islands. The ensuing conflict, which ended in the islands' liberation and the downfall of military rule in Argentina, was the first clear evidence for years that Britain's leaders had anything more positive to offer than the orderly management of decline. The resolute approach of Margaret Thatcher had received a vindication in the chilly South Atlantic and, with inflation falling at home and the economy finally beginning to grow again, the Conservatives entered what would be an election year in 1983 with renewed purpose and popularity. The country went to the polls on 9 June.

Offering a refuge for pacifist-inclined idealists, the Labour Party was badly placed to benefit from the resurgent faith in British arms and self-belief unleashed by victory in the Falklands War. With some signs that the worst of the recession was over, increasing numbers of voters seemed prepared to give the hard Thatcherite economic medicine the chance to complete its work, rather than follow the purgative treatment with the risk of returning to rampant inflation and trade union militancy. Instead of adapting to these changing realities, Labour fought the 1983 election campaign on a programme that called for a massive extension of state control over the country.

In accordance with the rules that had been established, the Labour manifesto was drafted by the party's National Executive Committee and presented to the Shadow Cabinet as a *fait accompli*, rather than as a rough copy awaiting discussion and amendment. It promised Britain's unilateral nuclear disarmament and withdrawal from the European Community. Market forces were to be curtailed. Quotas and tariffs would be imposed to restrict imports. Exchange controls were

THATCHER'S REVOLUTION

1979 The Conservatives win the general election with Margaret Thatcher as the UK's first female prime minister. The basic rate of income tax is cut from 33 to 30 per cent and the top rate from 83 to 60 per cent. Exchange controls are abolished. Unemployment runs at 4 per cent (1.4 million), inflation at 13 per cent. Home ownership is at 54 per cent.

1980 The SAS storms the Iranian Embassy to release hostages from terrorists. Unemployment runs at 5 per cent, inflation at 18 per cent.

1981 The Social Democratic Party (SDP) is formed. Serious riots affect Brixton, Toxteth, Southall and other inner-city areas. Unemployment runs at 8 per cent (2.7 million), inflation at 12 per cent.

1982 The Falklands War is won. Unemployment runs at 9 per cent, inflation at 9 per cent.

1983 The Conservatives are returned at the general election. US Cruise missiles are installed at Greenham Common, generating protest. Unemployment runs at 10 per cent, inflation at 5 per cent.

1984 The year-long miners' strike begins. The IRA's Brighton bomb aims to kill Thatcher and her Cabinet. British Telecom is privatized. Unemployment runs at 11 per cent, inflation at 5 per cent.

1985 Riots hit Broadwater Farm estate, London. Unemployment is 11 per cent, inflation is 6 per cent.

1986 The 'Westland Affair' over defence procurement sees Cabinet resignations. British Gas is privatized. Unemployment peaks at 11 per cent (3.2 million people). Inflation runs at 3 per cent.

1987 The Conservatives win an historic third term. Rolls-Royce, British Airways and BAA are privatized. The stock market crashes on 'Black Monday'. Unemployment runs at 10 per cent, inflation at 4 per cent.

1988 The standard rate of income tax is reduced to 25 per cent, the top rate to 40 per cent. Thatcher delivers her Bruges speech condemning European federalism. British Steel is privatized. Unemployment runs at 8 per cent, inflation at 5 per cent.

1989 The Community Charge, soon dubbed the poll tax, is introduced in Scotland (and in England and Wales in 1990). Nigel Lawson resigns as chancellor. Revolutions across Eastern Europe bring down communist regimes and begin the end of the Cold War. Unemployment runs at 6 per cent, inflation at 8 per cent.

1990 Anti-poll tax riots in Trafalgar Square. Geoffrey Howe resigns as leader of the Commons. Thatcher resigns during a damaging leadership election. Unemployment runs at 6 per cent, inflation at 9 per cent. Home ownership is at 65 per cent. A quarter of the population owns shares. Average living standards have increased 30 per cent over the decade.

to be brought back to curb the international flow of capital and the major clearing banks were threatened that if they refused to 'cooperate with us fully . . . we shall stand ready to take one or more of them into public ownership'. Corporatism was to be reintroduced, with a new Department of Economic and Industrial Planning implementing a five-year plan. The limited privatization that had taken place would be reversed. Electronics and pharmaceutical companies were to be largely nationalized along with 'other important sectors, as required in the national interest'.

Leadership style: Michael Foot and Margaret Thatcher at the Cenotaph on Remembrance Day 1981.

Further expansion of private health care would cease, whilst private schools would be stripped of charitable status and 'integrated' into the local authority sector 'where necessary'. In contrast, trade unions would regain their former powers.

The result was that Labour gained only a little over a quarter of the popular vote, just 2 per cent more than the Alliance (although the first-past-the-post voting system translated this into 209 Labour MPs, with a mere 23 for the Alliance). The Tories won 397 seats. With an overall majority of 144, Margaret Thatcher was free to enact her programme of rolling back state control, taking telecoms, gas and British Airways into the private sector, increasing home ownership with the sale of council houses to their tenants, reducing income tax and defeating the once mighty trade unions. The Labour Party did not return to power for another fourteen years, by which time it, like Britain, had changed markedly.

From *The New Hope for Britain*, 1983

Emergency programme of action

Within days of taking office, Labour will begin to implement an emergency programme of action, to bring about a complete change of direction for Britain. Our priority will be to create jobs and give a new urgency to the struggle for peace. In many cases we will be able to act immediately. In others, which involve legislation, they will take longer to bring into effect. But in all cases we shall act swiftly and with determination.

This is what we plan to do. We will:

Launch a massive programme for expansion. We will:

Provide a major increase in public investment, including transport, housing and energy conservation.

Begin a huge programme of construction, so that we can start to build our way out of the slump.

Halt the destruction of our social services and begin to rebuild them, by providing a substantial increase in resources.

Increase investment in industry, especially in new technology – with public enterprise taking the lead. And we will steer new industry and jobs to the regions and the inner cities.

Ensure that the pound is competitive; and hold back prices through action on VAT, rents, rates and fares.

Introduce a crash programme of employment and training, with new job subsidies and allowances.

Begin to rebuild British industry, working within a new framework for planning and industrial democracy. We will:

Agree a new national economic assessment, setting out the prospects for growth in the economy.

Prepare a five-year national plan, in consultation with unions and employers.

Back up these steps with a new National Investment Bank, new industrial powers, and a new Department for Economic and Industrial Planning.

Repeal Tory legislation on industrial relations and make provision for introducing industrial democracy.

Begin the return to public ownership of those public industries sold off by the Tories.

Give a new priority to open government at local and national levels, and give local communities greater freedom to manage their own affairs. We will also introduce an early Bill to abolish the legislative powers of the House of Lords.

In international policy, we shall take new initiatives to promote peace and development. We will:

Cancel the Trident programme, refuse to deploy Cruise missiles and begin discussions for the removal of nuclear bases from Britain, which is to be completed within the lifetime of the Labour government.

Ban arms sales to repressive regimes.

Increase aid to developing countries towards the UN target of 0.7 per cent.

Re-establish a separate Ministry of Overseas Development.

Take action to protect the status of refugees in Britain.

We will also open immediate negotiations with our EEC partners, and introduce the necessary legislation, to prepare for Britain's withdrawal from the EEC, to be completed well within the lifetime of the Labour government.

A POLICY FOR IMPORTS

But we must also plan ahead so that, as the economy expands, we keep our exports and imports in balance. We must therefore be ready to act on imports directly: first, in order to safeguard key industries that have been seriously put at risk by Tory policy; and second, so as to check the growth of imports should they threaten to outstrip our exports and thus our plan for expansion. We will:

Use agreed development plans, which we shall negotiate with the large companies that dominate our economy, so as to influence their purchasing and development policies. Our aim will be to prevent excessive import penetration and promote our own exports.

Use public purchasing policy to help support our strategy.

Introduce back-up import controls, using tariffs and quotas, if these prove necessary, to achieve our objective of trade balance – upon which sustained expansion depends . . .

PRICES – CONTROLLING INFLATION

The Tories have used mass unemployment to control inflation. We completely reject this approach. We believe it is madness to keep people out of work deliberately. Our priority will be to expand the economy and create jobs. But we are also determined to prevent soaring prices. Expansion will in itself help cut the costs of production and therefore hold back prices. But we will use other measures to help restrain inflation. We will:

Use direct measures of price restraint, such as cutting VAT, and subsidies on basic products, to cut into inflation as and when necessary.

Stop using public sector charges, such as gas prices – up by 116 per cent since 1979 – as a back-door way of raising taxes, as the Tories have done.

Buy our food where it is cheaper, on world markets, following Britain's withdrawal from the EEC.

Give powers to a new Price Commission to investigate companies, monitor price increases and order price freezes and reductions. These controls will be closely linked to our industrial planning, through agreed development plans with the leading, price-setting firms.

Take full account of these measures in the national economic assessment, to be agreed each year with the trade unions. The assessment will also take account of the impact of cost increases on the future rate of inflation.

1991

THE VERDICT IN THE FACTORTAME (II) CASE

EUROPEAN JURISDICTION AND THE LIMITS OF BRITISH SOVEREIGNTY

In delivering its verdict in the Factortame case, the European Court of Justice not only overturned the will of the British Parliament, it also gave any individual in any European Union country the right to sue their government for breaching European law. This had profound implications for the sovereignty of Parliament.

Although the judgment's application was universal across the ever-expanding legal competences of the EU, the specific case that established the precedent concerned the fishing industry. In the late 1970s and early 1980s, Spanish fishing boats that had traditionally fished off the coasts of Ireland and the west coasts of England found themselves excluded by the imposition of a fishing exclusion zone designed to deny access to non-members of the European Community (as the EU was then called). Spain did not join the EC until 1985 and in the meantime its fishermen sought to get around the exclusion either by re-registering their Spanish vessels as British ones or by becoming the owners of British vessels. British opposition was initially muted because a rudimentary European Common Fisheries Policy was being established and it was in Britain's interests to demonstrate that its registered fleet landed large catches so that, when formal restrictive quotas were introduced, Britain would be given a large share.

However, following Spain's entry into the European Community and the imposition by Brussels of tight quotas on how much, and what type of, fish each country could catch, British fishermen discovered that a large proportion of their entitlement was effectively being taken by Spanish vessels merely flying a British flag of convenience. Westminster responded in 1988 with the Merchant Shipping Act, which reserved the right to own a British-registered fishing boat for British citizens, domiciled in the United Kingdom.

Factortame Limited, a Spanish-owned company operating 'British' fishing boats, claimed that the Merchant Shipping Act breached the European law's prohibition of discrimination between member states. The issue was complicated because the whole rationale behind the EU's national fishing quotas was predicated precisely upon recognizing separate national fishing fleets. What was the point of national quotas if there was not a nation-based definition of who was bound by them? The Treaty of Rome did not specify that a member nation no longer had the right to set rules on the entitlement to fly its flag for business purposes.

In June 1990, in what became known as the 'Factortame I' verdict, the European Court of Justice ruled that British courts could not withhold interim relief (such as an injunction) from a British Act of Parliament just because the applicability of European law had not yet been determined. Thus Factortame Limited was granted an injunction against the 1988 Merchant Shipping Act. In July 1991 came 'Factortame II' with the European Court's adjudication on the legality of the 1988 Act. It ruled that member states' rights to set rules on what constituted their national marine area of control did not extend to discriminating against those of a fellow European member state – in this instance, Spain. It therefore declared the Merchant Shipping Act void. 'Factortame III' followed in May 1996 when the European Court ruled that the British government was liable for damages for having steered through a law that the court subsequently deemed illegal. After further legal argument, the government eventually paid up.

It now seemed that, in an area of conflict, the 1972 European Communities Act (which made British law subservient to European Community law) overrode all subsequent legislation. Thus, the ancient notion that no Westminster Parliament could bind its successor was overturned. Nonetheless, a qualification remained. The Factortame case established that the European Court of Justice could strike down British Acts of Parliament that had been originally passed in the belief that they were in keeping with the spirit of European law – in this particular case national fishing quotas. It remained unclear what would happen if a British Act of Parliament was passed that not only broke European law but specifically stated its conscious intention to do so. The implications of the European Union's judiciary attesting that such a firm national declaration was illegal could one day produce a constitutional crisis in Britain.

Judgment of the European Court of Justice, 1991

THE COURT, in reply to the questions referred to it for a preliminary ruling by the High Court of Justice of England and Wales, Queen' s Bench Division, by order of 10 March 1989, hereby rules:

1. As Community law stands at present, it is for the Member States to determine, in accordance with the general rules of international law, the conditions which must be fulfilled in order for a vessel to be registered in their registers and granted the right to fly their flag, but, in exercising that power, the Member States must comply with the rules of Community law;

2. It is contrary to the provisions of Community law and, in particular, to Article 52 of the EEC Treaty for a Member State to stipulate as conditions for the registration of a fishing vessel in its national register: (a) that the legal owners and beneficial owners and the charterers, managers and operators of the vessel must be nationals of that Member State or companies incorporated in that Member State, and that, in the latter case, at least 75% of the shares in the company must be owned by nationals of that Member State or by companies fulfilling the same requirements and 75% of the directors of the company must be nationals of that Member State; and (b) that the said legal owners and beneficial owners, charterers, managers, operators, shareholders and directors, as the case may be, must be resident and domiciled in that Member State;

3. It is not contrary to Community law for a Member State to stipulate as a condition for the registration of a fishing vessel in its national register that the vessel in question must be managed and its operations directed and controlled from within that Member State;

4. The fact that the competent minister of a Member State has the power to dispense with the nationality requirement in respect of an individual in view of the length of time such individual has resided in that Member State and has been involved in the fishing industry of that Member State cannot justify, in regard to Community law, the rule under which registration of a fishing vessel is subject to a nationality requirement and a requirement as to residence and domicile;

5. The existence of the present system of national quotas does not affect the replies given to the second question.

1997

CONDOLENCE BOOKS AND POPULAR INSCRIPTIONS TO DIANA, PRINCESS OF WALES

THE DEATH OF PRINCESS DIANA AND THE WEAKENING OF THE NATION'S STIFF UPPER LIP

In the early hours of 31 August 1997, Diana, Princess of Wales, then just thirty-six, died from injuries sustained in a car crash in central Paris. Also killed in the accident were her boyfriend, Dodi Fayed – son of the Egyptian entrepreneur Mohamed Al-Fayed, owner of Harrods department store – and the car's driver, Henri Paul, deputy head of security at the al-Fayed-owned Paris Ritz, where Diana and Dodi had been staying. Diana's life had been a heady mixture of aristocratic privilege and modern celebrity glitz, compassion for the less fortunate and media savviness, mass adulation and personal unhappiness. Her death sparked an outpouring of public emotion so removed from the self-control displayed by her former mother-in-law Queen Elizabeth II and her generation that it seemed as if a social revolution was under way. Some believed the monarchy itself was briefly endangered.

The fact that her fifteen-year marriage to the Prince of Wales had ended in divorce in 1996 had done little to diminish Princess Diana's public profile, either in Britain, where as the mother of Princes William and Harry she could hardly fail to be newsworthy, or in the rest of the world, where she remained a fashion icon on a scale surpassing that achieved by any Englishwoman in history. She had developed from the shy, nineteen-year-old daughter of an earl who married the Prince of Wales in 1981 into a loving mother, a dangerously weight-conscious bulimic and an international superstar. Technically, she had not been the hardest-working member of the royal family, but her stylishness and natural sympathy for others – whether embracing Aids sufferers or campaigning for a worldwide ban of

A page from the Dodi and Diana condolence book at Harrods is depicted in the fourth plate section.

407

landmines – gave to her engagements and charitable undertakings a frisson that those merely doing their duty could not match.

With the unravelling of her marriage, she launched a media campaign to both put her side of the story and discredit the Prince of Wales, first by providing private briefings to a friendly biographer, Andrew Morton, who turned out the best-selling *Diana – Her True Story*, and then, even more sensationally, by questioning whether her former husband was up to the job of kingship in a carefully choreographed television interview. In the broadcast, she cast herself as a 'queen in people's hearts'. It was a theme that the newly elected prime minister, Tony Blair, embellished when giving his public reaction to her death: 'People everywhere, not just here in Britain, kept faith with Princess Diana. They liked her, they loved her, they regarded her as one of the people. She was the People's Princess and that is how she will stay, how she will remain in our hearts and our memories for ever.'

The royal family was holidaying at Balmoral when the tragedy struck. The queen considered it her first duty to remain on the Scottish estate with her bereaved grandchildren, away from the public glare. The public mood elsewhere in the kingdom switched from grief at the cruel death of a beautiful and well-intentioned young woman to anger at the queen's failure to venture down south and visibly join in the emotional display. Realizing that private reflection was not what the public wanted, Blair was among those who persuaded the queen to make a hasty return to her capital, broadcast an appropriate tribute and ensure that Diana received a full public funeral. These late interventions did much to retrieve the House of Windsor's faltering standing.

Even so, suspicion of 'the Establishment' manifested itself, for a while, in the widespread credence given to a bizarre conspiracy theory in which the accident – caused in reality by a drunken chauffeur trying to shake off motorcycle photographers – had been an assassination carried out by Britain's security services. Resentment was also apparent at the funeral in the burst of applause, first outside and then inside Westminster Abbey, when Diana's brother Earl Spencer delivered a eulogy critical of the royal family's perceived lack of interpersonal skills.

Well over one million mourners gathered in Hyde Park or lined the route of Diana's coffin as it made its way to the Spencer family seat of Althorp in Northamptonshire. Across the world, an estimated 2.5 billion people watched the funeral on television. A sea of floral tributes was laid beyond the gates of Kensington Palace, Diana's former home. Candles were placed next to makeshift shrines, illustrated with cuttings of the princess from glossy magazines. Queues formed to sign books of condolence at St

James's Palace and at other points around the country. The Britain of self-control, of a stiff upper lip, of quiet Protestant understatement appeared to have been replaced by a temperament previously associated with Catholic Latin America. While many rejoiced that the emotionally repressed national caricature was giving way to one newly confident in expressing its feelings, others were aghast at what appeared, rather, to be the symptoms of a collective nervous breakdown.

The days of public mourning for Diana have become an indelible moment of shared national consciousness, like VE-Day or the England football team's 1966 World Cup victory. Measuring the extent to which the event shaped, or exemplified, changes in British society perhaps needs a longer perspective. The style of the public tribute was unprecedented, but its impressive scale needs putting in context. Vast crowds turned out to pay their respects at the state funeral of Field Marshal Earl Haig in 1928, yet his reputation proceeded to diminish almost continuously over the following half-century. At any rate, the damage done to the mystique of monarchy – which, after all, had once been part of Diana's own appeal – was certainly not apparent when, in 2002, joyful nationwide celebrations marked the Queen's Golden Jubilee.

Diana attracted huge crowds all over the world. These admirers are Russian.

1998

THE SCOTLAND ACT AND THE GOVERNMENT OF WALES ACT

A NEW SETTLEMENT FOR THE UNITED KINGDOM, OR THE BEGINNING OF ITS BREAK-UP?

I n 1999, the Scottish Parliament was restored, 292 years after it had voted itself out of existence, and Wales gained a democratic national assembly for the first time in its history. What was unclear was whether these developments marked a long-delayed recognition that Scottish and Welsh nationhood could coincide with allegiance to the United Kingdom or whether the new institutions would eventually tear the Union apart.

This was not the first time that home rule for part of the UK had been tried. Between 1921 and 1972, Northern Ireland's internal affairs had been largely determined by its Parliament in Stormont. Yet Ulster was a special case. It was not part of the mainland and its particular sectarian troubles led to its Parliament being suspended. It was supposed to be restored following the 1998 Good Friday Agreement, although it was not until 2007 that the basis for cross-community trust was sufficient to permit Stormont's resumption.

The fact that Wales and Scotland were not just, for administrative purposes, an extension of England had been recognized by the establishment of the Scottish Office in 1885 and the Welsh Office in 1965, with their own secretaries of state, separate bureaucracy and tailored legislation. These arrangements allowed for a devolved approach to implementing policy set by a government answerable to Westminster, but they did not involve Scottish and Welsh politicians taking decisions for which they were accountable to their own legislatures and voters.

The case for devolved authority was attacked on two sides: by those who felt that separate parliaments would create the sort of conflicts with Westminster that could ultimately disunite the kingdom; and by supporters of outright independence, who regarded them as paltry half-measures. The independence movements were led by

Plaid Cymru, the Party of Wales, which was founded in 1925, and by the Scottish National Party (SNP), which was created out of two smaller groups in 1934. Neither party initially attracted widespread support. During the 1950s, the SNP had scarcely more than 1,000 members and, in the 1959 general election, less than 1 per cent of the Scottish vote.

While the extent of public backing for nationalist parties waxed and waned, the principle of devolution *within* the United Kingdom did command support. In 1949, 2 million Scots (almost half the nation's adult population) signed a new 'Covenant', which combined a pledge of loyalty to the British Crown with a request for the restoration of a Scottish legislature. Neither successive Conservative nor Labour governments did much to acknowledge this sentiment, and the 1950s proved to be a period in which Scotland seemed relatively at ease with its existing constitutional arrangements. By the late 1960s, however, endorsement for the SNP was spreading rapidly. The discovery of North Sea oil became the separatists' strongest argument in asserting that a country of only 5 million people could successfully go it alone. In the October 1974 general election, support for the SNP peaked at 30 per cent of the Scottish vote and eleven MPs.

The Labour government of 1974–9 felt compelled to offer devolution (without separate tax-raising powers), but a parliamentary amendment made the adoption of home rule conditional on the support of 40 per cent of the electorate in a referendum. In March 1979, the 'yes' campaign won the most votes, but since the narrow margin of victory equated to only 33 per cent of the Scottish electorate, it failed to clear the qualifying margin. In Wales, the devolutionists were crushed by 956,000 votes to 243,000. The opposition to home rule of Margaret Thatcher and John Major blocked new initiatives between 1979 and 1997.

During this period, the Conservative vote collapsed in Wales and Scotland. Particularly resented was the decision to introduce the ill-fated poll tax to Scotland a year before England. It caused widespread outrage as well as simple refusal to pay it. In 1989, representatives of the Scottish Labour and Liberal parties, together with trade unions, local authorities, churches and other interested entities, met as a 'Constitutional Convention' to draw up fresh proposals for a new Scottish Parliament.

The proposals formed the basis for legislation when Labour won the 1997 general election. Although Tony Blair had little interest in devolving power, he felt unable to dilute the commitment made by John Smith, his Scottish predecessor as Labour leader. Concluding that it was a step towards their goal of independence, the SNP tactically supported devolution when it was proposed in the September

From the Scotland Act and the Government of Wales Act, 1998

SCOTLAND ACT

Part I The Scottish Parliament

(1) There shall be a Scottish Parliament.

(2) One member of the Parliament shall be returned for each constituency (under the simple majority system) at an election held in the constituency.

(3) Members of the Parliament for each region shall be returned at a general election under the additional member system of proportional representation provided for in this Part and vacancies among such members shall be filled in accordance with this Part.

(4) The validity of any proceedings of the Parliament is not affected by any vacancy in its membership.

(5) Schedule 1 (which makes provision for the constituencies and regions for the purposes of this Act and the number of regional members) shall have effect.

Part II The Scottish Administration

(1) There shall be a Scottish Executive, whose members shall be—
   (a) the First Minister,
   (b) such Ministers as the First Minister may appoint under section 47, and
   (c) the Lord Advocate and the Solicitor General for Scotland.

(2) The members of the Scottish Executive are referred to collectively as the Scottish Ministers.

GOVERNMENT OF WALES ACT

Part I The National Assembly for Wales

(1) There shall be an Assembly for Wales to be known as the National Assembly for Wales or Cynulliad Cenedlaethol Cymru (but referred to in this Act as the Assembly).

(2) The Assembly shall be a body corporate.

(3) The exercise by the Assembly of its functions is to be regarded as done on behalf of the Crown. . . .

Part II Assembly functions

21 Introductory

The Assembly shall have the functions which are—
   (a) transferred to, or made exercisable by, the Assembly by virtue of this Act, or
   (b) conferred or imposed on the Assembly by or under this Act or any other Act.

22 Transfer of Ministerial functions

(1) Her Majesty may by Order in Council—

(a) provide for the transfer to the Assembly of any function so far as exercisable by a Minister of the Crown in relation to Wales,

(b) direct that any function so far as so exercisable shall be exercisable by the Assembly concurrently with the Minister of the Crown, or

(c) direct that any function so far as exercisable by a Minister of the Crown in relation to Wales shall be exercisable by the Minister only with the agreement of, or after consultation with, the Assembly.

1997 referendum. This time a simple majority was sufficient and Scotland voted by three to one in favour of a parliament and by two to one that it should also be granted the right to vary income tax by three pence in the pound from the rate set at Westminster. Eight days later, the verdict was far more muted in Wales, with the devolutionists winning by the thinnest of margins, a mere 6,712 votes.

The Scotland Act was largely the work of Blair's secretary of state for Scotland, Donald Dewar (1937–2000). It devolved all competences to Scotland other than those specifically listed as 'reserved' for Westminster. In contrast, the presumption of the Wales Act was that all powers remained at Westminster except those specifically listed as moving to Cardiff. The sixty-member Welsh Assembly, which was not given powers to vary income tax, was primarily concerned with adapting Westminster legislation to Welsh circumstances rather than, as was the case with the Scottish Parliament, instigating its own laws (although Cardiff did gain some primary legislative powers, subject to London's veto, in 2006). In 1999, the Scottish Parliament began sitting in Edinburgh, with Dewar as first minister. Elected by a system of proportional representation that made coalition likely, the Parliament had 129 representatives and enjoyed legislative powers over such domestic affairs as health, education, transport, housing and social security. The commanding heights of economic policy, foreign affairs and defence remained the prerogative of London.

Neither unionists nor separatists imagined that this represented a final and irrevocable settlement. After the SNP formed a minority administration in 2007, they retitled the Scottish Executive in a telling linguistic sleight of hand as the 'Scottish Government' and pursued a legislative and cultural agenda that accentuated the division north and south of the border. Still awaiting a convincing answer was the 'West Lothian question' posed by the pro-Union Scottish Labour MP Tam

Dalyell, who wondered whether it was equitable for Westminster's Scottish MPs to vote on legislation that applied only to England when their English colleagues could not legislate for Scotland. The seemingly obvious solution of excluding the votes of Scottish MPs worked smoothly solely when the government's majority was not dependent on Scottish seats, which historically it often was. It risked legislative confusion, if not havoc, at some stage in the future.

In the past, Britain has always emerged, grumbling yet united, from far more severe trials. In the decades ahead, it will be up to its constituent peoples to decide whether they still believe, as so many of their forebears did, that Britain remains greater than the sum of its parts and an ideal of cooperation worth fighting to preserve.

2002

IRAQ'S WEAPONS OF MASS DESTRUCTION: THE ASSESSMENT OF THE BRITISH GOVERNMENT

TONY BLAIR'S CASE FOR WAR WITH IRAQ

The most controversial act of British foreign policy since the 1956 Suez Crisis was the decision to join the US invasion of Iraq in 2003. Although it did not provide the only justification for the attack, the government's decision to release an intelligence assessment suggesting that Iraq had the ability to launch weapons of mass destruction (WMD) within forty-five minutes of an order being given was one of the critical influences in persuading the House of Commons to sanction the invasion despite divided public opinion. Too late, the central claims of the report were found to be false.

Following al-Qaeda's terrorist attacks on New York and Washington, which killed 2,976 people on 11 September 2001, President George W. Bush's administration was determined not only to confront the militant Islamist perpetrators of the assault, together with the Taliban government of Afghanistan that had given them shelter, but also to remove another thorn in the side of American foreign policy – the dictatorship of Saddam Hussein in Iraq. In Tony Blair, Bush found the most resolute of allies. British forces joined the American-led invasion of Afghanistan in October 2001.

The plan to occupy Iraq was more controversial, since, despite the country's clear hostility towards the United States and other Western countries, not to mention the viciousness of its ruler, it was not implicated in the September 2001 terrorist outrages. Saddam Hussein had deployed chemical weapons in his war with Iran between 1980 and 1988, but his regime had received a major setback with the American-led coalition's repulsion of his occupation of Kuwait in 1991 and

BLAIR'S BRITAIN

1997 Labour wins the general election with 418 seats, ending eighteen years of Conservative rule. Diana, Princess of Wales, is killed in a Paris car crash. Wales and Scotland vote for devolved powers in referenda. There are about 10 million mobile phone subscriptions in the UK. The average house price is £68,525, the average household debt £16,155.

1998 The Belfast ('Good Friday') Agreement is signed. The Human Rights Act is passed. A national minimum wage is introduced.

1999 The UK joins in NATO airstrikes against Serbia during the Kosovo War. The first elections to the Scottish Parliament and the Welsh Assembly take place. About 20 per cent of households have internet access.

2000 The newly constructed Dome in London is the national focus for celebration – and criticism – during the commemoration of the new millennium. The first directly elected mayor of London, Ken Livingstone, takes office. British troops are sent into Sierra Leone.

2001 Labour wins a second term with 413 seats. The Conservative leader, William Hague, resigns and is replaced by Iain Duncan Smith. British troops join NATO forces in an invasion of Afghanistan following the al-Qaeda terrorist attacks on New York and Washington, DC.

2002 Blair makes the case for invading Iraq with the help of inaccurate intelligence information about Iraq's weapons of mass destruction.

2003 Over 1 million protesters march through London to condemn the proposed war in Iraq. British forces participate in the invasion of Iraq and take control of Basra. Iain Duncan Smith is replaced by Michael Howard as Conservative leader.

2004 The Hutton Report into the suicide of defence analyst David Kelly criticizes BBC journalism and controls. But the Butler report faults British intelligence's contribution in preparation for the Iraq war. The Civil Partnership Act gives same-sex relationships the legal entitlements of marriage.

2005 Labour wins a third term in the general election with 356 seats and a majority reduced to 64. Michael Howard resigns as Conservative leader and is replaced by David Cameron. Fifty-two innocent civilians are killed and hundreds injured in Islamist suicide bomb attacks in London.

2006 The 'cash for honours' investigation looks into the ethics of Labour fund-raising.

2007 The Scottish Nationalist Party (SNP) emerges as the largest party in the 2007 elections for the Scottish parliament. Alex Salmond heads a minority SNP administration. Tony Blair resigns as prime minister and is succeeded by Gordon Brown. Over 60 per cent of households have internet access. There are over 60 million mobile phone subscriptions in the UK. The average house price is £205,102, the average household debt £54,318.

the subsequent international efforts to restrict his war-making potential. When his obstructionism of UN weapons inspectors caused them to abandon their investigative mission in 1998, the assumption remained that he had something to hide. Under threat of military action, Iraq reluctantly allowed back UN inspectors in November 2002. While the inspection team was given wide access, the regime's failure to respond promptly to some requests played into the hands of those who had decided that regime change in Baghdad could alone solve the problem.

In September, Tony Blair's government had recalled Parliament early from its summer break to discuss the crisis and had issued its intelligence assessment on Iraq's WMD. The report asserted that Saddam's regime still had biological and chemical weapons, some of which could be deployed within forty-five minutes. The report also claimed that Iraq had recommenced work on a nuclear programme and was trying to get hold of uranium from Niger.

It further drew upon various private briefings provided to the Cabinet by its Joint Intelligence Committee (JIC). A furious row later developed over whether the government had strengthened the JIC's language ('sexed up' became the buzz-phrase of the moment) in order to strengthen the case for intervention. This was what the BBC journalist Andrew Gilligan inferred from a private briefing by a government weapons expert, David Kelly. In the subsequent media frenzy following the government's release of his identity, Kelly committed suicide.

Special Relationship: Tony Blair in step with President George W. Bush.

From *Iraq's Weapons of Mass Destruction: The Assessment of the British Government*, 2002

THE CURRENT POSITION: 1998–2002

1. This chapter sets out what we know of Saddam Hussein's chemical, biological, nuclear and ballistic missile programmes, drawing on all the available evidence. While it takes account of the results from UN inspections and other publicly available information, it also draws heavily on the latest intelligence about Iraqi efforts to develop their programmes and capabilities since 1998. The main conclusions are that:

- Iraq has a useable chemical and biological weapons capability, in breach of UNSCR 687, which has included recent production of chemical and biological agents;

- Saddam continues to attach great importance to the possession of weapons of mass destruction and ballistic missiles which he regards as being the basis for Iraq's regional power. He is determined to retain these capabilities; Iraq can deliver chemical and biological agents using an extensive range of artillery shells, free-fall bombs, sprayers and ballistic missiles;

- Iraq continues to work on developing nuclear weapons, in breach of its obligations under the Non-Proliferation Treaty and in breach of UNSCR 687. Uranium has been sought from Africa that has no civil nuclear application in Iraq;

- Iraq possesses extended-range versions of the SCUD ballistic missile in breach of UNSCR 687 which are capable of reaching Cyprus, Eastern Turkey, Tehran and Israel. It is also developing longer-range ballistic missiles;

- Iraq's current military planning specifically envisages the use of chemical and biological weapons;

- Iraq's military forces are able to use chemical and biological weapons, with command, control and logistical arrangements in place. The Iraqi military are able to deploy these weapons within 45 minutes of a decision to do so;

- Iraq has learnt lessons from previous UN weapons inspections and is already taking steps to conceal and disperse sensitive equipment and documentation in advance of the return of inspectors;

- Iraq's chemical, biological, nuclear and ballistic missiles programmes are well-funded.

Certainly, Alastair Campbell, the prime minister's director of communications – famous for being able to put the most favourable 'spin' on any story concerning the Labour government – was involved in the report's presentation. Nonetheless, John Scarlett, the JIC chairman, later gave evidence maintaining that the report was faithful to the briefings the security services had provided.

Whatever view is taken on how the Blair government presented both the report and the case built from it for invading Iraq, the fact remains that the document represented a colossal failing of information assessment by Britain's secret services. The ensuing occupation of Iraq uncovered no WMD, let alone those able to be deployed within forty-five minutes, nor a restarted nuclear programme. The likelihood of Niger successfully delivering uranium to Iraq was discounted.

These disclosures came too late to prevent the invasion. Having failed to secure a UN resolution explicitly endorsing military action, Tony Blair faced the House of Commons on 18 March 2003 and repeated his case, drawing substantively on the JIC's September 2002 report. Impressed by that evidence, Iain Duncan Smith, the leader of the opposition, pledged his party's support on the grounds that 'Saddam Hussein has the means, the mentality and the motive to pose a direct threat to our national security'. Upon these misapprehensions, MPs endorsed the prime minister's actions and voted down an amendment 'that the case for war against Iraq has not yet been established' by 396 to 217. Two days later the invasion began.

The bloody insurgency and the cost, in both human and diplomatic terms, of sustaining a democratic Iraqi state in the chaos that followed Saddam Hussein's overthrow naturally had the most far-reaching effects in the Middle East. In Britain, the consequences were political as well as psychological. There was a widespread – if disputed – claim by the war's opponents that military action was illegal without a specific UN resolution sanctioning it. To this charge was added the accusation that, in basing so much of his case for invasion on the WMD claims, Blair had effectively gone to war on the back of a conscious deceit, rather than merely poor advice. These were grave accusations that Blair and those closest to him strongly refuted when giving evidence to the Chilcot Inquiry in 2010. Yet they were manifestations of growing dissatisfaction not just with the 'New Labour project' but – more alarmingly – with the probity of those in public life more generally. In this sense at the very least, *Iraq's Weapons of Mass Destruction: The Assessment of the British Government* unquestionably had a toxic legacy.

2005

LIFE IN THE UNITED KINGDOM, QUESTION PAPER

TESTING BRITISHNESS

During the early years of the twenty-first century, several research projects were undertaken to track the genetic history of the British people. The preliminary results were surprising. It seemed that around 80 per cent of modern white Britons could trace their genetic make-up all the way back to ancestors who were already settled in the British Isles at the end of the Ice Age – 12,000 years ago.

The findings were particularly startling, not just because they suggested that the political and cultural influence of Anglo-Saxon, Viking and Norman settlers was far greater than their actual numbers, but also for the perspective placed upon more recent immigration. Between the twelfth century and the end of the nineteenth century, the only really huge influx to the mainland came not from abroad but from Ireland, which was at the time of the greatest migration (during and after the Irish potato famine of 1845–51) fully incorporated into the United Kingdom. From beyond the British Isles, the level of migration was continuous but never overwhelming. By 1700, Protestant Huguenots who had escaped religious persecution in France represented about 0.7 per cent of the British population and, a few decades later, the black population was thought to have peaked at about 0.2 per cent of Britons. Indeed, in the early decades of the twentieth century, there were thought to have been scarcely more than 10,000 non-white people in Britain, while the proportion of German and Italian-born residents in the country was put at about 0.2 per cent in 1911. The Jewish community, fleeing first tsarist and then fascist persecution, still represented less than 1 per cent by the end of the 1930s.

The picture began to change more rapidly after the Second World War with large-scale immigration from the 'New Commonwealth' countries of the Caribbean, Africa and the Indian subcontinent. Even so, by the mid-1970s these

'New Commonwealth' immigrants comprised only 3 per cent of the UK population of 55 million. By the 1980s, the majority of them were British-born. It was in the 1990s and, especially, in the first years of the twenty-first century that the most radical change became manifest. By 2006, official net immigration was running at an annual rate of about 300,000 (equivalent to the population of a city the size of Coventry) and one in four children born in Britain had a foreign parent. On top of this, by 2009 there were estimated to be around three-quarters of a million illegal immigrants in the country, all from outside the European Union.

This level of cultural impact was without precedent since the Norman Conquest. Whilst the dramatic influx of workers from Eastern Europe was curtailed by the onset of economic recession in 2008, there were still considerable numbers arriving from other parts of the world. Despite the size – and speed – of the influx, the newcomers were largely welcomed by Tony Blair's government and by businesses keen to tap new talents, filling positions left vacant because of skill shortages among British-born workers as well as ensuring that competitive pressures restrained wage growth. From the arts to the less glamorous jobs, the new arrivals quickly made their mark. Many observers welcomed this new diversity as a source of strength. There was even hopeful talk of creating a British version of the 'American Dream'.

Those more sceptical about the benefits of multiculturalism were less clear that it created a common community, seeing rather a process of atomization and alienation. Indeed, some of the social and religious attitudes introduced with immigration seemed to be at odds with the innate liberalism and tolerance that was supposedly Britain's great appeal. Evidence of divided communities, militant Islamic fundamentalist attitudes (even extending to the planning of Islamist terrorist attacks) and renewed recruiting by racist groups suggested that, for all the achievements, the ideal sometimes fell short of reality. These tensions also triggered reactionary political developments. The belief that Britain had lost control of its borders was among the reasons cited by politicians urging mandatory identity cards and other forms of heightened surveillance.

The governments of Tony Blair and Gordon Brown found themselves trying to celebrate the new diversity while searching for ways to channel it towards a common British identity – one that was simultaneously under threat from the re-emergence of Scottish, Welsh and Irish nationalism, recognized by devolution in Edinburgh and Cardiff, and power-sharing in Belfast. Defining a positive British identity was easier said than done. Aspects of British history that might once have been a source of pride, such as an empire that covered a quarter of the globe, often had a

---

A selection of sample test questions

1. When will the British Government adopt the euro as the UK's currency?
A 2010
B 2015
C Never
D When the British people vote for it in a referendum

2. What percentage of Christians in the UK are Roman Catholic?
A 10 per cent
B 20 per cent
C 30 per cent
D 40 per cent

3. What type of constitution does the UK have?
A A legal constitution
B A written constitution
C An amended constitution
D An unwritten constitution

4. How might you stop young people playing tricks on you at Hallowe'en?
A Call the police
B Give them some money
C Give them sweets or chocolate
D Hide from them

5. What proportion of the UK population have used illegal drugs at one time or another?
A One quarter
B One third
C One half
D Two thirds

6. Who is the monarch not allowed to marry?
A Anyone who is not of royal blood
B Anyone who is not a Protestant
C Anyone who is under the age of 25
D Anyone who was born outside the UK

7. What year did women in the UK gain the right to divorce their husband?
A 1810
B 1857
C 1901
D 1945

8. All dogs in public places must wear a collar showing the name and address of the owner. Is this statement true or false?
A True
B False

less positive resonance for those who had not been on the side of the conquerors. The same applied to celebrated military victories against European neighbours. In an attempt to define Britishness without offending anyone, the government suggested it was about the spirit of 'fair play', although even this observation implied a certain degree of self-satisfied chauvinism. A 'public consultation' on devising a national motto only managed to provoke derisive suggestions and the widespread reaction that the very idea was distinctly un-British.

One Cabinet minister in particular made constructive efforts to address the future of Britishness: David Blunkett (b. 1947). As a student, he had studied at Sheffield University under the professor of politics there, Bernard Crick (1929–2008). A socialist and constitutional reformer, Crick was the author of *In Defence of Politics* and a strong believer in the active participation of the citizen. Appropriately from this perspective, Britain was nothing if not four nations bound by political institutions. On becoming education secretary in 1997, Blunkett appointed Crick chairman of the Teaching of Citizenship and Democracy in Schools advisory group. The result was that 'citizenship' became part of the school national curriculum. In 2001, Blunkett became home secretary and Crick was again appointed, this time to chair the commission advising on how a test might be devised for those seeking British citizenship.

Previously, the process of British naturalization had been a purely bureaucratic procedure, but, inspired by American practice, the decision was taken to turn it into more of an event, complete with a formal ceremony. The general criteria for applicants included stipulations that they should have lived in Britain for five years (or three years if married to a Briton), be 'of good character', have a basic competency in the English language and pass a citizenship test. The examination was an entirely new initiative in which applicants answered multiple-choice questions on subject matter laid out in a Home Office publication, *Life in the United Kingdom*. Crick had written the history section and, inevitably, immediately drew accusations from professional historians that he had got some of his facts wrong.

Whatever the legacy of the citizenship test, it was clearly the product of a United Kingdom wrestling with a crisis of identity. The prospect of it being torn apart and Balkanized back into its constituent nations has become real for the first time in generations. The very notion of 'British documents' may soon be seen as a dated concept. Yet come what may, those collated in this book represent a rich bequest and, if we are fortunate, may prove an enduring inspiration with which to shape the future.

ACKNOWLEDGEMENTS

A work of this kind is made possible by the custodians of the documents themselves and I would naturally like to thank the keepers and archivists at all the libraries and museums for their help, without which there could have been neither study nor reproduction of the manuscripts in their care. For providing expert knowledge on the extent of collections and the whereabouts of particular documents, I would especially like to thank Professor Richard Aldous, Kate Grimond, Dr Christopher de Hamel, Simon Gough, Dr Peter Jones, Neil Robinson and Robert Seatter. Eamon Dyas and Nick Mays at *The Times* archive must also be thanked for all their wise counsel and forbearance over the years, as must the staff of the London Library for their guidance and assistance.

I am particularly indebted to Anthony Cheetham and Richard Milbank for conceiving this project and to my agent, Georgina Capel, for her zest and stalwart support. At Atlantic Books, Richard Milbank and Sarah Norman have provided invaluable editorial advice, expertise and great professionalism. I should also like to thank Rich Carr, Mark Hawkins-Dady, Celia Levett and Amanda Russell.

For their hospitality and kindness I particularly wish to record my gratitude to Jane Clark at Saltwood and to Mark Craig and Nicole Wright in London. Paul Stephenson has been a source of seasoned sagacity, whether conveyed from long distance or across a dinner table. This book is dedicated to my nephew and godson, Rufus Stewart.

Graham Stewart
Saltwood
Kent

27 June 2010

SELECT BIBLIOGRAPHY

The place of publication is London unless otherwise stated.

THE DARK AGES

GENERAL STUDIES:
Guy de la Bédoyère, *Roman Britain, A New History* (2006); Michael Lapidge et al (eds.), *The Blackwell Encyclopaedia of Anglo-Saxon England* (Oxford 1999); Peter Salway, *Roman Britain* (Oxford 1981); Simon Schama, *A History of Britain: At the Edge of the World? 3000BC–1603* (2000); F. M. Stenton, *Anglo-Saxon England* (Oxford 1971 edn.); Dorothy Whitelock, *English Historical Documents, c.500–1042* (1979 edn.)

SPECIFIC STUDIES:
Robin Birley, *Vindolanda: a Roman Frontier Post on Hadrian's Wall* (1977); Alan K. Bowman, *Life and Letters on the Roman Frontier: Vindolanda and its People* (2003); John Blair, *The Church in Anglo-Saxon England* (Oxford 2005); Michelle Brown, *The Lindisfarne Gospels: Society, Spirituality and the Scribe* (2003); Leo Sherley-Price (trans.), The Venerable Bede, *History of the English Church and People* (1955); Seamus Heaney (trans.), *Beowulf* (1999); Benjamin Thorpe (trans.), *Beowulf* (1889); G. N. Garmonsway (trans.), *The Anglo-Saxon Chronicle* (1953); Alfred P. Smyth, *King Alfred the Great* (Oxford 1995)

THE MEDIEVAL AGE

GENERAL STUDIES:
Robert Bartlett, *England Under the Norman and Angevin Kings, 1075–1225* (Oxford 2000); David C. Douglas and G. W. Greenaway, *English Historical Documents, 1042–1189* (1981 ed); E. F. Jacob, *The Fifteenth Century, 1399–1485* (Oxford 1961); May McKisack, *The Fourteenth Century 1307–1399* (Oxford 1959); Alec R. Myers, *English Historical Documents 1327–1485* (1969); Austin Lane Poole, *From Domesday Book to Magna Carta 1087–1216* (Oxford 1955 edn.); Sir Maurice Powicke, *The Thirteenth Century, 1216–1307* (Oxford 1962 edn.); Michael Prestwich, *Plantagenet England 1225–1360* (Oxford 2005); Harry Rothwell, *English Historical Documents 1189–1327* (1975); Simon Schama, *A History of Britain: At the Edge of the World? 3000BC–1603* (2000)

SPECIFIC STUDIES:
Carola Hicks, *The Bayeux Tapestry, the Life History of a Masterpiece* (2006); J. C. Holt, *Magna Carta* (1965); Sir Ivor Jennings, *Magna Carta and its Influence in the World Today* (1965); Richard Vaughan (ed.), *The Illustrated Chronicles of Matthew Paris* (Stroud 1993); John Field, *The Story of Parliament in the Palace of Westminster* (2002); J. R. Maddicott, *Simon de Montfort* (1994); James A. MacKay, *Robert Bruce, King of Scots* (1974); Michael Brown, *The Wars of Scotland, 1214–1371* (Edinburgh 2004); Anthony Kenny, *Wyclif* (Oxford 1985); Tim Card, *Eton Established, a History from 1440 to 1860* (2001); Christopher Brooke and Roger Highfield, *Oxford and Cambridge* (Cambridge 1988); Elisabeth Leedham-Green, *A Concise History of the University of Cambridge* (Cambridge 1996); Christopher Morris, *King's College: A Short History* (Cambridge 1989); Elizabeth Archibald and Ad Putter, *The Cambridge Companion to the Arthurian Legend* (Cambridge 2009); Alan Lupack, *The Oxford Guide to Arthurian Literature and Legend* (Oxford 2005)

RELIGION AND RENAISSANCE

GENERAL STUDIES:
S.T. Bindoff, *Tudor England* (1950); J. B. Black, *The Reign of Elizabeth, 1558–1603* (Oxford 1959 edn.); C. S. L. Davies, *Peace, Print and Protestantism, 1450–1558* (1976); G. R. Elton, *England Under the Tudors* (1955); Douglas Price, *English Historical Documents, 1558–1603* (1966); Simon Schama, *A History of Britain: At the Edge of the World? 3000BC–1603* (2000); C. H. Williams, *English Historical Documents, 1485–1558* (1967); Penry Williams, *The Later Tudors, England 1547–1603* (Oxford 1995)

SPECIFIC STUDIES:

David Daniell, *William Tyndale, a Biography* (New Haven, CT, 1994); Brian Moynahan, *If God Spare My Life: William Tyndale, the English Bible and Sir Thomas More* (2002); C. S. Knighton and D. M. Loades (eds.), *The Anthony Roll of Henry VIII's Navy* (Aldershot 2000); G. W. Bernard, *The King's Reformation, Henry VIII and the Remaking of the English Church* (New Haven, CT, 2005); Diarmaid MacCulloch, *Tudor Church Militant, Edward VI and the Protestant Reformation* (1999); Diarmaid MacCulloch, *Thomas Cranmer, A Life* (1996); Thomas Stuart Willan, *The Early History of the Muscovy Company 1553–1606* (Manchester 1956); Gordon Donaldson, *Mary, Queen of Scots* (1974); Antonia Fraser, *Mary, Queen of Scots* (1969); A.E. MacRobert, *Mary Queen of Scots and the Casket Letters* (2002); Edmund H. Fellowes, *William Byrd* (1948 ed.); Nicholas Canny (ed.) *The Oxford History of the British Empire: The Origins of Empire* (Oxford 1998); *Lawrence James, The Rise and Fall of the British Empire* (1994); John Keay, *The Honourable Company: a History of the English East India Company* (1991)

STUART BRITAIN

GENERAL STUDIES:

Andrew Browning, *English Historical Documents, 1660–1714* (1953); Godfrey Davies, *The Early Stuarts 1603–1660* (Oxford 1959 edn.); Sir George Clark, *The Later Stuarts 1660–1714* (Oxford 1956 edn.); Julian Hoppit, *A Land of Liberty? England 1689–1727* (Oxford 2000); Simon Schama, *A History of Britain: The British Wars 1603–1776* (2001)

SPECIFIC STUDIES:

Nick Groom, *The Union Jack, The Biography* (2006); Anthony James West, *The Shakespeare First Folio: the History of the Book* (2001; 2003); Stanley Wells and Gary Taylor (gen. eds.), *The Oxford Shakespeare, The Complete Works* (Oxford 2005 ed); John Adamson, *The Noble Revolt: The Overthrow of Charles I* (2007); Tristram Hunt, *The English Civil War: At First Hand* (2002); Diane Purkiss, *The English Civil War: A People's History* (2006); A. L. Rowse, *The Regicides and the Puritan Revolution* (1994); C. V. Wedgwood, *The Trial of Charles I* (1964); Austin Woolrych, *Britain*

in Revolution 1625–1660 (2002); Blair Worden, *The English Civil Wars 1940–1660* (2009); David S. Katz, *The Jews in the History of England, 1485–1850* (Oxford 1994); W. D Rubinstein, *A History of the Jews in the English-Speaking World: Great Britain* (Basingstoke 1996); Bill Bryson (ed.), *Seeing Further: the Story of Science and the Royal Society* (2010); Lisa Jardine, *The Curious Life of Robert Hooke, the Man Who Measured London* (2003); John Miller, *James II, A Study in Kingship* (1978); Edward Vallance, *The Glorious Revolution 1688: Britain's Fight For Liberty* (2006); T. M. Devine, *The Scottish Nation, 1700–2000* (1999); Michael Fry, *The Union: England, Scotland and the Treaty of 1707* (Edinburgh 2007)

HANOVERIAN BRITAIN

GENERAL STUDIES:

D. B. Horn and Mary Ransome, *English Historical Documents, 1714–1783* (1957); Paul Langford, *A Polite and Commercial People, England 1727–1783* (Oxford 1989); Simon Schama, *A History of Britain: The British Wars 1603–1776* (2001); Simon Schama, *A History of Britain: The Fate of Empire 1776–2000* (2002); J. Steven Watson, *The Reign of George III, 1760–1815* (Oxford 1960); Basil Williams, *The Whig Supremacy 1714–1760* (Oxford 1962 edn.)

SPECIFIC STUDIES:

Linda Colley, *Britons: Forging the Nation 1707–1837* (New Haven, CT, 1992); James Boswell, *The Life of Samuel Johnson* (1991 ed.); Henry Hitchings, *Dr Johnson's Dictionary, the Extraordinary Story of the Book that Defined the World* (2005); Jack Lynch (ed.) *Samuel Johnson's Dictionary* (2002); Niall Ferguson, *Empire: How Britain Made the Modern World* (2003); A. J. Youngson, *The Making of Classical Edinburgh* (Edinburgh 1966); James Buchan, *Capital of the Mind: How Edinburgh Changed the World* (2003); Richard L. Hill, *Richard Arkwright and Cotton Spinning* (1973); Steven King and Geoffrey Timmins, *Making Sense of the Industrial Revolution: English Economy and Society, 1700–1850* (Manchester, 2001); Hugh Thomas, *The Slave Trade: the History of the Atlantic Slave Trade* (1997); Steven M. Wise, *Though the Heaven's May Fall: The Landmark Trial that led to the end of*

Human Slavery (2006); Gavin Kennedy, *Adam Smith, a Moral Philosopher and his Political Economy* (2008); P. J. O'Rourke, *On the Wealth of Nations* (2007); *The History of The Times: The 'Thunderer' in the Making* (1935) and successive volumes (now running to seven in total) of the newspaper's official history; Tony Lewis, *Double Century: a Story of MCC and Cricket* (1987); David Underdown, *Start of Play: Cricket and Culture in Eighteenth Century England* (2000); John Major, *More than a Game: the Story of Cricket's Early Years* (2007)

THE YEARS OF REFORM

GENERAL STUDIES:
A. Aspinall and E. Anthony Smith, *English Historical Documents, 1783–1832* (1959); Boyd Hilton, *A Mad, Bad, and Dangerous People? England 1783–1846* (Oxford 2006); Simon Schama, *A History of Britain: The Fate of Empire 1776–2000* (2002); J. Steven Watson, *The Reign of George III, 1760–1815* (Oxford 1960); Sir Llewellyn Woodward, *The Age of Reform 1815–1870* (Oxford 1962 edn.)

SPECIFIC STUDIES:
Janet Todd, *Mary Wollstonecraft, a Revolutionary Life* (2000); Richard Godfrey, *James Gillray: the Art of Caricature* (2001); William Hague, *William Pitt the Younger* (2004); Paul Bew, *Ireland, the Politics of Enmity 1789–2006* (Oxford 2007); Roger J. P. Cain, John Chapman and Richard R. Oliver, *The Enclosure Maps of England and Wales, 1595–1918* (Cambridge 2004); J. M. Neeson, *Commoners: Common Right, Enclosure and Social Change in England, 1700–1820* (Cambridge 1993); W. G. Hoskins, *The Making of the English Landscape* (1955); L. T. C. Rolt, *George and Robert Stephenson: The Railway Revolution* (1960); Wendy Hinde, *Catholic Emancipation: a Shake to Men's Minds* (Oxford 1992); M. D. R. Lays, *Catholics in England 1559–1829 A Social History* (1961); Linda Colley, *Taking Stock of Taking Liberties* (2008); Robert Stewart, *The Foundation of the Conservative Party 1830–67* (1978); Robert Blake, *A History of the Conservative Party from Peel to Major* (1997); Douglas Hurd, *Robert Peel, a biography* (2007); David Jones, *Chartism and the Chartists* (1975)

THE VICTORIAN AGE

GENERAL STUDIES:
R. C. K. Ensor, *England 1870–1914* (Oxford 1936); W. D. Handcock, *English Historical Documents, 1874–1914* (1977); K. Theodore Hoppen, *The Mid-Victorian Generation, England 1846–1886* (Oxford 1998); Simon Schama, *A History of Britain: The Fate of Empire 1776–2000* (2002); A. N. Wilson, *The Victorians* (2002); G. M. Young and W. D Handcock, *English Historical Documents, 1833–1874* (1956); Sir Llewellyn Woodward, *The Age of Reform 1815–1870* (Oxford 1938)

SPECIFIC STUDIES:
Steven Brindle, *Brunel, the Man Who Built the World* (2005); Peter Ackroyd, *Dickens* (1990) and his *Introduction to Dickens* (1991); Michael Leapman, *The World for a Shilling: How the Great Exhibition Shaped a Nation* (2001); Kate Colquhoun, *A Thing In Disguise: The Visionary Life of Joseph Paxton* (2003); Jonathan Glancey, *Lost Buildings: Demolished, Destroyed, Imagined, Reborn* (2008); Geoffrey Green, *The History of the Football Association* (1953); Richard Holt, *Sport and the British, a Modern History* (Oxford 1989)

FROM EMPIRE TO WELFARE STATE

GENERAL STUDIES:
Peter Clarke, *Hope and Glory: Britain 1900–1990* (1996); Simon Schama, *A History of Britain: The Fate of Empire 1776–2000* (2002); G. R. Searle, *A New England? England 1886–1918* (Oxford 2004); Richard Shannon, *The Crisis of Imperialism, 1865–1915* (Oxford 1974); A. J. P. Taylor, *English History 1914–1945* (Oxford 1965)

SPECIFIC STUDIES:
John Charmley, *Splendid Isolation? Britain, the Balance of Power and the Origins of the First World War* (1999); Simon Heffer, *Power and Place: The Political Consequences of Edward VII* (1998); Martin Pugh, *The March of the Women: A Revisionist Analysis of the Campaign for Women's Suffrage, 1866–1914* (2000) and his *The Pankhursts* (2001); David Cannadine, *The Decline and Fall of the British Aristocracy,* (New Haven, CT, 1990);

Roy Jenkins, *Asquith* (1964); John Grigg's *Lloyd George*, vols: II. *The People's Champion 1902–1911* (1978), III. *From Peace to War 1912–1916* (1985) and IV. *War Leader 1916–1918* (2002); Niall Ferguson, *The Pity of War* (1998); Henry Pelling, *A Short History of the Labour Party* (1968 ed.); Sheila Lawlor, *Britain and Ireland 1914–23* (Dublin 1983); J. J. Lee, *Ireland 1912–1985: Politics and Society* (Cambridge 1989); Kenneth O. Morgan, *Consensus and Disunity, the Lloyd George Coalition Government 1918–1922* (Oxford 1979); Niall Ferguson, *Empire: How Britain Made the Modern World* (2003); Judith M. Brown and Wm. Roger Louis (eds), *Oxford History of the British Empire: The Twentieth Century* (Oxford 1999); Tony Judd, *Empire, the British Imperial Experience from 1765 to the Present* (1996); Asa Briggs, *The BBC, the First Fifty Years* (Oxford 1985); Ian McIntyre, *The Expense of Glory: a Life of John Reith* (1993); Philip Ziegler, *King Edward VIII, the Official Biography* (1990); Jonathan Glancey, *Spitfire, the Biography* (2006); John Terraine, *The Right of the Line, the Royal Air Force in the European War, 1939–1945* (1985); R.A.C. Parker, *Chamberlain and Appeasement* (Basingstoke, 1993); John Charmley, *Chamberlain and the Lost Peace* (1989); Graham Stewart, *Burying Caesar, Churchill, Chamberlain and the Battle for the Tory Party* (1999); David Faber, *Munich, the 1938 Appeasement Crisis* (2008); Paul Addison, *The Road to 1945: British Politics and the Second World War* (1975); Kevin Jefferys, *The Churchill Coalition and Wartime Politics, 1940–1945* (Manchester 1995 ed.); Nicholas Timmins, *The Five Giants, A Biography of the Welfare State* (1995); Robin Woolven (int.), *The London County Council Bomb Damage Maps 1939–45* (2005); Angus Calder, *The People's War Britain: 1939–45* (1969); Philip Hoare, *Noel Coward, a Biography* (1995); Sarah Street, *British National Cinema* (1997); Robert Winder, *Bloody Foreigners, The Story of Immigration to Britain* (2004); Eric Richards, *Britannia's Children, Emigration from England, Scotland, Wales and Ireland since 1600* (2004); Peter Hennessy, *Never Again: Britain, 1945–51* (1992); Alan Bullock, *Ernest Bevin*, vol. III (1983);

Ben Macintyre, *For Your Eyes Only: Ian Fleming and James Bond* (2008); Lord Kilmuir, *Political Adventure, the Memoirs of the Earl of Kilmuir* (1964)

ELIZABETH II'S BRITAIN

GENERAL STUDIES:
Peter Clarke, *Hope and Glory: Britain 1900–1990* (1996); Brian Harrison, *Seeking a Role: the United Kingdom 1951–1970* (Oxford 2009); Peter Hennessy, *Having It So Good, Britain in the Fifties* (2006); Dominic Sandbrook, *Never Had It So Good, A History of Britain from Suez to the Beatles* (2005); Dominic Sandbrook, *White Heat, A History of Britain in the Swinging Sixties* (2006); Simon Schama, *A History of Britain: The Fate of Empire 1776–2000* (2002); Alan Sked and Chris Cook, *Post-War Britain: A Political History* (1993 edn.)

SPECIFIC STUDIES:
David Reynolds, *Britannia Overruled, British Policy and World Power in the Twentieth Century* (1991); David Carlton, *Britain and the Suez Crisis* (Oxford 1988); D. R. Thorpe, *Eden: the Life and Times of Anthony Eden* (2003); Ian MacDonald, *Revolution in the Head: The Beatles' Records and the Sixties* (1994); Tim Pat Coogan, *The Troubles: Ireland's Ordeal 1966–95 and the Search for Peace* (1995); J. J. Lee, *Ireland 1912–1985: Politics and Society* (Cambridge 1989); John Campbell, *Edward Heath, a Biography* (1993); Ben Pimlott, *Harold Wilson* (1992); David Butler and Dennis Kavanagh, *The British General Election of 1983* (1984); Kenneth O. Morgan, *Michael Foot, A Life* (2007); Sarah Bradford, *Diana* (2006); T. M. Devine, *The Scottish Nation, 1700–2000* (1999); Con Coughlin, *American Ally: Tony Blair and the War on Terror* (2006); Anthony Seldon, *Blair Unbound* (2007); David Miles, *The Tribes of Britain: Who Are We? And Where Do We Come From?* (2005)

WHERE TO FIND THE DOCUMENTS

The Vindolanda Tablets
British Museum

The Lindisfarne Gospels
British Library

Bede's *Historia Ecclesiastica Gentis Anglorum*
Among the early copies are those held by the British Library, Cambridge University Library, the Bodleian Library, Oxford and the St Petersburg Public Library, Russia

Beowulf
British Library

The Treaty of Alfred and Guthrum
Corpus Christi College, Cambridge

The Anglo-Saxon Chronicle
The Parker Chronicle is at Corpus Christi College, Cambridge. The Laud (Peterborough) Chronicle is at the Bodleian Library, Oxford. The Abingdon, Canterbury and Worcester Chronicles are at the British Library

The Bayeux Tapestry
Musée de la Tapisserie de Bayeux, Bayeux, France

The Domesday Book
The National Archives

The Assize of Clarendon
Roger of Howden's *Chronica* in the British Library and the Bodleian Library, Oxford

Magna Carta
Four 1215 copies survive: two in the British Library and one each at Lincoln Cathedral and Salisbury Cathedral

Chronicles of Matthew Paris
The *Chronica Majora* is at Corpus Christi College, Cambridge. The *Historia Anglorum* is in the British Library

Medieval parliamentary election writs
The National Archives

The Statute of Rhuddlan
The National Archives

The Declaration of Arbroath
The National Archives of Scotland

Wyclif's Bible
British Library and John Rylands University Library, University of Manchester

Henry VI's charter for Eton College
Eton College

Henry VI's charters for King's College, Cambridge
King's College, Cambridge

Caxton's edition of Malory's *Morte d'Arthur*
British Library

Tyndale's New Testament
British Library

Parliament's petition to the pope
Vatican Archives

The Anglo-Welsh Act of Union
Parliamentary Archives

The Anthony Roll
British Library and Magdalene College, Cambridge

The Book of Common Prayer
British Library

The royal charter of the Muscovy Company
The original document was lost in the Great Fire of London 1666 but a copy of it exists in the London Metropolitan Archives

Foxe's *Book of Martyrs*
British Library

The Thirty-Nine Articles
Corpus Christi College, Cambridge

The Casket Letters
The National Archives

My Ladye Nevells Book
British Library

The royal charter of the East India Company
British Library

The Elizabethan Poor Law
Parliamentary Archives

The Monteagle Letter and Guy Fawkes's Confession
The National Archives

Union Jack designs
National Library of Scotland

The King James Bible
British Library

Shakespeare's First Folio
British Library

The Petition of Right
Parliamentary Archives

The Scottish National Covenant
The National Archives of Scotland

The record of the Putney Debates
Worcester College, Oxford

The death warrant of King Charles I
Parliamentary Archives

The Instrument of Government
The original document was lost during the Restoration though its contents were published. Text in C. H. Firth, R. S. Rait (eds.), *Acts and Ordinances of the Interregnum, 1642–1660*.

Menasseh Ben Israel's Humble Petition
National Archives

Memorandum of the Royal Society
Royal Society

The Clarendon Code
Parliamentary Archives

The Immortal Seven's Invitation to William of Orange
Text in Sir John Dalrymple, *Memoirs of Great Britain and Ireland*, Appendix I

The Bill of Rights
Parliamentary Archives

John Locke's *Two Treatises of Government*
British Library

The royal charter of the Bank of England
Bank of England

The Act of Settlement
Parliamentary Archives

The Act of Union
Parliamentary Archives; exemplification in the National Archives of Scotland

God Save the King, *Gentleman's Magazine*
British Library

Samuel Johnson's *Dictionary*
British Library

The Declaratory Act
Parliamentary Archives

James Craig's plan for Edinburgh's New Town
National Library of Scotland

Arkwright's water frame patent
The National Archives

The Somerset Judgment
Howell's *State Trials*, British Library

Adam Smith's *The Wealth of Nations*
British Library

First edition of *The Times*
British Library

Marylebone Cricket Club's Code of Laws
The original document was lost after publication. The revised laws of 1795 are in the MCC Library.

Mary Wollstonecraft's *A Vindication of the Rights of Woman*
British Library

The Anglo-Irish Act of Union
Parliamentary Archives

The General Enclosure Act
Parliamentary Archives

James Gillray's *The Plum-Pudding in Danger*
National Portrait Gallery, London

Sketch of *Rocket's* **boiler**
Science Museum, London

The Catholic Emancipation Act
Parliamentary Archives

The Great Reform Act
Parliamentary Archives

The Tamworth Manifesto
Published in *The Times*, British Library

The People's Charter
British Library

Engine design for SS *Great Britain*
Science Museum

Charles Dickens's *A Christmas Carol*
Morgan Library and Museum, New York

The 'Crystal Palace' design
Victoria & Albert Museum

The Rules of Association Football
Football Association Archives

The Married Women's Property Act
Parliamentary Archives

Charles Booth's poverty maps
British Library

The Anglo-French Entente Cordiale
The National Archives

Nominations for the peerage
Bodleian Library, Oxford

NUWSS 'Fourteen Reasons' appeal
British Library

War recruitment poster
Imperial War Museum, London

Clause IV of the Labour Party Constitution
Labour Party Archives, The People's Museum, Manchester; Passfield Archive, London School of Economics

The Anglo-Irish Treaty
The National Archives

Map of the British Empire
The National Archives

The royal charter of the BBC
BBC Written Archives Centre, Reading

Edward VIII's Instrument of Abdication
The National Archives

Design for the Supermarine Spitfire
Mark I factory drawings at the RAF Museum, Hendon. Mitchell's original Mark I drawings are no longer extant but his chalk drawings for the Prototype are held at the Solent Sky Museum, Southampton. Other material is held in the Supermarine/ Vickers-Armstrong Archive at the RAF Museum.

Hitler and Chamberlain's Munich note
The National Archives

The Beveridge Report
British Library

London County Council map of London war damage
London Metropolitan Archives

Brief Encounter **film script**
British Film Institute

The British Nationality Act
Parliamentary Archives

The North Atlantic Treaty
National Archives, Washington DC, General Records of the U.S. Government

The European Convention on Human Rights
Council of Europe Archives, Strasbourg

Ian Fleming's manuscript for *Casino Royale*
Ian Fleming Will Trust

The Sèvres Protocol
Bodleian Library, Oxford

Department of Education Circular 10/65
Published by Her Majesty's Stationary Office

The Beatles' *Sgt. Pepper* **album cover**
University of Leeds, School of Music

The Accession Treaty to the EEC
The National Archives

The Communiqué of the Sunningdale Agreement
The National Archives

The New Hope for Britain **Labour election manifesto**
British Library

Factortame (II) verdict
European Court of Justice

Diana, Princess of Wales condolence books
Althorp House and Harrods

The Scotland Act
Parliamentary Archives

The Government of Wales Act
Parliamentary Archives

Iraq's Weapons of Mass Destruction: The Assessment of the British Government
Published by the Stationery Office

Life in the United Kingdom, **question paper**
Published by the Stationery Office

INDEX